Lewis and Clark's
GREEN WORLD

The Expedition and its Plants

A. SCOTT EARLE   JAMES L. REVEAL

FARCOUNTRY PRESS

Cover images:
FRONT COVER TOP: Bitterroot, *Lewisia rediviva* JAMES L. REVEAL (SEE PAGE 188)
FRONT COVER BOTTOM: Ragged robin, *Clarkia pulchella* JAMES L. REVEAL (SEE PAGE 167)
BACK COVER: Camas (*Camassia quamash*) "lake". A. SCOTT EARLE (SEE PAGE 151)
COVER SPINE: Bitterroot, *Lewisia rediviva* A. SCOTT EARLE (SEE PAGE 188)
COVER BACKGROUND: Pacific silver fir, *Abies amabilis* JAMES L. REVEAL (SEE PAGE 102)
DUST JACKET BACK FLAP: James L. Reveal C. ROSE BROOME
ENDPAPERS: Camas prairie near Weippe, Idaho JAMES L. REVEAL

ISBN 1-56037-250-8

Library of Congress Control Number: 2003100446

© 2003 Farcountry Press

Photographs © by individual photographers as credited

Text © A. Scott Earle and James L. Reveal

Illustrations credited to *Intermountain Flora* are from Cronquist, et al., *Intermountain Flora: Vascular Plants of the Intermountain West, U.S.A.*, Vol. 3, Part A: *Subclass Rosidae (except Fabales)* (Bronx, NY: The New York Botanical Garden, 1997), and Vol. 3, Part B: *Fabales* (Bronx, NY: The New York Botanical Garden, 1989).

All journal quotations in this volume, unless otherwise noted, are from: *Meriwether Lewis and William Clark, The Journals of the Lewis and Clark Expedition*, 13 volumes. Edited by Gary E. Moulton. Lincoln, Nebraska: The University of Nebraska Press, 1983-2001. The first volume is the oversized atlas, the last an index.

Created, designed, and published in the USA. Printed in Korea.

Table of Contents

Acknowledgments

I would like to thank those whose helped me while I was working on this book. Jim Mack, Landscape Operations Coordinator at the Holden Arboretum in Kirtland, Ohio, found osage oranges and took us to a grove of these interesting trees. Lilian Pethtel in Kamiah, Idaho—who is well informed, indeed, about Lewis and Clark and their plants— told me exactly where to go to find several elusive plants. Trudy Armstrong and Ann Pryor in Lincoln, Montana, were interested in our project and Ann was kind enough to take us to where the bitterroot—and several other Lewis and Clark plants—flowered. Special thanks go to Jane Lundin whose sharp eyes found many of the plants pictured here, and who was kind enough to proofread the manuscript of this book. Thanks also to the folks at Farcountry Press—Barbara Fifer, Bob Smith, Julie Schroeder and especially Kathy Springmeyer—who initiated this project—for their support, creative assistance and encouragement. I am especially grateful for the privilege of working with my co-author, Jim Reveal—whose enthusiasm was contagious, whose vast knowledge was always on tap, and without whom this book would never have seen the light of day. Finally, for her enthusiastic support, companionship during many hundreds of miles of travel, and her unending patience during months spent putting this book together, I extend loving thanks to my wife Barbara.

A. Scott Earle

Reveal would like to acknowledge the opportunity permitted in 1998 by The Academy of Natural Sciences to study and publish (in 1999) on the collections of plants made by Lewis and Clark. That institution's support is allowing him to photograph and collect examples of the plants seen and collected by the explorers during the growing seasons of 2002 and 2003. He is grateful to both Dr. A. Ernie Schuyler and Dr. Richard M. McCourt of the Department of Botany at the Academy for these opportunities. Numerous botanists have answered difficult questions regarding the identity of certain specimens. Some of that continues. In particular, queries on nomenclature matters have dealt with speedily by K. N. Gandhi of Harvard University and Dr. D. II. Nicolson at the Smithsonian Institution. Access to critical literature was made possible through the kindness of the staff at the National Agricultural Library, Beltsville, Maryland, the LuEsther T. Mertz Library at the New York Botanical Gardens, and the Ewell Sale Stewart Library at the Academy. Help in the field, in 2002, was provided by David Graves and Hope Station in Nehalem, Oregon, and by Dick and Sarah Walker in Peck, Idaho. I am grateful to my usual collecting and traveling partner, Rose Broome, for once again putting up with me in the field or my being away from all the animal chores in Montrose. Finally, to Scott Earle, who somehow converted my academic musings into ordinary English and put up with my bemoaning that not everything conceivably known about Lewis and Clark plants could make it into the final manuscript.

James L. Reveal

Prologue

Historical Background

The Lewis and Clark expedition is a landmark event in the history of the United States. It put the young nation's stamp on the territory that lies between the Mississippi River and the Pacific Ocean. Upon the bicentennial of this journey, our nation is becoming increasingly aware of just how important the Corps of Discovery's achievements were to the fledgling country. Starting in 1803, Meriwether Lewis (1774-1809) and William Clark (1770-1838), working together in perfect rapport, led a small band of men (and one woman) whose performance was exemplary even when they faced nearly impossible conditions. The expedition returned in 1806 with a wealth of information that influenced many disciplines: ethnology, linguistics, geography, geology, zoology, and botany. This book is about the last of these, for the expedition—and Meriwether Lewis especially—contributed substantially to botanical knowledge.

The men who made up the Corps of Discovery came from diverse backgrounds, yet all had three things in common: They were superb woodsmen who possessed many skills, they were quite aware of the importance of their mission, and every man was resolute in his desire to go on. In the end, twenty-eight men, and one young Native American woman and her infant child, traversed more than two thousand miles of terrain —by boat, on horseback and on foot—from Fort Mandan in present-day North Dakota to the Pacific coast and then retraced their steps over much the same route. The party's only casualty probably was the result of a ruptured appendix—a condition that even today is associated with appreciable morbidity and occasional mortality. Other members of the expedition suffered serious injuries, sicknesses, and an accidental gunshot wound; all recovered. One man was lost for three weeks, but he returned to the party. Native Americans that the expedition met, for the most part, accepted the explorers; some even welcomed them. One encounter provoked by misunderstanding ended with the death of two Indians—the only episode of violence between the two cultures.

For many in modern America, the Lewis and Clark expedition is thought of as a great adventure into an unexplored land. It was a great adventure, but the land was certainly not unexplored. For centuries, Native Americans crisscrossed the continent, blazing trails and roads, establishing communities large and small. The expedition acquired vital knowledge and resources from Native Americans. It depended on their roads and trails in crossing the Rocky Mountains; on their horses for transportation; on their dogs for food; and on their knowledge of plants for survival. The expedition was an exercise in discovery, but it also reported carefully detailed facts and observations that had already been made by Native Americans. To be sure, the information was new to those of European ancestry, but it is important to remember that while we now apply "modern" names to the plants described here, many species had ancient names that reflected a different tradition.

Thomas Jefferson (1743-1826), with whom the story begins, was a "curious" man in both senses of the word. First, curious implies oddness, strangeness, or even eccentricity. These traits have recently provided fodder for historians. To whatever extent these flaws existed, however, they had little effect on the expedition and its success. But curious has a second meaning, for it also implies a desire to learn and an eagerness to see and to know—in brief, inquisitiveness. Jefferson had these traits in full. Seemingly he wanted to know everything—especially everything that pertained to the natural sciences and their practical applications: meteorology and weather; architecture and building; mineralogy and fossils; geography and cartography; exploring and surveying; the natural sciences, especially botany and horticulture; and above all agriculture. Each was a passion. He read voraciously, and his drive to learn led him to amass what was at the time the largest personal library in North America (his library of more than three thousand books became the foundation of the Library of Congress). Jefferson's curiosity and his compulsion to learn were principal ingredients in the expedition's success.

The phrase *manifest destiny* would not be coined for more than four decades, but the idea certainly existed in Jefferson's day. The Lewis and Clark expedition (several authors have noted that the expedition could as well have been named the "Jefferson expedition") reflected the inevitability of our country's westward expansion. The Louisiana Purchase, fortuitously ratified just as the expedition prepared to depart, coupled with Jefferson's zeal to explore the American West, laid the groundwork for the nation's continued growth.

In 1783, Thomas Jefferson, while serving in Congress, wrote to Revolutionary War hero George Rogers Clark (1752-1818) asking him to consider leading an expedition to explore the territory west of the thirteen original states. Clark supported Jefferson's plan, but tangled personal affairs prevented him from accepting. Later, while minister to France, Jefferson met an American adventurer, John Ledyard (1751-1789), who had served with Captain James Cook (1728-1779) during the exploration of North America's Pacific coast in 1778. Jefferson suggested that Ledyard might travel eastward across Russia and then accompany Russian traders from Vladivostok to the trading post at Nootka Sound, on the western shore of what later became known as Vancouver Island. From there, Jefferson reasoned, Ledyard could simply cross the North American continent to the Missouri's headwaters and float down to St. Louis. The intrepid Ledyard set out across Russia and almost reached Vladivostok, only to be recalled by an emissary dispatched by Catherine II the Great (1729-1796), empress of Russia, who

feared that the adventurer might be a spy.

Jefferson did not give up easily. As secretary of state under Washington, and president of the American Philosophical Society in Philadelphia, he let it be known in December 1792 that funds raised by subscription from fellow members of the society would be made available to any naturalist who knew the western United States, and who was willing to explore farther west. Meriwether Lewis, a young man of nineteen and a neighbor of Jefferson's in Albemarle County, Virginia, applied for the assignment. André Michaux (1746-1803), a capable French botanist who had collected plants as far north as Hudson's Bay in Canada, was considered more suitable, and he was chosen. Michaux reached Kentucky, but he was recalled for political reasons by the French minister to the United States, the troublesome Edmond-Charles-Édouard Genet (1763-1834).

Jefferson persisted. By the end of 1802, he was ready to ask Congress for funds to be used for western exploration, believing he now had the ideal man to lead an expedition. By then the United States was growing. Vermont joined the original thirteen states in 1791, followed by the frontier states of Kentucky (1792), Tennessee (1796), and Ohio (early 1803). Continuing westward expansion was inevitable. The English provided further motive for American exploration. In 1793-1794, a party led by explorer Alexander Mackenzie (1764-1820), of Canada's North West Company, crossed the Rocky Mountains, descended the Fraser River, and reached the Pacific Coast near today's Vancouver. He and his party were the first known non–Native Americans to cross the North American continent north of Mexico. Mackenzie published his journals in 1801—and was knighted the following year. While Mackenzie's party worked its way across the continent by land, George Vancouver (1757-1798), a captain in the British Royal Navy, conscientiously explored and charted the Pacific Coast by sea during the years 1792-1795, ranging as far north as Alaska. The English, with fur trading and settlement in mind, clearly were interested in the American Northwest. Jefferson knew of Mackenzie's crossing and of Vancouver's explorations, and Great Britain's presence in the Pacific Northwest made it obvious that there should be Americans there as well.

Shortly before his inauguration in March 1801, Jefferson sent a letter to his former neighbor, Meriwether Lewis, now a twenty-seven-year-old career army captain serving as a paymaster in the Army of the West. Jefferson wrote: "The appointment to the Presidency of the U.S. has rendered it necessary for me to have a private secretary, and in selecting one I have thought it important…to contribute to the mass of information which it is interesting for the administration to acquire. Your knolege [sic] of the Western country, of the army and of all its interests and relations has rendered it desirable that you should be engaged in that office."[1] Lewis quickly accepted. Two years later, when Jefferson offered Lewis the leadership of the project, the young officer enthusiastically accepted that, too.

The president was fully aware of what was—and was not—known of the land west of the Mississippi River. The extent of exploration had been plotted on contemporary maps. These showed the United States and its settlements as far west as the border of "Louisiana," first a Spanish, then a French, and soon to be an American possession. Louisiana was an enormous territory extending far to the west. Its borders were obscure, and it was largely unexplored by Europeans or by citizens of the United States. To the north, the Missouri River had been mapped as far as the site of Mandan Indian villages in central North Dakota. Maps ended there, leaving a great uncharted void that extended west to a rim of land along the Pacific coast, the site of Spanish holdings in California, and the northwest coast charted by a series of Spanish, French, British, and even American explorers. A few other Europeans, mainly those interested in the fur trade, had traveled as far west as the Rocky Mountains. With the exception of Mackenzie and the coastal expeditions, however, their contributions amounted to little. For Jefferson, the West was terra incognita in the truest sense of the term.

The prevailing belief was that the Continental Divide, an entity that had to exist, separated the Atlantic and Pacific ocean drainages. It was presumed to consist of a single pyramidal height of land—a mountainous continental backbone not unlike that of the Andes of South America. In fact, until the 1840s the Rocky Mountains were often termed the Andes of the North. It was thought that the Missouri River must originate there and flow eastward. The Columbia River, or its branches, should, it was argued, arise only a short distance to the west and flow to the Pacific. The Columbia had been discovered only a few years earlier, in 1793, by an American, Captain Robert Gray (1755-1806). Gray took his merchantman, the *Columbia Rediviva*, across the bar at the river's mouth and explored upstream. Gray named the river for his ship and then claimed it for the United States.

Jefferson, for political reasons, held off asking for congressional approval for his (and by now, Meriwether Lewis's) expedition until January 1803. He then sent a secret communication to Congress asking for an allotment of $2,500 to pay for an expedition that he and his secretary had been quietly planning for some months. Although Jefferson wrote vaguely about looking into the possibility of purchasing territory from the Indians, the heart of his message was that "The River Missouri and the Indians inhabiting it are not as well known as is rendered desirable," and he pointed out that the river might permit "a single navigation from its source, and, possibly with a single portage" it might provide a route to the

FRITILLARIA PUDICA, PURSH'S FLORA

Pacific Ocean.[2] The funds were forthcoming, and with them came implied congressional approval of the expedition.

Jefferson could now act. His instructions to Lewis were clear. He wrote: "The object of your mission is to explore the Missouri river, & such principal stream of it, as, by its course and communication with the waters of the Pacific ocean, whether the Columbia, Oregan, Colorado, or any other river may offer the most direct & practicable water communication across this continent for the purposes of commerce."[3]

Clearly, the president hoped that the origins of the two major rivers would lie close enough to allow an easy portage between them, constituting a de facto Northwest Passage, one that would permit trade between East and West. In point of fact, as the Lewis and Clark expedition would discover, the northern Rocky Mountains are made up of many mountain ranges. The explorers were able to thread their way through, with great difficulty, only by following the courses of swift-flowing rivers. While their return route was more direct, and while there are even easier routes across the northern Rockies, an unalterable geographic fact remains: There are approximately 450 straight-line miles between

navigable water on the Missouri (below the Great Falls in Montana) to open water on the Columbia (below today's The Dalles in Oregon). The explorers, in the end, were able to answer the most important question: There was no Northwest Passage by land; there were only hard and harder ways to cross the mountains. That negative knowledge in itself justified the expedition.

That was only the first of many of Jefferson's charges; many more followed. He ordered Lewis to observe and to note carefully "the names of [Native American] nations" and their territorial limits, languages, occupations, "food clothing & domestic accommodations." Lewis was also to map the route and note the soil types, animals, fossils, minerals, "volcanic appearances," climate (temperature, wind, rain and snow), and "the dates at which particular plants put forth or lose their flower, or leaf, times of appearance of particular birds, reptiles or insects."[4] Jefferson's instructions continued, becoming more and more detailed. Lewis accepted these charges. He and his co-commander, William Clark, tried to follow Jefferson's orders faithfully throughout the course of their journey.

Meriwether Lewis Goes to Philadelphia

In the last week of February 1803, Jefferson—who was still the president of the American Philosophical Society—wrote to several members of the society. The content of his letters was much the same. They introduced his secretary, Captain Meriwether Lewis of the U.S. Army, and asked the recipients to help him prepare for an expedition: Its purpose was the exploration of the Missouri River and thence west to the Pacific Ocean. The letter that Jefferson sent to Dr. Benjamin Smith Barton (1766-1815), professor of botany and materia medica at the University of Pennsylvania, mirrors the others. Jefferson wrote "I have appointed Capt. Lewis my secretary to conduct [the expedition]. It was impossible to find a character who to a compleat science in botany, natural history, mineral-

ogy & astronomy, joined the firmness of constitution & character, prudence, habits adapted to the woods, & a familiarity with the Indian manners & character, requisite for this undertaking. All the latter qualifications Capt. Lewis has. Altho' no regular botanist &c. he possesses a remarkable store of accurate obsevation on all the subjects of the three kingdoms [animal, vegetable, mineral], & will therefore readily single out whatever presents itself new to him in either. . . ." Jefferson noted that "He will be with you in Philadelphia in two or three weeks, & will wait on you, and receive thankfully on paper, and any verbal communications on botany, zoology, or Indian history which you may be so good as to make to him."[5]

At the end of May, Lewis wrote Jefferson to tell him that

he had met Dr. Barton. They had gotten on well, and the doctor had even suggested that he might accompany Lewis on his journey down the Ohio as far as Illinois, although because of his poor health, he was in the end unable to do so. Barton was a complex man who never quite fulfilled the promise of his youth; he was better at starting projects than he was at finishing them. He "read medicine" as an apprentice to Dr. William Shippen Jr. (1736-1808), a founder of the medical school of the College of Philadelphia (the country's first medical school; it became a part of the University of Pennsylvania in 1791). Then, in the fashion of the day, he had gone abroad, attending lectures in Edinburgh, where he was awarded a Harveian prize for a dissertation on *Hyoscyamus niger*, the European henbane, a plant in the Solanaceae, or nightshade family.[6] Barton then went to Germany where he submitted a thesis (possibly the same one) on medical botany and received his doctorate from the University of Göttingen in 1789. The same year, on his return to Philadelphia, he began lecturing in botany, which was then a prerequisite for anyone going into medicine. A short while later he was appointed professor of natural history and botany. In 1797, the university decided that botany would be an elective course. Materia medica, an important part of medical education in that era, consisted mostly of applied botany, so the decision made sense. (Two centuries ago, materia medica was the equivalent of pharmacology today.) It was a decision that would have left Dr. Barton out of the mainstream of medical education. Fortunately, however, the professor of materia medica, Adam Kuhn (1741-1814), resigned and Barton was appointed to his chair.

Dr. George W. Corner, in *Two Centuries of Medicine: A History of the School of Medicine at the University of Pennsylvania*, wrote that Professor Barton "appeared to his students a mixture of bumbling personal pretentiousness with scientific abilities amounting almost to genius. An excellent naturalist in both zoology and botany, Barton put materia medica on a broad scientific basis and awoke in many of his pupils a genuine love of natural history."[7] Despite occasional differences with his colleagues, Barton had their respect, for he was remarkably knowledgeable both in botany and in American Indian studies. He also possessed, at the time, the largest collection of natural history books in America.

It is difficult today to guess how much Lewis absorbed during his short association with Dr. Barton, but he probably learned a lot. Later, in journals kept during the expedition, Lewis described plants using botanical terms that were technically far beyond what one might expect a layman to use, even a layman with a special interest in botany. Lewis may also have learned from Barton how to collect seeds—for many that the expedition collected were later disseminated to interested growers—and how to preserve plant specimens. To establish a traveling herbarium of several hundred dried specimens during the course of the expedition, as Lewis did, meant that he had to be able to recognize new plants when he saw them, and then collect, press, and label the dry specimens—a painstaking process. He would have needed a special kind of absorbent paper in which to dry and then store and protect them. We do not have an exact figure for the number of plants that Lewis actually collected, for many were cached at the Great Falls of the Missouri, and later on the Beaverhead River, during the summer of 1805, and these did not survive spring flooding. Nonetheless, over two hundred plant specimens survived the unavoidable mishaps—rain, dampness, overturned boats, stumbling horses, and more. Today,

BERBERIS AQUIFOLIUM, PURSH'S FLORA

these are primarily in the Lewis and Clark Herbarium at the Academy of Natural Sciences in Philadelphia.

Lewis obtained all of the expedition's supplies, other than its military equipment, in Philadelphia. Barton could have told Lewis what items he needed to preserve his plants and where to go in the city to buy them. In Lewis's lists of supplies and equipment there is no mention of articles that were clearly intended for preserving plant specimens, such as the "bibulous paper" favored by botanists. However, the various boxes and oiled linen that the expedition carried would have been used to transport the dried plant specimens safely.

Two books unequivocally related to botany are on Lewis's lists of items that he purchased. The first was "Miller's edition of *Lineus* in two Vol." Johann Sebastian Mueller (1715-1780) published the two volumes of *An Illustration of the Sexual System of Linnaeus* in London in 1779-1789.[8] It would have provided a comprehensive list of plants, and their Latin names, arranged according to the Linnaean method of classification. One wonders how much Lewis used this reference, for he resisted using Latin words in his plant descriptions.

The other item was "1 Copy Bartons Bottony" for which he paid six dollars. Barton had just published his *Elements of Botany; or, Outlines of the Natural History of Vegetables* (1803). It seems rather odd that he did not simply give Lewis a copy. One can argue that students usually are expected to buy their professor's books, but a more likely explanation is that Barton was stingy, a trait for which he was well known. In all fairness, we should mention that the doctor did give (or lend) Lewis a copy of *The History of Louisiana* by Le Page Du Pratz, which Lewis carried to the Pacific and back, as he noted on the book's flyleaf when he returned it four years later. (The book, with both Lewis's and Barton's signatures, is now in the archives of the Library Company of Philadelphia.) Dr. Barton is discussed later, in our epilogue, for he had a pivotal—and negative—role in determining the fate of the plant specimens that the expedition returned.

Many others in Philadelphia were deeply interested in botany. Bernard M'Mahon (ca. 1775-1816), an enterprising horticulturist, had emigrated from Ireland in 1796 and started a seed store and nursery. He must have been an engaging individual, for his store became a popular meeting place for any and all who had an interest in plants. M'Mahon published a popular gardening book and catalog, *The American Gardener's Calendar* (1806) that, with his son's revisions, went through eleven editions over the next fifty years. M'Mahon corresponded often with Jefferson, who was also a dedicated horticulturist, and many of the seeds and plants that Lewis collected found their way into M'Mahon's garden.

Several other prominent botanical figures were also active in Philadelphia in 1803. A young German botanist, Freidrich Traugott Pursch (1774-1820) (he anglicized his name to Frederick Pursh), had arrived from Germany in 1799 and worked as a gardener and plant collector for Dr. Barton. While Lewis may not have met him on his first visit to the city, he had dealings with him later. Pursh scientifically described the expedition's specimens in his 1813 *Flora Americae Septentrionalis*. Whenever the plants of the Lewis and Clark expedition are discussed, Frederick Pursh's name is the one most frequently mentioned, after those of Lewis and Clark. His importance to the history of the Lewis and Clark expedition's plants cannot be overemphasized.

Dr. Caspar Wistar (1761-1818) was another personage Jefferson wanted Lewis to meet. Wistar taught anatomy at the University of Pennsylvania and later published *System of Anatomy* (1811), the country's first anatomical text. He had a special interest in fossils (as did Jefferson), and while the president did not mention fossils in his letter, presumably it was a subject that Lewis and the doctor discussed.

Lewis may also have met the engaging and popular Quaker merchant Zaccheus Collins (1764-1831). Collins, later a member of the Philosophical Society, did much to support the study of botany, and he became a close friend of Thomas Nuttall (1786-1859), one of the most productive of all of the many early Philadelphia-based botanists who collected plants in North America. Lewis may well have met Collins during his visit to Philadelphia in 1803. Later, Nuttall gave Collins's name to a new genus of American plants (one of the species that Lewis collected, *Collinsia parviflora*, small-flower blue-eyed Mary, is a member of the genus).

Many Philadelphians clearly were interested in botany. Evidence of how important botany was to Philadelphia, and vice versa, is that all the persons mentioned here in conjunction with Lewis's visit, including President Jefferson and both explorers, had their names attached to genera of plants. Wistar's name, for example, is perpetuated in *Wisteria*, the lovely purple-flowered climbing ornamental vines. (The name, bestowed in 1822 by Thomas Nuttall, should have been "Wistaria," but botanical names don't always follow set rules. Nuttall, when queried about the discrepancy, said that *Wisteria* was more euphonious!)

Several other botanists also were active in Philadelphia at the time. Of these, William Bartram (1739-1833) especially deserves mention. His father, John Bartram (1699-1777), is sometimes spoken of as "the father of American botany." The Bartrams, father and son, had traveled through the southern colonies in the years 1765-1766. William later described his own four-year journey through the South (1773-1777) in his book *Travels through North and South Carolina, Georgia, East and West Florida, the Cherokee Country, etc.* (1791), a work recognized today as a literary and scientific classic. The Bartram garden, on the banks of the Schuylkill River, sent seeds and plants to many prominent European botanists—including, indirectly, to Carl von Linné, or Carolus Linnaeus (1707-1788), who described the elder Bartram as a great botanist. After his father's death, William maintained the garden and encouraged many young botanists, including Thomas Nuttall. He also provided most of the thirty drawings that Dr. Barton used to illustrate the first edition of his *Elements of Botany*. It would have been surprising if Lewis had not visited the famed garden, for it was (and remains) a Philadelphia landmark, and he might well have met William at that time.

While we are primarily interested in the botanical aspects of Lewis's stay in Pennsylvania, he had much more than that to occupy his mind. He had left Washington in the middle of March, stopping first at Harper's Ferry, Virginia. He stayed three weeks there, arranging for the expedition's military supplies and spending more time than he should have overseeing the fabrication of a portable canoe of his own design. The artificers at the armory constructed a light, portable, skeletal framework that weighed only ninety-nine pounds (Lewis's ill-fated "leather boat" later cost the expedition precious time). On April 19, he arrived in Lancaster, then the capital of Pennsylvania. His mission there was to study with Andrew Ellicott (1754-1820), a recipient of another of Jefferson's letters. Ellicott was an astronomer, mathematician, and the surveyor who laid out Washington, D.C. His skill as a surveyor was one the expedition needed. Their course had to be mapped, and the accuracy of the maps would depend on what we call today "global positioning." This was not a simple matter two hundred years ago, for it depended on accurate measurement of both longitude and latitude. It is beyond our scope to go into the intricacies and instrumentation needed to carry this out—suffice it to say that navigation was not easy, and the captains never did feel completely comfortable with it.

After three weeks with Ellicott, Lewis went on to Philadelphia, where, in addition to the doctors Barton and Wistar, he called on Robert Patterson (1743-1823). Patterson, a brilliant Irishman, was the professor of mathematics and navigation at the University of Pennsylvania. He reinforced what Lewis

TRIFOLIUM MACROCEPHALUM, PURSH'S FLORA

had learned from Ellicott and helped him choose the scientific instruments the expedition would need, including sextants and a chronometer for determining longitude. The chronometer cost $250, the single most expensive item that Lewis purchased. Some of the later difficulties in determining the expedition's position resulted from problems with the chronometer, for it did not keep accurate time, probably because it could not withstand the vicissitudes of hard travel. It was then necessary to turn to astronomical observations and celestial tables that he had brought, for help in calculating their longitude. In spite of their troubles, the maps that William Clark made during the expedition were remarkably accurate and remained a standard reference for many years.

Dr. Benjamin Rush (1745-1813) was the final member of the American Philosophical Society with whom Jefferson had corresponded. Rush and Jefferson had, in the past, been closely associated. The doctor graduated from Princeton College and then studied for six years as an apprentice to John Redman (1722-1808), a prominent Philadelphia physician. He was also one of the ten pupils who attended the opening lectures that William Shippen gave in anatomy at the Medical College of Philadelphia in 1762, its founding year. Rush then traveled abroad and received his medical degree from the University of Edinburgh. He returned to Philadelphia in 1769, joined the faculty of the new Medical School as professor of chemistry, and a year later, in 1770, published the country's first chemistry textbook, *Syllabus of a Course of Lectures on Chemistry*. In 1796, Rush was appointed to the chair of theory and practice of medicine. Benjamin Rush was not only a prominent physician but he was also a patriot, active in politics. He and Jefferson were both members of the Continental Congress, representing Pennsylvania and Virginia respectively, during the exciting days that led up to the Revolution, and Rush joined the list of prominent Americans who signed the Declaration of Independence.

Rush's practice was enormous. He was well known for the selfless treatment that he provided to patients during a devastating yellow fever epidemic in 1793, surviving the disease himself. His treatment methods—and he defended them vigorously—seem barbaric today, for they consisted primarily of bleeding and purging. It is likely that his devotion to his patients did more good than the calomel and lancet that he used so freely. Rush apparently converted Meriwether Lewis, for the expedition's medicine chest mirrored the doctor's pharmacopoeia, and those who became ill on the expedition were all bled and purged. All survived (excepting the one death from a ruptured appendix)—a testimony to their youth and good health.

After meeting Lewis, Rush came up with two lists. The first, dated May 17, consisted of many questions that he hoped Lewis would be able to answer concerning the country's Native Americans. Rush wanted the men of the expedition to investigate the Indians' "physical history & medicine," their morals, and their religion, including many detailed questions about Indian customs. The second list, dated June 11, was given "to Capt. Lewis for preserving his health." His suggestions were, on the whole, rather impractical and included "Washing the feet every morning in cold water [to] fortify them against the action of cold"; if, in spite of this practice, one's feet did become cold, "it will be useful to wash them with a little spirit."[9] One can imagine the mens' reaction to this; they surely would have favored internal, rather than external, use of the expedition's "spirits."

Lewis, at this time, must have been occupied during every waking minute. Not only did he learn from the prominent scientists that Jefferson had introduced to him, but he also managed to complete the purchase of the expedition's supplies and arrange for transporting the military stores and equipment that the army provided. He returned to Washington early in June. On June 19, 1803, he wrote the most important letter of his life, addressing it to a former army acquaintance, William Clark, a younger brother of George Rogers Clark, asking him to join the expedition.[10]

Preparations and Departure, 1803

Lewis spent all of the money Congress authorized for the expedition during his stay in Philadelphia, although the final cost was far more (estimated to be almost $39,000). Jefferson's secretary of war, Henry Dearborn (1751-1829)—also a physician—had given Captain Lewis what amounted to unlimited access to the army's resources and stores. As a result, Lewis was able to obtain vastly more supplies and equipment for the expedition than the size of the congressional appropriation would suggest. The speed with which the project went forward during the spring and summer of 1803 suggests that the president and his secretary had been planning their expedition for many months. Lewis's mind and his pockets must have been full of lists; things to purchase and things to do. That matters proceeded as smoothly as they did is a tribute to his organizational genius. In a short time, he managed to come up with almost everything that his expedition would need to navigate thousands of miles of uncharted rivers and to cross hundreds of miles of rugged mountain terrain.

Lewis began to organize the expedition after he relinquished his position as secretary to the president early in the winter of 1803. He accumulated maps and charts that showed all that was then known of the Louisiana Territory west of the Mississippi and of the continent's northwest coast. He arranged to have a fifty-five-foot "keelboat" (a keeled flatboat—essentially a galley—of his own design) constructed in Pittsburgh. It would carry men and supplies down the Ohio River, then up the Mississippi River to St. Louis, and finally ascend the Missouri River.

Practically given carte blanche by the army, he visited both the Harper's Ferry armory and the Schuylkill armory near Philadelphia. The Harper's Ferry armory supplied most of the arms that the expedition required: muskets, as well as fifteen of the newest Model 1803 flintlock rifles, a piece that had not yet been issued to regular troops. Lewis

had the rifles altered to his own specifications—they were made shorter, more rugged, and had a larger bore (.54 caliber) than the extremely accurate "Kentucky rifle" on which they were based (his modifications were later incorporated into the rifles that were issued to troops). He had the expedition's gunpowder stored in ingenious lead vessels, also of his own design. The containers could be melted down and made into balls. He obtained flints, patches, shot pouches, powder horns, tomahawks (these also according to his specifications) that would be issued to each man, three swivel guns (small cannons), and several "blunderbutts" (short-range scatterguns) to be mounted on the boats, as well as pistols to back up the single-shot rifles.

He added tools: spades, axes, adzes, saws, files, blacksmithing supplies, and much more, an almost endless list amounting to what has been called "a veritable mobile hardware store."[11] The expedition's inventory was formidable: ink powder, metal pens, paper, sealing wax, paper, crayons, journals, scales, medications, cloth for tents, scientific instruments, and on and on. Lewis bought a brace of pistols for himself—one saved his life when the time came to use it.

From the Schuylkill armory, he obtained packs, hooded coats, "rifle frocks" and "fatigue frocks," blankets, shirts, and stockings (only two pairs for each man!), and flannel for patching old clothes and making new. He saved weight by taking few comestibles, for he planned to live off the land. Those that he did take included spices, salt, two hundred pounds of "portable soup" for emergencies (this was a standard item for long naval voyages and apparently was a powder, or, more likely, a highly concentrated sludge), and—of course—whiskey. If the items mentioned above seem like a lot, they were only a small part of what the expedition carried—his lists go on for pages.[12]

Items to be used as gifts and for trading with the Indians

were of the greatest importance to the expedition—as Lewis recognized at the outset. The total cost of these, almost $900, represented the largest part of the $2,500 that Congress allotted. Still, this was one of the few areas in which the expedition ran short. The items selected included a miscellany of beads, mirrors, inexpensive finery such as ribbons and "nonsopretty" (colorful trimming for dresses), medals in two sizes that showed Jefferson's profile on one side and the clasped hands of friendship on the other, fishhooks, "giggs" (fish spears), awls, vermilion paint, burning glasses, brass curtain rings, and brass buttons—this list also goes on and on. The Indians that the expedition met wanted, first of all, firearms—which could not, for the most part, be supplied—but after arms, the Indians wanted blue and white glass beads. As it turned out, the expedition ran out of trade goods on the way home. Their return journey would have been less stressful if only they had brought more beads.

In June 1803, when Lewis returned to Washington, the president gave him news that he had received only that month: France would sell the Louisiana Territory to the United States. It was intelligence that gave a new legitimacy to the expedition's plans to explore what until then had been a foreign possession.

Early in July, Lewis set out with heavily laden horses and wagons loaded with the expedition's supplies (he estimated 3,500 pounds, altogether). He arrived in Pittsburgh two weeks later, and then he had to wait for six frustrating weeks, stewing impatiently and urging hard-drinking boat builders to keep working on the expedition's keelboat. On the morning of August 31, almost a month later than planned, Lewis and a river pilot started down the Ohio River, accompanied by an escort of seven soldiers and three volunteers for the expedition. The journey downstream was difficult and time consuming. Because of the delay in delivering the keelboat, the river was low and the boat had to be dragged over exposed sandbars and through shallow riffles. They pushed on, past Wheeling, Marietta, and Cincinnati, reaching the Falls of the Ohio—real falls in those days—at Louisville on October 15. William Clark, waiting at nearby Clarksville, joined the expedition here. Lewis also hired George Drouillard (?–1810) the son of a French father and a Shawnee mother. It was a good choice; Drouillard, or "Drewyer" as he was referred to in the journals, turned out to be one of the expedition's most important members. He was a skilled hunter, a fine scout, and an able interpreter.

When Lewis had written to Clark toward the end of June, asking him to share leadership of the expedition, he had mentioned his difficulty in recruiting suitable men. Thus, even before the keelboat started down the Ohio, Clark had started to recruit experienced frontiersmen. The expedition's destination was still secret, so he told recruits that they were going to explore the headwaters of the Mississippi. His men included the famed "nine young men of Kentucky" (inaccurately named, for Clark's slave York [ca. 1770–ca. 1830]—whom Clark often referred to as "my servant"— was a tenth young man). More recruits came on board along the way; a few more joined in St. Louis.

In the spring of 1805, when the expedition left Fort Mandan (in today's North Dakota), it included all who would go to the Pacific and back: the two leaders; twenty-six soldiers; the interpreter Toussaint Charbonneau (1758-1843); his Shoshone wife, Sacagawea (ca. 1788-1812), and their infant child, Jean-Baptiste (1805-1866); George Drouillard; and Clark's "man," York. Jefferson had recognized from the first that Lewis

GAULTHERIA SHALLON, PURSH'S *FLORA*

would be the expedition's naturalist. He was knowledgeable in natural history and shared Jefferson's interest in plants. The president was sufficiently impressed by his secretary's abilities that he did not to feel the need to appoint a professional naturalist to accompany the expedition. Although both Lewis and Clark frequently mention the animals and plants that they saw in their journals, we have no way of knowing whether any of the expedition's enlisted men (save one of the sergeants, John Ordway [ca. 1775–ca. 1817]) shared the captains' deep interest in natural history.[13] Clark at one point wrote that York swam to an island on the Missouri to collect greens, so he clearly had some knowledge of edible plants. Sacagawea also provided the expedition with edible plants. Yet in the end, Lewis was the expedition's naturalist, just as Clark was its cartographer.

Once past the falls at Louisville, the party made better time. The keelboat reached the mouth of the Mississippi near present-day Cairo, Illinois, on November 13, and then worked its way upstream to St. Louis. Jefferson and Lewis had expected—hoped really—that they would spend the first winter three hundred miles farther along, on the banks of the Missouri. That was not to be. They located a suitable campground on the eastern bank of the Mississippi, twelve miles above St. Louis, and built winter barracks on the River DuBois. (It has been assumed that the name—later Americanized to "Wood River"—came from the locality's forested surroundings, but more likely, DuBois was the name of an early French settler.) The expedition-to-be settled in, preparing to depart in the spring as soon as the rivers were free of ice.

Frederick Pursh's Flora Americae Septentrionalis

Frederick Pursh came to the United States from Germany in 1799 and moved to Philadelphia soon afterwards. He was at the time one of the most thoroughly educated botanists and horticulturists in the United States. Because of a strange chain of events, Frederick Pursh gained access to the expedition's plants; many were unknown to science. His scholarship included 132 of the plants found by Lewis and Clark, and he proposed 94 new names based, at least in part, on their collections.[14] All together Pursh accounted for more than 3,000 North American plants in a two-volume compendium published in London in late December 1813. Its title, a long one in the fashion of the times, was *Flora Americae Septentrionalis; or, a Systematic Arrangement and Description of the Plants of North America, Containing, besides what have been Described by Preceding Authors, many new and rare Species, Collected During Twelve Years Travel and residence in that Country.* Had not Frederick Pursh written this book, and described in it the specimens that Lewis and Clark collected, the explorers almost certainly would not have been given credit for their botanical discoveries.

The descriptions in Pursh's book of the various plants in the Lewis and Clark Herbarium represent only a part of the story, however. Lewis and Clark's journals, as well as the published diaries of other members of the expedition, tell more—especially about where and when certain plants were found, and what Native Americans used them for. Pursh's published observations, taken in part from Lewis's original field notes, as well as later conversations that he had with Lewis (and likely with Clark after Lewis's death), provide additional insights. While our interest in Pursh's *Flora* is limited to those plants that Lewis and Clark collected, we should also mention that the *Flora* was an important contribution to the botanical literature of the time. It would have been so, even if he had not included the expedition's plants. Although Pursh proved to have certain character defects, he was not lacking in either industry or botanical knowledge, and his *Flora* was a great improvement over André Michaux's recently published *Flora Boreali-Americana* (1803).[15]

15

A Note on Nomenclature

The authors have worked to make this book readable, both for those who know little about plants, and for those who are knowledgeable—at any level—about botany. It has not always been an easy task. We have elected to use proper scientific nomenclature throughout. Thus we have included the italicized binomial name of each plant (usually derived from Latin or Greek root words), followed by the name(s) of the naturalist(s) who described it, in keeping with established botanical rules. We recognize that these names may mean little or nothing to many readers. We hope, therefore, that the following brief explanation of how scientific names are derived will be of some help.

There are, worldwide, over 250,000 species of flowering plants. Each plant has a scientific name that consists of its genus (generic) name (such as *Lewisia*), followed by its species name ("specific epithet") (such as *rediviva*). Together the two words comprise the scientific name or "binomial" of a plant (thus, *Lewisia rediviva*). This binomial refers to this plant only, no matter if the plant or the speaker is in Kalamazoo or Timbuktu. The "common," or vernacular, name for this species, in English, is "bitterroot."

Each species is assigned to a genus (there are approximately 13,500 genera of flowering plants, worldwide). The genera are assigned to families (globally, there are about 465 families). Typically family names end in *-aceae* (*Lewisia rediviva* is a member of the portulaca family, the Portulacaceae). The endings of generic names (the first part of the binomial) vary. Species names (the second part of the binomial) usually end with the same termination as the generic names, as in *Lewisia rediviva* (feminine ending), *Ceanothus sanguineus* (mas-

culine ending), or *Lomatium triternatum* (neuter ending). Names proposed in recognition of the direct contribution to science by an individual end in *-ae* (feminine), or *-ii* (masculine), as in *Linum lewisii* for Lewis's blue flax. Names proposed to honor individuals of prominence or ones who made an indirect contribution relative to the discovery of the plant end in *-ana*, *-anus*, or *-anum*, as in *Frangula purshiana* for cascara, or the false buckthorn, a plant named in honor of Pursh. The terminations *-ense* (neuter) or *-ensis* (masculine and feminine) express a geographic location, as in *Lonicera utahensis*, for the Utah honeysuckle. One ancient Latin tradition is still followed today: All trees are considered to be "feminine," no matter the gender of the generic name (thus, *Pinus ponderosa*). Another Latin custom that is followed is the use of a single terminal "*i*" after a vowel or an "*r*," as in *Anemone piperi* and *Poa canbyi*. Unlike the rules governing the naming of animals, in botany the genus determines the termination so that when *Lilium pudicum* was reassigned to the genus *Fritillaria*, its species name was altered to become *Fritillaria pudica*.

In addition to the binomial, each complete scientific name also indicates the identity of the person who first validly published a description of a plant and gave it its binomial scientific name, all according to rules formulated in the *International Code of Botanical Nomenclature*.[16] For example, the full scientific name of bitterroot is *Lewisia rediviva* Pursh. The name "Pursh" refers to Frederick Pursh, who was the first to describe the plant formally. He published its name in late December 1813, along with the names of many other plants brought back by the Lewis and Clark expedition, in his *Flora Americae Septentrionalis*.

CLARKIA PULCHELLA, PURSH'S FLORA

Some authors' names are abbreviated. Modern botanical nomenclature began in 1753 with the publication of *Species Plantarum*, by the Swedish naturalist Linnaeus; the names of plants he described are followed simply by the abbreviation "L." Other author abbreviations include "Hook." for William Jackson Hooker (1785-1865), "Michx." for André Michaux, "Nutt." for Thomas Nuttall, and "Torr." for John Torrey (1796-1873), just to mention four of the many prominent botanists whose names are attached to binomials found in this book.

Occasionally a species is transferred from one genus to another. For example, Pursh described antelope-brush in 1813 and gave it the scientific name *Tigarea tridentata* Pursh. Later, the French botanist Augustin-Pyramus de Candolle (1778-1841) pointed out that the plant was not a *Tigarea*. Instead, it represented a new genus, so he suggested the new generic name *Purshia*. Therefore, antelope-brush would be *Purshia tridentata* (Pursh) DC. In this case, Pursh's name is placed in parenthesis so that his contribution remains attached to the scientific name. Candolle (abbreviated "DC.") proposed the name *Purshia*, but he did not get around to publishing it; instead, it was validly published by another French botanist, Jean Louis Marie Poiret (1755-1834; abbreviated "Poir."). Poiret credited Candolle with coining the name *Purshia*; at this point, the full authorship of the binomial is reflected as *Purshia tridentata* (Pursh) DC. ex Poir. This notation is somewhat complicated, but it provides in a nutshell the history of how antelope-brush received its scientific name.

Each unique plant can have one, and only one, correct scientific name. On the other hand, each may have many common names. Some common names are firmly established. Douglas-fir is an example. Other trees found in the Pacific Northwest have several different common names (a few, used by loggers, are not printable here). We have tried to use English language names that have been proposed in an effort to standardize common names, but unfortunately many are obscure or seem contrived. While on one hand there is much to recommend the use of standardized common names formulated by botanists, on the other hand, it would seem impractical—for the chances that folks in Montana will refer to their "huckleberry" as a "square-twig blueberry" are about as great as their using the plant's scientific binomial, *Vaccinium membranaceum*, in everyday speech. Additionally, many common plant names reflect a folk heritage that should not be put aside in the interest of uniformity. To accommodate both viewpoints, we have used common names that are in widespread use, and indicated others (both proposed standardized names, and alternate vernacular names).

Finally, in defense of binomials, we should mention that, while they are not for everyone (Meriwether Lewis, for example, used a binomial for only one plant of the many he described), one does become familiar with them and learns, in time, what they mean. They are often quirky—those who proposed them clearly were not always knowledgeable in Latin, and even less in Greek, and often the two languages are mixed together helter-skelter. They are sometimes amusing, for names were given to honor family members, friends, patrons, or prominent individuals who had nothing whatsoever to do with the plant. As one starts to associate scientific names with various plants, it becomes second nature to use them, and in this way one avoids any ambiguity about the plant being described.

Lake Sakakawea
FORT MANDAN
BISMARCK

NORTH DAKOTA
Lake Oahe

MOBRIDGE

Lake Oahe

PIERRE
Missouri

CHAMBERLAIN

SOUTH DAKOTA

River

Niobrara River
NIOBRARA

IOWA
SIOUX CITY

N

OMAHA

Missouri River

KANSAS

ST. JOSEPH

MISSOURI

Kansas River
KANSAS CITY

Missouri River

WOOD RIVER
ST. LOUIS

JEFFERSON CITY

Mississippi River

SILVER BUFFALOBERRY	*Shepherdia argentea*
RUSSET BUFFALOBERRY	*Shepherdia canadensis*
SNAKEWEED	*Gutierrezia sarothrae*
BUR OAK	*Quercus macrocarpa*
LACY TANSY-ASTER	*Machaeranthera pinnatifida*
INLAND WILD RICE	*Zizania palustris var. interior*
RABBITBRUSH	*Ericameria nauseosa*
FOUR-WING SALTBUSH	*Atriplex canescens*
GARDNER'S SALTBUSH	*Atriplex gardneri*
WINTERFAT	*Krascheninnikovia lanata*
TALL GAYFEATHER	*Liatris aspera*
CATTAIL GAYFLOWER	*Liatris pycnostachya*
PRAIRIE WILD ROSE	*Rosa arkansana*
CANADA MILK VETCH	*Astragalus canadensis*
MISSOURI MILK VETCH	*Astragalus missouriensis*
LOOSEFLOWER MILK VETCH	*Astragalus tenellus*
GROUNDPLUM MILK VETCH	*Astragalus crassicarpus*
LANCELEAF SAGE	*Salvia reflexa*
AROMATIC ASTER	*Symphyotrichum oblongifolium*
FIRE-ON-THE-MOUNTAIN	*Euphorbia cyathophora*
SLIM SCURF PEA	*Psoralidium tenuiflorum*
LEMON SCURF PEA	*Psoralidium lanceolatum*
SILVER-LEAF SCURF PEA	*Pediomelum argophyllum*
SKUNKBUSH SUMAC	*Rhus trilobata*
INDIAN TOBACCO	*Nicotiana quadrivalvis*

OSAGE ORANGE	*Maclura pomifera*
OSAGE PLUM	*Prunus angustifolia*
WHITE PRAIRIE CLOVER	*Dalea candida*
PURPLE PRAIRIE CLOVER	*Dalea purpurea*
ROCKY MOUNTAIN BEEPLANT	*Cleome serrulata*
CLAMMY WEED	*Polanisia dodecandra*
CURLYCUP GUMWEED	*Grindelia squarrosa*
MEADOW ANEMONE	*Anemone canadensis*
CAROLINA ANEMONE	*Anemone caroliniana*
FIELD HORSETAIL	*Equisetum arvense*
WILD FOUR-O'CLOCK	*Mirabilis nyctaginea*

Wood River to Fort Mandan
Winter 1803-1804 to November 30, 1804

When the winter of 1803-1804 was over, the men of the Corps of Discovery prepared to leave their bivouac on the River Dubois, now called the Wood River. The captains had sited the expedition's winter encampment there for several reasons: The Wood emptied into the Mississippi just across from the mouth of the Missouri (although today the mouth of the Wood River is several miles farther upstream), and there was timber for barracks and fuel. The site was also acceptable to the French, who did not want a military encampment on their side of the Mississippi, given that the Louisiana Territory would not become an American possession for several months.

The winter had been productive, the leaders had an opportunity to evaluate their men and to train them in army ways and marksmanship, to fine-tune the company's roster and organization, and to establish discipline—responsibilities that fell mostly on Clark's shoulders. Lewis spent much of the winter in St. Louis, gathering and organizing supplies, maps, and intelligence, while acting as a representative of the president during the ceremonies surrounding the transfer of the Louisiana Territory to the United States.[1] Finally, winter turned into spring. The journals note that "the buds of the Spicewood [*Lindera benzoin*] appeared, and the tausels [tassels] of the mail [male] Cotton wood [*Populus deltoides*] were larger than Mulberry and . . . the grass begins to Spring."

On April 1, Clark noted that the "Spicewood is in full bloom, dogs tooth violet [*Erythronium albidum*], and may apple [*Podophyllum peltatum*] appeared above ground." By the fifth, domestic fruit trees, apples and cherries, were budding, as was the wild "Osage Plumb" (*Prunus angustifolia*), although the buds of the Osage Apple (*Maclura pomifera*) had not yet appeared. By the seventeenth, they noted "Peach trees in full Bloome, the Weaping Willow has put forth its leaves…the *Violet* the *doves* foot & *cowslip* [a shooting star, *Dodecatheon meadia*] are in bloe…the Gooseberry which is also in this country"—this might refer to either the cultivated European gooseberry, *Ribes uva-crispa* var. *sativum*, the native Missouri gooseberry, *Ribes missouriense*, or both—"and lilak [*Syringa vulgaris*] have put forth their leaves."[2]

In March, Lewis sent dormant cuttings of the "Osage apple," (we know it as Osage orange today) and the Osage plum to Jefferson. The fate of the plum cuttings is unknown, but the Osage orange flourished.

On May 14, 1803, the expedition left its winter encampment and began to work its way up the Missouri River. The men paused at St. Charles, a few miles above St. Louis, where Meriwether Lewis, who had been attending to last-minute details, joined the party, and on May 20, the expedition began the three-hundred mile crossing of what is now the state of Missouri, traveling upriver from east to west in the built-to-order, and now further modified keelboat—the men called it a "bateau"—and the two pirogues. The keelboat was, in effect, a galley fifty-five feet long with benches for twenty-two oars. The men propelled it against the current by using whatever method worked best under changing conditions—by tow ropes pulled by men on the bank, by poling in shallower water, by rowing, and even, occasionally, by sail with a following wind. Clark spent most of his time onboard, attending to navigation and mapping the expedition's progress. Lewis more often walked along on shore, hunting, taking note of the fauna and flora, and reconnoitering the countryside. Their passage was marked by squalls, sandbars, bank cave-ins, hidden snags, meeting fur traders heading downriver, and the tributaries that they passed: the Osage, the Salt, the Big and Little Manitous, the Big and Little Charitons, the Grand, the Crooked rivers, and then the Kansas. The expedition reached the site of today's Kansas City on June 26, 1804.

Lewis would have had his eye out for unusual plants. He may have collected some during this first segment of the journey, but if so, only one, a horsetail, has survived. Clark wrote, on June 8, that "Capt Lewis went out to the woods & found many curious Plants & Srubs" but he offered no further elaboration.[3] The plants named in the journals during these early weeks were ones the men already knew: oak, ash, walnut, sycamore, and cottonwood trees. Lewis collected cottonwood seeds (*Populus deltoides*), which was easy to do at that time of the year when the air was full of their floating "cotton"; we don't know what happened to these.

The journals also mention fruit trees and shrubs: Osage plums (*Prunus angustifolia*), blackberries and raspberries (*Rubus* spp.), and currants and gooseberries (*Ribes* spp.). One entry notes that York, Clark's "servant," swam to an island "to geather greens for our Dinner and returnd with a Suffcent quantity wild Creases [cresses] or Teng [tongue] grass."[4] Greens and berries when added to the mens' diet of meat would have been important in preventing scurvy. P. R. Cutright cites a document that Lewis apparently wrote after the expedition. In it Lewis referred to plants he found growing along the Missouri. The yellowroot or goldenseal (*Hydrastis canadensis*) was useful for treating "soar eyes," and a wild ginger, probably *Asarum canadensis*, acted as "a strong stomatic stimelent."[5]

The explorers camped for three days to rest and to dry their stores at the mouth of the Kansas River. The Missouri turns northward here and sequentially defines the borders of five future midwestern states. As one travels upriver, first are Missouri and Kansas. Above that, Nebraska replaces Kansas on the west bank, and Iowa is on the east. Still farther north, the river turns west, to define a portion of the boundary between Nebraska and South Dakota.

The expedition's journey upriver was plagued by summer heat and the river's endless surprises: shifting sandbars, hidden snags, and enormous, partly submerged trees carried downriver by the rushing current, endangering even the large boat. On land, clouds of "musquitors Ticks & Knats" made life miserable.[6]

The flora gradually changed as the Corps of Discovery went north and prairie replaced forestland. The travelers noted that trees and shrubs were increasingly confined to stream banks. Cottonwoods began to predominate, a trend that would continue until they would be the only large trees growing along the river. The expedition found that the prairie soil was rich and the prairie grass thick and green. On July 4, only a short distance below today's St. Joseph, Missouri, Clark—who occasionally got carried away—wrote with his freeform spelling: "The Plains of this countrey are covered with a Leek Green grass [big bluestem, *Andropogon gerardii*], well calculated for the sweetest and most norushing hay—interspersed with Cops [copses] of trees, Spreding ther lofty branchs over Pools Springs or Brooks of fine water. Groops of Shrubs covered with the most delicious froot is to be seen in every direction, and nature appears to have exerted herself to butify the Senery by the variety of flours…which Strikes & profumes the Sensation, and amuses the mind." And again, on August 1, Clark noted "the Praries Contain Cheres, Apple, Grapes, Currents, Rasp burry, Gooseberris Hastlenuts and a great Variety of plants & flours not Common to the US. What a field for a Botents [botanist] and a natirless [naturalist]."[7]

During the first few days of August, the captains held a council with Indians below some high bluffs a few miles above today's Council Bluffs, Iowa (the city took its name from this event). Clark wrote about the council on August 2, noting that the party sent the Indians "Som rosted meat Pork flour & meal, in return they Sent us Water millions." This note, and one by Sergeant Ordway, written on October 10 describing Arikara Indians, both mention watermelons grown by Native Americans.[8] This has occasioned some debate. Could watermelons, a plant native to Africa (*Citrullus vulgaris* or *Citrullus lanatus*), have been growing in Iowa and South Dakota in 1804? The answer is almost certainly "yes." Surely the men would have been able to recognize watermelons when they saw them. Apparently the Spanish introduced the plant into the Americas in the early 1500s and, understandably, it spread quickly. The French found Native Americans cultivating watermelon around the Great Lakes in the early 1600s, so likely it was in cultivation on the Great Plains soon thereafter.

On September 4, more than two months after leaving their encampment at the mouth of the Kansas River, the expedition reached the Niobrara River, thirty-five miles west of today's Yankton, South Dakota. A lot had happened that summer. The explorers had had their first council with Native Americans. Then, on August 23, Sergeant Floyd, the expedition's only casualty—and one of its best men—died, most likely of a perforated appendix. On that day, also, the men shot their first buffalo.

The Niobrara was known then as the "Qui courre," a corruption of the French name, L'Eau qui Court (meaning roughly "the Rushing River"). Clark noted then that there was now "a verry Cold wind from the S.S.E." Cold or not, it was a following wind, and the men took advantage of it. He wrote the next day that they had "Set up a Jury mast & Sailed."[9] As always, their course was marked by the unusual. The explorers saw their first pronghorn (*Antilocapra americana*), prairie dogs (*Cynomys ludovicianus*), mule deer (*Odocoileus hemionus*), and a white-tailed jackrabbit (*Lepus townsendii*), all new species. Lewis discovered the fossil of a giant fish-lizard—a plesiosaur. And Private Shannon, who had been lost for three weeks, rejoined the party on September 11, "nearly Starved to Death."[10]

Lewis stayed with the boats for the most part, but on September 17, he went ashore to reconnoiter. He returned with a magpie that he had shot, a bird that none in the party had seen before. The American magpie (*Pica hudsonia*) is a handsome bird, and all were impressed with its strikingly iridescent plumage; Clark referred to it in his journal as "a butifull thing." On the nineteenth, Clark noted "great quantities of the Prickley

Pear"—probably the brittle cactus, *Opuntia fragilis*—that grew along the shore, increasingly a source of trouble for the poorly shod men.[11] On the twenty-first, the expedition came to the Big Bend of the Missouri, one of the river's more notable landmarks—thirty miles around, yet the start and finish of the great loop are only a mile and a quarter apart. Then, on the twenty-fourth, the party came to a river that joined the Missouri from the west, close to a Teton Sioux Indian village—across from today's Pierre, South Dakota. They named the stream for the Indians, but the name failed to stick; today it is called the Bad River, which, considering the trouble the expedition would have with the Teton Sioux, is not an inappropriate name.

The party camped only one night near the mouth of the Teton. Then, two miles farther upstream, the boats came abreast of the first of two large Teton Sioux villages. The four days spent with the Sioux were harrowing. The Indians' behavior alternated between hospitable and threatening, aimed at abstracting as many presents as possible from the explorers, on one hand, and barring their passage upstream on the other. On two occasions standoffs came close to erupting into armed clashes. The captains managed to avoid bloodshed by making plain that they were willing to fight if necessary, and by diplomacy sweetened with gifts. As the party continued upriver, the Sioux followed along the banks, sometimes threatening, sometimes begging for tobacco and powder. From then on the captains always spoke disdainfully of the Teton Sioux, calling them, among other things, "the vilest miscreants of the saveage race"—an assessment that neighboring tribes also shared at the time.[12]

At an Arikara village above the mouth of the Grand River (near today's Mobridge, South Dakota), the party found a more peaceful people. The Arikara, unlike the Sioux, were sedentary and agrarian. Their gardens, worked by the women of the villages, grew sunflowers, melons, several varieties of squash, watermelons (see p. 20), corn (their principal food), beans, and tobacco. Sergeant Gass, in his journal, observed that Indian tobacco "answers for smoking, but not for chewing." Lewis "found it very pleasant" to smoke. The explorers received corn and other food from the Arikaras. Although Lewis gathered samples of the corn and sent them to Jefferson, this Native American cultivar now is extinct. Lewis was impressed by the hardiness of the Indians' corn and its ability to grow rapidly in a cool climate, a point that Pursh also noted in his *Flora*.[13] One of the more interesting foods they sampled was a bean, the American hog-peanut (*Amphicarpaea bracteata*), that the women of the tribe found in caches left by mice. Clark noted that when the Indian women robbed the mice of the tasty beans, they always left other food for the animals' winter stores.

The never-ending prairie winds grew colder and blew harder as the expedition continued upstream onto the high plains of today's North Dakota. The plants collected on this segment of their journey reflect the lateness of the season. Except for a late-blooming wild poinsettia (*Euphorbia cyathophora*) and a rabbitbrush (*Ericameria nauseosa*), the collected plants were ones that show little change from season to season, including sages (*Artemisia* spp.), junipers (*Juniperus* spp.), and others.

The party reached Mandan country at the end of October. The Mandans were the most settled of all of the Great Plains tribes, and they were used to white traders. Their villages, located about fifty miles above today's Bismarck, North Dakota, were strung along the Missouri where the river's course turns toward the west. Here, the party's maps, compiled by earlier explorers, ran out; the country beyond was terra incognita. Here, too, the captains planned to establish their winter encampment. They found a suitable location, and after an industrious three weeks, Fort Mandan was completed. The men moved in on November 30, 1804, and hunkered down for a long, bitter winter. There would be no further botanizing for five months.

MORACEAE (MULBERRY FAMILY)
Wood River encampment, winter 1804
OSAGE ORANGE, *MACLURA POMIFERA* (RAF.) C. K. SCHNEID.

The Osage orange is unusual. It is dioecious (from the Greek, meaning "two houses"; this is a botanical term that implies that there are male and female plants; only the female trees bear fruit). The hard, resilient wood is ideal for making bows and war-clubs (the tree is still sometimes known as bow-wood, or bodark, from the French "bois d'arc"). The trees have shiny, deep green, lanceolate to ovate leaves, each with a prominent thorn at the base. The fruit is also a deep green, becoming yellow late in the fall. In the past, topped trees, closely planted, were used as hedges, and rows of Osage oranges are still found in the Midwest, grown from hedges where they originally were used as long-lived, natural fences (hence another common name, hedge

Maclura pomifera

A. SCOTT EARLE

22

apple); some may also show scars on their trunks where they were used as fence posts and strung with barbed wire after the trees had died. The fruit has no food value except for squirrels, which are fond of the seeds. Even though inedible, the fallen "oranges" are gathered in the autumn for decoration and because their citruslike aroma is believed to repel insects and spiders.

The Osage orange cuttings that Lewis sent to President Jefferson in the spring of 1804 came from trees planted by Jean Pierre Chouteau, a prominent St. Louis trader who provided the expedition with supplies prior to its departure. He had introduced the trees into his garden from cuttings obtained from an Indian village three hundred miles up the Missouri. Jefferson planted the cuttings that Lewis and Clark sent back to him from Wood River at Monticello and gave some to Bernard M'Mahon, a seed seller and nurseryman of Philadelphia, who also grew the trees successfully. Although originally a native of the south-central United States, the home of the Osage Indians for whom the trees were named, it

is now found throughout the central and eastern parts of the country. The naturalist Constantine Samuel Rafinesque (1783-1840) recognized that the Osage orange was a hitherto undescribed plant. He named it *Ioxylon pomifera*; the name was later revised to *Maclura aurantiaca* by Thomas Nuttall, in honor of Philadelphia geologist William Maclure, president of The Academy of Natural Sciences of Philadelphia from 1817 until his death. The tree today is known as *Maclura pomifera* (the species name, *pomifera*, means "apple bearer").

The Osage orange belongs to the mulberry family (Moraceae), a group whose scientific name is derived from the word *morus*, the Latin name for the mulberry tree. One can debate whether the Osage orange—sent to Jefferson before the expedition actually departed—should be included as an expedition plant. Nevertheless, a specimen is found in the Lewis and Clark Herbarium at The Academy of Natural Sciences, apparently collected after the expedition was underway, although the site and date of the acquisition are unknown.

ROSACEAE (ROSE FAMILY)
Seen, but not gathered, on the south shore of the Missouri,
near present-day Glasgow in Chariton County, Missouri, on June 10, 1804
OSAGE PLUM, *PRUNUS ANGUSTIFOLIA* MARSHALL

The explorers had gone almost completely across the present state of Missouri and were near today's Glasgow. William Clark noted in his journal that the prairies abound with "a wild plumb of a Superior quallity, Called the Osages Plumb Grows on a bush the hight of a Hasel (and is three times the sise of other Plumbs,) and hangs in great quantity on the bushes."[14] The captains used the terms "cherry" and "plum" pretty much interchangeably in their journals. The Osage plum (*Prunus angustifolia*) is, as Clark mentioned, the largest wild cherry that grows in Missouri. Lewis

and Clark already knew the plant, for they had sent cuttings to Jefferson from their encampment on the Wood River.

This illustration below appeared in a portfolio published by the Smithsonian Institution. It was to have been used as an illustration in what proved to be an unfulfilled project of Asa Gray (1810-1888), one of the nineteenth-century's most prestigious American botanists. Gray's *Forest Trees of North America* was slated to be the newly founded Smithsonian's first publication, but Gray never managed to complete the project. The twenty-three plates that were completed eventually were published as a portfolio in 1891.

Two talented artists worked on these plates. Isaac Sprague (1811-1895), a well-known botanical illustrator who worked closely with Gray, first made drawings of the plants. The plates were then engraved and colored, between 1849 and 1851, by a talented and little-known German immigrant, Joseph Prestele (1796-1867), then living in upstate Ebenezer, New York. (Prestele later moved with his family to the religious community of Amana, Iowa.) He continued to work with Gray and Sprague, as well as with his sons, producing illustrations for textbooks, seed

Prunus angustifolia

GRAY'S FOREST TREES

companies, and other publications.[15]

A related species, the American plum (*Prunus americana*), is common today along this portion of the route. It forms dense thickets along creek banks and roadsides. Another early spring flowering shrub or small tree likely seen by Lewis was the Ohio buckeye (*Aesculus glabra*). Box elder or the ash-leaved maple (*Acer negundo*) is another tree that was well-known to members of the expedition as a streamside species. Those that grow along this portion of the Missouri River represent a distinct variety (*Acer negundo* var. *interius*) that was not named until late in the nineteenth century.

FABACEAE (PEA FAMILY)

Collected in Bon Homme County, South Dakota, or in Knox County, Nebraska, on September 2, 1804

WHITE PRAIRIE CLOVER, *DALEA CANDIDA* MICHX. EX WILLD.
PURPLE PRAIRIE CLOVER, *DALEA PURPUREA* VENT.

Lewis and Clark found both white and purple prairie clover in September 1804, probably in present-day South Dakota. Both plants were already known to science, but Lewis was not familiar with them—hardly surprising, as neither grow in Virginia. Lewis described the white and the purple species in a plant catalog that he compiled during the winter at Fort Mandan, to accompany the specimens he sent back in April 1805 on the keelboat to St. Louis and then overland to Philadelphia. Lewis's plants, numbered 15 and 16 on his list, were known until recently as *Petalostemon candida* and *Petalostemon purpurea*. They are now classified

as *Dalea*, although they retain their species' names, according to the rules of botanical nomenclature.[16]

In his list, Lewis wrote "No. 15. Was taken on the 20th of July, a pieniel [perennial] plant, an inhabitant of the open praries or plains, high situations, where the grass is low. the flower is a pale purple colour small form a kind of button of a long conic like form which terminate it's branches which are numerous—it grows abot 2½ or three feet high—it is a stranger to me.—the leaves are small and narrow, and divided into three on a stem." The next plant on his list was "No. 16. this is much the same as No. 15 with this difference that the

Dalea candida

JAMES L. REVEAL

Dalea purpurea

JAMES L. REVEAL

blume of the conic tausel are white in stead of purple and it's leaves single fewer and longer—."[17] Another specimen of *Dalea purpurea* was collected near Camp Disappointment, during Lewis's detour on the Marias River, on July 22, 1806.[18]

The prairie clovers are widely distributed, ranging from the eastern slopes of the Rocky Mountains north into the Canadian provinces of Saskatchewan and Manitoba, and south into Mexico. C. Leo Hitchcock wrote that "Although not choice ornamentals, our species are worth a place in the arid garden...though a little too large to be usable for the ordinary rockery."[19] Native Americans used the leaves of both plants for tea and chewed the inner portions of the roots.

CAPPARACEAE (CAPER FAMILY)

Collected above the mouth of the Vermillion River in Clay County, South Dakota,
or in Cedar or Dixon County, Nebraska, on August 25, 1804

ROCKY MOUNTAIN BEEPLANT, *CLEOME SERRULATA* PURSH
CLAMMYWEED, *POLANISIA DODECANDRA* (L.) DC. SUBSP. *TRACHYSPERMA* (TORR. & A. GRAY) ILTIS

It is not unusual to see the Rocky Mountain beeplant growing along dirt and farm roads on the Great Plains. Farther west, in the mountains, it is usually found at lower elevations, in open places, along washes, and in woodlands, where bees, flies, and other pollinators are frequent visitors. An annual, it occurs not only throughout most of the Great Plains where Lewis found it, but also westward to Washington, Oregon, and California, northward across southern Canada, and as far east as New England. It is now a weedy plant in portions of its range, having invaded the east only in recent decades, usually with the help of wildflower enthusiasts who want to see it growing in their areas. Cleomes are also found in ornamental gardens, where they also may escape and grow wild as weeds. A related species, the yellow spider flower (*Cleome*

25

lutea) has bright yellow flowers. Its lower leaves are divided into five leaflets, whereas the Rocky Mountain beeplant has only three leaflets. The yellow spider flower grows south of the route taken by Lewis and Clark, but it is sometimes seen in the Pacific Northwest; at times, both grow together on roadsides.

Lewis was apparently taken by this attractive prairie wildflower, for he collected the Rocky Mountain beeplant twice. The first time was on August 25, 1804, along the Missouri River near today's Vermillion, South Dakota. Four days later he gathered a second specimen near the White River in Lyman or Brule County, South Dakota. The Rocky Mountain beeplant usually has bright pink to purple flowers, although individual plants occasionally have all white flowers. Only one of Lewis's specimens has flowers, and those have faded so we are unable to tell what color they were originally. Pursh reported that Lewis saw both white and pale purple flowers. Lewis's notes indicated that the White River specimen's flowers were colored, so perhaps the ones obtained near Vermillion were white.[20]

Both species of *Cleome* were important food plants for

Cleome serrulata

JAMES L. REVEAL

Native Americans. Young plants were used as a potherb and boiled—apparently several times, because the plants have an offensive odor (explaining another common name, "stinkweed"). The boiled plants were eaten immediately or rolled into balls and dried for use at a later time. The plants' seeds may also be ground and used as meal.[21] "Cleome" was the name of a now unknown ancient Greek plant (possibly derived from the old Greek word *cleos*, meaning "glory") bestowed by Linnaeus when he named the genus.

Evidently Lewis did not know that there was a fragment of a clammyweed (*Polanisia dodecandra* subsp. *trachysperma*), another member of the caper family, included with one of his specimens of the Rocky Mountain beeplant. The clammyweed has a different fruit, and its stems and branches are sticky, but it also—like the beeplant—has purple or white flowers and three leaflets, so we can appreciate Lewis's confusion. *Polanisia* is fairly common throughout the Great Plains but is usually found farther south. The word *polanisia* was derived from the Greek words *poly*, for "many," and *anisos*, for "unequal," because the flowers' stamens are of unequal lengths.

ASTERACEAE (ASTER FAMILY)

Collected near the Omaha Indian village of Tonwontonga, Dakota County, Nebraska, on August 17, 1804

CURLYCUP GUMWEED, *GRINDELIA SQUARROSA* (PURSH) DUNAL

The mature flowers of curlycup gumweed resemble those of many similar yellow composite plants. It differs in one respect, however, for its cup-shaped buds are filled with a sticky, white gum. Knowing this, one will recognize gumweeds on first encounter. The chances of finding the bright yellow flowers along the Lewis and Clark Trail are high, for they grow on roadsides from Nebraska to Idaho—often in prodigious numbers—from midsummer on. *Grindelia squarrosa* is the most widespread of the several species of gumweed that grow in the United States.[22]

Lewis collected the curlycup gumweed on August 17, 1804, when the expedition was in the vicinity of Tonwontonga, a large "Maha" (Omaha) Indian village (the location in present day Nebraska would be about ten miles south of Sioux City, Iowa). He described the plant in the list of items sent to Jefferson from Fort Mandan as "No. 40. Taken on the 27th of August 1804. At our camp near the Old Maha village & is the growth of the Prairies."[23] Frederick Pursh recognized that Lewis's specimen was new to science. He classified it as a *Donia*—a now obsolete genus—mentioning that "The whole plant is viscous, and has a strong resiniferous or balsamic scent."[24] Later, in 1819, the French botanist Michel Felix Dunal (1789-1856) reclassified it as a *Grindelia*. The plant retained Pursh's species name, so it became *Grindelia squarrosa*, the name that it has today. The genus name honors the Russian botanist David Hieronymus Grindel (1776-1836). Its species name, *squarrosa*, means "right angle," for the plant's sharp, outward-turning involu-

Grindelia squarrosa

cral bracts (tiny leaflike segments of the involucrum, the cup that holds the many tiny flowers that make up the plant's compound inflorescence).

Not surprisingly, because of its aromatic smell, Native Americans and others have used the gum medicinally—topically for the rash of poison ivy and other cutaneous disorders, and internally for respiratory ailments, although there is no scientific evidence that would suggest that it has any therapeutic value. The latexlike gum also has no commercial use.

RANUNCULACEAE (BUTTERCUP FAMILY)

Collected near the Omaha Indian village Tonwontonga, Dakota County, Nebraska, on August 17, 1804

MEADOW ANEMONE, *ANEMONE CANADENSIS* L.
CAROLINA ANEMONE, *ANEMONE CAROLINIANA* WALTER

The expedition arrived in the vicinity of the Omaha village of Tonwontonga on August 13 and remained there until the morning of the twentieth. The captains set up their camp on a sandbar, some distance away from the village, and made observations of the latitude and longitude, while

the men fished, visited different locations, and traded with the Omaha villagers. On August 17, Clark wrote in his journal that he collected a grass—Canada rye, *Elymus canadensis*. He mentioned nothing about gathering other specimens, but it is possible that he found a meadow anemone

27

Anemone canadensis

blooms earlier in the summer. Might one or the other of the captains have received a dried plant from an Omaha Indian? We know that Native Americans used the plant medicinally, as a general panacea and to counter witchcraft, and so it would have been an important plant to collect.

Recognition of the various anemones, even today, is difficult, so it is not surprising that Frederick Pursh struggled with the material Lewis sent back to Jefferson in the spring of 1805. He seems to have confused Lewis's specimen with the Carolina anemone (*Anemone caroliniana*)—a plant that had already been described. He wrote in his *Flora* that Lewis found the plant on "the banks of the Missouri," but then he described it as having purple flowers and tuberous roots.[25] The meadow anemone has white flowers and arises from a rhizome (an underground root-like stem), whereas the Carolina anemone may have purple flowers and always has tubers. Further, *Anemone caroliniana* flowers in the early spring, so Lewis may have found the plant that Pursh described near St. Louis, and that specimen is now lost.

All of this shows how easy it is to become confused when dealing with the Lewis and Clark collection. One can still find meadow anemones near the site of the Omaha village, where they flower from late May well into July.

(*Anemone canadensis*) at the same time. Lewis did not list this specimen, which is now in the Lewis and Clark Herbarium, in the catalog of the plants that he sent to Jefferson in 1805, and there is no label in his handwriting on the specimen sheet—so, as with some of his other specimens, we just do not know where this anemone came from. There is, however, another possibility. It is unusual for the meadow anemone to flower in mid-August; it usually

---

LOASACEAE (LOASA FAMILY)
Collected near the Omaha village of Tonwontonga, Dakota County, Nebraska, August 1804
TEN-PETALED BLAZING-STAR, *MENTZELIA DECAPETALA* (PURSH) URB. & GILG EX GILG

The ten-petaled blazing-star is a coarse biennial or perennial plant with a flower that is hard to ignore. The plant may grow to be three feet tall and is notable for its large creamy-white flowers. The plants grow on clayey, sandy, or rocky soil, chiefly in disturbed places such as roadsides. The stems, arising from a stout taproot, have smooth, thin, white, exfoliating bark and the leaf margins are characterized by irregu-

lar coarse serrations—when touched the leaves feel like sandpaper. The showy ten-petaled flowers open fully in the late afternoon and close around midnight, depending on night-flying moths as pollinators. Numerous yellow stamens contribute to the flowers' impressive appearance. The fruit is a large, cylindrical capsule that can be up to two inches or more long and has numerous flattened, slightly winged seeds arrayed in five to seven vertical rows inside the capsule. These are dispersed by wind or by floating on water. A series of leafy, rough bracts may surround the capsule, so if it is broken off the plant—say by a grazing animal—the capsule and all of its seeds can become attached to the animal's fur and spread to other places.

We know that Lewis and Clark found the ten-petaled blazing-star (also known as the ten-petaled mentzelia, sand-lily, and gumbo-lily—the last has been suggested as a standardized name) near the Omaha village of Tonwontonga outside present-day Homer, Nebraska, where the Corps of Discovery camped between August 13 and August 20. The members of the party occupied themselves with fishing, hunting, trading with the Indians, and obtaining information about what lay farther upriver. On August 17, the day before Lewis's thirtieth birthday, someone in the party gathered *Anemone canadensis* and *Grindelia squarrosa*. Clark also noted that he collected at least three different grasses on that day, and he may have collected these wildflowers as well. If so, this may have been the only day on which either of the captains collected plants, for they would have been busy with Lewis's birthday celebration the next day, and Sergeant Floyd who was seriously ill "with a Beliose Chorlick" on the nineteenth.[26]

Pursh apparently took the Lewis and Clark specimen to

Mentzelia decapetala

JAMES L. REVEAL

London in 1811, where it disappeared. He had good reason to take it, for it was clearly a new species and perhaps a new genus. He did not anticipate that Thomas Nuttall and John Bradbury would ascend the Missouri River in 1811, and that Nuttall would return to London the following year with seeds and specimens of many of the same new species that Lewis and Clark had found. Worse yet, within months, garden specimens of the ten-petaled blazing-star were flowering in the garden of the Fraser Brothers at Sloane Square.

It appears that Pursh and Nuttall agreed to jointly publish a description of the plant and propose a new genus to honor their joint patron, Benjamin Smith Barton. We do not know why Pursh suddenly decided to publish *Bartonia decapetala* in Curtis's *Botanical Magazine* without Nuttall's knowledge. Understandably, Nuttall was disgusted and complained vociferously to whoever would listen, charging, among other things, that Pursh was stealing new species, ones that had not even been found by Lewis and Clark. Pursh responded in his *Flora*, writing that he "made a drawing and description of it" in 1807, and that he could not allow Nuttall the honor of describing the species because he (Pursh) wanted to preserve the "justice and propriety" due "the memory of M. Lewis, Esq."[27]

EQUISETACEAE (HORSETAIL FAMILY)

Collected in Burt County, Nebraska, or Monona County, Iowa, on August 10, 1804

FIELD HORSETAIL, *EQUISETUM ARVENSE* L.

The field horsetail, *Equisetum arvense* (the species name is a Latin word meaning "of the field") is interesting, for this group of primitive vascular plants has been around since the Carboniferous Era. Still, one wonders why the captains collected so common a plant. It would not have been new to them, for it is a circumpolar species widely distributed in the United States. The green, frilly plants are not unattractive, but they have little use other than as a browse for bear and wild ungulates (deer, moose, caribou, and so on). At times, they may grow in such abundance in moist areas that they are considered weeds.

Opinion differs as to whether humans can eat field horsetails, and they are included on some lists of poisonous plants. H. D. Harrington says, however, that the young shoots may be boiled and are palatable, and that Native Americans ate the field horsetail.[28] Unfortunately, the captains' journals do not explain what they had in mind when they gathered the specimens, and they mention the plant only once. On June 19, 1804, Clark wrote that the party came to a shallow lake, whose bottom was covered with what was almost certainly the field horsetail. It was, he wrote, a "place of great resort for Deer and fowls of every kind the bottom low & covered with rushes." The labels accompanying the two herbarium sheets note only that the specimens were collected on the banks of the Missouri. The explanatory list of items sent back to Jefferson from Fort Mandan in the spring of 1805 identify them as "No 31. Taken on the 10th of August, a species of sand rush, joined and so much branched as to form a perfect broom…it grows near the water's edge in moist sand." Lewis apparently collected the specimens both to document the plant's distribution along the Missouri River ("it is common to every part of this river at least as far as Latitude 42 N") and its potential use as animal fodder ("the horses are remarkably fond of it").[29] Frederick Pursh included *Equisetum arvense* in his *Flora* without mentioning the specimens that Lewis and Clark collected, probably because

Equisetum arvense

A. SCOTT EARLE

Equisetum arvense

JAMES L. REVEAL

they were not new plants—Linnaeus had named *Equisetum arvense* decades earlier.

Both of the Lewis and Clark Herbarium specimens are thick clumps—one is identified as being a sidebranch. They collected only the sterile or nonreproductive phase of the species. (In early spring, a brownish, nonphotosynthetic, fertile stalk appears, usually just as the green, sterile shoots are emerging from the moist ground.) Much of the floodplain along the lower Missouri River has been converted into farmland, so the bottomlands that the explorers saw are mostly gone. Large populations of field horsetail still grow, however, in some of the wildlife refuges along the river, where seasonal flooding is permitted. Only here can one appreciate the scene that Clark described.

NYCTAGINACEAE (FOUR-O'CLOCK FAMILY)
Collected in Bon Homme County, South Dakota, or Knox County, Nebraska, on September 1, 1804
HEARTLEAF FOUR-O'CLOCK, *MIRABILIS NYCTAGINEA* (MICHX.) MACMILL.

The heartleaf four o'clock is unusual, for its "flowers" consist of an involucre—a cuplike structure that resembles joined petals—borne in an umbrella-like cluster at the top of the main stem. The involucre is sometimes white, but often pink or purple, and contains several greatly reduced flowers that have no actual petals. The plant's lower leaves are opposite and heart-shaped—thus its common name. The upper leaves are lanceolate. Like other wild four-o'clocks, it grows on dry, open ground and may be found today along roads and railway tracks, blooming from midsummer on. Both the common name, "four-o'clock," and the species name, *nyctaginea* (from the Greek, meaning "night-opening"), reflect the plant's tendency to bloom late in the afternoon and early evening (dropping temperature, rather than light reduction, causes the flowers to open as evening approaches). The generic name, *Mirabilis*, means "marvelous"—in fact, the English term is derived from the Latin word.

On September 1, the expedition was working its way up the Missouri River after spending two days with the Yankton Sioux. A bit west of today's Yankton, South Dakota, Lewis found a four-o'clock that he did not recognize—hardly surprising, for at that time the plant grew only on the eastern Great Plains. Since then, it has spread over much of the United States and is clas-

Mirabilis nyctaginea

JAMES L. REVEAL

sified as a noxious weed in thirty-five states.

Frederick Pursh had a hard time with this specimen. He placed it in the genus *Allionia*, giving it the species name *ovata*. He noted that it was found "On the plains of the Missouri…[by] M. Lewis." He failed to recognize, however, that Lewis's specimen was the same plant that the French botanist André Michaux had described a decade before as *Allionia nyctaginea*—a plant that Pursh also included in his *Flora*.[30]

ELAEAGNACEAE (OLEASTER FAMILY)

Collected at the mouth of the Quicourre (Niobrara) River, Knox County, Nebraska,
or Bon Homme County, South Dakota, about September 4, 1804

SILVER BUFFALOBERRY, *SHEPHERDIA ARGENTEA* (PURSH) NUTT.
RUSSET BUFFALOBERRY, *SHEPHERDIA CANADENSIS* (L.) NUTT.

Few shrubs were more important to the Native Americans of the Great Plains than the silver buffaloberry (*Shepherdia argentea*). This large shrub or small tree is widely scattered on the prairie from Nebraska northward into Alberta and Manitoba. As with the related silverberry (*Elaeagnus commutata*, p. 200), tiny hairs give the leaves a silvery sheen. Look closely with a hand lens and you will see that the hairs are overlapping scalelike hairs, or elaborate star-shaped structures. The flowers of the two are similar; both are four-petaled, inconspicuous, and not likely to be noticed. Their fruit differs significantly; the silverberry's fruit is dry, mealy, and silvery, whereas those of the silver buffaloberry are sweet, succulent, and bright red. The branches of the latter are tipped with spines, so one must be careful in gathering the berries. The two genera (*Shepherdia* and *Elaeagnus*) are easily confused when in flower but not while they are fruiting. Both Lewis and Clark noted in their journals that buffalober-

ries made wonderful tarts. In 1832, while near old Fort Mandan, the artist George Catlin found that buffaloberry "bushes, which are peculiar to these northern regions, lined the banks of the river and defiles in the bluffs, sometimes for miles together; forming almost impassable hedges, so loaded with the weight of their fruit, that their boughs were everywhere gracefully bending down and resting on the ground."[31]

Lewis was impressed with the potential usefulness of the shrub, and he sent several live plants back to St. Louis on the keelboat in the spring of 1805. Lewis's original label for the dried specimens that he collected on September 4, 1804, reads, "obtained at the mouth of the River Quiccourre [the Niobrara River] from which place upwards it is abundant in the Missouri bottoms, it is a pleasant burry to eat—it has much the flavor of the cranbury and continues on the bush through the winter—this is an evergreen shrub." Frederick Pursh described the plant and put it into an established Eurasian genus as

Shepherdia argentea

JAMES L. REVEAL

Shepherdia canadensis

A. SCOTT EARLE

Hippophaë argentea.[32] Five years later, Nuttall—who saw the plant in 1811 and gathered its seeds—established a new genus, *Shepherdia*, to honor the curator of the Liverpool Botanic Garden, John Shepherd (1764-1836).[33] There is no record of what happened to the live plants that Lewis sent back from Fort Mandan, but cultivated specimens were soon growing in Europe, probably from seeds that Nuttall took to England, but possibly from seeds gathered by Lewis and Clark in 1804 as well. The Missouri's banks are now flooded by a series of dams, and the floodplains have been converted to productive agricultural fields, so that one no longer sees a continuous hedge of silver buffaloberry along the river's edges. Nevertheless, in late summer, one can still find the shrub and taste its berries.

The explorers would also have seen another, closely related plant, the russet buffaloberry (*Shepherdia canadensis*). The silver buffaloberry, described above, grows only to the east of the Rocky Mountains, as far as Minnesota, and is found mostly along watercourses and in other moist surroundings. Conversely, the russet buffaloberry (or soopalallie) is common in the northern Rocky Mountains, although it also grows from Alaska to Oregon and east to the Atlantic Coast.[34] It prefers a somewhat drier environment, often growing in open woods. The leaves are less silvery, more rounded, and are a scaly brown on their undersides. Its berries, like those of the silver buffaloberry, are red and also grow in clumps, but its branches lack spines. The berries are edible, but just barely. Because they contain saponin, a soaplike chemical, they are intensely bitter. Native Americans whipped the soopalallie berries with water to form a confection, or a topping like whipped cream, known as "Indian ice-cream." The russet buffaloberry also fruits during the summer. Lewis and Clark had to have seen the shrub along their trail in 1805, and especially while they were in the mountains. The otherwise unidentified "red berries" seen on July 16 and August 3, 1805, might have been this plant.[35] The captains both mention berries many more times in their journals, but trying to identify them often amounts to guesswork. Because the russet buffaloberry fruit was so bitter, Lewis may have thought that the plant was not worth collecting, or, more likely, he knew the plant from the East, as did Pursh, who included it in the *Flora* as *Hippophaë canadensis* (explaining his classification of Lewis's specimen of the clearly related silver buffaloberry).

ASTERACEAE (ASTER FAMILY)
Collected below the Big Bend of the Missouri in Lyman or Buffalo County, South Dakota, on September 19, 1804
SNAKEWEED, *GUTIERREZIA SAROTHRAE* (PURSH) BRITTON & RUSBY

Snakeweed is a low, resinous, unattractive shrub that often grows in dense patches. The plants are much branched, with small, narrow, sticky, alternate leaves. The composite flowers have only four to seven rays and are clustered into more or less discrete heads. The plant goes by several common names, and all seem to be in use: matchbrush, matchweed (from their dry woody stems and branches, and the ease with which the dry plants burn), broomweed, and snakeweed (the last seems to be preferred). The plant is a widely distributed perennial that spreads by root fragmentation and seeds. It is found all across the Great Plains, as far west as eastern Oregon, and from northern Canada to northern Mexico. Snakeweed has some minor browse value, for pronghorns and probably other Great Plains animals eat it. At times this may be important, as it usually grows in areas where there is little grass. Stockmen consider it a weed, because it may cause cows and ewes to abort their young, and it may even cause fatalities if cattle eat much of it. Overgrazing favors the snake-

Gutierrezia sarothrae

JAMES L. REVEAL

There are two snakeweed specimens in the Lewis and Clark Herbarium, apparently gathered on the same day, close to the mouth of the White River, near present-day Chamberlain, South Dakota. It is not mentioned in the expedition's journals, but the specimen sheets in the herbarium note that the plant was a "growth of high and bear prairies which produce little grass."

Frederick Pursh saw that it was a new species. He wrote in his *Flora* that the plant grows "On the plains of the Missouri" and classified it as a *Solidago* (a goldenrod), giving it the species name *sarothrae* (derived from the Greek *sarothron*, a word that means "broom," from the resemblance of the dried plant to an old-fashioned brushwood broom). Pursh also mentioned that the plant was one that Lewis had collected, for he was punctilious about giving Lewis credit for the expedition's plants included in his *Flora* (even though Clark and others undoubtedly collected some of them). The plant retained Pursh's species name, but it was later reclassified as a *Gutierrezia*.[36]

weed's growth, and it tends to become a dominant plant on poorly managed rangelands, displacing grass and sagebrush. It is still found today in relatively undisturbed sites, hanging on from a time a century or so ago, when sheep and cattle on the open western range numbered in the millions.

FAGACEAE (BEECH FAMILY)

Collected above the Niobrara River, Knox County, Nebraska, or Charles Mix County, South Dakota, on September 5, 1804

BUR OAK, *QUERCUS MACROCARPA* MICHX.

Full-grown bur oaks are majestic trees, big in all dimensions. They are second in size only to the eastern white oak (*Quercus alba*) among American oak trees. In the past bur oaks were reported to be up to 180 feet tall, with a basal diameter of six or seven feet. Their deeply incised leaves, and their acorns—up to two inches across—are larger than those of any other native oak. As might be expected, the wood has great commercial value. The bur oak is also an important ornamental tree. Although its original range was pretty much restricted to the Midwest, it has more recently been introduced into the eastern and southwestern parts of the United States and

beyond. Its majestic appearance, natural resistance to insects and disease, and adaptability, even in a city environment, make the bur oak one of our most important trees.

Lewis and Clark apparently did not realize that the tree had been described previously, and they—or most likely Lewis—collected it twice. Both of his specimens show the morphology of the leaves well, even after two hundred years.[37]

Pursh recognized Lewis's specimens as *Quercus macrocarpa*, a tree that the French botanist André Michaux had described during his twelve-year stay in North America (1785-1796). (The tree was included in a beautifully illustrated monograph

Quercus macrocarpa

JAMES L. REVEAL

Quercus macrocarpa

JAMES L. REVEAL

of North American oaks, *Histoire des chênes de l'Amérique*, published in 1801.) Pursh gave the tree's distribution accurately, noting that it grew on the Missouri and "within the mountains," although he did not mention Lewis or his specimens. The tree's range does extend to the Rocky Mountains (although it grows there only as a much smaller tree or shrub), but Pursh could have obtained this information only from one of the explorers. He used Michaux's scientific name, *Quercus macro-* *carpa*; the species name means "big fruit" and is the same one we use today. Pursh noted that it was known as the "Overcup White Oak by the inhabitants…the fruit is the largest of the American species; the wood is very excellent."[38] Today's common name, "bur oak" (or "burr oak"), refers to the prominent fringe of coarse hairs that grow on the cupule that holds the nut. The cupule usually covers more than two-thirds of the nut, explaining the common name "overcup oak."

ASTERACEAE (ASTER FAMILY)

Collected above the mouth of the White River, Lyman or Brule County, South Dakota, on September 15, 1804

LACY TANSY-ASTER, *MACHAERANTHERA PINNATIFIDA* (HOOK.) SHINNERS

The lacy tansy-aster is a taprooted perennial. Numerous long, usually woolly stems spring from a woody base. Its leaves are narrow and have sharp, bristle-tipped, spinelike little teeth. The flowers are yellow and look like tiny sunflowers. Interestingly, the sex cells of the pollen and ovary have only four chromosomes, yet this species is remarkably variable, and it includes several varieties and subspecies. The plant ranges from south-central Canada to northern Mexico.

Frederick Pursh based his description of the lacy tansy- aster on Lewis and Clark specimens, classifying it as *Amellus spinulosus* (the species name describing the spiny leaves). He noted that the plant was growing "In open prairies on the Missouri," adding that he had seen Lewis's specimen. He then described the plant at some length.[39] Oddly, *Amellus* is a genus found in southern Africa, and one wonders why Pursh went so far afield in trying to assign the plant. Over the years others have placed it in several other genera, most recently—in the 1960s—as a *Machaeranthera*

35

Machaeranthera pinnatifida

JAMES L. REVEAL

(from the Greek *machaira* meaning "sword," and *anthera* for "anther," for the sharp anthers of the disk flowers); this genus was described in 1832 to include asterlike plants with sharp-tipped anthers. The plant is known today as *Machaeranthera pinnatifida*;[40] some plant guides still list it under an older name, *Haplopappus spinulosus*.

Lewis collected three plants on September 15, 1804, of which the lacy tansy-aster was one. (The others were tarragon, *Artemisia dracunculus*, described here with the sages, and the Canada milk vetch, *Astragalus canadensis*.) That day he and Clark hiked up the White River in Lyman County, South Dakota, south of Oacoma—an area now under the waters of Lake Francis Case—and possibly he collected the plants then. The tansy-aster is still common throughout the Great Plains and flowers from late spring through early fall. You may find it growing along today's South Dakota State Highways 47 and 50, where those routes parallel the Missouri River, south of Interstate 90. The plant's present species name, *pinnatifida*, refers to the leaves, which are pinnatifid—deeply divided, like the barbs of a feather.

POACEAE (GRASS FAMILY)

Collected at various times and places

GRASSES OF THE GREAT PLAINS

The Great Plains that Lewis and Clark saw in 1804 was a grass-covered, flat to moderately rolling country dissected by tree- and shrub-lined streams. The explorers encountered tallgrass prairie in Missouri, but midgrass species were the rule along most of the Missouri River in Kansas and Nebraska. Only in northern portions of the Great Plains and in Montana did they see the short-grass steppes that are essentially all that is left today of the primeval Great Plains. Most of the tall- and midgrass prairie has been converted into the most productive farmland in the world.

The explorers were born to an agrarian society. They knew the value of grasses, especially those important for grazing and fodder production. Lewis and Clark did not consider the plains desolate. They accurately characterized them as potentially productive country. Zebulon Pike (1779-1813), Jefferson's questionable choice of an explorer to follow Lewis and Clark, destroyed that image and suppressed westward migration for more than thirty years. In 1810, he referred to the plains as "The Great American Desert." Another explorer, John Charles Frémont (1813-1890), known as the "Pathmaker of the West," altered that perception, and his reports, written in the early 1840s, were important in promoting western migration.

The mixed grasslands of the eastern and southern Great Plains were dominated by a series of highly productive perennial grasses. These were able to withstand drought,

Schizachyrium scoparium

JAMES L. REVEAL

Elymus canadensis

JAMES L. REVEAL

cold, wind, and extensive grazing by the great herds of pronghorn and buffalo that moved northward each spring and summer and returned south in the fall. Deer and elk joined these animals farther west on Montana's shortgrass steppes. Wildflowers dotted the landscape at different seasons of the year, and cottonwood, willow, and other shrubs lined the edges of clear-water streams. Birds were common on the grasslands, but unlike their eastern relatives, birds on the plains sing in flight, rather than from a perch.

Lewis collected at least eight grasses in 1804. All but one were among the first thirty specimens that he collected. All of these are now lost. The grasses that he probably gathered were big bluestem (*Andropogon gerardii* Vitman), little bluestem (*Schizachyrium scoparium* (Michx.) Nash), nodding wild rye (*Elymus canadensis* L.), and blue grama (*Bouteloua gracilis* (Kunth) Lag. ex Griffiths); all are com-

Bouteloua gracilis

JAMES L. REVEAL

Phalaris arundinacea

JAMES L. REVEAL

Koeleria macrantha

JAMES L. REVEAL

Hesperostipa spartea

JAMES L. REVEAL

Bouteloua curtipendula

JAMES L. REVEAL

mon on the Great Plains. We know that Lewis did collect specimens and seeds of reed canary grass (*Phalaris arundinacea* L.). He called it "wild prairie timothy"; these seeds did not survive. Here is how he described this plant, number 19, in his Fort Mandan catalog of plants: "[I]t grew in great abundance in the prarie from five to six feet high; it gave the plain much the appearance of an extensive timothy meadow ready for the sythe...."[41]

It is unlikely that the distinctive buffalo grass (*Bouteloua dactyloides* (Nutt.) Columbus), long known as *Buchloe dactyloises* (Nutt.) Engelm., or porcupine grass (*Hesperostipa spartea* (Trin.) Barkworth) would have escaped the explorers' attention. In marshy areas, they likely saw freshwater cordgrass (*Spartina pectinata* Link). Elsewhere, others, such as

yellow Indian grass (*Sorghastrum nutans* (L.) Nash) and June grass (*Koeleria macrantha* (Ledeb.) Schult.), would have been common. On the edge of the tallgrass prairie, they might have seen sideoats grama (*Bouteloua curtipendula* (Michx.) Torr.) and prairie dropseed (*Sporobolus heterolepis* (Gray) A. Gray). The inland wild rice (*Zizania palustris* L. var. *interior* (Fassett) Dore) is the only surviving specimen in the Lewis and Clark Herbarium of all of the grasses collected along the Missouri. Lewis gathered this grass on the Nebraska–South Dakota border (the northern edge of its known distribution) on September 8, 1804. Native Americans commonly used the seeds of this plant— we know them as "wild rice"—for food and used cordgrass for thatching.

ASTERACEAE (ASTER FAMILY)

Six specimens. Three from the Big Bend of the Missouri River in Lyman County, South Dakota, collected on September 21, 1804;
one from above the mouth of the Cheyenne River, Dewey or Sully County, South Dakota, collected on October 2, 1804.
Site and date of remaining two collections are uncertain.

RUBBER RABBITBRUSH, *ERICAMERIA NAUSEOSA* (PALL. EX PURSH) G. L. NESOM & G. I. BAIRD

The rubber rabbitbrush obviously fascinated the explorers, for the shrubs differed significantly from anything that they were familiar with in the East. They were acquainted with a few fall blooming yellow plants in the aster family, but most have petal like ray flowers with darker—sometimes blackish—tiny disk flowers in the center of the flower head, as in the native sunflower *Helianthus annuus*, for example. Rabbitbrushes, however, have no ray flowers, only bright yellow disk flowers. The shrubs may grow to be more than ten feet across and as much as six feet high. In the fall, they often dominate the sagebrush-covered hills of the American West with their bright yellow blooms. Rabbitbrushes were new to the explorers, new to Frederick Pursh, and new to science.

Describing plants that Lewis and Clark collected can be a challenge, but none more so than the rubber rabbitbrush. There are five specimens in varying states of preservation in the Lewis and Clark Herbarium at The Academy of Natural Sciences in Philadelphia. Classification of this plant can also be difficult, even in the field, for there are many varieties. Furthermore, the plant has had numerous scientific names assigned to it over the years, with changes ongoing right up to the present. And to top that off, we do not know where Lewis and Clark collected two of their six specimens. Lewis described the plants that he sent back from Fort Mandan in the spring of 1805 as plant number 32. He wrote, "Specimens of aromatic plants on which the atelope feeds—these were obtained 21st of Sept. 1805 at the upper part of the bigg bend of the Missouri—."[42]

Pursh did his best to classify the rabbitbrushes, assigning two or possibly three generic names to the specimens. These included *Chrysocoma nauseosa*—the generic name is obsolete, although we still use Pursh's species name. Today, we know rubber rabbitbrush (named for the sticky, white, rub-

Ericameria nauseosa

berlike sap that exudes from broken stems) as a highly complex species of about twenty varieties. Most are found in the cold desert between the Sierra Nevada and the Rocky Mountains, although some are found from southern Canada to northern Mexico. Lewis gathered two varieties along the Missouri River on the Great Plains, the hairy var. *nauseosa* and the smooth-foliaged var. *graveolens*. The rabbitbrush has, until recently, been classified in the genus *Chrysothamnus* (from the Greek, meaning "golden shrub"), and many guidebooks still use that name. In 1993, however, it was reclassified as *Ericameria* (a genus suggested by Thomas Nuttall in 1840). Thus, we have today's name, *Ericameria nauseosa*.

CHENOPODIACEAE (GOOSEFOOT FAMILY)

Atriplex canescens, *collected at the Big Bend of the Missouri River, Lyman County, South Dakota, September 21, 1804*
Atriplex gardneri, *collected at the Big Bend of the Missouri River, Lyman County, South Dakota, September 21, 1804,*
and on the Marias River, Toole County, Montana, July 20, 1806
Krascheninnikovia lanata, *collected at the Big Bend of the Missouri River, Lyman County, South Dakota, September 21, 1804 (specimen lost)*

FOUR-WING SALTBUSH, *ATRIPLEX CANESCENS* (PURSH) NUTT.
GARDNER'S SALTBUSH, *ATRIPLEX GARDNERI* (MOQ.) STANDLEY
WINTERFAT, *KRASCHENINNIKOVIA LANATA* (PURSH) A. MEEUSE & A. SMIT

September 21, 1804, was a chaotic day for the men of the expedition. It began at one o'clock in the morning when the sandbar the Corps of Discovery was camped on suddenly began to cave in. Clark was able to see the extent of the impending destruction by moonlight and quickly "ordered all hands on as quick as possible & pushed off…by the time we made the opsd. Shore our Camp fell in." The men made a second camp, and at daylight they moved into what was then "the Gouge of this Great bend," the Big Bend of the Missouri River. Clark sent two men to determine the distance between the closest points of the river's bend—some two thousand yards—although the river's course around the bend covered about thirty miles. Lewis went plant hunting, in what Clark described as rough gullies, and discovered two species of saltbush that he apparently confused. These are described in Pursh's *Flora*, as found "In the plains of the Missouri, near the Big-bend…Goats [pronghorn] delight to feed upon this shrub."[43]

Perennial saltbushes are not pretty but they are important as a source of browse for pronghorn, deer, and today's sheep; they also act as soil binders. Species of saltbushes tend to occur on barren flats, slopes, and bluffs, typically on alkaline soils throughout much of the arid West. The four-wing saltbush (*Atriplex canescens*), the plant that Lewis found that day in South Dakota, is the most widespread member of the genus *Atriplex* (*atriplex* is the Latin word for saltbush, while

Atriplex canescens

JAMES L. REVEAL

Krascheninnikovia lanata

JAMES L. REVEAL

canescens means "hoary" or "old and white"). The shrub, which may be three feet or more in height, is a greenish gray color. Its light tan fruit grow in an elongated cluster and have a distinct, four-winged appearance. Its leaves are covered with tightly arranged hairs. Although the species is widely scattered, it is found mainly in the western half of the Great Plains.

Lewis apparently did not recognize that his collection was actually a mixture of four-wing saltbush and Gardner's saltbush (*Atriplex gardneri*). Pursh did not know this, either, so his original description of *Atriplex canescens* in 1813 included features of both species. Lewis would gather Gardner's saltbush again on July 20, 1806, along the Marias River in Montana. Today, the plant is uncommon in South Dakota.

Lewis apparently gathered another species, known today

Atriplex gardneri

JAMES L. REVEAL

as "winterfat." Its scientific name, *Krascheninnikovia lanata*, honors the Russian botanist Ippolit Mikhailovich Krascheninnikov (1884-1947); the species name, *lanata*, means "woolly." Lewis also found this on September 21 while at the Big Bend. We can assume he gathered the plant, based on his notes, but we cannot be certain, for the specimen is lost.[44]

Winterfat was long known in the scientific literature as *Eurotia lanata* or *Ceratoides lanata*; it is one of the most important winter browse plants for grazing animals in the West. Although it still grows in the vicinity of the Big Bend, it is found more commonly along the Lewis and Clark Trail near the Missouri River in western North Dakota and Montana. The grayish to rusty, almost silky hairs that densely cover the plant, and especially its fruit, make the shrub easy to identify.

ASTERACEAE (ASTER FAMILY)

Liatris aspera, collected in Brule County, South Dakota, September 12, 1804
Liatris pycnostachya, collected above the mouth of the White River, Lyman or Brule County, South Dakota, September 18, 1804

TALL GAYFEATHER, *LIATRIS ASPERA* MICHX.
CATTAIL GAYFEATHER, *LIATRIS PYCNOSTACHYA* MICHX.

The gayfeathers, species of Liatris (the derivation of liatris is unknown), occur commonly on moist prairies and open woodlands throughout most of the Great Plains. They are erect, perennial herbs ("herb," when used botanically, refers to a nonwoody plant). The gayfeathers have large clusters of pink-to-purple (rarely white) flowers arranged in elongated, narrow, spikelike flower clusters. Typically they arise from solid, bulblike subterranean stems known as corms. There are perhaps thirty ill-defined species; all are found in eastern North America from southern Canada to northern Mexico.

41

Numerous naturally occurring hybrids may make identification difficult. The wandlike plants, waving in the prairie autumn winds, provide bright spots of color against the tan, dry, prairie grass.

Lewis collected two species of gayfeather along the Missouri River in 1804. He found the tall gayfeather (*Liatris aspera*) near the county line between Charles Mix and Brule Counties in South Dakota on September 12, 1804 (the plant's species name, *aspera*, is the Latin word for "rough"). The plant is not common there today; it grows more to the east, and much more abundantly to the south, in eastern Kansas and western Missouri. Lewis gathered the cattail gayfeather (*Liatris pycnostachya*) three days later near Chamberlain, in Brule County (the species name, *pycnostachya*, was derived from the Greek *pyknos* for "thick" and *stachys* for "spike"—for its prominent stems and flower clusters). The species does not grow in this area today. Lewis probably found the plants in the moist meadows that were near the Missouri River two centuries ago, meadows since obliterated by the impounded waters of reservoirs.

Liatris

JAMES L. REVEAL

Liatris

JAMES L. REVEAL

Frederick Pursh would have examined both of the expedition's specimens, but he probably saw that they were plants that André Michaux had previously collected, described, and named. Although Pursh included both the tall and the cattail gayfeathers in his *Flora*, he did not mention Lewis's specimens.[45]

ROSACEAE (ROSE FAMILY)

Collected above the Niobrara River, Knox County, Nebraska, or Charles Mix County, South Dakota, September 5, 1804, and near the mouth of the Cannonball River, Morton, Sioux, or Emmons County, North Dakota, October 1804

PRAIRIE WILD ROSE, *ROSA ARKANSANA* PORTER

The prairie wild rose has pink-to-white flowers, prickly stems, and alternate "odd-pinnate leaves" with seven to eleven toothed leaflets. ("Odd pinnate" refers to featherlike compound leaves that have varying numbers of opposing leaflets. These are borne on a central stemlet, the petiole. A single distal leaflet makes their total number odd—commonly seen in the rose, pea, and other plant families.) Overall, the plants have a low, shrublike appearance. Several flowers appear late in the summer on the end of the season's main branch, and sometimes on lateral branches as well. The plants are perennial and usually die back to ground level each year, depending on climatic conditions. The prairie wild rose is fairly common today on the Great Plains, although it is seen less often than in the past. It is native to the states east of the Rocky Mountains and ranges south to Texas.[46]

Meriwether Lewis sent back two specimens of wild rose from Fort Mandan in the spring of 1805, noting in his descriptive catalog, "N°. 50 Octobr 18th. The small Rose of the praries it rises from 12 to 14 Inches high does not vine." One would expect to find either two specimen sheets, or one sheet with two specimens, in the Lewis and Clark Herbarium, but all that remains is a single spray of leaves, and no bloom. A label in Frederick Pursh's hand appended to the remaining material gives no more information than what Lewis had written when he collected the plant: "Rosa Open prairies Septb: 5. 1804." The specimen may have

Rosa arkansana

JAMES L. REVEAL

been incomplete when Frederick Pursh examined it, for he did not include a western rose in his *Flora*.[47]

FABACEAE (PEA FAMILY)

Collected above the mouth of the White River, Lyman or Brule County, South Dakota.
Astragalus canadensis collected on September 15; Astragalus missouriensis on September 18;
also Astragalus crassicarpus on June 3, 1804; also Astragalus tenellus collected but specimen lost

CANADA MILK VETCH, *ASTRAGALUS CANADENSIS* L.
MISSOURI MILK VETCH, *ASTRAGALUS MISSOURIENSIS* NUTT.
GROUND PLUM MILK VETCH, *ASTRAGALUS CRASSICARPUS* NUTT.
LOOSEFLOWER MILK VETCH, *ASTRAGALUS TENELLUS* PURSH

The genus *Astragalus* makes amateur botanists cringe. It contains upwards of two thousand species; nearly forty are native to our Great Plains, and as many more are found in the Pacific Northwest. Moreover, differences between species are often so technical that precise identification can be difficult. Nonetheless, the plants do have common characteristics that help to place them, first, in the pea family, and then in the genus *Astragalus*. The pealike flower easily assigns them to the pea family as does their odd-pinnate leaves (defined on p. 42). They are distinguished from the true vetches (*Vicia* spp.), which have an even number of leaflets with a tendril (a threadlike extension that aids in the climbing habit of the vetches) at the end of their compound leaves, rather than a single leaflet. Closely clustered flowers, typical of those seen in other Fabaceae, are borne on the end of one or more stems. The fruit consists of pods—some have a bizarre shape—containing varying numbers of pealike seeds.

The term "milk vetch" is an old one, used in the British Isles for vetchlike members of the pea family (most notably the milk vetch, *Astragalus glycyphyllos*) that were believed to enhance milk production in goats that browsed on the plant. The common name spread to include related plants and more recently to embrace all plants in the genus *Astragalus*—a scientific name proposed by Linnaeus. The name apparently was derived from the Greek word for the ankle, *astragalos*, and specifically for the weight-bearing bone in the ankle that articulates with the tibia. It was applied initially to a now unknown leguminous plant of the Mediterranean region. One explanation for the name is that dry seeds rattling in the plant's pod resembled the sound of shaken dice, or "astragals," made from the anklebones of an animal—probably a sheep or goat.

Meriwether Lewis included three

Astragalus canadensis var. mortonii

A. SCOTT EARLE

milk vetches, which he had gathered in today's Missouri and South Dakota, with the other specimens that he sent back to President Jefferson in the spring of 1805. Frederick Pursh examined the specimens and saw that the Canada milk vetch, the plant with the widest distribution, was one that had been previously described. He included it in his *Flora* using Linnaeus's scientific name.[48]

Astragalus canadensis is a rather attractive plant. It stands up to two feet in height and has spreading dark stems. The many leaflets of its leaves, and its long, thin, off-white, clustered flowers (from 30 to as many as 150) are stacked closely together with almost geometrical precision. The plant ranges widely and is found in all of the northern states, from coast to coast, and south to Texas.

Astragalus missouriensis is very different. It is only about four inches high and has silvery green foliage and fewer leaflets (seven to fifteen). The

Astragalus crassicarpus var. paysonii

A. SCOTT EARLE

Astragalus tenellus

JAMES L. REVEAL

attractive, bright purple flowers with light centers are fewer and clustered more loosely than those of the Canada milk vetch. The Missouri milk vetch is restricted to the Great Plains, ranging north into Canada and south to Texas; it often grows on barren ground. Unfortunately, the Lewis specimen was so fragmentary that Pursh was unable to characterize it and thus did not attempt to describe the species. Thomas Nuttall named this new species in 1818 based on collections that he made along the Missouri River in 1811.

Astragalus crassicarpus, the ground or buffalo plum, is a different plant, for the fruit of the other two are recognizably similar to pea pods, while that of the ground plum is round, or nearly so, and thick walled. The plant itself—including the pods with their edible pealike seeds—often lies flat on the ground, explaining its various common names: ground plum, buffalo plum, pomme de terre, and so on. The scientific name comes from its peculiar pod, for *crassicarpus* is Latin for "thick fruit." The plant grows over a fairly wide area, from the Rocky Mountains, east to Missouri and Illinois, north into Canada, and south to Texas. It is characterized by frilly leaves with many leaflets, typical of the genus as a whole. Loosely clustered white to purple flowers are fairly large (an inch or more).

The ground plum was one of the first thirty plants that Lewis collected, plants that have since disappeared and are not now in the Lewis and Clark Herbarium. It was also the first of the three milk vetches that he found on "the 3rd of June above the mouth of the Osage river" in today's Missouri. He wrote that "it is a growth of the high dry open praries; rises to the hight of 18 inches or two feet puts forth many stems from the same root." He described how the Indians "frequently use the fruit of this plant to allay their thirst" noting that at the time he saw the plant, the pods were unripe and "about the sise of a pullet's egg…the seed are like pees…the pulp is crisp & clear" tasting much like a "gardin pee…[of a] fine red colour and sweet flavor."[49]

Astragalus tenellus is found mainly on the prairie from the Yukon to New Mexico, but its range extends as far east as Hudson Bay and as far west as the Great Basin. It is a spreading plant, seldom growing more than a foot above ground level. There are fewer than twenty creamy white flowers, and these are less than an inch long. The thin, membranous pod attracted Pursh's attention. The pods, borne on short stalks (stipes), are slightly longer than the flowers and contain up to twelve seeds.[50] Apparently Lewis's specimen was in late flower; its fruit was so distinctive that Pursh described the plant as a new species. In 1813, Pursh obtained additional specimens that John Bradbury had gathered along the Missouri two years earlier. Pursh incorrectly proposed a new name (*Ervum multiflorum*) for the same plant found previously by Lewis.[51]

LAMIACEAE (MINT FAMILY)
Collected at the Big Bend of the Missouri River, Lyman County, South Dakota, September 21, 1804
LANCELEAF SAGE, *SALVIA REFLEXA* HORNEM.

The lanceleaf sage is an annual, many-branched, leafy plant that often grows on disturbed ground and pastureland. While most of the Lamiaceae have numerous flowers arranged in discrete whorls (verticillasters) at intervals along their stems, the lanceleaf sage has only two opposite flowers (rarely more) in each verticillaster. Confusingly, the herb "sage" does not refer to sagebrushes (*Artemisia* spp.), but to the culinary sage (*Salvia* spp.).

Lewis collected two specimens of lanceleaf sage while the expedition was negotiating the Missouri River's big bend in

South Dakota. He would have recognized that the plant was in the mint family by its four-angled stems, opposing lanceolate leaves, and bilabiate flowers (that is, irregular five-petaled flowers, with upper and lower lips made up of joined petals). He had no reason to suspect that this plant would, in time, become a troublesome weed ("mintweed" is another common name).

Originally this plant grew on the Great Plains and south into northern Mexico, but it has spread as a seed contaminant throughout much of the United States and abroad as well. It even grows today as a troublesome weed in Australia's cotton fields. The plants are said to contain high concentrations of nitrates and have been known to poison livestock when present in chopped fodder, causing muscular weakness and sudden death. Fortunately, animals usually will not browse the plant as they are repelled by its strong odor.[52]

When Frederick Pursh examined Lewis's plant, he saw that it was a *Salvia* and named it *Salvia trichostemmoides* (his species name means "similar to *Trichostema*," a genus of North American herbs and shrubs).[53] Pursh did not recognize the plant as one already described by Jens Wilken Hornemann (1770-1841), a physician and professor of botany at Copenhagen. Hornemann based his 1806 description on a garden specimen—introduced into Europe from Mexico—giving it the scientific name that we know it by today.

ASTERACEAE (ASTER FAMILY)
Collected at the Big Bend of the Missouri River, Lyman County, South Dakota, September 21, 1804
AROMATIC ASTER, *Symphyotrichum oblongifolium* (NUTT.) G. L. NESOM

The aromatic aster (also called the aromatic American-aster) is a purple-flowered, daisylike plant that prefers dry surroundings. It is a densely glandular plant; the glands both provide an aromatic odor and make the plant sticky to the touch. A central stem (caudex) gives off several branches; each bears a loose cluster of showy purple "flowers"

Symphyotrichum oblongifolium

JAMES L. REVEAL

Symphyotrichum oblongifolium

JAMES L. REVEAL

with yellow disks. The leaves are short and blocky, explaining the species name, *oblongifolia*. Although leaves grow along the full length of the stem, the lower ones tend to fall away early. The plant grows from Pennsylvania to Alabama, and west to the Great Plains and New Mexico. Its presence on dry prairies supposedly indicates ground that has not been grazed.

In the past, this and many similar plants were classified as asters (*Aster* spp.), but recently that genus has been split and plants that formerly were assigned to *Aster* have been placed in other genera—*Symphyotrichum, Ionactis, Machaeranthera*, and so on—with most of them retaining "aster" as part of their common names. Many bloom late in the summer, and some retain their flowers well into the fall, as did those that Lewis collected on either side of the Rocky

Mountains. Although these plants are daisylike, they have a series of overlapping, layered, or "shingled" leaflike involucral bracts that make up the cuplike involucrum that holds the several flowers in a single composite cluster. Daisies (*Erigeron* spp.), on the other hand, have a single layer of bracts in their involucra. Such differences in the plants' involucra help to distinguish between the various genera.

Frederick Pursh—who listed seventy-eight species of *Aster* in his *Flora*, including some that had been collected by other explorers along the Pacific coast—did not realize that Lewis's specimen was new to science. Thomas Nuttall, who seemingly never took a walk without finding a new species of bird or plant, collected *Symphyotrichum oblongifolium* during an extended trip along the Missouri River in 1811, and he described it as an *Aster* in 1818.[54]

EUPHORBIACEAE (SPURGE FAMILY)

Collected October 1804 in Dewey or Potter County, South Dakota, or on October 15, 1804, in Sioux County, North Dakota

FIRE-ON-THE-MOUNTAIN, *EUPHORBIA CYATHOPHORA* MURRAY

This plant's bright red-tinged bracts surely would have caught Lewis's attention, prompting him to collect it. There is confusion surrounding the date that the plant was collected and disagreement about its classification, for the species has been known both as *Euphorbia heterophylla* and *Poinsettia cyathophora*. The species is found from the Dakotas southward to the Carolinas, Georgia, and Florida. Frederick Pursh knew it and listed it in his *Flora*—without mentioning Lewis's specimen—as *Euphorbia cyathophora*, the name that we know it by today. As its appearance suggests, it is related to the popular red-bracted Christmas ornamental, *Euphorbia pulcherrima*; our plant is sometimes referred to as a wild poinsettia.[55]

The Euphorbiaceae, or spurge family, is an important one, consisting of approximately three hundred genera and eight

Euphorbia cyathophora

A. SCOTT EARLE

47

thousand species worldwide, using the broadest definition of the family. We add this caveat because the latest summary of the family suggests that the Euphorbiaceae should be divided into three families.[56] No matter how it is defined, the family is diverse, with members ranging from small herbaceous weeds to giant African cactuslike succulents. Most have a toxic milky sap or latex. Many are economically important, including ornamentals like the poinsettia, food plants such as the manihot (cassava, tapioca), oil producers (tung, croton, and castor oil plants), and the medically important emetic derived from *Euphorbia ipecacuanhae*. Rubber plants are also in this family. The leafy spurge, *Euphorbia esula*, introduced from Europe, is a rapidly spreading weed in the American West, difficult to eradicate, and poisonous to livestock and wildlife.

The name *Euphorbia* is an old one, used first for certain African succulents. Euphorbus was physician to Juba II (50 B.C.-24 A.D.), king of Mauretania (a land roughly represented by today's Morocco). King Juba, husband of Antony and Cleopatra's daughter, wrote on many subjects including a resin derived from African succulents that acted medicinally as a powerful purgative. Juba gave this substance the name "euphorbium" to honor his physician, who presumably played some part in this saga. Euphorbus's name subsequently became attached to the plants now included in the genus *Euphorbia*. The species name of the plant shown here, *cyathophora*, was derived from two Greek words meaning "cup-bearing," for the shape of the plant's tiny flowers.

FABACEAE (PEA FAMILY)

Psoralidium lanceolatum *collected at an unknown time and place, probably on the Missouri River, in 1804;*
Psoralidium tenuiflorum *collected at the Big Bend of the Missouri River, Lyman County, South Dakota, September 21, 1804;*
and Pediomelum argophyllum *collected at an unknown time and place*

SILVER-LEAF SCURF PEA, *PEDIOMELUM ARGOPHYLLUM* (PURSH) J. GRIMES
YELLOW SCURF PEA, *PSORALIDIUM LANCEOLATUM* (PURSH) RYDB.
SLIM SCURF PEA, *PSORALIDIUM TENUIFLORUM* (PURSH) RYDB.

JAMES L. REVEAL
Psoralidium lanceolatum

The yellow scurf pea, *Psoralidium lanceolatum* (also known as the lance-leaved scurf pea, lemon scurf pea, and wild lemon-weed) is a low plant found in many western states, ranging east of the Cascade Range and the Sierra Nevada, in Washington, Oregon, and northern California, to Nebraska. Its pealike flowers are borne in clusters and are usually white with blue or purple markings. The leaves are palmately compound, with three leaflets whose shapes may vary from linear to ovate on the same plant. Because the plants are perennial, have many branches, and spread from an extensive root system, they often are found in "colonies," usually growing in sandy places, along roadsides, and on other disturbed ground.[57]

Psoralidium tenuiflorum

JAMES L. REVEAL

Pediomelum argophyllum

JAMES L. REVEAL

The slim scurf pea, *Psoralidium tenuiflorum* (the Latin species name means "slender-flower") is also commonly known as wild alfalfa and slender-flowered scurf pea. It is a fairly tall plant, up to two and a half feet. Its palmate leaves are made up of three to five (occasionally seven) leaflets. The light blue to purple flowers are borne in tight clusters. The pods, upper stems, and particularly the calyces of the flowers of yellow scurf pea and slim scurf pea are noticeably hairy, although the top of the leaves—unlike other *Psoralidium* species—are not. The slim scurf pea is also a plant of the western plains, found from the Rocky Mountains east to the Dakotas.

The silver-leaf scurf pea, *Pediomelum argophyllum* (the species name means "silver-leaf"), is last of this trio.[58] The plant has leaves that are covered—as Pursh noted—with a fine mat of white hairs, giving a silvery appearance. Its blue flowers are tightly clustered, and its leaves are pinnate, with three leaflets at the end of each petiole (leaf stem), although those on the main stem may have four or five leaflets. This plant, like the scurf peas, is a perennial. It ranges from the Rocky Mountains north into the central Canadian provinces,

east to Minnesota and Wisconsin, and as far south as New Mexico. The pods of all of the scurf peas are small, rounded, and may terminate in a small spine (a "beak"). Although each pod contains only one seed, there are so many flowers that there are plenty of seeds to ensure that the scurf peas continue to thrive.

Frederick Pursh recognized that these three plants were new to science. Lewis's specimen of the silver-leaf scurf pea is missing from the Lewis and Clark Herbarium—one of thirty plant specimens that disappeared after Lewis's 1805 shipment arrived in Philadelphia—and Pursh never saw it. He credited Lewis with collecting only the slim scurf pea, basing his description of the other two species on specimens that he saw in England, ones that Thomas Nuttall had collected in 1811. Pursh placed all three plants in *Psoralea* (the name is still used for these plants in many field guides), and he gave them the species names that we know them by today. He wrote that all were found "On the banks of the Missouri" and noted the color of their flowers. In describing the silver-leaved plant, he wrote that its tomentum (the dense, tangled, woolly hairs) gave it "a particularly handsome appearance."[59]

ANACARDIACEAE (SUMAC FAMILY)

Collected near the mouth of the Cheyenne River, Dewey, Sully, or Stanley County, South Dakota, October 1, 1804

SKUNKBUSH SUMAC, *RHUS TRILOBATA* NUTT.

Although the season was late, Lewis was still collecting plants. He added this species of sumac to his collection on October 1, 1804. In April of the following year, he sent the specimen with more than one hundred others to Jefferson. He

Rhus trilobata

JAMES L. REVEAL

wrote in the catalog that accompanied the shipment that this plant: "No. 57. October 1st 1804 first discovered in the neighborhood of the Kancez River—now very common, the growth of the little cops which appear on the steep declivities of the hills where they are sheltered from the ravages of the fire—."[60]

The skunkbush sumac—like its near relatives, poison ivy (*Toxicodendron radicans*) and the Pacific Coast poison oak (*Toxicodendron diversilobium*)—has compound leaves made up of three leaflets. The leaflets differ from those of poison ivy, however, for each is deeply incised to form three separate lobes, explaining the scientific species name *trilobata*. It is a shrubby plant, usually less than six feet tall, that has a pronounced odor, as the common name "skunkbush" suggests. The foliage is occasionally eaten by animals (such as mule deer), although it is not a preferred browse plant. Goats are said to be fond of the

leaves—but then, goats will eat almost anything. The plant's reddish orange fruit is highly acidic, yet birds devour the ripe berries in great numbers. The skunkbush sumac is found in the mountains of Idaho and Montana, eastward to Iowa, and westward to Oregon and California. It has at least a dozen regional names, including "stinking sumac," "squawbush," and "basketbush." The last two were bestowed because Indian women soaked and split its whippy branches for making baskets. It is, as Lewis noted, commonly found along watercourses or on shaded slopes. Unlike poison ivy and poison oak, *Rhus trilobata* is not considered to be a poisonous plant. Nevertheless, some people are more sensitive than others, and anyone with a history of skin irritation should avoid this and other sumacs.

Frederick Pursh did not include the skunkbush in his *Flora*, although he did describe eight other species of *Rhus* that grow in the East, including three varieties of poison ivy.[61] The specimen of *Rhus trilobata* in the Lewis and Clark Herbarium is in sad condition, consisting of only three twigs and as many leaves. It may be that it had succumbed to the vicissitudes of its long voyage even before Pursh examined it. In 1838, Thomas Nuttall re-collected *Rhus trilobata* and gave it the name that we know it by today.

Ask anyone what the derivation of the word *sumac* is, and most will guess that it is an American Indian name. In fact the name is from an Arabic word and it is used for various related plants. The name has been spelled in many different ways: "shoemake" (a form used by Lewis and Clark) "shumac," "sumach," and so on, although "sumac" seems to be preferred. The pronunciation also varies—some say that it is one of only three words in the English language in which an initial *s* is pronounced "sh."[62] The generic name *Rhus* is an old name going back to the Greek, used in times past for several Old World plants.

SOLANACEAE (NIGHTSHADE FAMILY)

Collected at the Arikara Indian villages, Campbell or Corson County, South Dakota, October 12, 1804

INDIAN TOBACCO, *NICOTIANA QUADRIVALVIS* PURSH

AZTEC TOBACCO, *NICOTIANA RUSTICA* L.

At the end of the first week of October 1804, the Corps of Discovery arrived at the Arikara villages—a site now inundated by the waters of the Oahe Reservoir in today's South Dakota. Unlike the Teton Sioux, the Arikaras were sedentary farmers. On August 12, 1804, William Clark wrote that the Indians "gave us about 7 bushels of Corn, some Tobacco of their own make, and Seed Legins & a Robe."[63] The specimen of tobacco in the Lewis and Clark Herbarium was almost certainly obtained at that time, dried and ready for use.

There are four tobacco plants of varying sizes on the specimen sheet. Lewis's ticket on the sheet reads "12th of October at the Ricare's town. This is the tobacco which they cultivate." Pursh studied the collection, realized that he was dealing with a new species, and noted that it grew "Cultivated and spontaneous on the Missouri; principally among the Mandan and Ricara nations....Flowers white, with a tinge of blue. The tobacco prepared from it is excellent. The most del-

icate tobacco is prepared by the Indians from the dried flowers."[64] The species name that Pursh gave our plant, *quadrivalvis*, refers to the four lobes of the seed capsule.

Lewis included more information when he sent plant and seed specimens to Jefferson in the spring of 1805. He described the Indians' method of cultivation and gave a description of the plant, its flowers, and preparation. Although all parts were probably smoked (never chewed or used as snuff), its carefully dried flowers were the preferred part of the plant. Lewis noted that these resembled green tea. He found them "very pleasant— . It dose not affect the nerves in the same manner that the tobacco cultivated in the U'S. dose—." He added "The smaller species of this plant differs but little from this just discribed...it is reather stronger than the large kind." Lewis sent back dried specimens of the larger type (*Nicotiana quadrivalvis*) and seeds of both large and small species (presumably *Nicotiana rustica*)

Nicotiana quadrivalvis

JAMES L. REVEAL

Nicotiana quadrivalvis

JAMES L. REVEAL

as well as a sample of dried flowers—an important trade item for the Arikaras.[65]

Bernard M'Mahon and others in Philadelphia planted both types of seed, and apparently they grew well at the time, although they were allowed to die out over the years. Because the plants are no longer grown, and because Lewis did not send back a specimen of the smaller species, we can only assume that it was *Nicotiana rustica*, a plant still in commercial use today.

Tobacco was important to the Indians; they cultivated it with as much care as they did their food plants. While not mentioning it specifically, the captains had probably sampled Indian tobacco earlier when they smoked the "pipe of peace" at various times during their journey upriver—most recently with the Teton Sioux.

For years the Great Plains form of *Nicotiana quadrivalvis* was thought to be extinct. The last specimens known were found in cultivation in the 1920s.[66] Therefore it was of some surprise when we came upon Indian tobacco growing in a plot at Fort Union National Historical Site, near the mouth of the Yellowstone River, in the fall of 2002 while photographing Lewis and Clark plants for this book. A local Native American farmer had given seeds to a member of the National Park Service a decade earlier. The seeds were planted and grown without anyone aware that as far as the botanical world was concerned the plant had disappeared. Fresh specimens and seeds were collected, with one of the specimens going to The Academy of Natural Sciences for comparison with the 1804 Lewis and Clark collection. They were the same.

Within days, seeds were being distributed to various botan-ical gardens from the University of California. An American botanist, Dr. Sandy Knapp, working on a monograph of *Nicotiana* at the Natural History Museum in London, reported that the Great Plains form of *Nicotiana quadrivalvis* was identical to wild populations long known as Bigelow's Indian tobacco (*Nicotiana quadrivalvis* var. *bigelovii*) found in southern Nevada and California. Furthermore, she was able to show that the long-thought-extinct Pacific Northwest form of the species (*Nicotiana quadrivalvis* var. *multivalvis*) was also identical to the wild plant. The two cultivated expressions of the species were not unique, and all of the forms were of a single species that should not be subdivided into varieties. As the year 2002 comes to an end, others are looking into how it came to be that Indian tobacco reached the Great Plains and when the local people first cultivated it. Detailed DNA studies of the modern plant and the original 1804 specimen are in the planning stages. It is hoped that this rather elegant annual will become a favorite of gardeners throughout the country.

The rediscovery—at least for the botanical world—of what was long thought to be the only plant found by the explorers that had gone extinct was a benefit neither of us expected when we set out to examine Lewis and Clark's green world.

The generic name *Nicotiana* honors Jean Nicot de Villemain, a French ambassador to the Portuguese court, who sent the plant to the queen mother of France in 1550. Tobacco has grown increasingly important since it was introduced into Europe—agriculturally, medically, and socially—but for our Native Americans, it has been culturally important for millennia.[67]

Osage orange, *Maclura pomifera*

NUTTALL'S *SYLVA*

KINNIKINNIK	*Arctostaphylos uva-ursi*
RED OSIER DOGWOOD	*Cornus sericea*
BRITTLE PRICKLY-PEAR	*Opuntia fragilis*
WESTERN PRICKLY-PEAR	*Opuntia polyacantha*
NIPPLE CACTUS	*Escobaria missouriensis*
LARGE INDIAN BREADROOT	*Pediomelum esculentum*
SILVER SAGEBRUSH	*Artemisia cana*
TARRAGON	*Artemisia dracunculus*
PRAIRIE SAGEWORT	*Artemisia frigida*

LONG-LEAF WORMWOOD	*Artemisia longifolia*
COMMON WHITE-SAGE	*Artemisia ludoviciana*
BIG SAGEBRUSH	*Artemisia tridentata*
RUSTY LUPINE	*Lupinus pusillus*
ROCKY MOUNTAIN JUNIPER	*Juniperis scopulorum*
CREEPING JUNIPER	*Juniperis horizontalis*
DWARF COMMON JUNIPER	*Juniperis communis* var. *depressa*

Fort Mandan to the Great Falls of the Missouri
December 1, 1804, to June 13, 1805

The Corps of Discovery remained at the Mandan villages for almost six months. Many neighboring villages along the Missouri had been abandoned—mute evidence of the devastating effect of the smallpox virus on Native Americans. Tribal entities, much reduced in size, coalesced. Altogether there were about 7,500 Indians resident in the Mandan villages. Most were Mandans, but there were also about 2,500 Hidatsas and several smaller tribes. Relations between the Indians and the white men were for the most part cordial. That winter was not wasted. Lewis wrote book-length notes on the country that the expedition had passed through, and on the tribes that lived along the Missouri. The captains also gathered information about what lay ahead from the Hidatsas, who ranged as far west as the Continental Divide. With this information and his own measurements, Clark completed a remarkably accurate map of the Missouri, almost to the Rocky Mountains.

The enlisted men kept busy, too, with hunting, camp maintenance, repairing old equipment and making new, and constructing dugout canoes, for the keelboat was to return to St. Louis in the spring, with the party's journals and the specimens (plant, animal, mineral, and Native American artifacts) that had been collected to this time. Although the season was bitterly cold, the men wintered well, excepting occasional frostbite and the venereal complications of frequent romps with friendly "squars." Game became scarce toward winter's end, but the Indians traded corn, squashes, beans, and roots for tools and trade items. Although the men could not have been aware of it at the time, the young Shoshone Indian woman, "Sac-ca-gar-we-a," the "wife" of interpreter Toussaint Charbonneau, was the expedition's most important addition that winter. Charbonneau had purchased her from the Hidatsas, who had captured her far to the west.

By April 7, 1805, the ice was off the river, and the Corps of Discovery resumed the journey upriver, passing, a few weeks later, through some of the most beautiful—and inaccessible—country in America. Lewis, scouting ahead of the main party, arrived at the cascades of the Missouri, the site of present-day Great Falls, Montana, on June 13, 1805.

Lewis and Clark had obtained only one plant, kinnikinnik (see p. 56), while at Fort Mandan. Lewis did, however, collect plants—probably many plants—in the course of the 550-mile segment between Fort Mandan and the Great Falls. He identified a few by number in his journal, while others are mentioned in his daily entries. Identifiable plants that he mentioned include a serviceberry (*Amelanchier alnifolia*), greasewood (*Sarcobatus vermiculatus*, re-collected by Lewis in 1806), narrow-leaved cottonwood (*Populus angustifolia*), and the Jerusalem artichoke (*Helianthus tuberosus*). Other plants, mentioned by date, include the creeping juniper (*Juniperus horizontalis*), specimen "No. 2," mentioned on April 12; Lewis described it accurately and noted that it would make "handsome edgings to the borders and walks of a garden." The golden pea (*Thermopsis rhombifolia*) was no. 3, April 18; wild licorice (*Glycyrrhiza lepidota*) and "white apple" (*Pediomelum esculentum*, now known as breadroot, scurf pea, or pomme blanche), on May 8; the first ponderosa pine on May 11; and the first Douglas-fir on May 23.[1]

At the falls, the explorers cached all of their plant specimens, along with Lewis's prized bearskins, the large pirogues, Lewis's "leather boat," excess supplies, and numerous other items. Regrettably, their cache was too close to the river. The following year's spring floods destroyed all of the plants, the bearskins, and much else besides. Lewis collected a few plants between Great Falls and Fort Mandan on his return trip in 1806, but we suspect that they were only a small fraction of those that were lost.

The country that Lewis and Clark passed through between Fort Mandan and the Great Falls of the Missouri is vastly different today. Much of the prairie along the Missouri River is now under cultivation or has been converted to rangeland. The river in the eastern part of this area is no longer a river; it is a series of lakes—its water has been impounded behind a string of dams. The flowering plants that the explorers saw are now found mostly on the edges of highways and especially along farm roads—and tradition has it that native plants also survive in family burial plots. Scattered state parks, wildlife preserves, and university-based research stations also provide some remnants of the native vegetation. The images painted by George Catlin and Karl Bodmer thirty years after Lewis and Clark show a landscape that is rarely seen today.

ERICACEAE (HEATH FAMILY)

Obtained at Fort Mandan, McLean County, North Dakota, in the winter of 1805

KINNIKINNIK, *ARCTOSTAPHYLOS UVA-URSI* (L.) SPRENG.

RED-OSIER DOGWOOD, *CORNUS SERICEA* L.

Kinnikinnik, or bearberry, is a circumboreal species, and those found in Europe and Asia are essentially the same as North American species. The plant grows in North America from Alaska to Labrador south to Virginia, South Dakota, New Mexico, and California. It is a low, prostrate shrub with numerous leathery evergreen leaves. The plant often forms mats up to six feet or more across. Its small flowers are usually white or pinkish, and, in common with those of many other members of the heath family, are urn-shaped, with five petals that roll outward at the tips. The red berries are often seen, particularly in good years; the flowers are seen less often, for they bloom early and may be buried by late snows. Kinnikinnik grows sparsely on the Great Plains. It is more common in northern North Dakota and on the short-

Arctostaphylos uva-ursi

JAMES L. REVEAL

Arctostaphylos uva-ursi

JAMES L. REVEAL

Cornus sericea

JAMES L. REVEAL

Cornus sericea

JAMES L. REVEAL

grass prairies of the western Dakotas. Both the generic and species names mean "bearberry"; the former is derived from the Greek, the latter from the Latin. The plant is said to be "one of the finest ground covers known."[2]

The label on the specimen sheet of the kinnikinnik in the Lewis and Clark Herbarium—apparently copied from Lewis's description—reads: "plants which grows in the open plains usually. the natives smoke its leaves mixed with tobacco Called by the french Engages *Sacacommis*—obtained at Fort Mandan." Frederick Pursh adopted Linnaeus's 1753 name *Arbutus uva-ursi*, noting that "On the plains of the Mississippi the Indians smoke the leaves under the name of *Sacacommis* and consider them of great medicinal value" (he neglected to mention that he had learned that from Lewis's label data).[3]

Lewis wrote in his journal that he "obtained" his specimen at Fort Mandan—where the plant does not occur. He probably received it as a gift from two trappers sent by Hugh Heney (or Hené) who arrived at Fort Mandan on February 28, 1805. Clark wrote that the two men brought "letters and Sacka comah," and it is likely that Lewis simply added a dried branch of kinnikinnik to his collection.[4]

Red osier dogwood is also a circumboreal species sharing essentially the same geographic range as kinnikinnik. The plant was already known to the expedition's French engagés (men hired to get the keelboat to Fort Mandan), for it is common in New England and southern Canada, and although Lewis certainly saw it, he apparently did not gather a specimen. The red osier dogwood is a fairly large shrub or small tree that bears large clusters of small four-petaled white flowers and off-white (occasionally blue) berries. It grows on stream banks and in moist woods. It is an attractive plant, and gardeners often use it today as an ornamental shrub. Native Americans apparently used the berries as food, although they are dry, bitter, and not at all palatable. As the common name "osier" suggests, the Native Americans made baskets from its flexible branches. The plant's species name, *sericea*, means "silky," although it is not apparent why it was applied to this plant.[5]

Native Americans of the upper Great Plains mixed both plants—the bearberry's leaves and the red osier dogwood's bark—with tobacco and then smoked the combination as part of a ceremony. Great Plains Indians may (as Pursh noted) have believed that the bearberry had medicinal value, but more likely the two adulterants served a practical purpose—they stretched the tobacco supply.

CACTACEAE (CACTUS FAMILY)

Not collected, but seen and mentioned ("great quantities of prickly pear of two kinds on the plains," Lewis, July 10, 1806)

CACTI ON THE GREAT PLAINS

There are no specimens of cacti in the Lewis and Clark Herbarium, although the explorers saw plenty of them on the Great Plains and made note of them frequently in their journals. Both men were familiar with the common eastern prickly-pear, or devil's-tongue (*Opuntia humifusa* Raf.), and they would have realized that the two common cacti that they encountered on the Great Plains—the brittle prickly-pear (*Opuntia fragilis* (Nutt.) Haw.) and the western prickly-pear (*Opuntia polyacantha* Haw.)—were different species. *Opuntia polyacantha* (the name "hairspine prickly cactus" has recently been suggested for this plant) grows from Missouri westward to eastern Oregon. The brittle prickly pear, *Opuntia fragilis*, is found in much the same area. Unlike the western prickly pear, the "pads" or "stem joints" of the former detach easily and adhere to whatever or whoever passes by. Its spines are armed with tiny barbs—lacking in *Opuntia polyacantha*— that serve to keep the spine from being withdrawn easily, a feature that helps to spread the detached segments. The flowers of both species are yellow, although those of the western prickly pear are occasionally pink or red.

On July 26, 1805, Lewis found another cactus, *Escobaria missouriensis* (Sweet) D. R. Hunt, commonly known as the nipple cactus (although the name "Missouri foxtail cactus" is also used), near the Three Forks of the Missouri, in what is now Gallatin County, Montana.[6] His journal entry notes that "the prickly pear also grow here as abundantly as usual. There is another species of the prickly pear of a globular form…." He then proceeded to describe the nipple cactus in considerable detail. *Escobaria missouriensis* is a small, rounded plant that bears a single greenish white flower and a red fruit. Its common name comes from its many spirally arranged "mammillate tubercles," each of which bears a symmetrical cluster of spines. Six years later Thomas Nuttall found the same plant near the Mandan villages in North Dakota and took live specimens back to London, where he introduced them to cultivation.[7]

Opuntia fragilis

A. SCOTT EARLE

Opuntia polyacantha

JAMES L. REVEAL

Fabaceae (Pea Family)

Collected at an unknown place and date, probably on the Missouri River

Large Indian breadroot, *Pediomelum esculentum* (Pursh) Rydb.

Frederick Pursh recognized that the plant Lewis referred to in his journal as the "white apple" was new to science (other common names include pomme blanche and prairie apple). Pursh's description in his *Flora* of 1813 is essentially an abstract of a far longer one that Lewis wrote on May 8, 1805, probably while camped above the mouth of the Milk River near today's Fort Peck Dam in Montana. Pursh's entry reads:

*The present plant produces the famous **Bread-root** of the American Western Indians, on which they partly subsist in winter. They collect them in large quantities, and if for present use, they roast in the ashes, when they give a food similar to yams: if intended for winter use, they are carefully dried, and preserved in a dry place in their huts. When wanted for use, they are mashed between two stones, mixed with some water, and baked in cakes over the coals. It is a wholesome and nourishing food, and, according to Mr. Lewis's observation, agreeable to most constitutions; which, he observed, was not the case with the rest of the roots collected by those Indians for food. This root has been frequently found by travellers in the canoes of the Indians, but the plant which produces it has not been known until lately.*[8]

This plant was known until recently as *Psoralea esculenta*, and it is listed

Pediomelum esculentum

JAMES L. REVEAL

under that name in older guidebooks.[9] It is a deep-rooted perennial, and its root is quite large as the illustration suggests. The roots are rich in carbohydrates; they have a starch content of 70 percent and a sugar content of 5 percent, according to one assay, and they are quite palatable, especially when boiled.[10] The plants often grow in hard soil, and the roots can be difficult to retrieve true of many of the roots eaten by Native Americans. Undoubtedly, those who depended on the roots for sustenance were far more proficient at gathering them than modern botanists.

GOODALE/SPRAGUE, *AMERICAN WILDFLOWERS*

59

ASTERACEAE (ASTER FAMILY)

Twelve specimens of Artemisia, collected at various times along the Lewis and Clark Trail

WORMWOODS, SAGEWORTS, AND SAGEBRUSH (*ARTEMISIA* SPP.)

On April 14, 1805, two weeks out from Fort Mandan, Meriwether Lewis wrote in his journal, "on these hills many aromatic herbs are seen…one resembling the camphor in taste and smell, rising to the hight of 2 or 3 feet; the other about the same size, has a long, narrow, smooth, soft leaf of an agreeable smel and flavor; of this last the Atelope is very fond; they feed on it, and perfume the hair of their foreheads and necks with it by rubing against it."[11] Lewis was describing the big sagebrush (*Artemisia tridentata* Nutt.) and the silver sagebrush (*Artemisia cana* Pursh). They were new plants, both for the men of the expedition, and to science as well. During the next year and a half the explorers would spend much of their time in the close company of various sages and their relatives, all members of the genus *Artemisia*.[12]

Few plants are as evocative of the American West as sagebrush. It was not easy then for Lewis and Clark—nor is it for most of us today—to discriminate among the various species and varieties. There are more than one hundred species in the genus *Artemisia*. Many are found in the arid regions of the Northern Hemisphere. The genus may be subdivided into three informal groups: the wormwoods, the sageworts, and the sagebrushes.

The wormwoods: The wormwoods are common throughout the range of the genus. Most are considered medicinal plants, largely because of their strong, aromatic odor (like tarragon). They are extremely variable and taxonomically complex. The explorers knew the wormwoods, and references to them appear with some frequency in the captains' journals. Lewis collected tarragon (*Artemisia dracunculus* L.) near the mouth of the White River in Lyman or Brule County, South Dakota, on September 15, 1804, and the long-leaf wormwood (*Artemisia longifolia* Nutt.) above the mouth of the Cheyenne River on October 3, 1804. Lewis's specimens of both are extant, but the Great Plains wormwood (*Artemisia campestris* L. subsp. *caudata*

Artemisia tridentata

JAMES L. REVEAL

Artemisia cana

JAMES L. REVEAL

Artemisia dracunculus

JAMES L. REVEAL

Artemisia longifolia

JAMES L. REVEAL

Artemisia frigida

JAMES L. REVEAL

(Michx.) Hall & Clements), a plant that Pursh mentioned in his *Flora*, is now lost.[13] Lewis also collected varieties of the common white-sage (*Artemisia ludoviciana* Nutt.), one of the most common species of wormwood of the Great Plains, on October 1, 1804, near the mouth of the Cheyenne River in South Dakota, and along the Columbia River, near The Dalles, Oregon, probably on April 10, 1806.

The sageworts: The prairie sagewort (*Artemisia frigida* Willd.) is the most common sagewort found in the American West. Lewis collected this little shrub twice, once near present-day Springfield, South Dakota (October 2, 1804), and again above the Cheyenne River (October 3, 1804), also in South Dakota. This plant is also found in Siberia, and it was from specimens gathered there that the species was described in 1803.

The sagebrushes: The sagebrushes are the most common of the western artemisias. They can be difficult to identify visually, but with experience and a good nose (for their odors differ), one can tell them apart. Lewis and Clark probably collected several examples in 1805, but only the silver sagebrush collected the year before (*Artemisia cana*) reached Philadelphia—where it proved to be a new species. Frederick Pursh named the plant, based on the two specimens that Lewis collected. The silver sagebrush is common, found mainly along stream drainages in the northern Great Plains as far west as the foothills of the Rocky Mountains in western Montana. It may be recognized easily, for its leaves, unlike those of most of the other species of *Artemisia*, are nearly always entire (meaning that the leaf margins are not toothed, lobed, or otherwise divided). Strangely, the most common sagebrush of all, the big sagebrush, *Artemisia tridentata*, is not represented in the Lewis and Clark Herbarium. There are several varieties of *Artemisia tridentata*, distinguished by minor differences, but all have the three-lobed leaf blade that gives the species its name.[14]

FABACEAE (PEA FAMILY)
Collected on an unknown date, "On the banks of the Missouri"
RUSTY LUPINE, *LUPINUS PUSILLUS* NUTT.

The rusty lupine (*Lupinus pusillus*) is an annual flower that blooms from May into August. It is easily recognized, for it is the only annual lupine that grows on the dry sandy soil of the prairies in North Dakota and eastern Montana. It is a low, sprawling, diffusely branched plant, only two to eight inches tall, quite unlike the erect perennial lupines that the explorers collected in the mountains of Idaho and Montana. Its flowers, growing in loose clusters, are usually light blue to purple, but occasionally they are white or cream colored.

Until recently a specimen in the Royal Botanic Gardens in Kew, England, was assumed to be the one that Lewis and Clark collected, but we know now that Thomas Nuttall actually gathered this specimen of *Lupinus pusillus* in 1811. Nevertheless, we also know that the captains did bring back a specimen, because Pursh noted that he saw a dry specimen of the plant in Lewis's herbarium. We just do not know where or when it was collected, beyond the little information included in Pursh's description: "On the banks of the Missouri…Flowers small, a fine blue mixed with some red."[15] Anything more, necessarily, is an educated guess.

Whatever the actual circumstances surrounding this Lewis and Clark specimen and its fate, it remains that the rusty lupine was a plant new to science when Pursh described it. He gave it the species name *pusillus*, a Latin word that means "very small." Today, this small plant makes a fine addition to a spring and early summer garden.

CUPRESSACEAE (CYPRESS FAMILY)
Collected along the Missouri and in the mountains of Montana, 1804 and 1806
ROCKY MOUNTAIN JUNIPER, *JUNIPERUS SCOPULORUM* SARG.
CREEPING JUNIPER, *JUNIPERUS HORIZONTALIS* MOENCH
DWARF COMMON JUNIPER, *JUNIPERUS COMMUNIS* L. VAR. *DEPRESSA* PURSH

For whatever reason, Lewis had a special interest in junipers, for he sent specimens of three species to President Jefferson from Fort Mandan in the spring of 1805. Possibly he was prescient enough to realize that they would make good ornamentals. He was acquainted with the eastern red-cedar (*Juniperus virginiana*), a common species in the eastern United States, and he would have seen it growing all along the preliminary part of his journey, from Washington to St. Louis, and then along the lower Missouri River into Nebraska. It is a medium-sized tree, common on prairie hillsides and in pastures, where it can become a troublesome invader when rangeland is not properly managed. Because Lewis knew the eastern red-cedar, he did not collect a specimen.

Rocky Mountain juniper (*Juniperus scopulorum*), a western relative of the eastern red-cedar, was the first of the three new

Juniperus horizontalis

A. SCOTT EARLE

Juniperus scopulorum

JAMES L. REVEAL

junipers that Lewis collected. He found it on October 2, 1804, growing on a bluff above the Missouri River, near the mouth of the Cheyenne River (along today's Sully-Potter county line in South Dakota). It was not the best time to be gathering specimens, for the party had recently encountered the Teton Sioux, yet the trees were so large—Lewis wrote "6 feet in the girth" on the specimen label (as copied by Pursh)—that they were too unusual to ignore. The tree no longer grows along this section of the Missouri, but it may still be seen farther south, in Brule and Lyman Counties. Lewis saw the Rocky Mountain juniper much more frequently in Montana, in the Rocky Mountains, along today's eastern border of Idaho and Montana, and along the Columbia River east of the Columbia Gorge.

Lewis found the creeping or horizontal juniper (*Juniperus horizontalis*) next, near Little Beaver Creek in present-day Emmons County, North Dakota. The label on the specimen in the Lewis and Clark Herbarium, in Lewis's hand, reads "Dwarf Cedar, never more than 6 inches high, open prairies. Octbr: 16. 1804." He probably had not seen the species before, for it is primarily a Canadian shrub, although it is also found in widely scattered locations in the United States. A

dwarf juniper that was only a few inches high was unusual enough to catch his attention. He was unaware of it, but the plant was already known to science, although not yet in cultivation. It is commonly seen today as an ornamental, growing in gardens and along borders; nurseries often feature several attractive creeping juniper cultivars. Pursh considered Lewis's plant to be a new variety of a European species of juniper, *Juniperus sabina*, and he wrote for some reason that it was found on "the banks of the waters of the Rocky-mountains."[16] The plant does occur high in the mountains, and it is not uncommon in western North Dakota and eastern Montana. Perhaps Lewis told Pursh that he had seen it growing there.

Lewis collected his last previously unknown juniper species, the dwarf common juniper (*Juniperus communis* var. *depressa*), just below the mouth of the Cannon Ball River in Sioux County, North Dakota, on October 17, 1804. On their return trip almost two years later, either Clark or, more likely, Lewis collected the plant again, on July 7, 1806. On that day, both captains were going east, across the Continental Divide. Lewis crossed over the Lewis and Clark Pass on his way to the Great Falls, and Clark crossed over Gibbons Pass,

63

Juniperus communis var. *depressa*

A. SCOTT EARLE

Juniperus communis var. *depressa*

JAMES L. REVEAL

just above today's Montana-Idaho border, heading for the Beaverhead River. The dwarf common juniper grows in both places. Pursh described var. *depressa* in his *Flora*, but he did not mention either of the Lewis and Clark specimens.[17] He knew it from his own specimens gathered along the Hudson River in New York. Today, botanists recognize several varieties of the common juniper, classifying them according to the plants' size and growth pattern. Var. *depressa* is usually less than three feet tall, with a semierect main stem and branches that spread out and eventually lie on the ground. It

grows in the mountains of western Montana and Idaho, although it is more common in the eastern United States.

The first two species mentioned above (*Juniperus virginiana* and *Juniperus scopulorum*) are erect, upright trees with scale-like needles. The other two are shrubs that have small awl-like (acicular) needles. The creeping juniper forms a ground-hugging mat, and the dwarf common juniper is a taller, flat-topped shrub, about the height of late snow cover. The fierce mountain and prairie winds are probably an important influence in determining the morphology of these low shrubs.

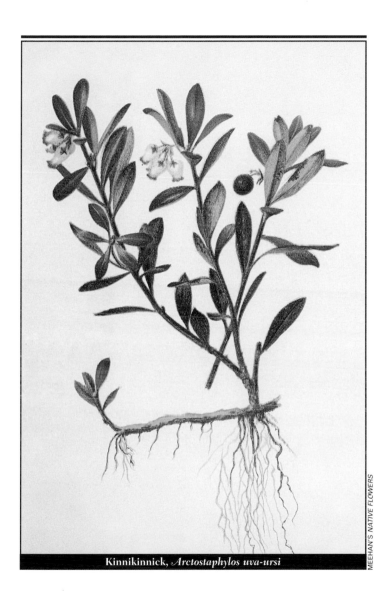

Kinnikinnick, *Arctostaphylos uva-ursi*

MEEHAN'S NATIVE FLOWERS

Golden currant	*Ribes aureum*
White wild onion	*Allium textile*
Geyer's onion	*Allium geyeri*
Brandegee's onion	*Allium brandegee*
Lyall's angelica	*Angelica arguta*

Lewis's monkey-flower	*Mimulus lewisii*
Cascade mountain-ash	*Sorbus scopulina*
Smooth snowberry	*Symphoricarpos albus var. laevigatus*
Western snowberry	*Symphoricarpos occidentalis*
Rocky Mountain honeysuckle	*Lonicera utahensis*

Great Falls to Travelers' Rest
June 14 to September 9, 1805

On June 14, 1805, Meriwether Lewis, reconnoitering ahead of the others, arrived at the lowest of the five Missouri River falls at today's Great Falls, Montana. The main party arrived several days later and began a grueling portage around the falls, while Lewis worked on his "leather boat," built on the light iron frame made for him in Harper's Ferry. The boat, covered with stretched and dried animal hides, sank almost as soon as it was launched above the falls. It took ten days to replace it with dugout canoes made from the trunks of large cottonwood trees.

Leaving their camp above the falls on July 15 in eight heavily laden canoes, the men battled the Missouri's current as they worked their way upstream, arriving at the Three Forks of the Missouri on July 27. The captains decided, correctly, to ascend the westernmost branch—they named it the Jefferson—continuing in a southwesterly direction until they came to its largest tributary, the Beaverhead River. The men battled it out, dragging the canoes upriver and struggling with dense stands of willows and sandbars. It was time to continue by land.

It was imperative to find Indians to get the horses they needed to carry their baggage and equipment. With three men, Lewis trekked toward the west, following willow-lined creeks in otherwise open country, coming eventually to a small spring near the summit of Lemhi Pass. This, they declared, was the source of the mighty Missouri.[1] On that day, August 12, 1805, Lewis stood on the Continental Divide looking west. He saw "immence ranges of high mountains still to the West of us with their tops partially covered with snow."[2] If he was dismayed by what lay ahead, it is not reflected in his journal. Now he could answer Jefferson's most pressing questions; the Rocky Mountains were not a single height of land, and there was no interior Northwest Passage.

Lewis and his party met Shoshone Indians a short distance west of the pass in present Lemhi County, Idaho, on August 13. He convinced them to return with him to the Beaverhead to wait for Clark, who was still working his way up the Beaverhead River with the main party, including Sacagawea and Charbonneau. Clark finally met Lewis on August 17. The reunion of Sacagawea with her brother, the leader of this group, and her people may be the journey's most dramatic moment. The whole party was now together at "Camp Fortunate," in today's Beaverhead County, Montana. They remained with the Shoshone for eight days, trading for the horses that they needed. The party crossed the pass again on August 26 and worked its way down the Lemhi River to the Salmon River (near today's Salmon, Idaho).

Now, it was Clark's turn to explore. Miles downstream he found that the Salmon was impassable—as the Indians had warned. It was imperative that they find a navigable branch of the Columbia. With an elderly Shoshone, "old Toby," as their guide, the party headed up the North Fork of the Salmon (today's U.S. Highway 93 follows their trail, more or less), and bushwhacked across Lost Trail Pass into the Bitterroot Valley, flanked on either side by imposing snow-covered peaks. They followed the Bitterroot River north to a point a few miles south of today's Missoula, Montana. There, on September 9, they established a camp, naming it "Travelers' Rest."

The flora between Great Falls and Travelers' Rest is far different from that of the Great Plains. Lewis saw new flowers, new shrubs, and new trees. He wrote that he collected the plants that he saw, although only three specimens are in the Lewis and Clark Herbarium from this segment of the trail. Evidently most of the specimens that he collected after leaving Great Falls were cached on August 20 at Camp Fortunate in Beaverhead County, Montana, a location now covered by the waters of the Clark Canyon Reservoir. When Clark opened the cache on July 8 of the following year, he could salvage only a single specimen—the golden currant. The plants considered below, collected on this segment of the journey, are ones that Lewis had to have gathered after leaving this encampment.[3]

GROSSULARIACEAE (GOOSEBERRY FAMILY)

Collected July 29, 1805, near Three Forks, Gallatin County, Montana

GOLDEN CURRANT, *RIBES AUREUM* PURSH

The captains, in their journals, often mentioned berries that grew on or near riverbanks, especially currants, comparing one with another, or with domestic currants. On August 2, a few days after collecting the golden currant near Three Forks, Lewis wrote that "we feasted suptuously on our wild fruit particularly the yellow courant…which I found to be excellent." Lewis and Clark became aware of the plant at the end of April in 1805 when Sacagawea "found & brought me [Clark] a bush Something like the Current, which She Said bore a delicious froot and that great quantities grew on the Rocky Mountains, this Srub was in bloom has a yellow flower with a deep Cup, the froot when ripe is yellow and hangs in bunches like Cheries, Some of those berries yet remained on the bushes."[4]

Plants in the genus *Ribes*—wild currants and gooseberries—are found throughout the West; there are over thirty species in the Pacific Northwest alone. The golden currant is one of the more commonly encountered species. It is characterized by five-petaled yellow blossoms, and usually yellow to orange semitranslucent berries. There may be considerable variability in the color of the fruit, however, ranging from

Ribes aureum

JAMES L. REVEAL

Ribes aureum

JAMES L. REVEAL

bright yellow through golden orange (most commonly) to dark red. The berries are edible, tasty, and an important food for birds and other animals. Characteristically, the leaves are lobed and resemble those of the related domestic gooseberry (the family name "Grossulariaceae" comes from the Latin word for *grossularia*, "gooseberry.") The generic name *Ribes* (pronounced "RY-beez") is derived from a Persian word, *ribas*, meaning "acidic," for the taste of the fruit.

The currant that Lewis collected on July 29, 1805, is in the Lewis and Clark Herbarium at The Academy of Natural Sciences in Philadelphia. It consists today of a twig and a few fragments of leaves. Nonetheless, this is enough material to show that his specimen is the golden currant *Ribes aureum*,

and it was probably fruiting when Lewis gathered it. The following year, on April 16, he found the plant in flower at The Dalles, Oregon, along the Columbia River. Two sheets of the latter collection still exist, one in Philadelphia and the second at the Royal Botanic Gardens at Kew, England. Frederick Pursh took the latter specimen with him when he went to Europe. It is in excellent shape, consisting of a branch with numerous leaves and flowers. All that remains in Philadelphia (or perhaps all that Pursh left) are a few flowers.[5]

Today, golden currant is often grown as an ornamental, var. *villosum* more so than var. *aureum*. Its fruit is made into jams or a sweet wine, but mostly they are eaten straight off the bush, just as the explorers did.

ALLIACEAE (ONION FAMILY)
Various species collected along the upper Missouri and westward, 1805-1806

GEYER'S ONION, *ALLIUM GEYERI* S. WATSON
WHITE WILD ONION, *ALLIUM TEXTILE* A. NELSON & J. F. MACBR.
BRANDEGEE'S WILD ONION, *ALLIUM BRANDEGEEI* S. WATSON

The selection of onions listed in the heading above are only a representative few of the many species that grow along the expedition's route—thirty or more grow in the Pacific Northwest alone.[6] Most onions along the Columbia, Snake, and Clearwater rivers flower during the early spring, and one may find them in many locations, but most often on slopes moist from recent snowmelt. As one proceeds into the higher mountains, onions flower later in the spring and early summer. Their small flowers range in color—they are usually white but are sometimes pink or purple—and are always arranged in umbel-like clusters (an "umbel" is a flower cluster in which all of the stemlets, or pedicels, arise from a common point on the main stem).

Members of the Corps of Discovery were always on the lookout for wild onions to perk up their monotonous diet.

Although the taste of their roots varies, the addition of any kind of onion could only improve the taste of the party's boiled roots, dried fish, and whatever fresh meat was available. Finding wild onions in the spring and early summer when they bloom in abundance is easy, but finding them in other seasons is not. Native Americans collected onions when they were blooming and sometimes used them later in the season as trade items. Lewis first took note of onions in his journal on July 22, 1805, while the party was working its way up the Missouri River, a few days after passing through the Gates of the Mountains in present-day Montana. He wrote: "I passed though a large Island which I found a beautifull level and fertile plain about 10 feet above the surface of the water and never overflown, on this Island I met with great quantities of a smal onion [possibly

Allium geyeri

JAMES L. REVEAL

Allium brandegeei

A. SCOTT EARLE

Brandegee's or Geyer's onion] about the size of a musquit ball and some even larger; they were white crisp and well flavored I geathered about half a bushel of them before the canoes arrived. I halted the party for breakfast and the men also geathered considerable quantities of those onions. its seed had just arrived to maturity and I gathered a good quantity of it. This appears to be a valuable plant inasmuch as it produces a large quantity to the squar foot and bears with ease the rigor of this climate, and withall I think it as pleasantly flavored as any species of that root I ever tasted. I call this beatifull and fertile island after this plant Onion Island."[7]

Lewis mentioned onions on several other occasions, but he only returned with a single specimen, and that is now so

Allium textile

JAMES L. REVEAL

damaged as to render exact identification difficult without DNA analysis of the leaves. Even the information on the label is confused; the location is given as "On the waters of the Kooskooskie"—today's Clearwater River in Idaho—whereas the date is given as "April. 30th 1806." The date would place the Corps at the mouth of the Walla Walla River in Washington. Most likely the place is correct and the date is wrong; we suspect that the plant is Geyer's onion, collected on May 30, 1806, while the party was at Camp Chopunnish. On that day, Lewis wrote, "one of the men brought me today some onions from the high plain of a different species from those near the borders of the river as they are also from the shive or small onion noticed below the falls of the Columbia."[8]

APIACEAE (PARSLEY FAMILY)

*Collected on the Lost Trail Pass, near the Idaho-Montana border, on September 3, 1805,
and on the Lolo Trail, Idaho County, Idaho, on June 25, 1806*

LYALL'S ANGELICA, *ANGELICA ARGUTA* NUTT.

Angelicas are commonly seen from midsummer through early fall in the mountains of Idaho and Montana, typically growing along streams and in nearby wetlands. They are rather tall plants, standing as high as three feet or more, and one may identify them by their spreading white clusters of small flowers borne on umbels, and by their compound pinnate leaves. The petioles are often slightly bent at the point that their leaflets are attached, and these "knees" may aid in the identifying the plants, as will the sheath at the base of the leaf stem (think of related celery or fennel plants)

The herbarium sheet for this plant in the Lewis and Clark Herbarium has two notations. The first, in Frederick Pursh's handwriting, says "Angelica within the Rocky mountains in moist places. Jun: 25th 1806. The flowering one taken in Septb: 3rd. 1805." A second notation, in Thomas Meehan's hand, says simply "all gone!" The missing plant is presumed to have been Lyell's angelica, a common plant in the areas mentioned, but either—or both—may also have been the similar Dawson's angelica (*Angelica dawsonii*). Both are found along the North Fork of the Salmon River (Lewis and Clark's "Fish Creek") and in moist surroundings on Lost Trail Pass (Lemhi County, Idaho, and Ravalli County, Montana) where the explorers were on September 3, 1805. Lewis collected angelica again on Hungery Creek while on their return crossing of the Lolo Trail on June 25, 1806. Both specimens are missing, either destroyed by insects while stored over the years, or taken by Pursh (most likely the former, as the plant is not included in the *Flora*).

Angelicas are common in the northern Rocky Mountains (*Angelica arguta* occurs more to the south, *Angelica dawsonii* is found farther north, although the species overlap).

Ours are related to Old World angelicas, known from early times as the "angelic herb," whence both common and scientific names were derived, and also as the "root of the Holy Ghost." They have been used medicinally for centuries.[9] Lewis, who had learned the use of herbs from his

Angelica arguta

JAMES L. REVEA

mother, would have recognized the Rocky Mountain plants as relatives of the eastern species with which he was familiar (*Angelica triquinata*, a plant common in the Virginian piedmont). This might have prompted him to collect the plants that he saw in the West. We would be remiss if we failed to mention one more thing: Our angelicas resemble another member of the Apiaceae, *Cicuta douglasii*, the North American water hemlock, a plant that grows in a similar environment. It is the most poisonous of all western North American plants. One must be cautious in dealing with wild plants in this family![10]

PHRYMACEAE (LOPSEED FAMILY)

Collected "On the head springs of the Missouri, at the foot of Portage Hill," August 1805

LEWIS'S MONKEY-FLOWER, *MIMULUS LEWISII* PURSH

Frederick Pursh's description of this plant in his *Flora* reads "Not above eight inches high; flowers two or three, larger than any known species [of *Mimulus*], of a beautiful pale purple."[11]

Mimulus lewisii

A. SCOTT EARLE

His description is accurate as far as it goes, although the plants are frequently several feet high and are often covered with deep pink-to-purple blooms. They sometimes grow in large patches, always close to mountain streams or seep springs. It is one of our most beautiful mountain wildflowers. The flower is irregu-

lar, with a prominent, three-petaled lower "lip" marked with bright yellow spots. The flowers are shed before they wither, and nearby streams are often filled with deep pink blossoms caught on logs and floating in backwaters. Pursh wrote that the plants bloom in August. This suggests that Lewis's specimen was collected fairly well up in the mountains, for usually they will have ceased blooming by then at lower altitudes.

Although Lewis's monkey-flower was described and named by Frederick Pursh in honor of Meriwether Lewis, the specimen that he used as a reference has disappeared. Pursh's note in his *Flora* says that his description was based on Lewis's dried specimen. His description is accurate, and the illustration in the *Flora* is a good representation of how it might have looked if drawn from the dried plant. No doubt Pursh took the specimen to London, but its fate is a mystery. Ewan has suggested that "the artist [William Hooker; not related to the eminent botanist of the same name] did not return the specimen after providing the drawing." Herbarium beetles also frequently attack herbarium specimens—they are especially fond of species of *Mimulus*—and may destroy specimens quickly. A third possibility is that the plant is resting in some herbarium, but—lacking information as to its origin and importance—it has gone unnoticed. In any case, it has not turned up.[12]

ROSACEAE (ROSE FAMILY)

Collected on the North Fork of the Salmon River, Lemhi County, Idaho, September 2, 1805,
and between Bald Mountain and Spring Hill, Lolo Trail, Idaho County, Idaho, June 27, 1806

CASCADE MOUNTAIN-ASH, *SORBUS SCOPULINA* GREENE

The Cascade mountain-ash, a member of the rose family (Rosaceae), is a montane to alpine shrub or small tree that

grows in the West from Alaska south to northern California and east to the Dakotas. White blossoms appear in early

Sorbus scopulina

JAMES L. REVEAL

Sorbus scopulina

JAMES L. REVEAL

spring in tight, flat-topped clusters made up of seventy to more than two hundred tiny flowers. These mature into bright red-orange berries that are a favorite food for birds but are considered inedible for humans. Lewis correctly referred to this mountain-ash as "a handsome growth," for each odd-pinnate leaf has nine to thirteen finely serrated, distinctly pointed leaflets, about three times as long as they are wide. In the aggregate they give the shrub a pleasing fernlike appearance that explains its popularity as an ornamental, a use that Lewis probably had in mind when he collected it.[13]

It is evident from Lewis's two tickets on the herbarium sheet of the mountain-ash that he collected the plant twice, although there is certainly nothing about the collection itself to support this conclusion. The specimens consist only of some stem and branch fragments, a portion of a single leaf, and part of an inflorescence. These—such as they are—are consistent with the plant as identified. Lewis wrote of the earlier collection "found on the 2d day of Sepbr. 1805. a small growth only rising to the hight of 15. feet moist situation it

seems to prefer. it is a handsome growth." On September 20 he described in his journal the same plant and with it a bird that was "feeding on the buries of a species of shoemake or ash which grows common in [this] country & which I first observed on 2d of this month."[14]

Although Pursh listed two other species of *Sorbus* in his *Flora*, for some reason he did not account for Lewis's specimen. Quite likely it was incomplete when it arrived in Philadelphia, and being a difficult genera, Pursh declined to describe it as a new species. The Cascade mountain-ash grows today along U.S. Highway 12 near Lolo Pass, on the boundary between Idaho and Montana. It is much more common than Sitka mountain-ash (*Sorbus sitchensis* M. Roem.), which grows today only along the Lolo Motorway.

The mountain-ashes take their common name from the resemblance of their leaves to those of (unrelated) ash trees that grow in the east and elsewhere throughout the Northern Hemisphere, particularly the white ash (*Fraxinus americana*). *Sorbus* is an old Latin term for the related serviceberry.[15]

Caprifoliaceae (Honeysuckle Family)

Seen and collected at unknown places and times (specimens missing)

Smooth snowberry, *Symphoricarpos albus* (L.) Blake var. *laevigatus* (Fernald) Blake
Western snowberry, *Symphoricarpos occidentalis* Hook.

No specimens of snowberry are in the Lewis and Clark Herbarium, yet the captains collected at least two of them, the smooth snowberry (*Symphoricarpos albus* var. *laevigatus*) and probably the western snowberry as well (*Symphoricarpos occidentalis*, also known as "wolfberry"). Lewis had just crossed Lemhi Pass on August 13, 1805, and he wrote that he had seen "a species of honeysuckle much in its growth and leaf like the small honeysuckle of the Missouri only reather larger and bears a globular berry as large as a garden pea and as white as wax."[16] If he gathered the plant—as one would expect, given the note in his journal—it has not survived (it may have been lost during the winter of 1805-1806 when the cache at Camp Fortunate was damaged by water). He probably did collect the seeds, for these reached Philadelphia. We know that the smooth snowberry was in cultivation in Philadelphia by 1812, because Bernard M'Mahon wrote to Thomas Jefferson suggesting that the plant be given a name.[17]

Pursh, using the name *Symphoria racemosa*, described yet another plant in his *Flora*, noting that Lewis had found it in August (year not specified) "On the banks of the Missouri," and indicated that he had seen a dried specimen in Lewis's herbarium. This may have been the western snowberry, found on the return trip in August 1806, between the Musselshell River in Montana and the South Dakota–Nebraska state line, where it is common.[18]

Another related plant, the Utah mountain snowberry (*Symphoricarpos oreophilus* var. *utahensis*) is similar to the smooth snowberry. It is common in the mountains of Idaho to fairly high elevations. Its berries are more oval than round. Both plants have oval, bluish green leaves; these, with their white berries, make them easy to identify, at least generically. Their white flowers are small and appear early in the spring. Like the berries, the flowers are borne in pairs, a trait of the Caprifoliaceae in general. Although the fruit of some plants in the honeysuckle family—the elderberry for example—is edible, the mushy white berries of the snowberry are not.

The genus *Symphoricarpos* was established by the French botanist Henri Louis Duhamel du Monceau (1700-1782) in

Symphoricarpos occidentalis

JAMES L. REVEAL

Symphoricarpos albus var. *laevigatus*

A. SCOTT EARLE

1755. The name was derived from the Greek *symphoros* and *karpos* and means, more or less, "fruit together," for the tendency of the berries to be borne in pairs. Snowberry is a common ornamental. Children brought up in northern states are often acquainted with the garden plant because when they step on the berries, they are rewarded with a satisfying "pop."

CAPRIFOLIACEAE (HONEYSUCKLE FAMILY)
Collected on the North Fork of the Salmon River, Lemhi County, Idaho, September 2, 1805
ROCKY MOUNTAIN HONEYSUCKLE, *LONICERA UTAHENSIS* S. WATSON

The Rocky Mountain honeysuckle that Meriwether Lewis collected on the North Fork of the Salmon River is a shrub that may grow as high as six feet. It has smooth, usually nonhairy (glabrous) leaves and small clusters of paired, creamy to pale yellow flowers. Its flowers are fragrant and are nearly regular in the sense that its five fused petals are not arranged into two sets of two and three petals each (that is, unlike the flowers of many other honeysuckle species, they are not bilabiate). Another distinctive feature, although not unique to *Lonicera utahensis*, is that its mature paired berries are tightly fused together at the base. The shrubs fruit in mid- to late summer. Their berries are bitter and supposedly toxic if eaten in any quantity, although birds and other animals apparently eat them with impunity.

When Lewis collected the plant on September 2, 1805, the expedition was on the North Fork of the Salmon River (their "Fish Creek"). They were moving north to the head of the valley where they would cross today's Lost Trail Pass into the Bitterroot River drainage. Now they had horses to carry baggage and they had to choose a route where the animals could go. The captains were anxious to reach the main Columbia River, so collecting plant specimens probably was not high in their priorities. Nevertheless, when Lewis saw the honeysuckle shrub with its bright red berries, he gathered a specimen and added it to his new collection of dried plants. His label, apparently cut from the original paper that contained the dried specimen, states "found on the waters of the columbia Sept: 2nd 1805 the growth of a moist situations seldom rises higher than 6 or 8 feet—puts up a number of succulent sprouts forming a thick bush."[19]

Lonicera utahensis

A. SCOTT EARLE

Lonicera utahensis

JAMES L. REVEAL

ROCKY MOUNTAIN LODGEPOLE PINE | *Pinus contorta* var. *latifolia*
ENGELMANN SPRUCE | *Picea engelmannii*
WESTERN LARCH | *Larix occidentalis*
ROCKY MOUNTAIN SUBALPINE FIR | *Abies bifolia*

WHITEBARK PINE | *Pinus albicaulis*
WESTERN RED-CEDAR | *Thuja plicata*
SITKA ALDER | *Alnus viridis* var. *sinuata*
BLACK HAWTHORN | *Crataegus douglasii*

Travelers' Rest to Canoe Camp
September 10 to September 26, 1805

The expedition spent two days at Travelers' Rest, at today's Lolo, Montana, to prepare for the mountain crossing that lay ahead. They shot two deer, only enough to satisfy present needs; little remained for the days to follow. On the afternoon of September 11, the party headed west into the Bitterroot Mountains. The day was warm, but the mountains on either side were snow covered, a warning of what was to come.

Their trail was difficult from the first. Steep slopes, sudden drop-offs, deadfall, lost and falling horses, and absence of game made each day's ordeal worse than the one before. They saw Indian "roads," but none clearly indicated the way. Old Toby, their Shoshone guide, lost his way, leading the party down to the Lochsa River to a fishing camp (near today's Powell Ranger Station on U.S. Highway 12). Passage downstream from there was impossible, and the men had to climb 3000 feet back up to the heights. Then it began to snow. Unless one has experienced similar circumstances, it is difficult to comprehend what the men were enduring, struggling along in bitter cold, in deep snow on top of old snowpack, in inadequate clothing and footwear. Some of the horses gave out and had to be abandoned. On October 14, they killed a colt, for their food was nearly gone. Clark noted that the "road as bad as it can possibly be to pass."[1] Two days later they killed another horse and then a third one on the day after that.

On September 16, Clark wrote in his journal that the party was in "a thickly timbered Countrey of 8 different kinds of pine, which are So covered with Snow, that in passing thro them we are continually covered with Snow, I have been wet and as cold in every part as I ever was in my life…."[2] The captains seem to have used the term "pine" as a synonym of "conifer." We can only guess which eight of many possible species he was referring to. Some of the possibilities include Rocky Mountain lodgepole pine (*Pinus contorta* var. *latifolia*), subalpine fir (*Abies bifolia*), Engelmann spruce (*Picea engelmannii*), whitebark pine (*Pinus albicaulis*), western larch (*Larix occidentalis*), western white pine (*Pinus monticola*), western red-cedar (*Thuja plicata*), Rocky Mountain ponderosa pine (*Pinus ponderosa* var. *scopulorum*), Rocky Mountain Douglas-fir (*Pseudotsuga menziesii* var. *glauca*), mountain hemlock (*Tsuga mertensia*), and the western yew (*Taxus brevifolia*). The explorers probably also saw the dwarf common juniper (*Juniperus communis* var. *depressa*), a plant that Pursh named eight years later, although Lewis would not have considered this a "pine."

By the eighteenth, the men were living on horseflesh, "portable soup" purchased in Philadelphia almost two years earlier, tallow candles, and bear grease. That day Clark took six hunters to reconnoiter ahead of the main party, and he was elated to see open prairie in the distance. On September 20, Clark emerged onto high meadows near present-day Weippe, Idaho, where he met the "Chopunnish or Pierced Noses." They gave him food: camas root bread, dried meat, and salmon. That evening Clark wrote that he found himself "very unwell…from eateing the fish & roots too freely."[3] Four days later, Lewis and the rest of the party arrived. Nearly starving, they too ate the food proffered by the Nez Perce, and in short order many became ill. Some, including Lewis, were very much so. The men blamed the roots that they had eaten (although most physicians today would assume that food poisoning was more likely responsible for their severe gastrointestinal symptoms, the result of eating poorly preserved fish and meat). Nevertheless, the men were grateful. They praised the Nez Perce as the finest of all the Native Americans that they had met, and decided to overwinter their horses with them, to be reclaimed on the return journey.

Even though Lewis and many of the men were still sick, the party moved off the heights and down to the Clearwater River. On September 26, they established a camp—"Canoe Camp," west of today's Orofino, Idaho—where the Clearwater becomes navigable. They were not quite home free, but it must have seemed so at the time. Understandably, given the uncertainties and hardships that the men faced, few plants were collected between Travelers' Rest and Canoe Camp. Those shown on the next few pages are an amalgam, including the trees noted above and a few other plants mentioned in the journals.

PINACEAE (PINE FAMILY)
Observed on various dates along the Lolo Trail in Missoula County, Montana, and Idaho County, Idaho

The expedition spent September 9 and 10 at Travelers' Rest on today's Lolo Creek, a short distance east of the main Bitterroot River, preparing for their mountain crossing. On the morning of the twelfth, as they ascended Lolo Creek, Clark noted "The Timber is Short & long leaf Pine Spruce Pine and fur."[4] There are a number of trees that fit Clark's list in this area and at this altitude. Clark's "long leaf Pine" is Rocky Mountain ponderosa pine (*Pinus ponderosa* var. *scopulorum*, see p. 92); his "short…leaf Pine" is Rocky Mountain lodgepole pine (*Pinus contorta* var. *latifolia*), and his "Spruce Pine" is Engelmann spruce (*Picea engelmannii*). The "fur" is the Rocky Mountain or inland Douglas-fir (*Pseudotsuga menziesii* var. *glauca*), similar to the coastal Douglas-fir (*Pseudotsuga menziesii* var. *menziesii*) seen at Fort Clatsop (see p. 106). On September 14, Lewis mentioned the western larch (*Larix occidentalis*) and the next day saw "pines" that were quite likely the Rocky Mountain subalpine fir (*Abies bifolia*) and the whitebark pine (*Pinus albicaulis*), as both are trees found along the expedition's route at higher elevations.

Observed on Lolo Creek, Missoula County, Montana, on September 12, 1805
ROCKY MOUNTAIN LODGEPOLE PINE, *PINUS CONTORTA* DOUGLAS EX LOUDON VAR. *LATIFOLIA* ENGELM.

The Rocky Mountain variety of lodgepole pine grows throughout the Pacific Northwest from southern Alaska and Yukon, Canada, south into Rocky Mountains of Utah and Colorado. An isolated population also grows in the Black Hills of South Dakota. Its needles average about two inches in length. The bark of mature trees is composed of many thin, irregular scales. The tree's straight trunk gave the lodgepole its name, for Native Americans used it for their tepees and lodges. When growing as solitary trees, lodgepoles may have trunks up to three feet in diameter and grow as tall as 150 feet. More often the trees grow close together in dense "stands" in sites where fires are common. Forest fires burn all vegetation, but lodgepole cones are especially fire resistant and the heat prompts the release of large numbers of seeds. Lodgepole seedlings soon form pure stands of small, ruler-straight, high-crowned trees whose trunks are seldom more than eight inches in diameter. While some are suitable for lumber, more often they are used for railroad ties, fence rails, cabin logs, and fuel. The trees usually do well, but they are not disease resistant, and parasites—various fungi and especially pine bark beetles—can destroy large numbers of trees in localized areas.

Why does a tree as tall and straight as the lodgepole pine have a species name—*contorta*—that implies "misshapen" or "twisted"? The answer is that there are three varieties of lodgepole pine. One was described and named *Pinus contorta* by the British nurseryman John Loudon (1783-1843) in 1838, adopting a name proposed by the David Douglas (1798-1834), the great Scottish plant hunter. In an 1829 manuscript, Douglas wrote that the tree grew near the coast and was "greatly twisted in every direction." This variety, called shore pine or sometimes scrub pine, is frequently stunted and always gnarled. The variety Lewis and Clark saw grow-

Pinus contorta var. latifolia

JAMES L. REVEAL

ing along the Lolo Trail is a tall tree that is never gnarled, and thus is similar to the Sierran lodgepole pine (*Pinus contorta* var. *murrayana*), an even taller tree that reaches its northern limits near Mount Hood in Oregon. Lewis and Clark's tree was described and named var. *latifolia* by George Engelmann (1809-1884) in 1871, who based his description on specimens gathered in the Uintah Mountains in Utah by the King expedition in 1868. The shore pine that Lewis and Clark saw along the Pacific Coast is a smaller tree (rarely over thirty feet), and its foliage is a deep green compared to the yellow-green needles of the inland variety.

Lewis noted the Rocky Mountain lodgepole pine on September 14, 1805.[6] He called it a "pitch pine" because of its resemblance to the longer-needled pitch pine (*Pinus rigida*) of Virginia and elsewhere in the East.

Observed on Lolo Creek, Missoula County, Montana, on September 12, 1805

ENGELMANN SPRUCE, *PICEA ENGELMANNII* PARRY EX ENGELM.

Engelmann spruce is the only spruce found in the northern Rocky Mountains. It closely resembles its near relative, the Colorado blue spruce (*Picea pungens*), a tree that grows farther south. Despite the resemblance, the two species are different and they do not hybridize. Engelmann spruce may be distinguished from Rocky Mountain subalpine fir (*Abies bifolia*) because the spruce's conical configuration is noticeably wider at the base than the firs's. Also, the foliage of the spruce has a decidedly bluish hue that the fir does not possess. The spruce's needles are short (about an inch, more or less), and they grow around the circumference of the branches, unlike those of the subalpine fir, where the needles tend to grow on the lateral sides of the twig. The spruce's needles are ridged, front and back, giving them a four-sided appearance. Grasp one of the tree's branches and you will find that the needles are painfully sharp. The bark is thin and scaly. Like the blue spruce, Engelmann spruce is a handsome tree and often planted as an ornamental; it is also popular as a Christmas tree. Even though the scientific generic name for spruce, *Picea*, was derived from the Latin word *pix* for "pitch," the wood of Engelmann spruce is relatively low in resin, which makes it especially useful as pulp for paper making. The wood is used for soundboards on stringed instruments, including pianos. As with Douglas-fir and whitebark pine, spruce trees often live hundreds of years.

The Engelmann spruce's species

Picea engelmannii

A. SCOTT EARLE

name (or "specific epithet") honors German-born George Engelmann, a physician who emigrated to the United States in 1832 and settled in St Louis. He became increasingly interested in botany, especially in ferns, in conifers, and in grape culture. Despite his busy medical practice, Engelmann wrote several detailed botanical monographs and in time became one of the country's best-known botanists. His extensive plant collection served as a foundation for the Missouri Botanical Garden's herbarium.

Encountered on the Lolo Trail in Idaho County, Idaho, on September 14, 1805
WESTERN LARCH, *LARIX OCCIDENTALIS* NUTT.

On the fourteenth of September, as the men struggled to cross the Bitterroot Range, Clark noted in his journal: "The Mountains which we passed to day much worst than yesterday the last excessively bad & Thickly Strowed with falling timber & Pine Spruc fur Hackmatak & Tamerack, Steep & Stoney our men and horses much fatigued."[7]

The tamerack (also known as "hackmatac"—both are American Indian words) that the explorers saw was the western larch, *Larix occidentalis*, similar enough to the eastern species that they had no difficulty in recognizing its characteristic appearance. The larches are trees of northern forests. They grow between elevations of 2000 and 6000 feet. The western larch may live to be seven hundred years old and grow to be more than two hundred feet high. The trees are

Larix occidentalis

A. SCOTT EARLE

characterized by their short needles, fifteen to forty in a bundle, located at the base of small (from one and a half to two inches long) reddish cones, or at the end of short twiglike "spur shoots." The unusual arrangement of the needles, the tree's tall, straight trunks, and its high, symmetrically rounded crowns give the tree a distinctive appearance, making it easy to identify even from a distance. Unlike other conifers, larches are deciduous, meaning that its needles fall off each year. In the autumn the needles turn a bright yellow and then fall away to be replaced by new ones in the spring. The western larch's heavy cinnamon-brown bark is resistant to moderate fire, so the trees often survive when other trees are lost. Their wood is heavy, durable, and resistant to rot; it is used for railroad ties, for telephone poles, and for both rough and finished lumber. *Larix* is derived from the Latin word for "larch"; *occidentalis* means "of the west." The western larch was observed in 1826 by David Douglas but was not described or given a scientific name until Thomas Nuttall named it in the third volume of his *North American Sylva*, published in 1849.

Encountered on the Lolo Trail, Idaho County, Idaho, September 14 and 16, 1805

ROCKY MOUNTAIN SUBALPINE FIR, *ABIES BIFOLIA* MURRAY

The expedition was now in high country. It was late in the season and the men were having a miserable time as they worked their way across the Bitterroot Range, yet Clark noted a "fur" among other trees that he listed in his journal. Growing as thin, symmetrical spires, Rocky Mountain subalpine firs look as if they belong in the mountains. They are found at higher elevations throughout the Rocky Mountains, from about 6000 feet (or higher, depending on the latitude) to timberline. Unlike the true pines (*Pinus* spp.), the subalpine fir's needles are short and blunt, its cones are a dark bluish purple before they mature, and its bark is thin and gray, lacking the usual roughness of other mature conifers. In the fall of the year,

Abies bifolia

A. SCOTT EARLE

Rocky Mountain subalpine fir; it is the only thin, steeple-shaped evergreen that grows in Idaho and Montana's high-altitude forests. The tree's perfect profile is sometimes altered, however, when the lowermost branches, weighed down by heavy winter snow, take root and give a bushlike "skirt" that spreads out from the base of the tree. A similar phenomenon occurs at timberline where the subalpine zone gives way to alpine tundra. Here, one finds trees in dense clusters of low, windshaped, bushy masses. Although these are the same trees, they are completely unlike the stately spires one sees lower down. These bushy forms are known as "elfinwood," or "krummholz," a word derived from

as the cones reach maturity, those of fir fall completely apart, whereas those of pine remain together, as a real pine cone should. Usually only a glance is required to identify the the German meaning "crooked wood" (other trees also form krummholz, even those in the tropics). Alpine firs are too slender to use for lumber, although they are occasionally harvested as Christmas trees—a practice now prohibited on government lands except by individual permit. The generic name, *Abies*, comes from the Latin name for fir trees. The species name, *bifolia*, means "two leaves," from the tendency of the needles to grow on opposing sides of their branches.

Noted near Lolo Pass, Montana-Idaho border, September 16, 1805
WHITEBARK PINE, *PINUS ALBICAULIS* ENGELM.
CLARK'S NUTCRACKER, *NUCIFRAGA COLUMBIANA* (WILSON)

Like the Rocky Mountain subalpine fir, the whitebark pine is a tree of higher altitudes. It grows in Idaho and Montana, from about 7000 feet to treeline. The tree takes both its common and scientific species name, *albicaulus* (Latin, meaning "white bark"), from the light gray bark of the branches and trunks of younger trees. Its needles typically grow in bundles of five. The whitebark pine is a survivor, often the highest tree at timberline. There they exist, like the intermountain bristlecone pines of the Great Basin (*Pinus longaeva*), often dwarfed and twisted; both may live for two or three thousand years.

The whitebark pine has particular relevance for the expedition, for it is intimately linked to Clark's nutcracker, a bird that Lewis described on August 22, 1805. *Nucifraga columbiana* is a member of the crow family (Corvidae). It resembles a small crow, although only its wings are black; the body is gray. The seeds of the whitebark pine are the bird's principal food, obtained by forcing open the scales of the cones with its beak. Bird and tree were both new to science, but a specimen of only the bird reached Philadelphia.

The whitebark pine and Clark's nutcracker have coevolved.

Pinus albicaulis

A. SCOTT EARLE

The bird harvests the seeds, stores them in a capacious pouch beneath its tongue, and then caches them underground for later use, remembering exactly where they are hidden. A few seeds inevitably are not retrieved, however, and under the right conditions these germinate and grow—a form of natural reforestation. It is unusual to see a single whitebark pine; they almost always grow in clusters of two or more, all of the same size. Often, the trunks are so close together—for all have originated from one seed-cache—that they fuse. The tree's roundish cones are moderately large, and unlike those of other Pinaceae, the seeds remain in the cone waiting for the birds to harvest them.[9]

Given its relative inaccessibility, whitebark pine is not commercially important, although in the past the trees were used by miners working at higher altitudes as "stopes"—beams for shoring up mine shafts—and for their cabins. The seeds, cached by birds and squirrels, are important food for other animals, and bears especially depend on whitebark pine seeds as an important part of their food supply. These unique trees seem to be holding their own, although avalanches, fire, and disease, including white pine blister rust, exact a toll.

Clark's nutcracker, drawn by ornithologist Alexander Wilson (1766-1813) from a specimen returned by the expedition. On August 22, 1805, at the entrance of the North Fork of the Salmon River (Lewis and Clark's "Fish Creek," close to the site of today's North Fork, in Lemhi County, Idaho), Lewis wrote the first description of Clark's nutcracker: "I saw today a speceis of woodpecker, which fed on the seeds of the pine. it's beak and tail were white, it's wings were black, and every other part of a dark brown. it was about the size of a robin...."[10]

CUPRESSACEAE (CYPRESS FAMILY)
Noted on the Lolo Trail, September 20, 1805
WESTERN RED-CEDAR, *Thuja plicata* DONN EX D. DON

On September 20, 1805, Meriwether Lewis wrote: "the Arborvita is also common and grows to an immence size, being from 2 to 6 feet in diameter." The following day he added that the tree "increases in quantity and size. I saw several sticks [trunks] large enough to form eligant perogues of at least 45 feet in length."[11] His description of the western red cedar still holds, at least for the protected trees found in the DeVoto Grove on U.S. Highway 12 west of Lolo Pass.

Lewis was also correct in describing the tree as an arborvitae, for it is in the Cupressaceae (cypress family). The name "western red cedar" (or "red-cedar") is firmly entrenched in common usage, but the less commonly used "western arborvitae" is a better name for this tree.

Typically, western red-cedar grows in dense, well shaded, moist forests throughout the American and Canadian northwest.[12] The trees are long-lived, reaching ages of more than a thousand years. Many giant old-growth trees have been lumbered over the past two hundred years, but some may still be seen, as noted above. The wood of the western red-cedar, as with other so-called cedars, resists rot and has many uses: lawn furniture, caskets, shingles, and boards for general building purposes. Native Americans also found many uses for the trees. Their great size and straight trunks made them

Thuja plicata

JAMES L REVEAL

ideal for the dugout canoes—some as much as fifty feet long—used by coastal Indians, and for totem poles. Their soft inner bark was used for clothing and ropes. The word *Thuja* is from an ancient Greek word for a now unknown evergreen. The name *plicata* is Latin and means "folded" or "furrowed," presumably for the fluted bark of mature trees.

BETULACEAE (BIRCH FAMILY)
Seen on the Lolo Trail, Idaho County, Idaho, September 20, 1805
SITKA ALDER, *ALNUS VIRIDIS* (VILL.) DC. VAR. *SINUATA* REGEL

On September 20, Lewis mentioned several plants in his journal, including an "alder common to the Atlantic states."[13] The alder he saw was most likely the Sitka (or wavy-leaf) alder, for it closely resembles eastern smooth alder (*Alnus serrulata*). The Sitka alder (often called *Alnus sinuata* or *Alnus sitchensis* in the older literature) is common throughout much of Idaho and Montana, growing at all elevations. Its range extends from eastern Siberia to western Canada and south to California. Typically the trees are found along watercourses in the mountains. The high bushes, or low trees, have leaves with wavy (sinuous) margins, with superimposed tiny teeth from which the plant derives its varietal name. The trees bear both male and female catkins. The former are long and dependent, growing at the end of the

Alnus viridis var. sinuata

JAMES L. REVEAL

branches in early spring. The female catkins are more often seen. These are shorter, ovoid, and are borne on short stems that arise at the base of a leaf, with three or four catkins to a branch. They resemble miniature pine cones and persist well into the summer. The bark is a reddish brown, becoming gray as the trees age. The Sitka alder is a pioneer species, being one of the first to occupy a disturbed site, especially after an avalanche, local flooding, or fire.

The expedition might have encountered the Sitka alder anywhere along the passage through the mountains, for the trees grow along the banks of streams, ponds, and shaded moist slopes. The family name is derived from *betula*, an old Latin word for "birch," the alder's near relative.

ROSACEAE (ROSE FAMILY)

Collected at the mouth of the Walla Walla River, Walla Walla County, Washington, on April 29, 1806

BLACK HAWTHORN, *CRATAEGUS DOUGLASII* LINDL.

On September 22, 1805, after crossing the snow-covered Bitterroot and Clearwater mountains, the main party reached the Nez Perce village on Weippe Prairie. Sergeant Joseph Whitehead apparently was the only man to notice that the Native Americans ate two different kinds of hawthorn berries. He wrote in his journal that "the Indians belonging to this Village, brought us such food, as they had, which consisted of Roots of different kinds, which has a sweet taste & was good also Red & black haws & some Salmon." "Haws" refers to the fruit of hawthorns, in the genus *Crataegus* (an ancient Greek name, derived from *kratos* meaning "strong" or "powerful," referring to the strength of the wood). Although mostly found in eastern North America, a few species occur as far west as the Pacific Coast; others are found south to the Andes.[14]

The berries that Whitehead ate were black haw (*Crataegus douglasii*) and red haw, which is also known as Piper's hawthorn (*Crataegus chrysocarpa* var. *piperi* or *Crataegus columbiana*). The black haw is a large shrub or small tree growing to twenty feet or so, with shiny, dark red thorns up to 1½ inches long, and white flowers with ten (or fewer) stamens. The round fruit is purplish black. The "red haw," as Whitehead called it, has longer thorns (1½ to 3 inches long) and a dark red fruit that is not quite as round.

The following spring, Lewis collected a "purple haw" on April 29, 1806, near the mouth of the Walla Walla River in present-day Washington. The label on the specimen in the Lewis and Clark Herbarium reads "Deep purple Haw. Columbia R. Aprl. 29th 1806." Frederick Pursh was unable to make out the plant's features and thought that it was the yellow hawthorn of the southeastern United States, and he identified it as such in his *Flora*.[15] Years later, the plant was again collected, seen to be a new species, and named *Crataegus douglasii* in 1835 for David Douglas.

The black hawthorn grows from British Columbia and Ontario in the north, south to California, Arizona, and New Mexico, and east to Minnesota and Michigan, although it is

Crataegus douglasii

JAMES L. REVEAL

common only in the Pacific Northwest. The "red haw" is more restricted; it is found only in southwestern Canada and the Pacific Northwest. The red haws that Whitehead ate probably were gathered farther west along the Clearwater River, as it is not known to occur at Weippe. Both species flower from late April into early June, and their fruit mature over the summer months. Although these hawthorns are sometimes planted as ornamental trees, they are less commonly used than more attractive nonnative species. Dried haws are edible but are not particularly appetizing. Still, after weeks of eating nothing but meat including dogs and horses—the men probably found them quite good. We assume that haws, like related rose hips, contain a significant amount of vitamin C, a nutrient conspicuously lacking in an all-meat diet. Finally, we should mention that the thorns of the hawthorn are sharp and dangerous; care should be taken to avoid injury, especially to the eye.

ROCKY MOUNTAIN PONDEROSA PINE	*Pinus ponderosa* var. *scopulorum*
PACIFIC MADRONE	*Arbutus menziesii*
SALAL	*Gaultheria shallon*
VINE MAPLE	*Acer circinatum*
BIGLEAF MAPLE	*Acer macrophyllum*
ROCKY MOUNTAIN MAPLE	*Acer glabrum*
DULL OREGON GRAPE	*Berberis nervosa*

Pacific Ocean

FORT CLATSOP

WASHINGTON

Snake River

Columbia River

IDAHO

RICHLAND PASCO

KENNEWICK LEWISTON

WALLA WALLA

PORTLAND CLARKSTON

THE DALLES

KAMIAH

PENDLETON

OREGON

SHINING OREGON GRAPE	*Berberis aquifolium*
CREEPING OREGON GRAPE	*Berberis repens*
MOUNTAIN-BOX	*Paxistima myrsinites*
EATON'S ASTER	*Symphyotrichum eatonii*
COLUMBIA TICKSEED	*Coreopsis tinctoria* var. *atkinsoniana*
GRAY TANSY-ASTER	*Machaeranthera canescens* var. *incana*

Canoe Camp to Fort Clatsop
September 27 to December 10, 1805

On September 27, 1805, the Corps of Discovery set up camp on the Clearwater River a few miles west of today's Orofino, Idaho, possibly where its North Fork joins the main Clearwater. The large Rocky Mountain ponderosa pines (*Pinus ponderosa* var. *scopulorum*) that grew there were perfect for making the dugout canoes that the expedition needed. Three-quarters of the men, Lewis included, were still ailing, their gastrointestinal problems prolonged by the Nez Perce's diet of camas roots and dried salmon. Even though inconvenienced by diarrhea, most of the men were able to go about the business of chopping down trees and hollowing out the trunks to make dugout canoes. On October 7, 1805, the party launched its flotilla of five canoes and resumed its westward journey. If the men expected to float downstream on placid waters, they would be vastly disappointed. There were rapids and cascades—lots of them—ahead.

The expedition spent four days navigating the Clearwater and six days on the Snake River, where they nearly lost one canoe when it struck a rock. Kettles, bedding, powder, and personal possessions disappeared overboard. Nevertheless, they made good time, passing the site of today's Lewiston, Idaho, and Clarkston, Washington, and across the southeast corner of Washington to join the Columbia River near present-day Kennewick, Washington.

Their diet gradually changed. The Nez Perce's camas roots were replaced by Columbia River salmon, augmented by dogs purchased from the Indians along the river—forty dogs from one village alone! Most of the men considered dog meat a delicacy. The party's journals for this segment include many observations on the Native Americans that they met. Sacagawea's reassuring presence smoothed their way, as the Indians knew that a woman would never be part of a hostile party.

Falls and rapids were the expedition's greatest hindrance. They negotiated these by a combination of portaging, lowering the boats with elk hide ropes, and relying on plain guts as they shot rapids that the local people considered impossible. On October 30 they reached tidewater. Seven days later Clark penned the famous line "Ocian in view, O! the joy."[1] It was, in fact, the broad estuary of the Columbia River. Finally, after battling high winds and ocean waves, they saw the Pacific shore a week later, traveling the last miles on foot. The party then crossed to the southern shore of the Columbia estuary. On December 10 they camped on a sheltered bluff a few miles from the ocean. Here they built Fort Clatsop, named for the local Indians. A long, wet winter lay ahead.

Considering the difficulties that the expedition met, and the lateness of the season, it is surprising that any plants were collected during this segment, other than the ponderosa pine (*Pinus ponderosa* var. *scopulorum*) that they used for their dugouts. Nevertheless, a few, mostly fruiting specimens, are preserved in the Lewis and Clark Herbarium.

PINACEAE (PINE FAMILY)

Collected at Canoe Camp on the Clearwater River, October 1, 1805

ROCKY MOUNTAIN PONDEROSA PINE, *PINUS PONDEROSA* C. LAWSON VAR. *SCOPULORUM* ENGELM.

As the expedition's naturalist, Lewis could not have ignored the Rocky Mountain ponderosa pine. He and everyone else involved in the business of hollowing out ponderosa logs must have been covered with the trees' sticky pitch. They had encountered the tree earlier, in the Salmon and Clearwater river valleys, although contact with the trees there could hardly have been as intimate as it was at Canoe Camp.

Ponderosa pine has long needles that grow mostly in packets of three. Two varieties are found in the Pacific Northwest, the Rocky Mountain *Pinus ponderosa* var. *scopulorum* that we are describing here, and the more western *Pinus ponderosa* var. *ponderosa*. The latter tree was named by David Douglas.[2] Douglas had found the tree along the Spokane River in northern Washington in 1826, but it was not named until 1836, two years after his death. Var. *ponderosa* has needles in bundles of three to five that are mostly six to twelve inches long, whereas the needles of var. *scopulorum* are two or three per bundle and typically more

Pinus ponderosa var. scopulorum

JAMES L. REVEAL

than seven inches long.

Unlike the whitebark pine, the Rocky Mountain ponderosa pine grows rapidly and has a shorter life span, less than six hundred years. The trees are not as common today as they were formerly. Their thick red bark protects them from fires that kill other species—but wildfires now are controlled. Wildfire control favors trees like the Douglas-fir that would otherwise die as wildfires sweep through the forest. Because of this, Douglas-firs persist and have, to an extent, replaced ponderosa pines in their combined range. Given recent changes in fire control policy, however, we may see a resurgence of ponderosa pine in the future. Ponderosa pine is also cultivated as a timber tree. Its wood, like that of the related eastern yellow pine, is soft but still suitable for lumber, boxes, crating, and so on. Interestingly, the trees were a source of food for the Indians. While camped at Travelers' Rest on November 12, 1805, Clark wrote, "the Indians have pealed a number of Pine for the under bark which they eate…in the Spring."[3]

Ericaceae (Heath Family)

Arbutus menziesii collected at the Cascades of the Columbia River, November 1, 1805;
Gaultheria shallon collected in the vicinity of Fort Clatsop, January 20, 1806

Pacific madrone, *Arbutus menziesii* Pursh
Salal, *Gaultheria shallon* Pursh

Lewis and Clark were not the first to botanize along the coast of Oregon and Washington. Surgeon-naturalist Archibald Menzies (1754-1843) gathered plants in the Straits of San Juan de Fuca in 1792.[4] Menzies returned to England with several hundred plant specimens that he had found along the Pacific Coast, from 1791 until 1794. His carefully prepared specimens went to Sir Joseph Banks, and he, in turn, made them available to Frederick Pursh to examine while he prepared his *Flora Americae Septentrionalis.* Menzies had previously found several of the plants that Lewis collected during the expedition's stay at Fort Clatsop. Having two sets of specimens meant that Pursh could describe more carefully those plants that he believed were new to science. His *Flora* included two species of heath that both Lewis and Menzies had collected.

The first of these, the Pacific madrone (or madroña, *Arbutus menziesii*), is an odd tree. Some are twisted and gnarled, and others may be straight and stately, depending on their environment. Their bark is smooth and paper-thin. It is chartreuse in young trees but becomes reddish and finally thick and dark brown as the trees age. Their shiny dark green leaves make the trees easy to recognize. Small (one-quarter inch long), white, spring-blooming flowers resemble those of much smaller heathers, yet they grow on a tree that can be 120 feet tall. The tree usually is found in the company of old-growth forest conifers on rich, wooded slopes. Lewis gathered his specimen at the Cascades of the Columbia River on the first of November in 1805, probably doing a bit of botanizing while the others moved canoes and baggage over a "bad Slippery and Rockey way." A month later he wrote a brief description of the tree: "the tree which bears a red burry in clusters of a round

form and size of a red haw. the leaf like that of the small magnolia, and brark smoth and of a brickdust red colour."[5] The madrone's clustered red berries are edible, but only barely (although birds are fond of them), and eating more than a few may cause intestinal cramping. Madrone makes an excellent ornamental shrub or tree, although it sheds both bark and

Arbutus menziesii

leaves almost continuously and so may be "somewhat messy."[6]

The Lewis and Clark journals mention the second of Menzies specimens, salal (or shallon, *Gaultheria shallon*) several times. On February 8, 1806, Clark sketched this shrub and Lewis provided a description. He wrote: "The *Shallon* is the production of a shrub which I have heretofore taken to be a speceis of loral and mentioned as abounding in this neighbourhood and that the Elk fed much on it's leaves." He went on to provide a detailed and precise description—too long to quote here in its entirely—of the plant's red

89

Gaultheria shallon

JAMES L. REVEAL

Gaultheria shallon

JAMES L. REVEAL

shoots, its branches, leaves, and edible fruit.[7] The plants that he saw were fruiting, and he speculated, on his label (now attached to the specimen sheet in the Lewis and Clark Herbarium), that salal might be a species of huckleberry.[8]

The berries were eaten by Native Americans along the Columbia during winter months, and they are still sought. This evergreen shrub, with its shiny green leaves, pink flow-

ers, and dark purple fruit, also grows at reconstructed Fort Clatsop "under the shade of close pine forests, where scarcely any other plant thrives."[9] As the description suggests, salal is an attractive plant, and gardeners use it in landscaping. When David Douglas arrived on the Columbia, the first collection he made was of salal in honor of Menzies and of Lewis and Clark.

SAPINDACEAE (SOAPBERRY FAMILY)

Collected at the "Great Rapids" (Cascades) of the Columbia River, Skamania County, Washington, or Hood River County, Oregon on October 30 or 31, 1805, and on April 10, 1806. Rocky Mountain maple seen, but if collected no specimen extant.

VINE MAPLE, *ACER CIRCINATUM* PURSH
ROCKY MOUNTAIN MAPLE, *ACER GLABRUM* TORR.
BIGLEAF MAPLE, *ACER MACROPHYLLUM* PURSH

The two maples Lewis collected along the Columbia River were unlike any maples that he had ever seen in Virginia.[10] The first was a reclining, sometimes twisted, and even vine-like shrub or small tree. Pursh named the species *circinatum*, a Latin word that means "curled at the apex." He appar-

ently was referring to the curled branch noticeable in Lewis's herbarium specimens (the generic name *Acer* means, simply, "maple" in Latin). It must have been a surprise to Lewis to find a sprawling shrub half the height of the shrubby striped maple (*Acer pensylvanicum*), the smallest of the

Acer circinatum

Acer glabrum var. douglasii

Acer macrophyllum

several maples that grow in Virginia. His specimens of vine maple were gathered in October 1805 "On the great rapids of the Columbia river," as the expedition worked its way downstream.[11] On February 10, 1806, while at Fort Clatsop, he entered a detailed description of the maple into his journal and made a small sketch of a leaf. It was well known to the local Native Americans who used the flexible twigs in open weave carrying baskets and fish traps. He saw it again on April 12 when the party stopped at "the Cascades" near present-day Cascade Lock, Oregon. Here, against a backdrop of Douglas-fir, western hemlock, and western redcedar, the diminutive maple would have stood out in marked contrast to the surrounding giants.

Lewis did not recognize the bigleaf maple as a maple, even when he saw it in flower. No maple could have such large leaves! Pursh named this tree *Acer macrophyllum*—the species name means "big leaf" in Latin. Lewis had also described bigleaf maple on February 10, noting that he had seen individuals up to fifty feet tall with trunks three feet in diameter. This stately species was more akin to his Virginia maples except for its huge leaves: "8 inches in length and 12 in bredth."[12] Although Lewis wrote about this tree at Fort Clatsop, apparently he did not collect a specimen there. The one that Pursh examined was gathered at "the Cascades" on April 10, 1806, on the journey home. Both maples grow today along the Columbia River west of the Cascade Range wherever there are remnants of forest. Both are also in cultivation, *Acer circinatum* more than *Acer macrophyllum* because of its smaller size and brilliant fall color.

Lewis first mentioned Rocky Mountain maple (*Acer glabrum*) on August 13, 1805, while on the west side of Lemhi Pass in Lemhi County, Idaho, where he "saw near the creek some bushes of the white maple." This was var. *glabrum*, a plant with grayish branches and deeply lobed leaves. On the return trip, Lewis saw the species again on the Lolo Trail in the Clearwater Mountains on June 16, 1806. Here he mentioned a "small speceis of white maple."[13]

JAMES L. REVEAL

This time it was the Douglas's maple, *Acer glabrum* var. *douglasii*, a plant with reddish stems and shallowly lobed leaves. If Lewis collected a specimen of *Acer glabrum* in 1805, it would have been destroyed with the other plants cached at "Camp Fortunate." Unaware of this, he did not collect another specimen in 1806. The Rocky Mountain maple is widely distributed; it grows from Alaska to California and New Mexico, with var. *douglasii* being common in the Far West and var. *glabrum* more common in the Rocky Mountains.

BERBERACEAE (BARBERRY FAMILY)

Collected at the Cascades of the Columbia River, Skamania County, Washington, or Hood River County, Oregon, possibly on October 31, 1805 (Berberis nervosa), *and April 11, 1806* (Berberis aquifolium)

SHINING OREGON GRAPE, *BERBERIS AQUIFOLIUM* PURSH
DULL OREGON GRAPE, *BERBERIS NERVOSA* PURSH
CREEPING OREGON GRAPE, *BERBERIS REPENS* LINDL.

Three species of Oregon grape grow in the Pacific Northwest. Figure what the chances were of collecting two of the three species at the same place—the Cascades of the

Berberis aquifolium

JAMES L. REVEAL

Columbia—and finding one fruiting in the fall, and another flowering the next spring! Although the two species are quite similar, Lewis, a keen observer, would have realized that he was not collecting the same plant twice. He documented his findings carefully, judging from the information on the label on the specimen now in the Lewis and Clark Herbarium. He wrote this about the shining (or holly-leaf) Oregon grape (as copied by Pursh): "The flowering stem springs up from near the ground & is upright; the infertile shoots trail along the ground.—Rich Soil among rocks. Great rapids of Columbia. Apr. 11th 1806." Pursh, in his 1813 *Flora* description of the two new species, noted that the plants were alike, but the dull (or Cascade) Oregon grape's leaves have more leaflets (nine to nineteen), the teeth on the margins of the leaflets were serrated, and the leaflets had three palmate nerves (veins). The shining Oregon grape, on the other hand, had fewer leaflets (five to nine), the teeth were coarser and sharper, and each leaflet had only one nerve. He assigned the two plants to *Berberis* as *Berberis nervosa* and *Berberis aquifolium* (the latter name means "waterleaf," probably for the shiny surface of the leaflets) and included an illustration of both plants.[14]

A third species, the creeping Oregon grape, *Berberis repens*, is a smaller and more sprawling plant. It is found more to the east and at higher altitudes than the others, although their distributions overlap. We know the explorers saw creeping Oregon grape while they were in the moun-

Berberis nervosa

JAMES L. REVEAL

Berberis repens

A. SCOTT EAFLE

tains, because they collected its seeds.

All three Oregon grapes have small, densely clustered yellow flowers that mature into grapelike bunches of deep blue berries. The berries are edible but are not particularly palatable; those of *Berberis repens* are sweeter than the others. Native Americans valued the plants for their berries and for a bright yellow dye that they extracted from the stems. The roots of Oregon grapes are poisonous.[15]

All three species were soon in cultivation in Philadelphia, New York, and eventually in London. *Berberis repens* was named in 1828, when described by John Lindley, the Librarian of the Royal Horticultural Society. Seeds of the plant came to the society from a nursery in New York (probably the Elgin Botanic Garden), which had obtained its plants, in turn, from Bernard M'Mahon, the Philadelphia nurseryman who grew out the Lewis and Clark seeds.[16]

CELASTRACEAE (STAFF-TREE FAMILY)
Collected near the Pacific Ocean, Pacific County, Washington, on November 26, 1805
MOUNTAIN-BOX, *PAXISTIMA MYRSINITES* (PURSH) RAF.

There are two herbarium sheets of the mountain-box, *Paxistima myrsinites*, one in the Lewis and Clark Herbarium in Philadelphia; the other is at the Royal Botanic Gardens in Kew outside of London—the latter presumably purloined by Frederick Pursh to use in writing his *Flora*. Recognizing that it was a new plant, Pursh struggled with the species. He mentioned that it was found "On the Rocky-mountain and near the Pacific Ocean" and went on to describe it: "This curious

shrub, of which I have likewise observed a specimen in the museum of A.B. Lambert, Esq., collected by A. Menzies, deserves to be examined in the living plant ... I refer it to *Ilex* [holly] at present, till further observations will decide to which genus it belongs, or whether it may not form one by itself."[17]

The roving French botanist Constantine Samuel Rafinesque-Schmaltz (1783-1840) decided that it did deserve its own genus, and in 1838 he proposed *Paxistima*, a word derived from the Greek *pachos*, meaning "thick," and *stigma*.[18] The scientific name of this plant should have been *Pachystigma*, but that name was already used for a genus of African plants. The spellings used in many publications prior to the 1970s were *Pachistima* and *Paxhystima*. The botanical literature was filled with discussions from 1943 on about which spelling ought to be correct. A formal international ruling was made to retain Rafinesque's original spelling, even though it was probably an inadvertent misspelling.

Pursh's species name *myrsinites* refers to the small, evergreen leaves of some species of *Myrsine*, notably the cultivated ornamental *Myrsine africana*, a member of the myrsine family (Myrsinaceae). The staff-tree family (Celastraceae), to which this plant actually belongs, is mostly made up of tropical plants. Related to these are various species of *Euonymus*, popular as ornamental trees

Paxistima myrsinites

JAMES L. REVEAL

and shrubs, and the much-publicized psychoactive stimulant khat, *Catha edulis*, whose fresh leaves are chewed in great amounts in parts of Africa.

The information that Pursh copied from Lewis's now discarded label for the mountain-box specimen at Kew reads: "Near the pacific ocean, Evergreen about 4. feet high; berry deep purple. Novbr 16. 1805." It is, as he noted, an attractive evergreen plant with deep green, glossy leaves that make it an exceptionally attractive ornamental or hedge shrub—probably the reason that Lewis collected it. He obviously was impressed with the plant, for conditions were hardly conducive to botanizing. The men were having a miserable time. The weather was windy and cold and it had been raining for days. They were looking for a place to winter over—a place where they could finally dry out; perhaps gathering specimens of this plant was a diversion.

ASTERACEAE (ASTER FAMILY)

Collected on "Lewis's River" (Snake River), Washington, October 1805

EATON'S ASTER, *Symphyotrichum eatonii* (A. GRAY) G. L. NESOM

COLUMBIA TICKSEED, *Coreopsis tinctoria* NUTT. VAR. *atkinsoniana* (DOUGLAS EX LINDL.) H. PARKER EX E. B. SM.

The men of the Corps of Discovery left Canoe Camp on October 7, 1805, and worked their way down the Kooskoosky (Clearwater) River in their newly minted dugouts. They reached the Snake River on October 10 (at today's Lewiston, Idaho, and Clarkston, Washington). The party made good time on the Snake, shooting one rapid after another, even dangerous ones that they probably should have portaged, arriving finally at the Columbia on October 16. Sometime during their six days on the Snake, where it crosses the southeastern corner of today's Washington State, Lewis—or it could have been another of the men—gathered two late-blooming, ray-flowered plants. Lewis added these to his collection, and in time they ended up in the Lewis and Clark Herbarium in Philadelphia. Pursh's annotations on both specimen sheets, taken from Lewis's original label, are basically the same: "On Lewis's R. Octbr: 1805." Obviously, Pursh examined the specimens—both were new—but he did not include either with the other Lewis and Clark plants in his *Flora* of 1813.

The aster family is the largest of all the flowering plant families. There are more than 1,500 genera and nearly 24,000 species, ranging from tiny herbs to large trees. Even in 1813 the family was enormous and complex. Well-preserved flowers, moderately mature fruits, and some idea as to the plant's overall appearance are necessary if one is to classify members of the family properly. Further, the two specimens collected along the Snake River were clearly related to the genus *Aster*—a group of plants that may require microscopic examination of reproductive parts for correct classification. Given the poor condition of both specimens, Pursh showed good sense in not attempting to name either one.

The first of these, the golden (or plains) tickseed, *Coreopsis tinctoria* var. *atkinsoniana* (also known as *Coreopsis atkinsoniana*) is a colorful plant, as its name tinctoria suggests (from the Latin, it translates as "used in dyeing"). Typically the plants are one to three feet high. They grow along the banks of larger rivers in the Pacific Northwest, blooming in late summer. Their divided, linear leaves are rather sparse. Each plant has several to many flower heads; each flower head typically has eight yellow-orange rays with deep red or brownish bases. The centrally positioned disk flowers are dark, raised, and prominent. Linnaeus proposed the genus *Coreopsis* in 1753; the name, derived from two Greek words, means "looks like a bug," from the appearance

Coreopsis tinctoria var. atkinsoniana

A. SCOTT EARLE

of the seeds (achenes). David Douglas proposed the plant's name to honor his brother-in-law, Thomas Witlam Atkinson (1799-1861), or possibly his father-in-law, William Atkinson—both were prominent British architects.

Lewis also gathered an Eaton's aster, a plant now classified as a *Symphyotrichum*. Asters and their relatives, including *Symphyotrichum* species ("American-asters") typically bloom late in the season; this feature sometimes helps to distinguish them from look-alike daisies (*Erigeron* spp.). Many of the aster relatives that grow in the Pacific Northwest have purple rays, but Eaton's asters have white or pink rays, a characteristic that helps to separate the plant from others found in the region. Because the species was long confused with similar ones, it was not classified as a distinct species until 1900 even though it is found from southwestern Canada to California and New Mexico.[19]

ASTERACEAE (ASTER FAMILY)
Collected on the Columbia River, October 1805
GRAY TANSY-ASTER, *MACHAERANTHERA CANESCENS* (PURSH) A. GRAY VAR. *INCANA* (LINDL.) A. GRAY

Machaeranthera canescens, or hoary tansy-aster (usually known simply as the "hoary aster"), is a highly variable species, and a total of ten varieties are presently recognized.

Machaeranthera canescens var. incana

The plant grows in western North America, ranging from western Canada to southern California and central Arizona and New Mexico. The variety that Lewis collected in October 1805 was the gray tansy-aster, var. *incana*, a robust plant with large heads and numerous (up to fifty) rays. It is known mainly from the eastern end of the Columbia River gorge, but it does extend into Idaho and California. This variety blooms in the late summer and fall of the year. In common with many xeric plants, it is covered with fine hairs (*canescens* and *incana* are both Latin and mean "hoary" or "gray," referring to the grayish cast of the hairs). Its sharp-tipped leaves are usually toothed and often appear "crisped"—common to plants in a dry environment. Each plant bears many flower heads that have stiff, outwardly turning, usually hairy bracts, deep purple rays, and a raised, bright yellow disk—the tansy-asters are attractive plants.

Lewis added this flowering composite to his collection of plants as the party worked its way down the Columbia River—he had already collected two late bloomers while on the Snake River, an Eaton's aster (*Symphyotrichum eatonii*), and a golden tickseed (*Coreopsis tinctoria* var. *atkinsoniana*) (see p. 96). Pursh wrote on this plant's specimen sheet (copying Lewis's terse description) that the plant was found "On the Columbia. Octbr. 1805." Not having further information we assume that Lewis found the plant somewhere on the dry grasslands of the Palouse Prairie, between the mouth of the Snake River and the Columbia Gorge. Pursh described the species in his *Flora* as *Aster canescens*, from material gathered by Thomas Nuttall near the site of Fort Mandan in 1811. He did not mention Lewis's specimen.[20]

Vine maple, *Acer circinatum*

NUTTALL'S SYLVA

Sitka spruce	*Picea sitchensis*
Western hemlock	*Tsuga heterophylla*
Grand fir	*Abies grandis*
Pacific silver fir	*Abies amabilis*
Douglas-fir	*Pseudotsuga menziesii*
Western white pine	*Pinus monticola*
Deer fern	*Blechnum spicant*
Spinulose wood fern	*Dryopteris carthusiana*
Pineland sword fern	*Polystichum munitum*
Western bracken fern	*Pteridium aquilinum* var. *pubescens*
Braun's giant horsetail	*Equisetum telmateia* subsp. *braunii*
Cattail	*Typha latifolia*
Wild licorice	*Glycyrrhiza lepidota*
Seashore lupine	*Lupinus littoralis*
Duck-potato or wapeto	*Sagittaria latifolia*
Edible thistle	*Cirsium edule*
Pacific silverweed	*Argentina anserina* var. *grandis*
Small cranberry	*Vaccinium oxycoccos*
Evergreen blueberry	*Vaccinium ovatum*
Oval-leaf blueberry	*Vaccinium ovalifolium*
Red blueberry	*Vaccinium parvifolium*
Western blue elderberry	*Sambucus cerulea*
Pacific red elderberry	*Sambucus racemosa* var. *arborescens*
White-stem raspberry	*Rubus leucodermis*
Pacific dewberry	*Rubus ursinus* var. *macropetalus*

Fort Clatsop
December 10, 1805, to March 23, 1806

On December 10, the expedition arrived at the site chosen for their winter quarters and immediately started work on their fort. Two weeks later, on the twenty-fourth, they moved in, naming it Fort "Clat Sop" for their Native American neighbors. Sketches in the journals show two opposing rows of cabins and a gated stockade. The day after they arrived at the site, Clark took five men and left for the ocean to find a place where they could build a "salt works." Lack of salt in their diet had been a hardship during the latter part of their journey, and salt also could be used to as a meat preservative. They chose a site on the Oregon coast where the town of Seaside is now located.

There were elk in the forests around Fort Clatsop. At first the hunters had no trouble finding all they needed, but as the weeks passed, game—probably as a direct result of the number they killed—became increasingly hard to find. Even though fires were kept burning constantly in the cabins, the area's extreme humidity meant that they could not jerk the meat that the hunters brought in. Game had to be consumed soon after animals were killed or it spoiled, and several notes in the journal refer to eating tainted meat. In January, visiting Indians told them that there was a beached whale on the shore nearby. Clark, several men, and Sacagawea, who all wanted to see the "monstrous fish," left for the coast, but local inhabitants had gotten there first and stripped the skeleton clean. They did not return empty-handed, for they were able to purchase three hundred pounds of blubber.[1]

During the previous winter at Fort Mandan, Indians had been generous with their food, but the coastal tribes were sharp traders who gave little away and expected a high return for the food, fish, furs, and other items they brought to the fort. While the men did not starve that winter, no one grew fat either. All in all, it was an unpleasant time. Visiting Indians brought fleas into the barracks and the men were never able to get rid of them. The chimneys did not draw, so their cabins were constantly filled with smoke. Some of the men contracted venereal diseases from the local women. Enough men were infected that Lewis strongly enjoined them all to resist the blandishments of the "squars."[2] And it rained constantly. Hunting parties were hard put to locate game, and when they managed to find some, the meat had to be transported over long distances, through swamps and dense woods, so it was often spoiled by the time the men got the meat back to the fort.

The enlisted men were kept busy with camp chores—gathering wood for the fires, repairing equipment, and making clothes and moccasins for the return trip (moccasins made from uncured hide during the trip west had lasted only a few days). When the expedition set off in the spring, the men had more clothing than at any other time during the journey. The captains also made good use of the enforced leisure. Clark compiled the data that the expedition had collected, and he made an accurate map—the first ever—of what became in later years the northern United States. Lewis, the expedition's naturalist, observed and recorded the world around him. He described new animals and plants, often accompanied by drawings in the captains' journals. Lewis also made ethnological notes on the area's native people. These, as P. R. Cutright has noted, were of special importance: "The plants and animals [Lewis] described at such painstaking length, are, by and large, still with us, whereas the Indians are not."[3] The captains also compiled carefully calculated tables of the distances they had traveled, along with estimates of Indian populations encountered along the way.

Although Lewis brought back only nine plant specimens—because of the dampness he was unable to preserve more—he wrote detailed and often lengthy descriptions of others, especially of the trees that he observed. Some are shown on the following pages.

As spring approached, the expedition prepared to leave Fort Clatsop. Although the captains knew that they could not cross the Bitterroot Mountains until the snowpack melted, they also knew that they had to be in the Nez Perce villages before the Indians departed for their annual buffalo hunt, else they would not be able to reclaim their horses. The men—long absent from home—must also have been anxious to get underway. Their departure was set for April 1, 1806, but they were in a hurry to leave and moved the date up one week. On March 23, 1806, the expedition set out for the United States.

PINACEAE (PINE FAMILY)
Described at Fort Clatsop, February 1806
THE CONIFERS OF FORT CLATSOP

By February 1806 the men of the expedition had settled into their winter routine, and Lewis could turn his attention to describing his surroundings. Starting on February 4, 1806,

Picea sitchensis

JAMES L. REVEAL

he began to describe the "sveral species of fir in this neighbourhood which I shall discribe as well as my slender botanicall skil will enable me."[4] Had Latin names been attached to the trees when his descriptions appeared in the edited journals (published in 1814 as *History of the Expedition under the Command of Captains Lewis and Clark*) Lewis would have been credited with describing and naming five of North America's grandest trees.

Of the six conifers described by Lewis only the Douglas-fir was named. Naval surgeon Archibald Menzies of the Vancouver expedition had previously collected it, and it was subsequently described and illustrated in *A Description of the Genus Pinus* (1803) by Aylmer Lambert (1761-1842), a wealthy and ardent English botanist. The other trees were new to science. Lewis's descriptions of the Fort Clatsop conifers were detailed and accurate enough, although if he collected any specimens they did not arrive in Philadelphia. Unfortunately, because he did not give the trees Latin names, and failed—or was unable—to return specimens, none of the conifers bears his name today.[5]

It is difficult to find old-growth forest today with the diversity and majesty of the trees that the members of the Lewis and Clark expedition saw. Fortunately a few scattered remnants remain, protected in state and national parks. Visiting them, one can still experience the feeling that Menzies, Douglas, and the members of the Lewis and Clark expedition must have felt when they saw these great trees.

SITKA SPRUCE (*PICEA SITCHENSIS* (BONG.) CARR.)

A fully grown Sitka spruce is a massive, tall tree characterized by its scaly bark and sharp, stiff needles that grow around the full circumference of the branches. It was the first of the conifers that Lewis described in 1806. Menzies had actually collected the tree in 1791, but for some reason it had remained nameless until botanist August Gustave Heinrich von Bongard (1786-1839) described it in August 1832 (antedating Rafinesque's publication by less than three months). Bongard based his description on specimens found by Russian explorers on Sitka Island in present-day Alaska. Today's reconstructed Fort Clatsop near Astoria, Oregon, is surrounded by magnificent Sitka spruce trees.

Tsuga heterophylla

JAMES L. REVEAL

Abies grandis

JAMES L. REVEAL

until 1898. The western hemlock is a widespread and important conifer. It is an excellent ornamental as well as an important commercial source of lumber.

WESTERN HEMLOCK (*TSUGA HETEROPHYLLA* (RAF.) SARG.)

The western hemlock is, like the other conifers described here, a tall, majestic tree. Its needles are short, flat, and irregular. Its cones—strangely for such a large tree—are less than an inch in length. From a distance the western hemlock can be identified by its drooping "leader"—the topmost part of the tree. Rafinesque suggested the name *Abies heterophylla* (meaning "different leaves," referring to the differently sized needles) in 1832, so the western hemlock is now known as *Tsuga heterophylla*.[6] Douglas and other early collectors believed that it was identical to the eastern hemlock (*Tsuga canadensis*), and it was not accepted as a different species

GRAND FIR (*ABIES GRANDIS* (DOUGLAS EX D. DON) LINDL.)

Lewis wrote that the men believed that his third conifer, the grand fir (*Abies grandis*), was identical to the balsam fir (*Abies balsamea*) of eastern North America. He observed that the trees around Fort Clatsop produced "considerable quantities of a fine clear arromatic balsam in appearance and taste like the Canadian balsam."[7] Douglas named the fir *grandis* for its large size; the grand fir is a stately tree growing up to 250 feet high. It differs little from its eastern counterpart, but its distribution is strictly western. It grows from Vancouver Island to northern California and inland onto the western slopes of the Rocky Mountains of Idaho and Montana.

PACIFIC SILVER FIR (*ABIES AMABILIS* DOUGLAS EX J. FORBES)

Lewis wrote only a brief note about his fourth tree. Some who have read his description suggest that the trees Lewis observed were small grand firs, but it does not seem likely that he would have made this error. More likely his description applies to the Pacific silver fir (*Abies amabilis*), an uncommon tree that does not grow today near the mouth of the Columbia River in Clatsop County, Oregon. The word *amabilis* means "lovely." Douglas used the name in 1829, but he delayed formal publication as he had not been able to obtain seeds. The tree was named in 1839 by the British gardener James Forbes (1773-1861), in the book *Pinetum Woburnense*, distributed as a gift to visitors who came to the Duke of Bedford's Woburn Abbey. Only one hundred copies were printed.

DOUGLAS-FIR (*PSEUDOTSUGA MENZIESII* (MIRB.) FRANCO)

On May 23, 1805, while a short distance west of the Musselshell River in central Montana, Lewis noted in his journal "Some spruce pine of small size appears among the pitch pine."[8] It was the first appearance of Douglas-fir (*Pseudotsuga menziesii*), a tree that comes into its own in Pacific coastal forests. He saw Douglas-fir along most of the route from western Montana to the Pacific Ocean, although he waited until he was at Fort Clatsop to write a detailed description. It was the fifth conifer on his list. He described it and even added a sketch in his journal of its cone with its distinctive three-lobed bracts.

There are two varieties of Douglas-fir. The tree that Lewis saw in Montana is the Rocky Mountain Douglas-fir (*Pseudotsuga menziesii* var. *glauca*). The coastal variety that

Pseudotsuga menziesii

JAMES L. REVEAL

Abies amabilis

JAMES L. REVEAL

Pseudotsuga menziesii

JAMES L. REVEAL

he found at Fort Clatsop is known simply as Douglas-fir (*Pseudotsuga menziesii* var. *menziesii*). Douglas-fir is one of the world's most important lumber trees.

WESTERN WHITE PINE
(*PINUS MONTICOLA* DOUGLAS EX D. DON)

Lewis noted that this large pine growing near Fort Clatsop was similar to the eastern white pine (*Pinus strobus*). In describing the western tree, he wrote that "I see no difference between this and that of the mountains in Virginia; unless it be the uncommon length of the cone of this found here, which are sometimes 16 or 18 inches in length and about 4 inches in circumference."[9] The observation was accurate, as the eastern species differs only slightly from the western white pine (*Pinus monticola*) even though the two are widely separated geographically. Douglas knew the tree mainly from the Cascade Range, and thus his choice of a name, *monticola*, meaning "mountain-dweller," is appropriate.

Lewis may have never actually observed the tree. Clark wrote in his journal, "I saw a few on Haleys bay [now Baker Bay in Pacific County, Washington] on the North side of the Columbia River, a fiew scattering on the Sea coast to the

Pinus monticola

JAMES L. REVEAL

North on one of which I engraved my name—and Some on the S S E Side of E *co la* Creek [Ecola Creek near Cannon Beach, Clatsop County, Oregon] near the Kil â mox [Tillamook] nation."[10] Today it grows in the coastal ranges of Washington and British Columbia, and inland to the Cascade Range, Sierra Nevada, and in northern Rocky Mountains. White pines—both eastern and western species—are also among our most important lumber trees. Their wood has many uses. It had an important use in the past for the masts of sailing vessels; also, the wood is extremely serviceable, especially when used for fine woodworking.

VARIOUS FAMILIES OF FERNS

Collected January 20, 1806

DEER FERN, *BLECHNUM SPICANT* (L.) SM.
SPINULOSE WOOD FERN, *DRYOPTERIS CARTHUSIANA* (VILL.) H. P. FUCHS
WESTERN BRACKEN FERN, *PTERIDIUM AQUILINUM* (L.) KUHN VAR. *PUBESCENS* UNDERW.
PINELAND SWORD FERN, *POLYSTICHUM MUNITUM* (KAULF.) C. PRESL

Meriwether Lewis collected the expedition's only ferns on January 20, 1806.[11] He mentioned others, including the local bracken fern and the sword fern, in his journals, and he may have collected them during his stay at Fort Clatsop; if so, they did not escape the ravages of molds and mildews in the moist environment.

Ferns have confused botanists for centuries. The deer fern has had many names—we know it today as *Blechnum spicant*.[12] The species has a circumboreal distribution but occurs in North America only along the west coast from Alaska to northwestern California.

The spinulose wood fern has also had many names over the years.[13] It is now known as *Dryopteris carthusiana*. It is found throughout much of Eurasia and North America, reaching its southern limits in Oregon (in the west) and Alabama (in the east).

The illustration of *Blechnum spicant* is from a print in *Native Flowers and Ferns of the United States*, published by Thomas Meehan from 1878 to 1880. Meehan was a successful nurseryman and author who also wrote the *Handbook of Ornamental Trees* (1853). He had more than a casual relationship with the plants of the Lewis and Clark expedition, for he discovered that many of the specimens were stored—neglected and deteriorating—in rooms at the American Philosophical Society in Philadelphia.[14] Meehan's last years were spent in sorting and classifying this material, and bringing the collection to The Academy of Natural Sciences in Philadelphia, where it became today's Lewis and Clark Herbarium.

Neither of these ferns is particularly common in the Fort Clatsop area, and that may have been the reason that Lewis gathered them. The western bracken fern and the pineland sword fern are the most common ferns found there today. While both grow in deep shade under the great conifers, Lewis also encountered the bracken "in the open uplands and prairies where the latter are not sandy and consist of deep loose rich black lome."[15] He wrote that the root was edible, noting that when it was "roasted in the embers is much like wheat dough and not very unlike it in flavour, though it has also a pungency which becomes more visible after you have chewed it some little time." The bracken fern is one of the most widely distributed of all of the vascular plants. Several of its twelve varieties can be weedy. The immature fronds (crosiers) are edible, although some contain carcinogenic compounds.

Lewis described the sword fern (*Polystichum*

BLECHNUM SPICANT, MEEHAN'S NATIVE FLOWERS

Dryopteris carthusiana

JAMES L. REVEAL

Polystichum munitum

JAMES L. REVEAL

munitum) in detail on February 13, 1806, adding a sketch of a single pinnule (the leaflike segment of the frond) to his journal.[16] Like the deer fern, the sword fern is evergreen, in the sense that the fronds do not die in the winter, unlike those of the wood fern and bracken fern. Although Lewis did not mention it, the sword fern was also used locally both for food and as a medicine. The pineland sword fern is strictly a western North American species, occurring from British Columbia to California eastward to Montana, with a separate population in the Black Hills.

VARIOUS FAMILIES

Collected or described, Fort Clatsop, winter of 1805-1806

BRAUN'S GIANT HORSETAIL, *EQUISETUM TELMATEIA* SUBSP. *BRAUNII*
WILD LICORICE, *GLYCYRRHIZA LEPIDOTA*
SEASHORE LUPINE, *LUPINUS LITTORALIS*
DUCK-POTATO OR WAPETO, *SAGITTARIA LATIFOLIA*
EDIBLE THISTLE, *CIRSIUM EDULE*
PACIFIC SILVERWEED, *ARGENTINA ANSERINA* VAR. *GRANDIS*
CATTAIL, *TYPHA LATIFOLIA*

Native American life on the Columbia was based in large part on commerce up and down the river. The Indians were traders and could drive a hard bargain. Roots were an important part of Indian commerce, and as the winter of 1805-1806 wore on, those that the men of the expedition were able to obtain from the Indians became increasingly important—although they had to live with their aftereffects. Most had experienced troublesome gastrointestinal upsets after eating camas root, so they were apprehensive whenever they ate unknown roots. Still, things worked out, and Clark noted on December 27, 1805, that "roots and berries are timely and extreamly

Equisetum telmateia subsp. *braunii*

JAMES L. REVEAL

Equisetum telmateia subsp. *braunii*

JAMES L. REVEAL

greatfull to our Stomachs, as we have nothing to eate but Spoiled Elk meat."[17]

Over time Lewis learned the Indian names of most of the roots.[18] He described some and collected two. Four of the ones that he described were the western bracken fern described above (*Pteridium aquilinum* var. *pubescens*), a rush (Braun's giant horsetail, *Equisetum telmateia* Ehrh. subsp. *braunii* (J. Milde) Hauke), a licorice-like plant variously identified as wild licorice (*Glycyrrhiza lepidota* Pursh) or seaside lupine (*Lupinus littoralis* Douglas), and duck-potato or wapeto (*Sagittaria latifolia* L.).[19] The two that

Glycyrrhiza lepidota

A. SCOTT EARLE

Lewis collected are the edible thistle (*Cirsium edule* Nutt.)—he called it "black root" because it turned dark when boiled—and the Pacific silverweed (*Argentina anserina* (L.) Rydb. var. *grandis* (Torr. & A. Gray) Rydb.). His note on the specimen label for the silverweed reads: "The roots are eat[en] by the natives, & taste like Sweet Potatoes." Both of these were new to science, but Pursh was unable to determine their importance, for they were not flowering when Lewis gathered them.

By far the most important plant, both for the Native Americans and for the men of the expedition, goes by many names: duck-potato, arrowhead,

Lupinus littoralis

JAMES L. REVEAL

and wapeto (variably spelled wapetoo, wapeto, wappato, whapto, wapto, wapito, and wapata); they all describe *Sagittaria latifolia*—a plant so important for the men of the expedition that Lewis apparently could not bring himself to save one as a specimen (or possibly, because the plant is widely distributed, he did not think it necessary to collect it).

On New Year's Day of 1806, Lewis wrote "at present we were content with eating our boiled Elk and wappetoe." Two months later they were able to "live sumptuously on our wappetoe and Sturgeon," and a few days later "we once more live in *clover*; Anchovies fresh Sturgeon and Wappetoe." Later, during the ascent of the Columbia, while in the vicinity of their "wappetoe island" (today's Sauvie Island), Lewis had more to say about the plant. On March 29, 1806, he wrote "the wappetoe furnishes the principal article of traffic with these people which they dispose of to the nations below in exchange for beads cloth and various articles. the natives of the Sea coast and lower part of the river will dispose of their most valuable articles to obtain this root." On the same day, Clark wrote: "the nativs inform us they Collect great quantities of pappato, which the womin collect by getting into the water, Sometimes to their necks holding by a Small canoe and with their feet loosen the wappato or bulb of the root from the bottom from the Fibers, and it imedeately rises to the top of the water, they Collect & throw them into the Canoe, those deep roots are the largest and best roots." Boiled or baked, the egg-sized root was eaten much as we would eat a potato. Indians and explorers were not the only ones to value the roots, for Lewis wrote on the twenty-ninth of March that "great numbers of large and small swans, gees and ducks…feed much on this bulb."[20] These references to wapeto are only a few of those that are scattered throughout the journals. At the time of the expedition's stay at Fort Clatsop, the area had one of the densest Indian populations in western North America.

Sagittaria latifolia

JAMES L. REVEAL

Clearly the Columbia River's plenty—game, salmon, and edible roots—were what supported this population.

We should mention one more Fort Clatsop root, for it might well have supported the party if matters had become truly desperate. On March 1, 1806, Lewis wrote that "The Indians of this neighbourhood eat the root of the Cattail or Cooper's flag. it is pleasantly taisted and appears to be very nutricious. The inner part of the root which is eaten without any previous preperation is composed of a number of capillary white flexable strong fibers among which is a mealy or starch like substance which readily desolves in the mouth and separate from the fibers which are then

Typha latifolia

JAMES L. REVEAL

Sagittaria latifolia

GOODALE/SPRAGUE, AMERICAN WILDFLOWERS

Argentina anserina var. grandis

JAMES L. REVEAL

rejected. It appears to me that this substance would make excellent starch; nothing can be of a purer white than it is.—" The ubiquitous cattail, *Typha latifolia* L., was called "Cooper's flag" because, as Moulton notes, "coopers placed the plant's long leaves between barrel staves…to make the barrels watertight."[21] The cattail has long been known as a valuable food plant, one that has a prominent place in survival manuals. Essentially all parts are edible at various stages of the plant's growth. Not only the roots are edible, as Lewis noted, but also the young shoots can be used as greens, and the plant's copious powdery pollen makes a satisfactory flour substitute.

VARIOUS FAMILIES

Vaccinium oxycoccos collected at Fort Clatsop, January 20, 1806, and Vaccinium ovatum *collected in the vicinity of Fort Clatsop, Clatsop County, Oregon, January 27, 1806, and other berries eaten but not collected*

SMALL CRANBERRY, *VACCINIUM OXYCOCCOS* L.
EVERGREEN BLUEBERRY, *VACCINIUM OVATUM* PURSH
OVAL-LEAF BLUEBERRY, *VACCINIUM OVALIFOLIUM* SM.
RED BLUEBERRY, *VACCINIUM PARVIFOLIUM* SM.
WESTERN BLUE ELDERBERRY, *SAMBUCUS CERULEA* RAF.
PACIFIC RED ELDERBERRY, *SAMBUCUS RACEMOSA* L. VAR. *ARBORESCENS* (TORR. & A. GRAY) A. GRAY
WHITE-STEM RASPBERRY, *RUBUS LEUCODERMIS* DOUGLAS EX TORR. & A. GRAY
PACIFIC BLACKBERRY, *RUBUS URSINUS* CHAM. & SCHLTDL. VAR. *MACROPETALUS* (DOUGLAS EX HOOK.) S. W. BR.

As we have noted before, given the miserable winter weather, it is not surprising that Lewis collected only a few plants during the expedition's four-month stay at Fort

Vaccinium oxycoccos

JAMES L. REVEAL

Clatsop—two ferns, two plants with edible roots (he may have obtained the roots from visiting Indians), one grass, and four plants in the heath family.[22] We have described one of the berry-bearing members of the heath family, salal (*Gaultheria shallon*), in another section (see page 91). Two others also bear edible berries, although neither was blooming or in fruit when Lewis collected his specimens. Both are evergreen plants; one is very small, the other large. The first, the small cranberry, *Vaccinium oxycoccosis*, seldom grows more than a foot high, whereas the other, *Vaccinium ovatum*, may be twelve or more feet tall. The plant is a blueberry. The captains' journals also mention several other berries that the men ate. If they were collected, the specimens did not survive.

There are about 450 species of *Vaccinium* (a term derived from the Latin word for "blueberry") widely distributed throughout the Northern Hemisphere and montane tropics. Many bear edible berries, including cranberry,

Sambucus racemosa var. arborescens

JAMES L. REVEAL

Rubus ursinus var. macropetalus

JAMES L. REVEAL

Vaccinium ovatum

A. SCOTT EARLE

whortle-berry, bilberry, blueberry, and huckleberry. Except for some individual species, most should be termed either "cranberry" or "blueberry."[23]

The small cranberry is a low, creeping shrub with a circumpolar distribution. It grows in boggy places mostly at low elevations, and bears small, nodding pink flowers and pink to red fruit. Lewis mentioned the plant on January 25, 1806, listing "the vineing or low Crambury, a light brown bury reather larger and much the shape of the black haw."[24] The label on the plant's herbarium sheet copied from Lewis's notes by Pursh reads "New Species. With a purple small berry eatable., an evergreen –Fort Clatsop. Jan. 20th 1806." As the plant had neither flowers or fruit (required to assign a species), Pursh did not include it in his *Flora*. It turned out not to be a "new species," but one that Linnaeus had described half a century earlier. Linnaeus's name for the species came from an old Greek generic name that referred to a sour berry.[25]

The evergreen blueberry, *Vaccinium ovatum*, on the other hand, was a plant new to science, as Frederick Pursh recognized. While Lewis's specimen was sterile—without flowers or fruit—the one that Archibald Menzies gathered in the 1790s at least had flowers. The distinctive combination of the leaves and flowers allowed Pursh to describe the new species, and he gave it the name that is has today, *Vaccinium ovatum*. He wrote only that it was found "On the Columbia River. *M. Lewis* [and] On the north-west coast. *Menzies*."[26] It is a handsome shrub, native to the Pacific Northwest, and found between the coast and the Cascade Range. Its branches bear horizontal rows of more or less oval, pointed, toothed leaves, and bright pinkish flowers in small clusters. The reddish brown to black berries are sweet and edible, so the plants are cultivated both as ornamentals and for their fruit. Lewis described this plant in considerable detail on January 26, 1806, mistakenly referring to it as a "Shal-lun," that is the salal, *Gaultheria shallon*.[27]

Two other species of *Vaccinium*, the oval-leaf blueberry (*Vaccinium ovalifolium* Sm.) and the red blueberry (*Vaccinium parvifolium* Sm.), grow in the moist forests near

Fort Clatsop and in nearby coastal mountains. The first is a low shrub to six feet high with large, edible, blue-black berries. The latter is an even taller shrub (to twelve feet) but with slightly sour red fruits. The members of the expedition may not have had an opportunity to eat the red blueberry, as the berries mature in late summer, falling off the plant soon thereafter. Lewis described the oval-leaf blueberry on February 7, 1806.[28] Archibald Menzies collected both species in the 1790s, and Sir James Edward Smith, president of the Linnean Society of London, named them in 1817.

Two elderberries are common in the coastal mountains near Fort Clatsop, but Lewis noted only one during the winter of 1805-1806. He described the western blue elderberry (*Sambucus cerulea*) on December 1, 1805, as a "large elder with skey blue buries." On February 7, 1806, Lewis expanded his remarks, noting that the difference between this species and the more widespread Canadian elderberry (*Sambucus canadensis*) of the East was in the color of the fruit ("pale sky blue" versus "a deep purple").[29] The Pacific red elderberry is common along the coast, and its elongated inflorescence (not flat topped) and bright red fruit (not sky blue) readily distinguish it from the western blue elderberry.

Two species of dark-fruited briar are common near Fort Clatsop. The white-stem raspberry (*Rubus leucodermis*) has fruit that is red initially, but these quickly turn purple and then black. It can be a tall shrub—to six feet—with arching branches armed with curved, flattened prickles. It may be the plant that Lewis described on February 13, 1806, as the stems can be "the size of a man's finger." It resembles the common red raspberry (*Rubus idaeus*) familiar to Lewis from the East.

The men may also have seen the Pacific blackberry (*Rubus ursinus* var. *macropetalus*).[30] It is a trailing plant with broad, curved prickles and sweet black fruit. Unfortunately, the competition for the fruit is intense when they form in July, so by the time the Corps of Discovery arrived in December 1805, probably few berries were left, even though they may remain on the plants well into the winter.

Vaccinium ovalifolium

JAMES L. REVEAL

Vaccinium parvifolium

JAMES L. REVEAL

Sambucus cerulea

A. SCOTT EARLE

Red alder, *Alnus rubra,* at reconstructed Fort Clatsop

A. SCOTT EARLE

OTHER FORT CLATSOP PLANTS
Observed in the neighborhood of Fort Clatsop,
winter of 1804-1805

Shore pine, *Pinus contorta*

JAMES L. REVEAL

Tough-leaf iris, *Iris tenax*

JAMES L. REVEAL

Oregon crabapple, *Malus fusca*

JAMES L. REVEAL

American lyme grass, *Leymus mollis*

JAMES L. REVEAL

111

GRAY'S LOMATIUM	*Lomatium grayi*
BARESTEM LOMATIUM	*Lomatium nudicaule*
COUS	*Lomatium cous*
WESTERN SWEET CICELY	*Osmorhiza occidentalis*
NINE-LEAF LOMATIUM	*Lomatium triternatum*
FERN-LEAVED LOMATIUM	*Lomatium dissectum* var. *multifidum*
NORTHERN YAMPAH	*Perideridia montana*
POET'S SHOOTING STAR	*Dodecatheon poeticum*
SERVICEBERRIES	*Amelanchier alnifolia* and varieties
PUGET SOUND LARKSPUR	*Delphinium menziesii*
RICE-ROOT CHECKER-LILY	*Fritillaria affinis*
WESTERN WAKE-ROBIN	*Trillium ovatum*
YELLOW BELL	*Fritillaria pudica*
THREADLEAF PHACELIA	*Phacelia linearis*
GARRY OAK	*Quercus garryana*
RED ALDER	*Alnus rubra*

Map showing the route along the Columbia River through Washington, Oregon, and Idaho, with locations including Pacific Ocean, Fort Clatsop, Portland, The Dalles, Richland, Pasco, Kennewick, Walla Walla, Pendleton, Clarkston, Lewiston, Kamiah. Highways: 5, 30, 84, 14, 82, 95, 12. Snake River, Columbia River.

WESTERN SPRING BEAUTY	*Claytonia lanceolata*	SHOWY PHLOX	*Phlox speciosa*
STREAMBANK SPRING BEAUTY	*Claytonia parviflora*	BIG-HEAD CLOVER	*Trifolium macrocephalum*
MINERS' LETTUCE	*Claytonia perfoliata*	SMALL-HEAD CLOVER	*Trifolium microcephalum*
SIBERIAN SPRING BEAUTY	*Claytonia sibirica*	GREEN RABBITBRUSH	*Chrysothamnus viscidiflorus*
SALMONBERRY	*Rubus spectabilis*	GLACIER LILY	*Erythronium grandiflorum*
WESTERN THIMBLEBERRY	*Rubus parviflorus*	DOUGLAS'S BRODIEA	*Triteleia grandiflora*
NUTTALL'S BITTERCRESS	*Cardamine nuttallii*	STRICT FIELD CHICKWEED	*Cerastium arvense* subsp. *strictum*
ARROWLEAF BALSAMROOT	*Balsamorhiza sagittata*	SYRINGA	*Philadelphus lewisii*
BLUE-EYED MARY	*Collinsia parviflora* var. *grandiflora*	RED CURRANT	*Ribes sanguineum*
RETRORSE FIDDLENECK	*Amsinckia menziesii* var. *retrorsa*	SPREADING GOOSEBERRY	*Ribes divaricatum*
NARROW-LEAF COLLOMIA	*Collomia linearis*	STICKY CURRANT	*Ribes viscosissimum*
SLENDER POPCORN FLOWER	*Plagiobothrys tenellus*	CUTLEAF DAISY	*Erigeron compositus*

Fort Clatsop to Camp Chopunnish
March 23 to May 14, 1806

The Corps of Discovery launched its canoes on March 23, 1806, and set out on the first leg of the long journey back to the United States. Their flotilla included two of the dugout canoes that had brought them down the Columbia River and two Indian canoes, one purchased and the other stolen a few days before. The captains justified the theft as payment for the times that the Indians had stolen elk shot by the expedition's hunters. The trip up the Columbia was enlivened by constant contact with coastal Indians, who were as comfortable on the river as they were on land. The expedition's hunters were able to provide game, but the men also traded with the natives for dried salmon, sturgeon, the candlefish they called anchovies, and seal meat.

The expedition made good time, traveling fifteen miles or more a day. On April 10, they came to the Cascades of the Columbia, and on the eighteenth they reached Celilo Falls (the site of today's The Dalles, Oregon). It took ten days to portage around the rapids and falls. All the while, they were bedeviled by obnoxious, arrogant, demanding natives who stole everything they could, managing to make off with a surprisingly large number of items. The final insult was the theft of Lewis's dog, Seaman. Seaman was retrieved, but by now the men were so angry at the Indians that the captains noted that they "seem well disposed to kill a few of them." These Indians, Lewis wrote, were "the greates theives and scoundrels we have met with."[1] Despite their righteous anger, they controlled the urge to retaliate and thus avoided bloodshed. The party completed its portage on April 20. Indians above the falls were far more reasonable. The expedition continued upstream by canoe until the first of May, when they managed, after long and hard bargaining over several days, to obtain enough horses (including an elegant white horse for Clark) to continue their journey overland.

At the junction of the Columbia and the Snake Rivers, Yakama Indians told them of a "road" that ran east, across today's southeastern Washington, to join the Snake River near the mouth of the Clearwater. The route was over rolling foothills of the Blue Mountains and avoided having to follow the tortuous Snake River. The expedition followed the Indians' advice and saved time, while traveling thirty miles or so each day. They rejoined the Snake River seven miles below the point at which the Clearwater River joins the Snake at today's Clarkston, Washington, and Lewiston, Idaho, on May 4. They were now in Nez Perce country and soon met the Chopunnish Indians with whom they had left their horses after their harrowing ordeal along the Lolo Trail six months before. On May 14, the party settled in to wait for the snow to melt in the high country, establishing their camp on a meadow located in today's Kamiah, Idaho, on the site of an older Indian encampment, signs of which were still present early in the twentieth century. The camp later became known as "Camp Chopunnish."[2]

Understandably, Lewis took more notice of animals, birds, and plants than he had when the expedition was outward bound. Nagging uncertainties about the expedition's route had been resolved, and it was spring. He knew that this would be the only opportunity to collect the many new plants that he saw each day. He gathered numerous specimens between Fort Clatsop and Camp Chopunnish. Many were new to science, and the collections from this part of the journey included several splendid spring wildflowers that grow in the Pacific Northwest.

APIACEAE (PARSLEY FAMILY)
Several species, collected at various sites and dates
APIACEAE OF THE NORTHWEST: EDIBLE UMBELLIFERS

The parsley or carrot family is a large one made up of approximately 3,500 species found throughout the world. These characteristically have flower clusters that are supported by stemlets (pedicels) of nearly equal length. The pedicels arise from a common point on the main stem and then diverge, to resemble the ribs of an inverted umbrella. The flower aggregates are known as "umbels" (from the Latin *umbella*, meaning "parasol" or "umbrella") a term from which the older, alternative family name, Umbelliferae, was derived. Many botanists prefer the newer name Apiaceae, derived from the Latin *apium*, a word that means "celery." Food plants in the family include parsley, carrots, celery, and parsnip, as well as many herbs that are used for flavoring: cilantro, fennel, chervil, aniseed, dill, cumin, coriander, and caraway.

When the party traded with the Native Americans for edible roots, they often had no way of knowing to which plant family the roots belonged. Now, with the arrival of the growing season, it was possible to match plants to the roots they had eaten earlier, including quamash or camas (*Camassia quamash*), wapeto (*Sagittaria* spp.), and "cows," obtained from the yellow-flowered *Lomatium cous*. Many other species of *Lomatium* grow in the American West—some sixty species are found in the Pacific Northwest alone. The terms lomatium, biscuit-root, and desert-parsley are all equally correct when used as common names for plants in this genus. Many, but not all, are edible. Lomatiums are difficult to classify. Some are quite similar, and examination of their small, pumpkinseed-shaped fruit is often necessary if one is to distinguish one species from another. Lacking this, positive identification may not be possible. There are seven specimens of lomatiums in the Lewis and Clark Herbarium, but only four can be classified with any degree of certainty. Several are shown here, as well as two other umbellifers— one that Lewis collected, and another that he saw and carefully described. While classification of the various Apiaceae at the species level may be difficult, all of the men would have recognized the plants shown here as relatives of such common eastern plants as the meadow parsleys (*Pastinaca* spp.), wild carrot or Queen Anne's lace (*Daucus carota*), and many others.

Collected "Near the Sepulchre rock" (near Lower Memaloose Island), Klickitat County, Washington,
or Wasco County, Oregon, April 14, 1806
GRAY'S LOMATIUM, *LOMATIUM GRAYI* J. M. COULT. & ROSE

Gray's lomatium (or mountain desert parsley) has compound leaves that are divided into many leaflets—sometimes more than a thousand. These lie in different planes, giving the leaves a distinctive "thick" appearance. The plant is common east of the Cascade Range, and it is found frequently in eastern Oregon and western Idaho, and occasionally as far east as Wyoming and Colorado. As Lewis's description suggests, it has a bulky taproot that gives rise to many, often woody or rootlike branches (caudices).[3]

There are some umbellifer specimens in the Lewis and Clark Herbarium that are so incomplete that their classification is difficult. Attempts to classify such plants, short of using DNA analysis, cannot be done with a great degree of confidence. Lewis and Clark's specimen of *Lomatium grayi* is an example. It consists only of a few fragments of plant material consistent with a lomatium. Lewis's comment (as transcribed by Pursh) says only that it is a plant with "A large fusiform root, which the natives prepare by baking;—Near the Sepulchre rock On the Columbia R.—Aprl. 14th. 1806."

Pursh wisely made no attempt to classify this plant. Various later comments on the specimen sheet add to our doubt about its identity. One note reads "This is apparently a mixture of material"; another, written in 1994, classifies the material as *Lomatium grayi*. In 1999, the plant was renamed *Lomatium cuspidatum*, based on Lewis's description of its fusiform root and the Indians' method of baking it.[4] We now believe, for several reasons—the chief one being that *Lomatium cuspidatum* does not grow where this plant was obtained—that the earlier classification, *Lomatium grayi*, is more likely the correct one for this plant.

Lomatium grayi

JAMES L. REVEAL

Collected in the vicinity of The Dalles of the Columbia River, Klickitat County, Washington, or Wasco County, Oregon, April 15, 1806

BARESTEM LOMATIUM, *LOMATIUM NUDICAULE* (PURSH) J. M. COULT. & ROSE

The barestem lomatium, or pestle-parsnip, was the first of the several lomatiums that Lewis collected in the spring of 1806. It is easily identified, for the stems and branches are long and bare. Although it is not immediately evident, the leaves are compound, made up of three or more long-stemmed, broadly oval, fan-shaped, or nearly round leaflets. Each plant bears from three to thirty leaflets. The species name means "bare stem," and the appearance of the plant is distinctive among the lomatiums. Frederick Pursh saw that the plant was a new one and classified it as a *Smyrnium nudicaule*.[5] He wrote on the specimen sheet, presumably from Lewis's field note, that the plant was "Supposed to be a Smyrnium the natives eat the tops & boil it sometimes with their soup. On the Columbia." He described the plant in his *Flora*, adding to Lewis's description that the Indians used the plant "the same as we use celery."[6] The barestem lomatium is also known as Indian-

consumption-plant, for Native Americans supposedly used it to treat tuberculosis.

Lomatium nudicaule

A. SCOTT EARLE

Collected at the mouth of the Walla Walla River, Walla Walla County, Washington, on April 29, 1806

COUS, LOMATIUM COUS (S. WATSON) J.M. COULT & ROSE

Native Americans commonly used the root of cous ("cows," "chapallel" or "shap-el-el") for food, beating the plants' globular roots to soften them, then roasting and fashioning them into cakes that could be kept for several years. They were reconstituted by boiling the cakes to make a thick soup or mush. "Cows bread" was an important trade item for the Indians of the Pacific Northwest, and it was an important food for the Corps of Discovery during its return journey. Pursh's copy of Lewis's description of the plant reads, "An umbelliferous plant of the root of which the Wallowallows make a kind of bread."[7]

The leaves of *Lomatium cous* resemble those of other plants in the genus—including several varieties of *Lomatium dissectum*—and while the appearance of the roots (included with the specimen in the Lewis and Clark Herbarium) is helpful, examination of mature fruit is necessary for firm identification. Lacking this, Pursh was unable to classify the plant. It has recently been suggested that Lewis may have obtained his plant from an Indian rather than gathering it himself.[8]

JRJ

CRONQUIST, *INTERMOUNTAIN FLORA*

Collected in Klickitat or Benton County, Washington, or Gilliam or Morrow County, Oregon, on April 25, 1806

WESTERN SWEET CICELY, OSMORHIZA OCCIDENTALIS (NUTT. EX TORR. & A. GRAY) TORR.

Lewis is assumed to have collected western sweet cicely (*Osmorhiza occidentalis*) on April 25, 1806. Most likely it was this plant that he had described on May 16, 1806, when he wrote "Sahcargarmeah geathered a quantity of the roots of a speceis of fennel which we found very agreeable food, the flavor of this root is not unlike annis seed, and they dispell the wind which the roots called Cows and quawmash are apt to create particularly the latter."[9]

We write "assumed to have collected," because—unfortunately—no plant material remains on the specimen sheet in the Lewis and Clark Herbarium. The copy of Lewis's field note (in Frederick Pursh's hand) reads: "A species of Fennel root eaten by the Indians of an Annis Seed taste. Flowers white. Columbia R. Aprl. 25th 1806." An additional note, written by Thomas Meehan, reads simply "All eaten." Although we have found nothing in Pursh's *Flora* that might help to positively identify the plant, Lewis's description on April 16 makes it seem likely that it was an *Osmorhiza*—probably *Osmorhiza occidentalis* (or possibly the less com-

Osmorhiza occidentalis

A. SCOTT EARLE

mon *O. chilensis*). *Osmorhiza occidentalis* is an attractive, leafy, yellow-flowered plant that grows from northwestern Washington south to California and as far east as Colorado. Although Cutright suggested that Lewis's plant may have been the northern yampah (*Perideridia montana*), described below, this is unlikely if the location and date of collection for the plant are correct, although the reference to the root tasting like anise would fit that species also.[10]

Several species of *Osmorhiza* grow in the eastern United States, although Lewis may not have been acquainted with them. The roots of some species of sweet cicely are edible (the true sweet cicely is a European plant, *Myrrhis odorata*). After sampling *Osmorhiza occidentalis*, H. D. Harrington wrote that its taste was so strong that he was unable to eat the root, although he felt that the root, if ground, or the seeds, would be suitable to use for flavoring other foods.[11] Edibility may decrease as plants age, however, and Lewis's specimen probably was immature when he gathered it.[12] Unfortunately, lacking a specimen, anything said of the missing specimen in the herbarium must remain conjectural.

Collected on the Clearwater River, Nez Perce County, Idaho, May 6, 1806

NINE-LEAF DESERT-PARSLEY, *LOMATIUM TRITERNATUM* (PURSH) J. M. COULT. & ROSE

Frederick Pursh dealt with the various lomatiums the best he could. In his *Flora* he accounted for two of the seven lomatiums that the expedition brought back; he could classify these two by their appearance. He believed that both were new species. One of these, the nine-leaf desert-parsley, is a moderately sized plant with grasslike leaves. On closer examination one finds that the leaves are actually compound, with each leaf dividing into three leaflets, and each of these in turn dividing into three more leaflets—the plant's leaves are "triternate," the botanical term from which Pursh derived the species name. He named it *Seseli triternatum*, placing it in a genus made up mostly of European umbellifers. Pursh's description, altered slightly from Lewis's original note, reads "On the waters of Columbia river. *M. Lewis*…. Flowers deep yellow. The fusiform root of this species is one of the grateful vegetables of the Indians: they use it baked or roasted."[13] Lewis's note indicated that he had collected the plant on the Kooskoosky River (today called the Clearwater River). He wrote that the roots were

"5 or 6 inches long eaten raw or boiled by the natives."

The nine-leaf desert-parsley is found today in parts of all four northwestern states and the adjacent Canadian provinces. Several varieties are recognized; our plant is var. *triternatum*.

Lomatium triternatum

JAMES L. REVEAL

Collected on the Kooskoosky (Clearwater) River, in the vicinity of Camp Chopunnish, Kamiah, Idaho County, Idaho, June 10, 1806

FERN-LEAVED LOMATIUM, *LOMATIUM DISSECTUM* (NUTT.) MATHIAS & CONSTANCE
VAR. *MULTIFIDUM* (NUTT.) MATHIAS & CONSTANCE

Although it comes in several sizes and forms, the fern-leaved lomatium is the largest member of the genus that grows in the vicinity of the expedition's camp. Var. *multifidum* is a tall plant with woody stems and narrow, dissected (deeply divided), compound leaves; it favors rocky slopes

Lomatium dissectum var. *multifidum*

A. SCOTT EARLE

that range from foothills to those at moderate elevations in the mountains. The plant may be seen today in late spring, lining the walls of the Clearwater Gorge, from Orofino to Kamiah, Idaho, where Lewis probably gathered his specimen. *Lomatium dissectum* grows all through the Pacific Northwest and the neighboring Canadian provinces south to

California and east to Colorado. The varieties differ considerably in appearance, with quite marked variations in foliage, flower color, and size. The single-seeded fruits, however, are all similar in appearance, regardless of the variety, and are small, flat, and oval with longitudinal striping, all features that unite the varieties into a single species.

Frederick Pursh's copy of Lewis's label for this plant reads "A great horse medicine among the natives. On the Koos Kooskee Jun: 10th. 1806.—grows on rich upland." There is not much left of Lewis's specimen today—several large stems, a portion of an umbel without flowers, and fragments of leaflets. We have no way of knowing how much of the plant was present when Pursh examined it, but evidently there was enough for him to include it in his *Flora*. He classified it as *Phelandrium aquaticum*, a species Linnaeus had named earlier. Pursh wrote that Lewis's plant was collected "On the waters of the Rocky-mountain. *M. Lewis....* The Indians of that country use it as a medicine in the diseases of horses"—a description similar to the one that Lewis had written on the original specimen sheet.[14] Lacking mature fruit, Pursh did not realize the plant was new. Thomas Nuttall re-collected the plant a few years later and recognized that it had not been described previously. He proposed *Leptotaenia dissecta* in 1840. As with the other biscuit-roots, it eventually ended up in 1942 as a *Lomatium*, while retaining Nuttall's name as *dissectum*.

Presumed seen, but not collected, on eastern slope of Lemhi Pass, Lemhi County, Idaho, August 26, 1805

NORTHERN YAMPAH, *PERIDERIDIA MONTANA* (BLANK.) DORN

The northern yampah is an attractive plant bearing white-flowered umbels. Its leaves are pinnate with a few narrow

leaflets. The plant grows in moist places throughout the Northwest, south to California and east to Colorado and

South Dakota. It blooms later in the year than other umbellifers, whose roots were important as a food source. Although it is one of the edible umbellifers that Lewis described in considerable detail, northern yampah is not, however, present in the Lewis and Clark Herbarium. Either it was not collected or, if it was, the specimen did not survive.

On August 26, 1805, Lewis observed "the indian women collecting the root of a speceis of fennel which grows in the moist grounds and feeding their poor starved children; it is really distressing to witness the situation of those poor wretches." He went on to describe the root. It is, he wrote, "of the knob kind ...bing about 3 or four inches in length and the thickest part about the size of a man's little finger."[15] The plants were three to four feet high with numerous small white flowers borne in umbels. The Indian women were almost certainly collecting roots of the northern yampah, now classified as *Perideridia montana*, but listed in many guides as *Perideridia gairdneri*.[16]

While the various species of *Lomatium* bloom early in

Perideridia montana

A. SCOTT EAFLE

the spring, many white-flowered umbellifers bloom later. Several white-flowered umbellifers grow near Lemhi Pass, including species of *Angelica* and the western water hemlock (*Cicuta douglasii*). The latter is an extremely poisonous plant and obviously was not the plant whose roots the Indian women were harvesting. It is possible, however, that they were harvesting the white-flowered cow parsnip, the long-forgotten *Heracleum maximum* Barton (listed in most guidebooks as *Heracleum lanatum* Michx.). This plant bears the largest leaves of any of the North American Apiaceae, and it is common in the mountains of Idaho. The stems of immature plants, peeled stems of mature plants, and the plant's roots are all said to be edible, being "much used by the Indians as food."[17] The plants have a distinctive and apparently not very pleasant taste. Presumably, the cow parsnip was a plant that Lewis would have known from the east, so it is unlikely that it was the "speceis of fennel" that he saw the Indian women gathering.

PRIMULACEAE (PRIMROSE FAMILY)

Collected near The Dalles of the Columbia River, Klickitat County, Washington, or Wasco County, Oregon, on April 16, 1806

POET'S SHOOTING STAR, *DODECATHEON POETICUM* L. F. HEND.

Lewis and Clark probably saw shooting stars blooming in the Northwest, from May to September, depending on the elevation. All shooting stars have strongly swept back petals, like those of the related European cyclamen. The filaments of the stamens and their anthers are joined, coming together to a point in front of the petals, giving the appearance of a comet. The anthers and filaments may be variously colored, to attract the small bees and flies that serve as pollinators. For those interested in wildflower gardening, seeds of some species are available through seed catalogs, but the plants require the right combination of exposure, shade, soil moisture, and patience to grow them.

The morphological differences among the various shooting stars are subtle, so the explorers probably thought that all of the shooting stars they saw were the same species. They might have seen three species in the Pacific Northwest. The Bonneville shooting star (*Dodecatheon conjugens*), the tall mountain shooting star (*Dodecatheon jeffreyi*), and the common dark-throat shooting star (*Dodecatheon pulchellum*) all grow in the mountain meadows of Idaho and Montana. Until recently, the plant that Lewis collected on the Columbia was thought to be the tall mountain shooting

Dodecatheon pulchellum

A. SCOTT EARLE

star (*Dodecatheon jeffreyi*), but now we know that it was the poet's shooting star, *Dodecatheon poeticum*, one of the rarest species. It was not found again until 1929, growing in essentially the same place that Lewis had found his specimen nearly 125 year earlier. Today, the poet's shooting star is restricted to springs and seeps originating around basaltic outcrops along both sides of the Columbia River in the general area of The Dalles. It flowers only briefly in April and May.

Pursh copied Lewis's original note onto the label that accompanied the specimen. It says that Lewis had found the plant "Near the narrows of Columbia R." From this it is obvious that Pursh saw the specimen, even though he made no mention of a separate western plant in his *Flora*.[18]

ROSACEAE (ROSE FAMILY)

Collected at The Dalles of the Columbia River, Klickitat County, Washington, or Wasco County, Oregon, on April 15, 1806

CASCADE SERVICEBERRY, *AMELANCHIER ALNIFOLIA* (NUTT.) NUTT. EX M. ROEM. VAR. *SEMIINTEGRIFOLIA* (HOOK.) C. L. HITCHC.
WESTERN SERVICEBERRY, *AMELANCHIER ALNIFOLIA* (NUTT.) NUTT. EX M. ROEM. VAR. *ALNIFOLIA*
CUSICK'S SERVICEBERRY, *AMELANCHIER ALNIFOLIA* (NUTT.) NUTT. EX M. ROEM. VAR. *CUSICKII* (FERN.) C. L. HITCHC.

Serviceberries were well known to the men of the expedition. Numerous species grow in North America, and their berries, although not much used today, were in the past eaten fresh, dried, made into preserves, and used to make wine. The men of the expedition had been seeing the western serviceberry (or saskatoon, *Amelanchier alnifolia*) all across the country. Lewis mentioned it (usually as "Sarvis berry") as growing along

the upper Missouri in notes that he compiled in Fort Mandan during the winter of 1804-1805. On July 17, 1805, above the Great Falls of the Missouri, he noted that "The survice berry differs somewhat from that of the U' States the bushes are small sometimes not more than 2 feet high and scarcely ever exceed 8 and are proportionably small in their stems, growing thicly ascosiated in clumps. The fruit is the same form but for

Amelanchier alnifolia var. alnifolia

A. SCOTT EARLE

Amelanchier alnifolia var. alnifolia

A. SCOTT EARLE

the most part larger more lucious and of so deep a perple that on first glance you would think them black."[19]

Western serviceberries (*Amelanchier alnifolia* var. *alnifolia*) are attractive plants. Their white, five-petaled flowers, borne in clusters at the end of the branches, bloom early in the spring. They have found their way into gardens and in the west have replaced the related shadbush (or eastern serviceberry, *Amelanchier canadensis*) as ornamental plants. The tree takes its name from the related European service tree, also a member of the rose family. The name is probably a corruption of the Latin name for the European tree, *sorbus*. The alternate use of the word *sarvis* presumably had a similar derivation. In the Chesapeake Bay region, the appearance of the flowers signified that the shad had started to run, which gave rise to another common name, "shadbush." The scientific name, *Amelanchier*, was adopted from *Amelancier*, the Savoyard word for the European medlar

tree, *Mespilus germanica*. The species name, *alnifolia*, means "alder-leaved," for the shape of the leaves.

Western serviceberries grow throughout northern North America, from Alaska to Nevada, mostly east of the Cascade Range and the Sierra Nevada, through the Rocky Mountains and Great Plains to Quebec. They vary in size from small shrubs to attractive trees, occasionally as much as twenty feet high. Their foliage characteristically—as with an identifiable specimen in the Lewis and Clark Herbarium—consists of broad, dark green leaves with serrated ends or margins. Given the plant's wide distribution, it is not surprising that there are several varieties. The plant that Lewis collected on the Columbia is *Amelanchier alnifolia* var. *semiintegrifolia*, the Cascade serviceberry. A second specimen, collected on the Clearwater River several weeks later, consists only of two twigs. Although it is probably a serviceberry, its identification remains uncertain.[20]

RANUNCULACEAE (BUTTERCUP FAMILY)
Collected on the Columbia River, near the mouth of the White Salmon River in Multnomah County, Oregon, April 14, 1806
MENZIES' LARKSPUR, *DELPHINIUM MENZIESII* DC.

Dioscorides, a Greek physician, first used the name *delphinion* to describe a larkspur.[21] The word was derived from the Greek word for "dolphin," because of a supposed resem-

Delphinium menziesii

A. SCOTT EARLE

blance of a part of the flower to the animal. Larkspurs are common plants, ones that members of the expedition would certainly have recognized. Like many other members of the Ranunculaceae, they are highly toxic if ingested and can kill grazing cattle, although for some reason sheep are not affected. Lewis, who was acquainted with herbal medicine, might also have known that their seeds, used topically, are an effective treatment for head lice ("lousewort" is the common name of a European larkspur, *Delphinium staphisagria*). The plants are hated by stockmen in the West but are a favorite of wildflower lovers everywhere—an example of the truism "my wildflower, your weed."

Lewis collected the Puget Sound or Menzies larkspur (named for Archibald Menzies, the surgeon-naturalist of the Vancouver expedition) on April 14, 1806; it is the only representative of this genus in the Lewis and Clark Herbarium. There is no mention of a larkspur in Lewis's journal for April 14, but Moulton believes that a "bearsclaw" that Lewis saw on April 2 ("I preserved a specemine it is in blume") might have been this larkspur.[22] We know that Frederick Pursh examined the specimen in the Lewis and Clark Herbarium, for there is a note on the specimen sheet, copied from Lewis's original label that accompanied the plant. It reads "A Sort of Larkspur with 3 styles. On the Columbia…" We do not know why he did not include it in his *Flora* as a new species.

LILIACEAE (LILY FAMILY)
Collected near the "Kooskooskee" (Clearwater) River, Nez Perce or Clearwater County, Idaho, on May 8, 1806
YELLOW BELL, *FRITILLARIA PUDICA* (PURSH) SPRENG.

It would have been hard for Meriwether Lewis to pass by these cheery little flowers, as they were evidence that spring had arrived in the mountains and that the expedition really was on its way home; furthermore, it was a plant he had not seen before. Although he did not describe it in his journal, one of the two dry specimens at The Academy of Natural Sciences in Philadelphia has a label taken from Lewis's original notes (as copied by Pursh) that says the bulb is in the "shape of a bisquit which the natives eat."

The yellow bell (also known as yellow fritillary or mission bell) occurs from the Cascade Range and Sierra Nevada east to Wyoming. The species name, *pudica*, is Latin for "modest"—the bright yellow, six-tepaled flowers seem always to be looking downward, in the manner of shy maidens.[23] The flowers appear soon after the snow melts from lowland meadows and sagebrush-covered slopes to well up into the mountains.

Frederick Pursh saw that Lewis's specimen represented a new plant. Although he believed that it might be a *Fritillaria*, he felt that it more closely resembled a lily and so named it *Lilium pudicum*. The new species was one of the fourteen expedition plants that he used in illustrating his *Flora Americae Sepentrionalis*, possibly because Lewis's specimens were in excellent condition—they look today much as they do in the illustration in Pursh's text. The yellow bell was

later renamed *Fritillaria pudica*, the name that we now know it by. The flowers do well in cultivation and may be used to bring early color into wildflower gardens.

Fritillaria pudica

A. SCOT EARLE

LILIACEAE (LILY FAMILY)
Collected on "Brant" (Bradford) Island, Multnomah County, Oregon, on April 10, 1806
RICE-ROOT CHECKER-LILY, *FRITILLARIA AFFINIS* (SCHULTES & SCHULTES F.) SEALY
WESTERN WAKE-ROBIN, *TRILLIUM OVATUM* PURSH

The ascent of the Columbia River was fraught with difficulties. What had been a tolerable, though challenging, ride down the river, now became a travail. Rapids and falls dominated the deep canyon that the river cut through the Cascade Range, and the loaded boats had to be hauled upstream by towrope. The morning of April 10, 1806, found the men on the south side of the Columbia near Brant (today's Bradford) Island, having camped the previous evening at what is now Bonneville, Oregon. Today, the rapids are gone, submerged by the waters impounded by the Bonneville Dam.

Lewis described the morning's activities: "We set out early and dropped down the channel to the lower end of brant Island

from whence we drew them [the canoes] up the rapid by a cord about a quarter of a mile...,"[24] One can imagine the scene: the men laboring to get their boats and provisions up the rapids while Captain Lewis went off botanizing!

He obtained three specimens that day: bigleaf maple (*Acer macrophyllum*; see p. 91) and two members of the lily family, the rice-root checker-lily, *Fritillaria affinis*, and a wake-robin (*Trillium ovatum*). All three were new, and Pursh described and gave names to each. The wake-robin grows today in widely scattered locations in the Pacific Northwest from near the coast to the higher mountains, usually in boggy places. It flowers from March to June. Its white—aging to

123

Fritillaria affinis

A. SCOTT EARLE

Trillium ovatum

JAMES L. REVEAL

pink and then light purple—flowers are on short stalks, and its ovate leaves are stemless (see also *Trillium petiolatum*, p. 177). Pursh described the plant as growing "On the rapids of the Columbia river.... Flowers pale purple." He gave it the same scientific name that we know it by today.[25]

The rice-root checker-lily is found on bluffs that overlook the Pacific Ocean to the eastern slope of the Cascade Range. Lewis's original note with the specimen (as copied by Pursh) reads, "obtained on Brant island 10th. of apl 1806, the the [sic] root of the plant is a squamous bulb and is eaten by the natives. the Clah-clel-lar opposite this Island call it tel-lak-thil-pah." This is the second fritillary that Lewis collected, and with its checkered pattern it is closer in appearance to

the European species (*Fritillaria meleagris*) that gave the genus its name. It is a plant with a pronounced checkerboard-like pattern on its tepals (*fritillus* is Latin for "game board").

Pursh saw that Lewis's plant was similar to the Kamchatka fritillary—known also as the northern rice-root, Indian rice, and black lily—*Fritillaria camschatcensis*. He confused the two plants and incorrectly named Lewis's plant *Fritillaria lanceolata* (for the narrow, lanceolate leaves).[26] Years later, botanists realized that Pursh's *Fritillaria lanceolata* was a synonym of *Fritillaria camschatcensis*, and Lewis's plant was given its present name, calling attention to the affinity between the two species. As Lewis noted, the plant's many bulblets are edible, explaining its common names "rice-root" and "Indian rice."

BORAGINACEAE (BORAGE FAMILY)

Collected at "Rock Fort" (Rocky) Camp, The Dalles, Wasco County, Oregon, on April 17, 1806

THREAD-LEAF PHACELIA, *PHACELIA LINEARIS* (PURSH) HOLZ.

On April 17, 1806, the expedition was bivouacked at the site of today's Bonneville Dam at The Dalles, under a

protected rocky outcropping that they had named "Rock Fort" when they stayed there the previous fall (October 25-28,

1805). Lewis was in his collecting mode. Although he mentioned only one plant, a "hiasinth," he gathered seven others, including a specimen of thread-leaf phacelia, all on April 17, 1806. Later, in Philadelphia, Frederick Pursh examined Lewis's specimen. He recognized that the plant was new and assigned it to *Hydrophyllum*, giving it the species name *lineare* for its narrow leaves. He reported the species as "Found on the banks of the Missouri."[27] By assigning the species to *Hydrophyllum*, its true identity was obscured, so the species was named again, in 1823, as *Phacelia menziesii*. That error was not discovered until 1895 when the combination *Phacelia linearis*—its present name—was published.[28]

Thread-leaf phacelia has attractive, five-petaled, pink to purple flowers that grow in loose clusters. Its long anther-tipped filaments protrude well beyond the petals, in common with those of many other species of *Phacelia*. The plant's leaves narrow toward the top of the stem; the basal leaves usually develop small lobes that protrude on either side of the leaf. *Phacelia linearis* typically grows in dry places, blooming from spring to early summer depending on the elevation. While Lewis collected it at The Dalles, he

Phacelia linearis

A. SCOTT EARLE

might also have seen the plant growing anywhere along the route that the expedition traversed between the Columbia and the Clearwater rivers. There is not much left today of the specimen in the Lewis and Clark Herbarium, and Lewis's label (as copied by Pursh), attached to the sheet, says only that he collected the plant at "Rocky Camp. Apr. 17th 1806."[29]

FAGACEAE (BEECH FAMILY)

Collected in Cowlitz County, Washington, or Columbia County, Oregon, on March 26, 1806

OREGON WHITE OAK, *QUERCUS GARRYANA* DOUGLAS EX HOOK.

The expedition was three days out from Fort Clatsop, on March 26, 1806, heading up the Columbia River. They passed Oak Point and saw "an Elegant and extensive bottom on the South side and an island [Crim's Island] near it's upper point which we call Fanny's Island and bottom…near the river towards the upper point we saw a fine grove of whiteoak trees."[30]

Lewis must have gathered his specimens of the Oregon

white oak (or Garry oak), *Quercus garryana*, here. Lewis's note (as copied by Pursh and attached to one of the specimen sheets) reads "A sort of white Oak Columbia March 26th 1806." This oak is an attractive, early maturing tree that may grow to be one hundred feet tall. Its leaves are typical of white oaks in general, with the lobes being rounded rather than pointed as in red oaks. Even though Lewis's specimens show the leaves well, Frederick Pursh, possibly

Quercus garryana

JAMES L. REVEAL

NUTTALL'S *SYLVA*

because he lacked the tree's fruit (an acorn), did not include the tree in his *Flora* of 1813.[31]

Thomas Nuttall later noted that the Oregon white oak is the only white oak found in the region. He described the tree as attaining "the height of ninety or one hundred feet, if not more, with a diameter from three to six feet…. The wood is remarkably white for an Oak, hard and fine-grained, and well suited for almost every kind of construction for which the White Oak or English Oak is employed."[32]

BETULACEAE (BIRCH FAMILY)

Collected in Cowlitz County, Washington, or Columbia County, Oregon, on March 26, 1806

RED ALDER, *ALNUS RUBRA* BONG.

Meriwether Lewis collected a specimen of an alder on March 23, 1806. One may reasonably ask, "why did he bother to collect this particular tree?"—for alders are usually

NUTTALL'S *SYLVA*

quite unspectacular shrubs or small trees that grow, often in large numbers, on the banks of rivers and in swamps. The captains' journals make no mention of collecting the tree. This is not unusual, for more often than not they made no notes of plants collected on certain days. Lewis does mention, however, in a list of trees that he had seen over the past few days, that "the black Alder appears as well on some parts of the hills as the bottoms."[33] His "black alder" almost certainly was the one we know today as the red alder. Lewis may have collected the tree because—far from being a streamside shrub—it grows as a fairly large tree near the Pacific Coast. When Frederick Pursh examined the specimen, he did not realize that it was from a hitherto unknown tree—he thought that it was the same as the black alder (*Alnus glutinosa*) of Europe, an introduced tree, now found throughout the eastern United States.

Thomas Nuttall visited the Pacific Northwest in 1834, and when he saw an alder growing "along the borders of small clear brooks, near the confluence of the Wahlamet," he realized that it was the same tree that Lewis had found; furthermore, he saw that it was not a black alder. When Nuttall published his *Sylva* (the book appeared in installments, starting in 1842, as a continuation of a similar work on North American trees published by François André Michaux forty years earlier) he named the tree *Alnus oregana* and gave it the common name "Oregon alder." The illustration on page 126 is the one that appeared in the two-volume edition of Nuttall's *North American Sylva* published in Philadelphia in 1857.[34]

Nuttall described the tree best. He noted that it may grow to be thirty to forty feet high (though individual trees have been known to exceed 75 feet). Its fine-grained wood was used for furniture, and the wood aged to a mahogany color. He felt that the wood could be used not only for fine furniture, but that the tree itself might serve as an ornamental. Nuttall also mentions that "The chips, boiled with copperas [ferrous sulfate, $FeSO_4$], give a black dye to wool: and the leaves have been used in tanning: sheep will browse on them and the smaller branches" suggesting that this is a tree of many uses.[35]

The red alder grows in moist lowlands along the Pacific Coast west of the Cascade Range from Alaska to California, and it is also found in Idaho. The trees may be identified by their long pollen-producing catkins in the spring and by their brown, oval, pineconelike fruits that persist into the winter. The leaves are unusually large for the genus (up to six inches long). They are wavy-margined, coarsely veined leaves and are significantly lighter on the underside than on the top

Alnus rubra

JAMES L. REVEAL

PORTULACACEAE (PURSLANE FAMILY)

Collected on the Columbia River, in March and April, and on the Clearwater River, June 1806

FOUR SPRING BEAUTIES (*CLAYTONIA* SPP.)

As the expedition worked its way east after leaving Fort Clatsop in the spring of 1806, the men kept seeing little white flowers blooming in moist places. Lewis, and probably many of the men, would have related them to the spring beauties (*Claytonia caroliniana* and *Claytonia virginica*) common throughout the eastern United States as far south as Georgia. The eastern species are predominately pink, and only sometimes white (or rarely orange), whereas in the West the opposite is true. In any event, the plants were easy to collect, and four made it back to Philadelphia to be examined and classified by Frederick Pursh. The genus *Claytonia* is named for an early American botanist, John Clayton (1693-1773), who lived in Virginia.[36]

Many species of *Claytonia*, and the closely related genus *Montia*, are found in the West.[37] Many are so similar that

127

identification can be difficult, especially at the species level. Spring beauties, montias (or candyflowers), and the bitterroots (*Lewisia*) are all members of the purslane family, Portulacaceae. All are edible, and many have enlarged roots that Native Americans and early settlers used for food. Plants in the purslane family usually may be distinguished from those in other families by their not having the same number of sepals (the outermost set of flower parts below the petals) as petals. For example, spring beauties may have five or more petals, but each flower has only two sepals. Below are notes on the four spring beauties in the Lewis and Clark Herbarium.

WESTERN SPRING BEAUTY (*CLAYTONIA LANCEOLATA* PALL. EX PURSH)

The western spring beauty is a small attractive plant. Its flowers (usually several bloom at a time) are white with red markings and shocking pink anthers. Some years—for reasons that are obscure to us—the red markings widen and the flowers appear to be a lovely overall deep pink. The rather thick, deep green leaves (common in the Portulacaceae) are lance shaped. The explorers collected the species on the Lolo Trail between Bald Mountain and Spring Hill in Idaho County, Idaho, on an affluent of the Kooskoosky (Clearwater) River on June 27, 1806. Later, Pursh wrote

Claytonia lanceolata

A. SCOTT EARLE

Claytonia parviflora

A. SCOTT EARLE

"On the Rocky-mountains. *M. Lewis*" and "In the collection of A.B. Lambert, Esq. I found a specimen collected by Pallas in the eastern parts of Siberia, perfectly agreeing with the present species."[38] An illustration of the species is found opposite page 175 in Pursh's *Flora*. The drawing was not made from the extant Lewis specimen, however, and Pursh makes no reference to having seen garden material, so it is unlikely that he saw the plant in cultivation. It may be that there is another Lewis and Clark specimen in some herbarium that has yet to be discovered, for the illustration is not that of any Siberian species.[39]

STREAMBANK SPRING BEAUTY (*CLAYTONIA PARVIFLORA* DOUGLAS EX HOOK.)

The streambank spring beauty seems to be the least common of the spring beauties. As the name suggests, the species grows in moist situations, often in deep shade. Its flowers are small, white or pink, and similar to those of other plants in the genus. The leaves are small and ovate, borne on the ends of long stems (petioles). The specimen in the Lewis and Clark Herbarium consists today of a single leaf. The associated label states: "On the Columbia in moist ground March 26 1806." At one time Lewis's collection probably consisted of several flowering plants. We do not know what happened to the dried plant to reduce it to its present condition, but probably the loss occurred prior to the collection reaching Pursh, for he did not write an account of the plant. Nonetheless, the species had already been collected. The Spanish botanist Josef Mariano Moçiño (1757-1820) visited Nootka Sound in 1792 and found the plant. Although he collected no specimens, drawings were made in the field from live material, and the resulting illustrations show all the details one could wish to see. That same year, Archibald Menzies gathered specimens at Nootka Sound and on Queen Charlotte's Island. In spite of this excellent material, the species went unnamed until 1826.

MINER'S LETTUCE
(CLAYTONIA PERFOLIATA DONN EX WILLD.)

Miner's lettuce is remarkable in that its opposite, stemless leaves are joined at their bases, so that the plant's stem seems to perforate a single, bilaterally symmetrical "leaf," explaining the name *perfoliata* (from the Latin, meaning "through the leaf"). The little five-petaled flower resembles those of all of the other spring beauties. Lewis collected this

delicate little plant at Rock Fort (Rocky) Camp near The Dalles, Wasco County, Oregon, on April 17, 1806. Pursh wrote in his *Flora* that Lewis found the plant "On the Rocky-mountains," which was not true, for The Dalles Narrows are at the base of the Cascade Range.[40] The species was well known even in 1813, having been in cultivation since the 1790s. It is likely that Archibald Menzies introduced the plant into England. Throughout most of the twentieth century, miner's lettuce was known as *Montia perfoliata*, the name used in many guidebooks today. The name "miner's lettuce" came from the use of the plant as greens by early western settlers. A similar, closely related plant, *Claytonia cordifolia*, is also found in the Northwest. It differs in having large, heart-shaped leaves.

SIBERIAN SPRING BEAUTY (CLAYTONIA SIBIRICA L.)

The Siberian spring beauty is the most commonly encountered member of this group of plants found along the expedition's route. It is often noticed as a profusion of white flowers growing from a bed of green made up of the plant's short stalked, thin, lanceolate leaves. Lewis gathered his speci-

Claytonia perfoliata

JAMES L. REVEAL

Claytonia sibirica

JAMES L. REVEAL

mens of this plant (it is also known as "western spring beauty," "Siberian montia," and "candyflower") above the mouth of the Sandy River, Multnomah County, Oregon, or Skamania County, Washington, on April 8, 1806 where it is still common today. Pursh said only that Lewis found the plant "On the Columbia River."[41]

ROSACEAE (ROSE FAMILY)

Salmonberry collected near the mouth of the Cowlitz River, Cowlitz County, Washington, or Columbia County, Oregon, March 27, 1806. Thimbleberry collected near The Dalles, Klickitat County, Washington, or Wasco County, Oregon, on April 15, 1806

SALMONBERRY, *RUBUS SPECTABILIS* PURSH
WESTERN THIMBLEBERRY, *RUBUS PARVIFLORUS* NUTT.

The genus *Rubus* contains plants that we are all familiar with, including raspberries, blackberries, and loganberries (a hybrid cultivar of the two). Many similar, but less well-known, brambly plants also belong to the genus, including the two plants described here, several dewberries, bartonberries, cloudberries, and various introduced wild raspberries and blackberries. Many have brambly stems, rather coarse, toothed leaves, five-petaled white (or occasionally pink to red, as with the salmonberry), saucer-shaped flowers with many anthers—traits typical of the rose family in general—and a fruit that consists of an aggregation of "drupelets" (the small, clustered fruits that make up the berry).

A traveler along the Columbia River today will see more species of *Rubus* than the men of the expedition encountered in 1806, for since then several introduced European species have escaped from gardens and now thrive in the wild. Nevertheless, there were native species, beyond the two mentioned above, that Lewis and Clark might have seen in 1806. These include the dwarf red raspberry (*Rubus pubescens*), the California dewberry (*Rubus ursinus*), and the white-stem raspberry (*Rubus leucodermis*).[42] Lewis did not collect any of these—perhaps because he thought they were the same species found in the East.

The two that he did collect are the showiest members of the native northwestern *Rubus* species. The salmonberry (or salmon raspberry), is a brambly plant that bears large, bright red blossoms—its species name, *spectabilis*, means "remarkable" or "notable." Lewis found the early-flowering salmonberry on March 27, 1806, three days after leaving Fort Clatsop. It grows in moist woods, in swamps, and along streams from Alaska to California, and east onto the lower slopes of the Cascade Range. The attractive flowers are pink to deep red, so the plants are used as ornamentals in the Northwest, but they do tend to escape and are difficult to eradicate. The sprouts are tender when they first appear—as

Rubus spectabilis

JAMES L. REVEAL

Rubus parviflorus

Rubus parviflorus

are those of related brambles and Native Americans ate them. The fruit resembles a raspberry and ripens from late spring to early summer. The fruits are edible but soft, difficult to gather, and tend to be insipid.

The western thimbleberry (*Rubus parviflorus*) is a similar shrub, although it is distributed far more widely than the salmonberry. It grows all along the Pacific Coast and east to the Great Lakes. Its loosely clustered flowers are white, and—despite a species name that means "small flowered"—they may be an inch or more across. The stems growing on the waist-high shrubs have no prickles, the leaves are large and resemble maple leaves, so identification is easy. Native Americans used both plants; for their edible shoots, as noted, and for their fruit.

Frederick Pursh, copying Lewis's notes, annotated the herbarium sheet for the salmonberry "Fruit like a Rasberry—Columbia. March 27th 1806," and the thimbleberry as "A shrub of which the Natives eat the yung sprout without kooking. On the Columbia. Aprl. 15th 1806." Pursh named the new species *Rubus spectabilis*. In his description he notes only that it is found "On the banks of the Columbia. M. Lewis." He mentioned that Archibald Menzies had also collected the plant "On the north-west coast." Pursh included an illustration of *Rubus spectabilis*. It is one of the nicest in his *Flora*, but it is drawn entirely from the Menzies collection.[43] Thomas Nuttall found the thimbleberry growing on Michilimackinack Island, in Lake Huron, and realized that it was a new species. He described it in his *Genera of North American Plants* (1818) giving it the name that it has today. Lacking flowers and fruits, Pursh had been unable to classify Lewis's specimen.

BRASSICACEAE (MUSTARD FAMILY)

Collected near the mouth of the "Quicksand" (Sandy) River, Multnomah County, Oregon, on April 1, 1806

NUTTALL'S BITTERCRESS, *CARDAMINE NUTTALLII* GREENE

In the early spring, the Pacific Northwest abounds in small plants with the four-petaled flowers and slim seedpods ("siliques") characteristic of the mustard family. Nuttall's bittercress or toothwort is one of many similar plants, although its deep pink or purple flowers are larger and more showy than those of many other crucifers.[44]

This plant's attractive flowers undoubtedly prompted Meriwether Lewis to collect the two specimens that are now in the Lewis and Clark Herbarium in Philadelphia. Frederick Pursh evidently believed that the plant was a new one; he described it as growing "On the banks of the Columbia," noting that it was "Very slender; leaves small; flowers purple." He named it *Dentaria tenella.* The same plant was later collected by

Cardamine nuttallii

A. SCOTT EARLE

Thomas Nuttall. As often happens with closely related and variable plants, the plant's classification has varied over the years; sometimes it is considered a separate species, and sometimes it is called a variety of *Cardamine pulcherrima.*[45]

The generic name, *Cardamine,* is an old one used in antiquity for a now unknown crucifer. The word is related etymologically (although not botanically) to the spice cardamom. The crucifers are all, more or less, edible. The common names of many crucifers include the word "cress" (bittercress, watercress, rockcress, and so on). Tasting the leaves can be helpful in identifying crucifers, for the wild plants taste similar to common vegetables of the mustard family—watercress, mustard greens, broccoli, and cabbage to name only a few.

ASTERACEAE (ASTER FAMILY)

Collected in Skamania or Klickitat County, Washington, or Hood River or Wasco County, Oregon, April 14, 1806,
and in the vicinity of Lewis and Clark County, Montana, July 7, 1806

ARROWLEAF BALSAMROOT, *BALSAMORHIZA SAGITTATA* (PURSH) NUTT.

The arrowleaf balsamroot is a good indicator of springtime, for it is spring whenever and wherever the balsamroot blooms, regardless of calendar date. For several weeks in April, bright clusters of the gold-flowered plants seem to migrate from the shore up the walls of the Columbia Gorge

and then to the upper plains. No doubt other northwestern plants could be used as ecological indicators, but the balsamroot is best because it is so conspicuous. On the slopes of high mountains in the north country, one can watch the plants slowly ascend, forming upward moving golden contour lines as the summer wears on. They will almost reach tree line in late July before giving up.

The arrowleaf balsamroot was a new plant to the explorers. They had probably not encountered it while outward bound in the summer of 1805, for it is fairly restricted, growing from the Pacific Coast east to Colorado and Montana. (A few grow in the Black Hills of South Dakota, well to the south of the expedition's route across the Great Plains.)[46] The plants were first mentioned in the journals on April 13, 1806, the day before someone in the expedition—probably Lewis—collected balsamroot specimens. Clark noted on that day that he saw "parties of women and boys in Serch of herbs & roots to Subsist on maney of them had parcels of the stems of the Sun flower."[47] It is not surprising that he referred to the balsamroot as a sunflower, for the flowers are similar. There can be little question, however, that the plant Clark was referring to was the balsamroot. It would have been in bloom then, and Native Americans are known to have eaten the young stems (and the roots, too). The true sunflower, *Helianthus annuus*, is a summer-blooming plant with a dry, inedible stem—although its seeds were an important part of the Native American diet. It is likely that the explorers continued to see balsamroot as they moved into the mountains, encountering—and collecting—it for the last time in early July, as Lewis approached today's Lewis and Clark Pass, west of the Great Falls.

It was a new plant also to Frederick Pursh. He noted on

Balsamorhiza sagittata

A. SCOTT EARLE

the specimen sheet that it was found in the "Rocky mountains. Dry hills July 7th 1806"; in another note, he reported that "The stem is eaten by the natives, without any preparation. On the Columbia. April. 14th 1806."[48]

The arrowleaf balsamroot—there are half a dozen or more species belonging to the genus—is easily identified. Its silvery, grayish green, arrow- or spear-shaped leaves are followed soon by the golden yellow flower heads, one to a stem. The rays are wide and vary in number; usually there are thirteen, but there may be as many as twenty-one.[49] The ends of the individual rays are often notched. The plant's scientific and common names both mean exactly the same thing.

ANTIRRHINACEAE (FIGWORT FAMILY)

Collected at "Rock Fort" (Rocky) Camp, The Dalles, Wasco County, Oregon, April 17, 1806

LARGE FLOWER BLUE-EYED MARY, *COLLINSIA PARVIFLORA* LINDL. VAR. *GRANDIFLORA* (DOUGLAS EX LINDL.) GANDERS & G. R. KRAUSE

This little plant with contradictory species and varietal names comes in two sizes.[50] The men of the expedition had

to have seen both varieties, but the smaller one, *Collinsia parviflora* var. *parviflora*, is so small (the species name, *parv-*

133

Collinsia parviflora

A. SCOTT EARLE

iflora, means "small flower") that it would hardly seem worth collecting. Its tiny flowers are only about an eighth of an inch long and are irregular but bilaterally symmetrical. Both varieties of blue-eyed Mary have opposite leaves and irregular flowers. Three of the flower's five petals are joined to form a lower "lip"; the flower tube, made up of petals joined at their base, comes off the calyx at an angle—a characteristic feature. The petals are an intense blue-to-violet color, with a white base. Its calyx (the modified leaves that cup the petals and reproductive parts of the flower) is also irregular, with five unequal lobes. Blue-eyed Mary appears in the spring, typically on sagebrush slopes still moist from snowmelt, at intermediate elevations and higher. It grows from southern

Alaska to California and eastward to Colorado and Michigan. Although the plant appears in large numbers, it may be unnoticed at first; then—once the flowers are seen—the tiny blue dots are everywhere underfoot.

This is not so with the large-flowered variety. One might suspect that there is a growth hormone in the rain that falls on our Pacific Northwest, for most plants are larger there. So it is with this flower. It grows along the Columbia River as far east as the Hood River, as far north as British Columbia, and south to California. Both blue-eyed Marys are attractive plants, but it takes a hand lens to see that with the smaller variety. The form that Lewis and Clark gathered, however, has flowers up to three-quarters of an inch in length. It is an annual spring plant that would brighten anyone's rock garden.[51]

When Frederick Pursh saw the Lewis and Clark specimen, he recognized that it was a plant new to science. He was unsure how to classify it; he placed it in an existing genus of similar plants, naming it *Antirrhinum tenellum* (thereby missing an opportunity to create a new generic name). Pursh wrote in his *Flora*, incorrectly, that it was found on the banks of the Missouri, but said, correctly, that its flowers are "bright blue, large in proportion to the size of the plant." He also wrote that he had seen Lewis's dry specimen as well as live plants, but where, he does not say. Possibly Lewis had brought seeds back with him. The plant might have been growing in Philadelphia, or in New York, where Pursh worked prior to leaving for England.[52]

BORAGINACEAE (BORAGE FAMILY)

Collected at "Rock Fort" (Rocky) Camp, The Dalles, Wasco County, Oregon, on April 17, 1806

RETRORSE FIDDLENECK, *AMSINCKIA MENZIESII* (LEHM.) A. NELSON & P. B. KENN. VAR. *RETRORSA* (SUKSD.) REVEAL & SCHUYLER

Menzies fiddleneck—also known as the small-flowered fiddleneck, or amsinckia—is a bristly plant with small, orange

flowers. It is not overly attractive, and because fiddlenecks—there are several species—may poison cattle when mixed

Amsinckia menziesii var. retrorsa

A. SCOTT EARLE

Amsinckia menziesii var. retrorsa

A. SCOTT EARLE

tially.[53] Lewis would have been acquainted with eastern plants that have similar growth patterns, but fiddlenecks did not grow in eastern North America in 1806, so it was new to the members of the expedition—and that, presumably, was the reason Lewis collected it. Amsinckias—possibly the same plants that Lewis collected—grow today in vast numbers east of the Columbia Gorge, sometimes turning fields yellow in the spring.

We know that Frederick Pursh examined Lewis's dried specimen. A note in his handwriting, presumably copied from Lewis's original notation, reads "Rocky Camp. Aprl. 17th 1806." He did not recognize that the plant was both a new genus and a new species, and he does not seem to have accounted for it in his 1813 *Flora*. The one known specimen remained in Philadelphia; Pursh did not take it to Europe as he did with many others of the expedition's plants.[54] Three varieties of *Amsinckia menziesii* are recognized. Two varieties—var. *menziesii* and var. *retrorsa*—occur in the Columbia Gorge.

with forage, they are considered weeds. Their presence on roadsides and in other dry, disturbed areas serves to reinforce that opinion. The plants are notable only for their spirally coiled, bristly flower clusters. As the stems lengthen and uncoil, the flowers, borne on the outer side, bloom sequen-

POLEMONIACEAE (PHLOX FAMILY)

Collected at "Rock Fort" (Rocky) Camp, The Dalles, Wasco County, Oregon, on April 17, 1806

NARROW-LEAF COLLOMIA, *COLLOMIA LINEARIS* NUTT.

On April 17, 1806, Lewis and Clark were having a wildflower day, for there were a lot of early spring flowers in bloom and many were new to them. One of these, the narrow-leaf collomia (or narrow-leaf mountain-trumpet) is a common plant found throughout the western and northern parts of North America. It blooms in early spring (remem-

bering that "early spring" in the mountains may be the end of June or even later). While the plants are usually scattered, they can also grow in large patches. Typically they favor open rocky soil, often in the company of sagebrush. There are about a dozen species of *Collomia*, with Lewis and Clark's *Collomia linearis* by far the most common.

135

Collomia linearis

A. SCOTT EARLE

The narrow-leaf collomia's flowers are typical of the phlox family in general, with five sepals, five petals, five anthers, and a long flower tube that flares at the end giving it a trumpet-shaped (salverform) appearance. Its leaves are narrow, or "linear," explaining its species name.

Frederick Pursh examined Lewis's specimen, but he neither recognized it as a new genus and species nor accounted for it in his 1813 *Flora*. As with many of the plants that Lewis collected, it was Thomas Nuttall who found the plant anew, growing on the upper Missouri River near the mouth of the Cheyenne River. He described and named it in his *Genera of North American Plants* (1818). Nuttall derived his genus name from the Greek *kolla*, meaning "glue," for he noted that the plant's seed became sticky when moistened (a property that is sometimes helpful in classifying different species within the phlox family).[55]

BORAGINACEAE (BORAGE FAMILY)

Collected at "Rock Fort" (Rocky) Camp, The Dalles, Wasco County, Oregon, on April 17, 1806

SLENDER POPCORN-FLOWER, *PLAGIOBOTHRYS TENELLUS* (NUTT. EX HOOK.) A. GRAY

Plagiobothrys tenellus

A. SCOTT EARLE

Captain Meriwether Lewis must have spent some time on his hands and knees on this day at the Narrows of the Columbia River, for several of his specimens are tiny plants. This one's flowers may be no larger than an eighth of an inch across, and the plant sometimes is only a few inches high. It is not a plant that one notices unless actively looking for every wildflower in the vicinity, as Lewis evidently was doing. The slender (or Pacific) popcorn-flower (the species name, *tenellus*, means "delicate"), like the fiddleneck (see p. 134), is a member of the borage family. This plant, like many other members of the Boraginaceae, is covered with stiff hairs, has five-petaled flowers in clusters that uncoil (helicoid cymes), and grows mainly in open places.

Evidently Frederick Pursh took no notice of it—the dried

specimen in Lewis's collection is not impressive—or else was uncertain where to place it, for he did not list it in his *Flora*. As with so many of the plants that Lewis and Clark collected, Thomas Nuttall subsequently found it growing along the Columbia River in 1834 (or possibly 1835), but he did not attempt to describe it, either. So this slender, tap-rooted, white-flowered annual remained undescribed until

the German botanist Karl Andreas Geyer (1809-1853) found it growing in the mountains along the Coeur d'Alene River of northern Idaho in the spring of 1844.[56] Some fifty species of *Plagiobothrys* grow in North and South America. A few can be troublesome weeds (though *Plagiobothrys tenellus* is not). Our plant ranges from British Columbia south to Baja California, and eastward into Idaho, Utah, and Arizona.

POLEMONIACEAE (PHLOX FAMILY)
Collected in Nez Perce County, Idaho, May 7, 1806
SHOWY PHLOX, *PHLOX SPECIOSA* PURSH

Botanists recognize sixty or so species of phlox, although there is considerable variability. Deciding how to classify the various species can be a challenge. While phlox species grow throughout eastern North America and a few are native to the northern parts of Asia, more are found in the American West than anywhere else. Lewis would have recognized the plant that he collected on April 17 as a phlox, for its appearance was similar to ones he knew from Virginia.

When Frederick Pursh examined Lewis's specimen, he recognized that the species was new and gave the plants the species name *speciosa*, a Latin term that means "showy" or "splendid." He may have gotten a bit carried away, for its flower is not much different from those of other species of phlox. The plant is of average height—to a foot and a half (not the four feet Pursh reported)—and usually has several to many branches growing from a woody base. The leaves are linear, and a few flowers form a loose cluster at the end of each branch, "in such abundance, that they cover the whole shrub."[57] The narrow flower tube is considerably longer than the sepals and—typical of the Polemoniaceae—the petals separate at the top of the tube and flare abruptly to form a shallow saucer-shaped flower. The ends of the pink or sometimes white petals are

Phlox speciosa

JAMES L. FEVEAL

usually more or less deeply notched, a distinguishing feature.

Although Pursh stated that the plant is native "to the Plains of Columbia," Lewis's two specimens were collected much farther to the east, demonstrating Pursh's (and others') lack of geographical understanding of the West at the time. The species today is found from the Pacific Northwest to the northern edges of the deserts in the American Southwest.

FABACEAE (PEA FAMILY)

Big-head clover collected at "Rock Fort" (Rocky) Camp, The Dalles on April 17, 1806;
Small-head clover collected at Travelers' Rest on July 1, 1806

BIG-HEAD CLOVER, *TRIFOLIUM MACROCEPHALUM* (PURSH) POIR.
SMALL-HEAD CLOVER, *TRIFOLIUM MICROCEPHALUM* PURSH

Lewis's criteria for collecting plants included not only ones that were new to science, but also ones that might have some practical value: grasses for fodder, fruit-bearing shrubs and trees, interesting ornamentals, and so on. That clovers are valuable fodder plants may explain why Lewis collected two species of clover. The first, found at The Dalles, was the big-head clover (its scientific name, *Trifolium macrocephalum*, has the same meaning as its common name). He certainly knew it was a clover, but it is most assuredly unlike any that he had seen before. All of the clovers the men knew from the East were European plants that were brought in with fodder for cattle being transported to the New World. This one, however, grows only in the Pacific Northwest. It is well named, for the head, made up of half-inch long pink flowers, may be two inches or more across. The plant is also unusual in that its palmate leaves bear more than three leaflets and resemble those of lupines. This resemblance also extends to its habitat—for it grows on rocky, sagebrush-covered slopes rather than the moist meadows preferred by most clovers.

Frederick Pursh was impressed by Lewis's specimen, and he chose the big-head clover to be one of the fourteen

TRIFOLIUM MACROCEPHALUM, CRONQUIST, INTERMOUNTAIN FLORA

TRIFOLIUM MICROCEPHALUM, CRONQUIST, INTERMOUNTAIN FLORA

illustrations he included in his *Flora*. Pursh recognized that it was new to science and described it carefully, noting that it was "very handsome and showy" although he said—incorrectly—that it grew "At the headwaters of the Missouri." In 1813 some authors distinguished between those clovers with three leaflets and those with more; accordingly, Pursh assigned his new species to the genus *Lupinaster*.[58] In 1817, the French botanist Louis Marie Poiret gave it the name that we know it by today.

Ten weeks after collecting big-head clover, Lewis collected a second clover, at Travelers' Rest. In size, this plant lies on the opposite end of the spectrum and more closely resembles the clovers that the men knew in the East. The flower head measures less than half an inch across, and the plants have the three leaflets for which the genus *Trifolium* is named. Pursh said the plant was found "On the banks of Clarck's river" and had "exceedingly small, pale purple" flowers. He named it *Trifolium microcephalum*.[59] This native western plant is found from British Columbia to Baja California eastward to Montana and New Mexico.

Asteraceae (Aster Family)

Collected on the "Kooskooskee" (Clearwater) River, Nez Perce County, Idaho, May 6, 1806

Green rabbitbrush, *Chrysothamnus viscidiflorus*

The rabbitbrushes as a group are characterized by their bright golden yellow, rayless flowers, their narrow, stemless, linear leaves, and their typically shrublike appearance. Like all species of rabbitbrush, green rabbitbrush (*Chrysothamnus viscidiflorus*) flowers and fruits in the late summer and fall of the year. Their many bright yellow flowers add a welcome autumnal color to the gray-green sagebrush-covered hills of the American West.

This small, aromatic shrub was unlike any member of the aster family that grew in eastern North America, and that alone may have attracted Lewis's attention to a shrub that was not even in flower. Perhaps there were a few seeds still on the plant and he thought it might make an attractive ornamental. More likely he was attracted by its pronounced medicinal odor, and he thought it would have some medicinal use. Unfortunately, the green rabbitbrush is difficult to grow from seed, and the plants are not known to have any therapeutic value. Further, not much remained of his specimen after months of hard travel from the Clearwater River in today's Nez Perce County, Idaho, to Philadelphia. Flowers are a key feature in understanding the relationships of angiosperms (flowering plants). Lewis's specimen had no flowers, so Pursh was unable to describe a new genus. It remained for Thomas Nuttall to establish the genus *Chrysothamnus* (meaning "golden shrub" in Greek) in 1840.

Like its counterpart, rubber rabbitbrush (*Ericameria nauseosa*, p. 39), green rabbitbrush is a highly variable and taxonomically complex species. It grows from southern British Columbia to southern California, northern Arizona,

Chrysothamnus viscidiflorus

JAMES L. REVEAL

and northern New Mexico at a wide variety of elevations and on many different kinds of soil. However, in this species there are only seven varieties rather than twenty as in *Ericameria nauseosa*. At least three varieties are found along the Lewis and Clark route, and all may be distinguished from rubber rabbitbrush by the almost varnished, exceedingly sticky nature of the flowering branches.[60]

LILIACEAE (LILY FAMILY)

Collected along the "Kooskooskee" (Clearwater) River, Nez Perce or Clearwater County, Idaho, on May 8,
and on the Lolo Trail, Idaho County, Idaho, 1806

GLACIER LILY, *ERYTHRONIUM GRANDIFLORUM* PURSH

Here is a pretty little spring charmer that goes by many common names: glacier lily (most commonly), pale fawn-lily, yellow fawn-lily, dogtooth-violet, trout-lily, avalanche-lily, and adder's-tongue, to list a few.[61] These suggest how

Erythronium grandiflorum

JAMES L. REVEAL

much this small, nodding, yellow lily means as an emblem of the coming of spring—and likely that is also how the men of the expedition regarded it when they first saw the flowers. Frederick Pursh got it right, too, for he recognized that the plant was new to science. Lewis's note (as copied

by Pursh) on one of the two specimens in the Lewis and Clark Herbarium says: "From the plains of Columbia near Kooskooskee R.—May. 8th 1806. the natives reckon this root as unfitt for food." He named the plant *Erythronium grandiflorum*, a name that it has retained to the present—unusual for a Lewis and Clark plant![62]

Glacier lilies favor open woodland, spilling over onto sage-covered slopes still moist from snowmelt. They usually are found scattered here and there, but sometimes are found growing in great numbers. The plants usually have two basal, prominently veined, broadly lanceolate leaves and one or two downward-looking flowers. Six identical, swept back tepals (the sepals and petals, collectively) range in color from white (var. *candidum*) through pale yellow to a rich gold. Oddly, the anthers also have a range of colors—white, red, and purple forms have been reported on plants growing in different areas. Its range includes all of the Pacific Northwest and extends eastward to Montana, Wyoming, and Colorado. Although Lewis implied that the roots are inedible, Harrington reports that they are tasty and may be eaten either raw or boiled—although he also notes that it is a pretty plant whose roots should be eaten only as emergency food, and, considering their alleged inedibility, even then with caution.[63]

Themidaceae (Cluster-lily Family)

Collected near The Dalles of the Columbia River, Klickitat County, Washington, or Wasco County, Oregon, April 17, 1806

Douglas's brodiaea, *Triteleia grandiflora* Lindl.

Douglas's brodiaea (or Douglas's triplet-flower) is a lovely lilylike plant that grows in dry open places, often in the company of sagebrush.[64] It is commonly seen in late spring in the Pacific Northwest and eastward into western Montana, Wyoming, and northern Utah. One, or usually more flowers are borne as an umbel atop a long bare stem. The tepals are white to light blue with darker blue markings. The plants have narrow, parallel-veined basal leaves and a tall naked stem topped by a hyacinth-like cluster of six-tepaled flowers.

Meriwether Lewis had the time and opportunity to look for plants while the men were portaging their baggage and canoes around the Narrows of the Columbia River, later known as The Dalles.[65] On April 17, 1805, Lewis noted in his journal that he saw "a species of hiasinth in these plains the bulb of which the natives eat either boiled baked or dryed in the sun," mentioning that he "preseved a specemine of it."[66] Confusingly, the date of actual collection of the two specimens in the Lewis and Clark Herbarium is given as April 20, and the location as "the plains of Columbia." On April 17, the captains were separated by some distance

Triteleia grandiflora

Triteleia grandiflora

JAMES L. REVEAL

along the rapids, but both were equally exasperated. They were trying to purchase horses with minimal success, and Lewis was trying to recover several items that the Indians had stolen the night before. Given the confusion, it is understandable that the dates do not match.

Frederick Pursh identified this "hyasinth" as *Brodiaea grandiflora*, the first—and at the time—the only species in a recently proposed genus. Pursh wrote in his *Flora* that Lewis had collected the plant, and that it grew "On the plains of the Columbia and Missouri rivers." He also noted that he himself had seen the plant growing, although he did not say where.[67]

CURTIS'S BOTANICAL MAGAZINE

CARYOPHYLLACEAE (PINK FAMILY)

Collected in Klickitat County, Washington, or Wasco or Sherman County, Oregon, on April 22, 1806

STRICT FIELD CHICKWEED, *CERASTIUM ARVENSE* L. SUBSP. *STRICTUM* (L.) UGBOROGHO

The strict field chickweed is a perennial that grows as a small shrub with branched, trailing stems. As with many other members of the pink family, its five petals are deeply

Cerastium arvense

JAMES L. REVEAL

notched at the outer end and it has opposite, narrow leaves that arise from small swellings (nodes) along the stems. The flowers are borne in loose clusters and may bloom from spring well into the summer. Some members of the pink family, particularly European plants, have showy, colorful flowers (the carnation, for example, is a cultivated form of the European clove pink, *Dianthus caryophyllus*), but those native to the American West do not.

Field chickweed is a cosmopolitan plant found in much of northern North America and in Europe. Linnaeus knew the plant and named it *Cerastium arvense*, deriving the

generic name from the Greek word *kerastos* ("a horn"), for the shape of the plant's seed capsule, and the species name *arvense*, from a Latin term that means "of the field." The name "chickweed" has been in use for centuries, and it was often applied to plants that chickens favor, including those in several other genera in the pink family (such as *Arenaria* and *Stellaria*). It is a bit surprising that Lewis did not recognize this plant, for it grows in the eastern United States as far south as Georgia (although it is uncommon in Virginia). As might be expected with a plant so widely distributed, there are variant forms, and in North America we have five subspecies, with subsp. *strictum* being the most common.[68]

The dried plant in the Lewis and Clark Herbarium is not a good specimen, consisting of little more than a single flowering stem. It is hard to guess what its condition might have been when Frederick Pursh examined it, but evidently it was not sufficient, even then, for him to recognize the plant as field chickweed. He listed *Cerastium arvense* in his *Flora* as an eastern species (presently subsp. *arvense* is confined mainly to Canada and Greenland) and gave the Lewis and Clark plant a new species name, *Cerastium elongatum*, noting only that it was found "On the plains of Columbia River."[69] Subsequently the Lewis and Clark specimen was recognized as field chickweed, and Pursh's name was discarded.

The family scientific name, Caryophyllaceae, is an old one, derived from a Greek word, *garyphallon*, which means "clove," from a fancied resemblance of the fragrance of the European clove pink (and its horticultural descendant, the carnation) to the spice that comes from *Syzygium aromaticum*.

HYDRANGEACEAE (HYDRANGEA FAMILY)

Collected on the "Kooskoosky" (Clearwater) River, Nez Perce County, Idaho, May 6, 1806,
and on the Blackfoot River above its confluence with the "Clarks River" (Bitterroot River), Missoula County, Montana, July 4, 1806

SYRINGA, *PHILADELPHUS LEWISII* PURSH

Syringa is the only widespread and common member of the hydrangea family found in the mountain West.[70] It ranges from British Columbia to northern California and eastward to Idaho and Montana. As with many other plants in the hydrangea family, it is prized today both as an ornamental and for its fragrance. Many other white-flowered shrubs and small trees bloom in the spring and early summer at the mid-elevations where syringa is found, and it may be hard at first glance to distinguish this plant from the others. Nevertheless, its fragrance and its large, four-petaled white blossoms clearly set it apart.[71] The names of both Idaho and Montana's state flowers—syringa (*Philadelphus lewisii*) and the bitterroot (*Lewisia rediviva*, p. 196)—honor the explorer who found them.

The sheet in the Lewis and Clark Herbarium for this plant has two specimens on it. Both are labeled in Frederick Pursh's handwriting (copied presumably from Lewis's field notes). The specimen on the left of the sheet is labeled "A Shrub from the Kooskoosky. May 6th 1806. An Philadelphus?" That on the right reads "On the waters of Clarks R. Jul. 4th 1806." When Frederick Pursh examined these two specimens, he recognized that they were the same and that both belonged in the genus *Philadelphus*, as Lewis

had suggested in his field note. In his *Flora*, Pursh mentioned only that the species was found on the waters of "Clarck's river"—a name that today is used only for the

Philadelphus lewisii

JAMES L. REVEAL

Bitterroot River; however, in the early nineteenth century the name was used for all its branches as well, possibly because of uncertainty about the location of its headwaters. Pursh did not mention that Lewis had gathered the same plant two months earlier, on the Kooskoosky (Clearwater) River.[72]

GROSSULARIACEAE (GOOSEBERRY FAMILY)
Collected in various places
WILD CURRANTS AND GOOSEBERRIES

There are four species of wild currants in the Lewis and Clark Herbarium. Lewis probably collected others, but so many of the expedition's specimens were lost, either from flooding of caches or later from other causes, that we have no way of knowing what other species he may have gathered. Certainly there was plenty of material available. Ten species of wild currants grow on the Great Plains, and well over thirty species occur in the Rocky Mountains and Pacific Northwest.[73]

The gooseberry family consists of a single genus, *Ribes*, a group found throughout the Northern Hemisphere and in the Andes of South America. The men of the expedition were familiar with its berries; they were important to them—as a source of plant vitamins, if not calorically. The fruit of all species of *Ribes* are edible, but only a few of these are palatable (although palatability may vary according to ripeness, locality, and degree of hunger). Numerous species of *Ribes* are in cultivation today, as ornamentals, as fruit, and because plant breeders use them to produce desirable cultivars. The following three representatives were all collected on the expedition's return trip. No doubt others were encountered and eaten.

Collected near the mouth of the Cowlitz River, Cowlitz County, Washington, or Columbia County, Oregon, March 27, 1806
RED CURRANT, *RIBES SANGUINEUM* PURSH

The red currant (also known as the blood currant and red-flowering currant) was blooming when Lewis collected it

Ribes sanguineum

JAMES L. REVEAL

near the mouth of the Cowlitz River on the lower reaches of the Columbia in 1806. Its bright red flowers were reason enough for him to include it in his traveling herbarium, for they stand out both when he found the plant growing in the wild and in today's gardens as attractive ornamentals. Its shiny black berries are, like those of many other wild currants, edible but unpalatable.

Frederick Pursh recognized that this was a new plant and gave it the name that it bears today. He noted that the plant was "*inerme*," a Latin term that means "unarmed," often used to describe plants in genera where some species have thorns, prickles, or bristles and others do not. Lewis wrote (as copied by Pursh) that it grew "On the Columbia River …Flowers beautiful, of a blood red or purple." Pursh noted that the plant bloomed in April and that he had seen Lewis's dried specimen.[74] Today that specimen may be seen in the Lewis and Clark Herbarium in Philadelphia, although little of the plant remains. Pursh very likely took a portion of the dried plant with him to London (now lost), and the years have taken their toll on the remainder, for the specimen consists only of a twig with a few small leaves and a flower.

Collected above the mouth of the Sandy River, Multnomah County, Oregon, or Skamania County, Washington, April 8, 1806

SPREADING GOOSEBERRY, *RIBES DIVARICATUM* DOUGLAS

The spreading gooseberry is a relatively localized species found from southern British Columbia south to California. Its berries are purple-black and edible. Because of its variability, three varieties are recognized today; the one that Lewis found in 1806 is var. *divaricatum*. While the plants are usually unarmed, bristly examples are sometimes found, suggesting that the spreading gooseberry represents a bridge between wild currants and gooseberries. This is one reason why all of the plants formerly in the genus *Grossularia* are now included in the genus *Ribes*.

The species name, *divaricatum*, means "diverging" or "spreading." Although Meriwether Lewis collected the plant,

Frederick Pursh did not recognize it as a new species. David Douglas later found the spreading (or coastal black) gooseberry growing on the "bank of streams near Indian villages, on the North West Coast of America" and gave it the species name *divaricatum* for its spreading, straggly branches.[75]

There is not much left of the specimen that Lewis collected—only one branch with emerging leaves. Frederick Pursh's note (copied from Lewis's description) on the herbarium sheet reads only "Deep purple Gooseberry—Columbia R. Aprl. 8th 1806." Given the paucity of material, Pursh was unable to assign the specimen to a species, so it remained for Douglas to rediscover the plant two decades later.

Collected near Hungery Creek, Lolo Trail, Idaho County, Idaho, June 16, 1806

STICKY CURRANT, *RIBES VISCOSISSIMUM* PURSH

Lewis found the sticky currant blooming along the Lolo Trail during the expedition's return trip. He would have recognized it as a *Ribes*, for the appearance of the shrubs and especially of their three-lobed leaves help in identifying them. This plant's yellowish white flowers are larger than those of most of the other wild currants, and when he touched its leaves he would have recognized immediately that it was different from other *Ribes*. As the name *viscosissimum* (which means "most sticky") suggests, this plant's leaves—especially when it is flowering—are sticky. While they may not be quite as sticky as flypaper, that substance comes to mind when one first touches them.

Lewis's dried specimens (there are two herbarium sheets, one in Philadelphia and the other at the Royal Botanic Gardens at Kew, outside London) are relatively complete and include terminal branches complete with leaves and flowers. Pursh's copy of Lewis's label on the Philadelphia specimen

reads, "Fruit indifferent and gummy. The hights of the rocky mountain." The description suggests that the men knew the

Ribes viscosissimum

plant from earlier—it is widely distributed throughout the West—because it would not have been fruiting when Lewis gathered his specimens in early June 1806. The deep bluish black berries are not ones that a person would seek out, unless forced by hunger to do so, for they are "rather dry and with a disagreeable taste and smell."[76] Pursh realized that this was a new plant; apparently, judging from his notes on the specimen sheet at Kew, he had initially wanted to name it *viscosum*, then altered this to *glandulosum* before finally settling on the name that we know it by today. This was fortunate, for both of the first two names had been published previously (in 1794 and in 1802) and therefore were not available for him to use.[77]

Asteraceae (Aster Family)

Collected on the "Kooskooskee" (Clearwater) River, Idaho, date unknown

Cutleaf daisy, *Erigeron compositus* Pursh

Surprisingly, given the large number of composite plants (members of the aster family) that the explorers had to have seen, Lewis collected only one true daisy—that is, a member of the genus *Erigeron*, typified by same-length leafy bracts subtending the flower head. He found the cutleaf daisy (or "dwarf mountain fleabane," as it is also called) growing somewhere along the Clearwater River. He did not give the date, but some assume—both from the dates the expedition spent on the Clearwater and because this is a plant that blooms early—that he collected it in late April or early May of 1806 (however, it is possible that it was collected the previous year).[78]

Pursh recognized immediately that Lewis's specimen was a daisy, and a new one at that. He named it *Erigeron compositus* (his species name means "compound," for the plant's frilly branching leaves) noting that it was found "On the banks of the Kooskoosky River" by "*M. Lewis*." He went on to say that the plant was "Not above a span high; flowers resembling a daisy exceedingly." It was a good description, for the plant is small (a "span" measures approximately nine inches—the distance between the tips of the outstretched thumb and little finger).[79]

We often see the cutleaf daisy today growing on rocks or in sandy places. It is a fairly widely distributed perennial that ranges across North America from Alaska to Greenland, and in our northern states and provinces as far east as Quebec. As with most plants this widely distributed, there are several varieties; Lewis's plant is var. *compositus*. The species is attractive and compact. It bears many flowers and grows in what would seem to be inhospitable surroundings. It would seem to be an ideal plant for use as an early-bloomer for rock gardens.

Erigeron compositus

A. SCOTT EARLE

Bristly black gooseberry, *Ribes lacustre*

A. SCOTT EARLE

Bristly black gooseberry, *Ribes lacustre*

A. SCOTT EARLE

Hudson's Bay currant, *Ribes hudsonianum*

A. SCOTT EARLE

Hudson's Bay currant, *Ribes hudsonianum*

A. SCOTT EARLE

Common eriophyllum	*Eriophyllum lanatum*	Ragged robin	*Clarkia pulchella*
Common camas	*Camassia quamash*	Narrow-leaved skullcap	*Scutellaria angustifolia*
Canby's bluegrass	*Poa canbyi*	Lance-leaf stonecrop	*Sedum lanceolatum*
Bluebunch wheatgrass	*Pseudoroegneria spicata*	Worm-leaf stonecrop	*Sedum stenopetalum*
Idaho fescue	*Festuca idahoensis*	Trumpet honeysuckle	*Lonicera ciliosa*
Western fairy-slipper	*Calypso bulbosa* var. *occidentalis*	Silvery lupine	*Lupinus argenteus*
Spotted coral-root	*Corallorhiza maculata*	Silky lupine	*Lupinus sericeus*
Green-leaf rattlesnake plantain	*Goodyera oblongifolia*	Varileaf phacelia	*Phacelia heterophylla*
Mountain lady's-slipper	*Cypripedium montanum*	Prairie smoke	*Geum triflorum* var. *ciliatum*
White rein-orchid	*Platanthera dilatata*	Pineapple weed	*Matricaria discoidea*
Hooded ladies'-tresses	*Spiranthes romanzoffiana*	American bistort	*Polygonum bistortoides*

Bunchberry	*Cornus canadensis*	Long-leaf suncup	*Camissonia subacaulis*
Pursh's wallflower	*Erysimum capitatum* var. *purshii*	Piper's anemone	*Anemone piperi*
Clustered elkweed	*Frasera fastigiata*	Purple trillium	*Trillium petiolatum*
Elegant mariposa lily	*Calochortus elegans*	Bear grass	*Xerophyllum tenax*
Woolly American yarrow	*Achillea millefolium* var. *lanulosum*	California false hellebore	*Veratrum californicum*
Wilcox's penstemon	*Penstemon wilcoxii*	Scarlet gilia	*Ipomopsis aggregata*
Shrubby penstemon	*Penstemon fruticosus*	Western mountain kitten's-tail	*Synthyris missurica*
Sugarbowl	*Clematis hirsutissima*	Redstem ceanothus	*Ceanothus sanguineus*
Cascara	*Frangula purshiana*	Snow-bush ceanothus	*Ceanothus velutinus*
Ocean spray	*Holodiscus discolor*	Western horsemint	*Agastache urticifolia*
Black chokecherry	*Prunus virginiana* var. *melanocarpa*	Western polemonium	*Polemonium occidentale*
Bitter cherry	*Prunus emarginata*	Showy polemonium	*Polemonium pulcherrimum*

Camp Chopunnish to Travelers' Rest
May 14 to June 30, 1806

For those with an interest in botany and in mountain flowers, the weeks the Corps of Discovery spent waiting to cross the Lolo Trail in the spring of 1806 are the most interesting of all. The snowpack was unusually heavy that year and the expedition could go nowhere until the snow melted in the mountains. There were the usual camp duties to attend to while they waited. The horses that they had left with the Chopunnish the previous fall had to be rounded up. Hunting parties ranged far afield looking for game. The expedition had almost nothing left to barter except the buttons from their army uniforms. Clark saved the day. As they ascended the Clearwater River, he had treated several Indians for various afflictions, and after two "cures" he found that he was, in the eyes of his grateful patients, a great physician. He wrote: "these two cures has raised my reputation and given those nativs an exolted oppinion of my Skill as a phician.... [I]n our present Situation I think it pardonable to continue this deception for they will not give us any provisions without Compensation in merchendize, and our Stock is now reduced to a mear handfull."[1] His reputation preceded him, and by the time they established "Camp Chopunnish," as many as fifty Indians a day showed up looking for relief from a variety of conditions.[2] They appreciated his ministrations and rewarded him with gifts of food and even a horse or two. Plants were in bloom everywhere. Except for a few notable exceptions, there is not much in the *Journals* that reflects how much time Lewis spent during these weeks collecting and preparing plant specimens—more than forty altogether. He searched for them, gathered the new ones he found, identified them as best he could, pressed and dried them, added a field note, and occasionally made a note in his journal about where he found them. His botanizing had to have kept him occupied for days.

It is clear from his journal entries that some of his men brought him specimens as well.

Although they kept busy, the men were anxious to get going. They were still more than two thousand miles from St. Louis, and they had to complete their descent of the Missouri before the river iced up. The Indians repeatedly told them that the snow was too deep to try to cross the Bitterroots, but the captains could wait no longer. On June 10, the party left Camp Chopunnish (on the site of today's Kamiah, Idaho). They returned to the Weippe Prairie where they had met the Nez Perce the previous year. Anyone who has driven the road from the Clearwater to today's Weippe, Idaho, negotiating one steep hairpin turn after another, realizes what their first day was like. The river's banks are steep and rise almost two thousand feet to the Weippe Prairie. Shrubs and small trees were blooming, and sprays of white flowers would have been everywhere—red elderberry (*Sambucus racemosa*), oceanspray (*Holodiscus discolor*), smooth snowberry (*Symphoricarpos albus* var. *laevigatus*), mallow-leaf ninebark (*Physocarpus malvaceus*), wild cherries (*Prunus* spp.), Cusick's serviceberry (*Amelanchier alnifolia* var. *cusickii*), mountain balm (*Ceanothus velutinus*), and many others that bloom each June. Lewis recognized some; others, such as the syringa or mock-orange (*Philadelphus lewisii*, the Idaho state flower) were new to him and to science.

At the prairie a new spectacle awaited the expedition. They had hit it just right, for the camas (*Camassia quamash*) was in full bloom. Each spring on the high prairies of Idaho and Montana a profusion of delicate gray-blue flowers grows on ground moist from melting snow; they grow in such numbers that from a distance they appear to form "lakes" on the prairies and "streams" alongside spring freshets. Lewis described this illusion: "the quawmash is now in blume and from the colour of its bloom at a short distance it resembles lakes of fine clear water, so complete is this desetption that on first sight I could have swoarn it was water."[3] They remained on the Weippe Prairie for four days.

On June 15, they started off following their trail of the previous fall heading into the mountains. As they approached the heights, spring turned back into winter. The snow grew deeper and deeper, until their "road" became totally impassi-

ble, and without a native guide the party could go no farther. On the seventeenth of June, the men turned back—their only retreat. They stashed everything they could, including their newly collected plants, and returned to the meadows at Weippe. Finally, for the price of two rifles, three Nez Perce agreed to guide them through the mountains. This time they completed the crossing in seven days, making good time on frozen corn snow. They arrived at Travelers' Rest on June 30. The hardest part of the return trip was behind them.

ASTERACEAE (ASTER FAMILY)

Collected on the "Kooskooskee" (Clearwater) River, Camp Chopunnish, Kamiah, Idaho County, Idaho, on June 6, 1806

COMMON ERIOPHYLLUM, *ERIOPHYLLUM LANATUM* (PURSH) FORBES

Eriophyllums (as with a number of other plants, such as impatiens and geraniums, the genus name is most commonly used as a common name) usually grow in open dry places where one does not expect to see such a bright flower. It is one of the Pacific Northwest's more attractive yellow-rayed composites. The flower heads bear wide, bright, orange-yel-

Eriophyllum lanatum var. integrifolium

JAMES L. REVEAL

low rays that catch one's eye when viewed against a background of dry summer grasses. The plant's leaves are covered with fine woolly hairs that give them a silvery green color. (The woolly leaves have given rise to another common name, woolly sunflower.) There are about a dozen varieties of eriophyllum, and both the number of rays and the shape of the leaves are important in identifying them; most are found in California. One species and two varieties are common in the Pacific Northwest. *Eriophyllum lanatum* var. *lanatum* usually has thirteen ray flowers and divided leaves. It ranges north into Canada, whereas the related *Eriophyllum lanatum* var. *integrifolium* typically has eight rays and undivided leaves, and its range extends farther south, into California. Both varieties grow along the Lewis and Clark Trail.

On one of the two herbarium sheets in the Lewis and Clark Herbarium, Frederick Pursh's label, copied from Lewis's original, reads: "On the uplands on the Kooskooskee R. Jun: 6th 1806." This is curious, for the word uplands is not associated with any other specimen gathered during Lewis and Clark's month-long stay at Camp Chopunnish.[4] Pursh did not realize that the plant represented a new genus. He added it to an existing genus, naming the new species *Actinella lanata* (the species name means "woolly").[5] In 1816, *Eriophyllum* was established for a Mexican plant (the name *Eriophyllum* was derived from the Greek *erion*, for "wool," and *phyllon*, for "leaf"), and this eriophyllum became a member of that genus in 1828, retaining Pursh's species name.

AGAVACEAE (AGAVE FAMILY)

Collected June 23, 1806, on the Weippe Prairie, Clearwater County, Idaho

COMMON CAMAS, CAMASSIA QUAMASH (PURSH) GREENE

Camassia quamash

JAMES L. REVEAL

As one follows the Corps of Discovery from St. Louis to the Pacific and back again, certain plants command more than passing notice. The cottonwood provided shade, fuel, and transportation while the party was on the Missouri. Dugout canoes made of ponderosa pine carried the men to the Pacific Ocean. Cous sustained them on their return trip up the Columbia, and camas root revived the starving party when they came off the Lolo Trail. The last of these, the common camas, is a lovely plant.[6] Its blue tepals (undifferentiated sepals and petals) are accented by prominent anthers shaped like bright yellow parentheses. While the tepals are most often a bluish gray, their color ranges from intense blue to a subdued light blue and even purple, according to conditions and locality. Wide, basal, parallel-veined leaves are similar to those seen in the lily family. Its fleshy roots were as important to the Nez Perce as salmon was to the coastal Indians.

In September 1805, the explorers saw enormous piles of camas roots on the Weippe Prairie, near today's Weippe, Idaho, and noted that they were "round and much like an onion which they call quamash...of this they make bread & Supe." Frederick Pursh recognized that the camas was new to science, as Lewis had suspected when he collected the plant on the day that the expedition set out to cross the Clearwater and Bitterroot Mountains. Pursh named it *Phalangium quamash*. His generic name *Phalangium* was soon supplanted by *Camassia*, a name proposed by John Lindley, derived from the English common name, producing the name by which we know it today, *Camassia quamash*. "This plant," Pursh wrote, "is known among the natives by the name *Quamash*, and the bulbs are carefully collected by them and baked between hot stones, when they assume the appearance of baked pears, and are of an agreeable sweet taste. They form a great part of their winter stores. Though an agreeable food to Governor Lewis's party, they occasioned bowel complaints if eaten in any quantity." Had Lewis read Pursh's description he probably would have considered "bowel complaints" an understatement. Lewis became extremely

Camassia quamash

JAMES L. REVEAL

sick after eating the root in the Nez Perce encampment. Later, he granted that "this root is palleatable" but added that it "disagrees with me in every shape I have ever used it."[7]

The roots should be harvested while the plants are in bloom to be able to distinguish them from those of the poisonous death camases (*Toxicoscordion venenosum* var. *gramineum* and *Toxicoscordion paniculatum*), for these plants grow in the same area and the bulbs are similar. On June 11, Lewis described the camas at great length, suggesting that he was fully aware that it was a plant new to science. Moulton credits Lewis's description as "an outstanding documentation of camas ethnobotany."[8]

POACEAE (GRASS FAMILY)

Collected near Camp Chopunnish, Kamiah, Idaho County, Idaho, on June 10, 1806

CANBY'S BLUEGRASS, *POA CANBYI* (SCRIBN.) HOWELL
BLUEBUNCH WHEATGRASS, *PSEUDOROEGNERIA SPICATA* (PURSH) A. LÖVE
IDAHO FESCUE, *FESTUCA IDAHOENSIS* ELMER

The explorers left Camp Chopunnish on the morning of June 10, 1806, and reached their old camp at the east end

Poa canbyi

JAMES L. REVEAL

of the Weippe Prairie the following day.[9] Lewis wrote in his journal that "the country through which we passed is extreemly fertile and generally free of stone, is well timbered with several species of fir, long leafed pine and larch."[10] He briefly described several species of shrubs and herbs and collected a few more. He did not mention that he saw any grasses along the way, yet he added three species to his traveling herbarium between today's Kamiah and Weippe Prairie, Idaho. These included the plant that we know today as Canby's bluegrass (*Poa canbyi*). It was (according to Frederick Pursh's copy of Lewis's note) the "most common grass through the plains of Columbia & near the Kooskooskee R. Jun: 10th 1806."[11] Pursh believed Lewis's specimen represented a new plant and named it *Aira brevifolia*. He named another grass collected the same day *Festuca spicata*; we know it now as bluebunch wheatgrass,

Pseudoroegneria spicata. He failed to recognize that the third grass, Idaho fescue (*Festuca idahoensis*), was new to science. In fact, this grass would go unnamed until 1903. Idaho fescue is now widely cultivated as a decorative bunchgrass, especially in arid regions of the West. Idaho fescue, Canby's bluegrass, and bluebunch wheatgrass are all important range and forage grasses. All three may still be seen growing on hillsides a few miles north of Kamiah.[12]

Pseudoroegneria spicata

JAMES L. REVEAL

Festuca idahoensis

JAMES L. REVEAL

ORCHIDACEAE (ORCHID FAMILY)

Western fairy-slipper collected on Hungery Creek, Lolo Trail, Idaho County, Idaho, June 16, 1806; Mountain lady's-slipper mentioned on June 30, 1806, along Lolo Creek in Missoula County, Montana. Other orchids may have been seen but were not collected

WESTERN FAIRY-SLIPPER, CALYPSO BULBOSA L. VAR. OCCIDENTALIS SALISB.
SPOTTED CORAL-ROOT, CORALLORHIZA MACULATA RAF.
MOUNTAIN LADY'S-SLIPPER, CYPRIPEDIUM MONTANUM DOUGLAS
GREEN-LEAF RATTLESNAKE PLANTAIN, GOODYERA OBLONGIFOLIA RAF.
WHITE REIN-ORCHID, PLATANTHERA DILATATA (PURSH) HOOK.
HOODED LADIES'-TRESSES, SPIRANTHES ROMANZOFFIANA CHAM.

Orchids are among the most attractive and prized of all plants. The word is derived the Latin *orchis* (and indirectly from the same Greek word) and means "testicle," for the shape of the pseudobulb of some species. With nearly 800 genera and perhaps 19,500 species, the orchid family is second only to the aster family (Asteraceae) in numbers. Lewis and Clark probably saw several species of orchids, but they mentioned only two and collected only one.

Lewis gathered the western fairy-slipper (*Calypso bulbosa*

var. *occidentalis*) on the Lolo Trail during his return journey. It ranges from southern Alaska to California and east to northern Idaho. The plant requires decaying leaf litter and the shade of cool forests to thrive, as do many other orchids. In the fall a corm (a short, bulblike underground stem) gives off a single leaf. This persists through the winter, and in early spring an erect shoot appears, topped by a small, magenta, spotted flower characterized by a slightly hairy bulbous lower petal or "lip" (explaining the species name, *bulbosa*). The generic name

153

Calypso was that of a secretive sea nymph in Greek mythology. Appropriately, the name means "hidden," for these orchids are secretive little plants.[13]

Lewis probably also saw the spotted coral-root, *Corallorhiza maculata* Raf., the most common species of coral-root in the West, while he was crossing Idaho and Montana. There are related species in the forests of Virginia, and this may explain why he did not collect the western plant. Coral-roots are saprophytic plants that grow in mixed conifer forests. They obtain their nutrients by attaching their bright red roots (whence their name) to those of other plants. The plants are reddish brown because their vestigial, scalelike leaves lack chlorophyll.[14]

We know that Lewis saw the mountain lady's-slipper (*Cypripedium montanum*), for he noted in his journal "I also met with the plant in blume which is sometimes called the lady's slipper or mockerson flower." Several days later, on July 2, while the party was camped at Travelers' Rest, Clark wrote, "Capt L. showed me a plant in blume which is Sometimes called the ladies Slipper or Mockerson flower. It is in shape and appearance like ours only that the corolla white marked with Small veigns of pale red longitudinally on the inner Side, and much Smaller."[15] The mountain lady's-slipper is rare today, and it will not survive transplantation from the wild. Lewis apparently thought that he had seen the same plant in Virginia, for he did not collect the western plant. David Douglas rediscovered the mountain lady's-slipper in the mid-1820s, and it was described in 1840.

Lewis might also have seen the green-leaf rattlesnake plantain (*Goodyera oblongifolia*), named for the British botanist John Goodyer (1592-1694). Its range extends from

Calypso bulbosa var. occidentalis

A. SCOTT EARLE

Cypripedium montanum

JAMES L. REVEAL

the subarctic regions of the Northern Hemisphere to the tropics—a remarkable distribution for any plant, and especially for an orchid. The western plant is related to the dwarf rattlesnake plantain (*Goodyera repens*) that Lewis would have known from the forests of Virginia. Both have two white-striped, flat green leaves that lie close to the ground. Their markings are thought to resemble those of a rattlesnake, making them easy to identify—a good thing, because the tiny flowers do not amount to much.

Bog- or rein-orchids (*Platanthera* spp.) are common along slow-moving streams and in moist meadows in the mountains of Idaho and Montana. The white bog orchid, *Platanthera dilatata* (listed as *Habenaria* in older guidebooks), is a plant that Lewis and the others probably saw frequently in moist settings along the expedition's route across the Lolo Pass and west of Lewis and Clark Pass.[16] There are three varieties, distinguished by differences in the

Corallorhiza maculata

A. SCOTT EARLE

Platanthera dilatata

A. SCOTT EARLE

Spiranthes romanzoffiana

A. SCOTT EARLE

appearance of the small greenish white flowers clustered at regular intervals along the thick spikelike stem.

Hooded ladies'-tresses, *Spiranthes romanzoffiana*, is not uncommon either, although Lewis did not mention this orchid in his journal. It is easily identified, for each of its tightly clustered white flowers is slightly offset from the one above and below along the plant's stem, giving the inflorescence a spiral appearance (*Spiranthes* means "spiral flowers").[17]

CORNACEAE (DOGWOOD FAMILY)

Collected on the Lolo Trail, June 16, 1806

BUNCHBERRY, *CORNUS CANADENSIS* L.

Three spring-blooming dogwoods grow along the western part of the Lewis and Clark Trail. The explorers collected one species and frequently mentioned another one, the red-osier dogwood (*Cornus sericea*), but they did not collect it (see p. 56). The third western species, *Cornus nuttallii*, is a tree that occurs along the coast in the Cascade Range and in northern Idaho. It looks so much like the eastern flowering dogwood, *Cornus florida*, that Lewis—who must have seen it in the spring of 1806—would have had no reason to collect it.[18] He did, however collect the bunchberry, *Cornus canadensis*, then in flower, during the party's first return attempt to cross the Clearwater and Bitterroot mountains. The bunchberry grows

Cornus canadensis

JAMES L. REVEAL

Cornus canadensis

JAMES L. REVEAL

in moist places across the present United States from the Rocky Mountains east to Labrador, and as far south as Virginia (where it is rare). If Lewis did not know the plant from the East, some of his men might well have been acquainted with it, so it is a bit surprising that he collected it.

The bunchberry is anomalous, for it is the only native herbaceous (nonwoody) member of the dogwood family that grows along the Lewis and Clark Trail; the other Cornaceae are all shrubs and trees. It is a low plant that bears five or six opposing, stemless leaves. These arise from the main stem so closely together as to resemble a whorl. The leaves

are thick and heavily veined. Above these there is what looks like a four-petaled white flower borne on a short stem. Look closely, however, and you will see that, like others in the family, the "petals" are actually bracts—modified leaves—that surround a cluster of tiny flowers. The ovaries of these flowers eventually become rich red drupes (berries) gathered together into a bunch—hence the plant's common name. Birds eat the berries, but they are considered inedible for humans. The bunchberry is an attractive plant in any season, and its white "flowers" and red berries make it a fine ornamental plant for shady gardens.

BRASSICACEAE (MUSTARD FAMILY)

Collected on the "Kooskookee" (Clearwater) River, Camp Chopunnish, Kamiah, Idaho County, Idaho, on June 1, 1806

PURSH'S WALLFLOWER, *ERYSIMUM CAPITATUM* DOUGLAS EX HOOK. VAR. *PURSHII* (DURAND) ROLLINS

Wallflowers are one of the more showy of the wild crucifers. Those found in our mountains are erect plants, usually standing less than two feet tall. They have bright yellow to orange four-petaled flowers that together form a loose inflorescence. In common with many other members of the family, the flowers and their resulting thin podlike fruit (siliques) are often seen on the plant at the same time. It is easy to recognize wallflowers, but further classification is difficult at the species and varietal levels. The form and growth patterns of the siliques are important for identification. Pursh's wallflower, *Erysimum capitatum* var. *purshii*, grows in Idaho's mountains, appearing in late spring. The plant prefers rocky ground and talus slopes and it grows almost to tree line. Lewis did not take note of the plant in his journal, but

Erysimum capitatum

A. SCOTT EARLE

someone collected it; possibly another member of the expedition found the plant on the rocky slopes above the Clearwater River.

Erysimum capitatum (of which Pursh's wallflower is one of several varieties) grows in most of western North America, from Alaska to central Mexico. The species has long been confused with the western wallflower, *Erysimum asperum*, a closely related Great Plains plant, and both names have been used more or less interchangeably for our mountain plant. It is not clear whether Pursh made use of the Lewis and Clark specimen, although he classified it in his *Flora* as *Erysimum lanceolatum*, the name of an Old World species. He noted (incorrectly) only that it grew on "the banks of the Missouri" and (correctly) that it flowered in June.[19]

GENTIANACEAE (GENTIAN FAMILY)

Collected on the Weippe Prairie, Clearwater County, Idaho, on June 14, 1806

CLUSTERED ELKWEED, *FRASERA FASTIGIATA* (PURSH) A. HELLER

The snow in the mountains was finally melting and the men of the expedition were getting ready to depart for home. Lewis was engaged in some last-minute botanizing on the Weippe Prairie, and the clustered elkweed was one

of the plants that he collected there. Pursh later copied Lewis's original note describing a plant that grew "In moist & wet places On the Squamash flats.—Jun: 14th 1806." Lewis didn't mention the clustered elkweed in his journal, but it would have been in full flower at the time. Clearly, he prepared the specimen carefully, because Pursh wrote that the flowers were blue—evidence that the plant dried quickly and the flowers kept their color.

The clustered elkweed is a tall, single-stemmed plant whose broad leaves form whorls of three or four at intervals as they ascend the stem. Many four-petaled blue flowers are gathered into a dense inflorescence at the top of the stem, explaining both its common and scientific names

Frasera fastigata

JAMES L. REVEAL

(*fastigata*, from the Latin, means "gathered together" or "bundled").[20] When Pursh saw the intact specimen, he realized that it was another plant new to science. Pursh assigned the clustered elkweed to the genus *Swertia*. It was later transferred to *Frasera* while retaining his species name.[21] The plant has a fairly restricted distribution; it is found only in the Blue Mountains of Washington and Oregon, and in northern Idaho, where Lewis discovered it.[22]

LILIACEAE (LILY FAMILY)

Collected on the "Kooskooske" (Clearwater) River, Camp Chopunnish, Kamiah, Idaho County, Idaho, May 17, 1806

ELEGANT MARIPOSA LILY, CALOCHORTUS ELEGANS

"A small bulb of a pleasant flavour, eat by the natives—On the Kooskooske.—May 17th 1806"; so reads Frederick

Calochortus elegans

JAMES L. REVEAL

Pursh's note, undoubtedly a paraphrase of Lewis's description, on the specimen sheet of this little flower. Pursh knew that he was dealing with a new plant when he saw the dried specimen. He must have thought carefully about a generic name, for he was unable to fit it into an existing genus and his name would be a new one. He derived it from two Greek words: *calo* ("beautiful") and *chortus* ("grass"). The name that he coined, *Calochortus elegans*, was well chosen, for this and other mariposa lilies are lovely plants.[23] Most bear one to several three-petaled flowers. The wide petals resemble butterfly wings, explaining the common name "mariposa lily," derived from the Spanish word for butterfly. Sixty or so species have since been identified; all are plants of the American West, occurring from British Columbia to Guatemala. They are usually found growing on dry ground. Mariposa lilies have many other common names: butterfly lilies, Mormon tulips, cat's ears, and sego lilies.

The last of these is often applied to a number of Rocky Mountain mariposa lilies, but it is a term that—strictly applied—should only refer to *Calochortus nuttallii*, the Utah state flower. The plant was a good choice as the state flower, for early Mormon settlers reputedly managed to stay alive in time of famine by eating sego lily bulbs. If so, they had to work hard for their sustenance, for the bulbs are small and lie deeper in the ground than the plants' size would suggest. And the ground is where the bulbs of all mariposa lilies should remain: They do not do well when transplanted into gardens. One description of the genus mentions that "despite the quantities of bulbs which have been dug in the wild and marketed during the last century, not a single species can be said to have been established in cultivation successfully."[24] Mariposa lilies, like many of our native wildflowers, should be admired and enjoyed where they grow.

ASTERACEAE (ASTER FAMILY)

Collected at Camp Chopunnish, Kamiah, Idaho County, Idaho, May 20, 1806

WOOLLY AMERICAN YARROW, *ACHILLEA MILLEFOLIUM* L. VAR. *LANULOSUM* (NUTT.) PIPER

Lewis collected the two yarrow specimens in the Lewis and Clark Herbarium at the "Cape [camp] on Kooskooske May 20th. 1806." The yarrow—Lewis apparently knew it as a "tansy"—is a circumboreal plant; it grows on all of the continents in the Northern Hemisphere. It has always been a favorite of herbalists, taking its scientific name from the Homeric hero Achilles, who used it topically to treat wounds during the Trojan War. The plant has a medicinal odor, explaining why it has been used to treat wounds, although there is no scientific evidence to suggest that it has any therapeutic value. Quite possibly Lewis's interest in the plant was derived from its reputed medicinal value, an interest acquired from his mother, Lucy Lewis Marks, who was well known in the Virginia Piedmont as an herbalist.[25]

The yarrow that grows in the West is a ubiquitous plant that grows at all elevations at least as high as tree line. It appears in early summer and blooms

Achillea millefolium var. *lanulosum*

A. SCOTT EARLE

Achillea millefolium var. *lanulosum*

JAMES L. REVEAL

well into the fall. While often found in disturbed areas and sometimes considered a weed, it is not a notably aggressive plant. On first encounter, because of its superficial resemblance to an umbellifer, one might think that it is a member of the parsley family (Apiaceae). However, a closer look reveals that its tiny "flowers" are made up of many tinier, individual flowers arranged in a head typical of the aster family (Asteraceae). The plant's species name, *millefolium*, literally means "a thousand leaves" in Latin, referring to its frilly foliage.

ANTIRRHINACEAE (FIGWORT FAMILY)

Penstemon wilcoxii *collected near Camp Chopunnish, Kamiah, Idaho County, Idaho, on May 20, 1806;*
Penstemon fruticosus *on the Lolo Trail in Idaho County or Clearwater County, Idaho, on June 15, 1806*

WILCOX'S PENSTEMON, *PENSTEMON WILCOXII* RYDB.
SHRUBBY PENSTEMON, *PENSTEMON FRUTICOSUS* (PURSH) GREENE

Although species of *Penstemon* grow in eastern North America, it is a genus that really comes into its own in the West. In the Pacific Northwest alone, there are some eighty species of *Penstemon*, and in the Intermountain West just to the south there are over a hundred species.[26] They are common from the Columbia River Gorge to the eastern foothills of the Rocky Mountains in Montana, flowering from late spring well into the summer. Penstemons are among our most beautiful wildflowers, and it must have pleased the explorers to see them blooming along their route.

Wilcox's penstemon was the first one that Lewis collected. One may identify the plant by its serrated leaves and the small stemlets, or pedicels, that arise on each side of the main stem above the plant's paired opposing leaves. The pedicels bear small clusters of bright purple flowers—a distinguishing feature, for more commonly penstemons have

Penstemon wilcoxii

A. SCOTT EARLE

Penstemon wilcoxii

JAMES L. REVEAL

Penstemon fruticosus

JAMES L. REVEAL

Penstemon fruticosus

A. SCOTT EARLE

whorled flower clusters (verticillasters) surrounding the main stem. Wilcox's penstemon is common on the dry foothills above the Clearwater River. It grows mainly in the tricorner area of Idaho, Oregon, and Washington, and eastward to northwestern Montana. Frederick Pursh did not recognize it as a new plant. His note on the specimen sheet, presumably copied from Lewis, says only that the plant was found while the expedition was camped on the "Kooskoosky" at Camp Chopunnish.[27]

Lewis gathered his specimen of the shrubby penstemon, *Penstemon fruticosus*, along the Lolo Trail, possibly on Eldorado Creek. The species is often found on rocky slopes growing mostly in open places. It is one of the most attractive of our western penstemons. The plant is unusual in that it grows as a low evergreen shrub (*fruticosus* means "shrubby" in Latin) from a woody base. Its irregular but bilaterally symmetrical flowers (common to the genus) are large—sometimes more than two inches long—and are a rich, light purple color with darker markings. The shrubby penstemon is found mostly in the Pacific Northwest, but it ranges east to Montana and Wyoming. It, like many penstemons, may hybridize with other species—a tendency that suggests to botanists that *Penstemon* is a genus that is still actively evolving. Frederick Pursh described this plant in 1813 and gave it the name *Gerardia fruticosa*. It is also one of the fourteen American plants illustrated in Pursh's *Flora*.[28]

RANUNCULACEAE (BUTTERCUP FAMILY)
Collected in the vicinity of Camp Chopunnish, Kamiah, Idaho County, Idaho, on May 27, 1806
SUGARBOWL, *CLEMATIS HIRSUTISSIMA* PURSH

The sugarbowl is a striking plant both for its color and its shape, and this is probably the reason it has so many common names: hairy clematis, vase flower, leather flower, lion's beard, Douglas's clematis, and so on. There should never be

161

Clematis hirsutissima

JAMES L. REVEAL

any problem identifying the plant; its nodding, hairy, purple, urn-shaped flower and its frilly, three-part leaves are unmistakable. It is fairly restricted geographically, found in the eastern parts of British Columbia, in Washington and Oregon, and eastward to Montana and Wyoming, and south in the Rocky Mountains to Colorado.

Lewis's specimen of this plant in the Lewis and Clark Herbarium has no "ticket" (a written label identifying the collector, the name of the plant, and the date and place of collection), but information about it is included in Frederick

Pursh's description of this new species in his *Flora* of 1813. Pursh noted that it is one "of the most common plants of the plains of the Columbia."[29] His description of its distribution and frequency of occurrence is a bit hyperbolic, although occasionally it does grow in fairly large numbers in moist open areas, soon after snowmelt.

Lewis probably saw two other purple clematises during his early summer crossing of the Bitterroots, although they are not among the specimens the expedition returned: the cut-leaf western blue virgin's bower, *Clematis occidentalis* var. *grosseserrata*, and the Columbian virgin's bower, *Clematis columbiana*. The two species are often confused, although their three-parted leaves differ (the leaflets of the former are serrated). Both occur along the Lewis and Clark Trail in mountains of the Northwest, and both are vining plants with moderately large flowers that consist of four thin, bright purple sepals that stand out in the somber woods and on the talus slopes where they grow.

The western virgin's bower (*Clematis ligusticifolia*), also called the white virgin's bower, is the most common western species of clematis that Lewis and Clark's would have seen. The small, unisexual flowers (the individual flowers are either male or female but not both) are white to cream colored, and the climbing plants often climb over other shrubs, fences, and even buildings. The species was used medicinally by Native Americans to treat various ailments.

Rhamnaceae (Buckthorn Family)

Collected on the "Kooskooskee" (Clearwater) River, Camp Chopunnish, Kamiah, Idaho County, Idaho, May 29, 1806

Cascara, *Frangula purshiana* (DC.) J. C. Cooper

Cascara is an attractive tall shrub (or small tree) characterized by silvery bark and deep green, ovate leaves. Parallel veins run laterally from the center of the leaves and are so prominent that the leaves almost look ridged. Clusters of tiny, five-petaled flowers develop adjacent to the leaf stems and mature into blue berries that are said to be edible. (Given the tree's cathartic properties, the berries are not ones that we would care to evaluate for edibility.) It is an attractive tree and might well fit into a landscaping plan as an ornamental.

Lewis collected two specimens of cascara. His field note on one—copied by Pursh—noted correctly that the shrub was "appierently a species of Rhamnus. About 12 feet high, in Clumps. fruit a 5-valved purple berry which the natives eat & esteen highly; the berry depressed globous.—On the waters of the Kooskooskee May. 29th 1806."

Interestingly, neither Pursh nor Lewis mentioned that the plant's usefulness extended beyond its edible berry. The tree's bark contains a cathartic known medically as Cascara sagrada (Spanish for "sacred bark") a name reputedly bestowed by a Spanish priest who learned of its effectiveness from Indians in California. The bark has a relatively gentle laxative property that does not produce the gripes that can occur with many other laxatives. Cascara (also known as false buckthorn, Pursh's buckthorn, and chittam bark) is often used today as the active ingredient in proprietary preparations and is grown commercially for that purpose. Apparently the captains were unaware of the bark's laxative action, and it was not used in traditional medicine until many decades later. It was not listed in either the U.S. Pharmacopeia or the National Formulary until the end of the nineteenth century.[30] The trees were harvested extensively for their bark in the past, so they are not as common today as they once were.

The cascara plant was known until recently as *Rhamnus*

Frangula purshiana

JAMES L. REVEAL

purshiana. Frederick Pursh recognized it as a member of the buckthorn family when he described it as a plant that was new to science; he named it *Rhamnus alnifolius*.[31] However, that name was already in use for a closely related tree. Because of this, the French botanist Augustin Pyramus de Candolle proposed a new name for Lewis's plant. The name that he chose, *Rhamnus purshiana*, honored Frederick Pursh.

The words *rhamnus* and *frangula*—both from the Latin—are names of Old World buckthorns. The bark of several related trees that grow in the Old World have always been known to have a cathartic effect, but they are not as gentle when used for that purpose as our tree.

ROSACEAE (ROSE FAMILY)

Collected on the "Kooskooskee" (Clearwater) River, Camp Chopunnish, Kamiah, Idaho County, Idaho, May 29, 1806

HILLSIDE OCEANSPRAY, *HOLODISCUS DISCOLOR* (PURSH) MAXIM.

Hillside oceanspray, *Holodiscus discolor*, is not difficult to identify, at least when the plant is in flower. Its ovate leaves are two to three inches long and coarsely lobed with

Holodiscus discolor

prominent veins. The leaves are green on top and a silvery gray beneath. When it is flowering, tightly compacted sprays of tiny, white-to-cream-colored flowers help to distinguish the plant. *Holodiscus* shrubs seldom grow to be more than eight feet high. Hillside oceanspray grows from British Columbia to southern California and as far east as western Montana.

It is one of the more attractive spring-blooming shrubs of the American West; it is regularly seen growing in ornamental gardens. Massed, foamy flower clusters give the plant its common name "oceanspray." There are five species in the genus, and these range from western North America to northern South America. Two species grow in the Pacific Northwest, and Lewis found one of them.[32]

Frederick Pursh recognized that the plant Lewis had collected along the Clearwater River near Kamiah, Idaho, represented a plant new to science. He named it *Spiraea discolor*. Its genus name was changed in 1879 when the Russian botanist and explorer Carl Johann Maximowicz (1827-1891) saw specimens of oceanspray in the garden in St. Petersburg; he established a new genus, *Holodiscus*, for Pursh's *Spiraea discolor*.[33] Lewis also seemed to recognize that oceanspray was a new shrub when he collected it. In his journal he mentioned it as a plant similar to, but different from ninebark (*Physocarpus* spp.), a rather similar plant in the rose family that he knew in the East.[34]

ROSACEAE (ROSE FAMILY)

Collected on the "Kooskoosky" (Clearwater) River, Camp Chopunnish, Kamiah, Idaho County, Idaho, May 28, 1806

BLACK CHOKECHERRY, *PRUNUS VIRGINIANA* L. VAR. *MELANOCARPA* (A. NELSON) SARG.

Chokecherries are easy to identify by their long sprays of small white flowers when they are blooming, and by their clustered dark red berries when they are in fruit. Their bark has the horizontal markings typical of cherry trees in general.

Toothed ovate or oblong leaves, pointed at the end, help to identify them. Several species of wild cherries grow all along the Lewis and Clark Trail. Chokecherries, especially, grow in great numbers and at all elevations in Idaho and Montana,

Prunus virginiana **var.** *melanocarpa*

JAMES L. REVEAL

Prunus virginiana **var.** *melanocarpa*

JAMES L. REVEAL

Berries borne by the western plant, *Prunus virginiana* var. *melanocarpa*, are such a deep red color that they often look black (*melanocarpa* means "black fruit"), whereas those of the eastern variety are a brighter red. At the higher elevations of the Lolo Trail black chokecherry seldom grows to be more than six feet tall, and it starts to flower while it is only a foot or two high. Elsewhere in the West, the plant can grow twenty feet or more in height. Both varieties of chokecherries have been characterized as "mostly worthful shrubs," whose flowers are attractive and whose fruit is alluring to birds—good enough reasons to find a place for them as ornamentals.[35]

Frederick Pursh copied Lewis's field note onto a specimen sheet. It reads "Prunus Choak or Pidgeon Cherry On the waters of Kooskoosky May 29th 1806." It is hard to guess today what the specimen looked like when it arrived in Philadelphia. It now consists only of a twig and a few leaves. Probably Pursh did not have enough material to see what he was dealing with even when it was fresh, so he had no reason to mention Lewis's specimen in the *Flora*. Furthermore, the eastern chokecherry, *Prunus virginiana*, had been described decades earlier. Given the poor quality of the specimen, we can hardly blame him for not recognizing that the black chokecherry, var. *melanocarpa*, was a new variety.

and one will often see fruit-laden trees along the Lewis and Clark Trail in late summer and early fall. Look for them on the western side of the Lemhi Pass in Idaho, and along the Lolo Trail in Idaho and Montana.

Anyone who has spent a childhood in the country knows that the plant is well named. Chokecherries have a sour-bitter-sweet taste, and yet people children especially—and animals consume great numbers. The western chokecherries at Camp Chopunnish were blooming when Lewis gathered his specimen, but the men would have seen the plants and eaten their fruit the previous summer in Idaho and Montana.

165

ROSACEAE (ROSE FAMILY)

Collected on the "Kooskooskee" (Clearwater) River, Camp Chopunnish, Kamiah, Idaho County, Idaho, May 29, 1806

BITTER CHERRY, *PRUNUS EMARGINATA* (DOUGLAS EX HOOK.) WALP.

The men of the expedition had seen fruiting shrubs and trees all across the country, and they took special note of several, including those presented in this chapter as well as the American plum, *Prunus americana*, and the bitter cherry, *Prunus pensylvanica* (see pp. 24, 216). Lewis may well have collected other specimens of *Prunus* (the word is Latin for "plum") as the party ascended the Missouri between Fort Mandan and the Great Falls of the Missouri but, if he did, they were lost with the flooding of their cache in the spring of 1806. Frederick Pursh did not include any of Lewis's specimens of *Prunus* in his *Flora* of 1813. He did not recognize *Prunus emarginata*—a species found mostly west of the Rocky Mountains—as a new species. He obviously examined it, for a note on the specimen (copied from Lewis's description) in his Germanic hand says "Prunus A Smaller Shrub than the Choak cherry, the natives count it a good Fruit." The fruit is in fact edible but smaller and very bitter.[36]

Our native plums and cherries tend to grow along waterways and near moist places as high shrubs or small trees. Their bark is similar to their cultivated relatives—mostly dark and smooth, with small horizontal markings and deep red twigs. Wild cherries may be confused with other shrubs in the rose family, most noticeably the western serviceberry, *Amelanchier alnifolia* (see p. 120). Wild cherry leaves are different, however, for they are broadly oval and serrated over their entire margin, whereas those of the serviceberry are more rounded, have no point, and are usually serrated only on the distal portion of the leaf. The leaves of *Prunus emarginata* are, like those of the chokecherry, oval and serrated over their entire margin, although they are not pointed. Their flowers, and later the fruits, are clustered on the ends of small branching twigs. Bitter cherry grows from southern British Columbia southward through Washington, Idaho, and western Montana to northwestern Mexico.

Prunus emarginata

Prunus emarginata

Onagraceae (Evening Primrose Family)

Collected on the "Kooskooskee" (Clearwater) River, Camp Chopunnish, Kamiah, Idaho County, June 1, 1806

Ragged robin, *Clarkia pulchella* Pursh

The expedition was at the site of present Kooskia, Idaho, where the south and middle forks of the Clearwater River join at the site of an Indian village that had been there for centuries. Meriwether Lewis wrote in his journal on June 1, 1806: "I met with a singular plant today in blume of which I preserved a specemine; it grows on the steep sides of the fertile hills near this place." He went on to describe the plant that we know today as the ragged robin (and by many other names as well, including pinkfairies, deerhorn, and elkhorns) in terms that showed that he possessed a knowledge of botany that far exceeded that of the average layman: "the radix is fibrous …the leaf is sissile, scattered thinly, nearly linear tho somewhat widest in he middle, two inches in length, absolutely entire, villose, obtusely pointed and of an ordinary green …the calyx is a one flowered spathe. the corolla superior consists of four pale purple petals which are tripartite, the central lobe largest and all terminate obtusely."[37] His description went on to describe the plant precisely, displaying observational and descriptive abilities that one has to envy.

Frederick Pursh, on examining Lewis's specimen, recognized it as a plant new to science—as Lewis undoubtedly had suspected—and described it in his *Flora* as "A beautifull herbaceous plant from the Kooskooskee [Clearwater] & Clarks [Bitterroot] R." On the opposite page he included an engraving of the plant. The illustration is far more extensive than the specimen in the Lewis and Clark Herbarium,

suggesting that there may have been a better specimen originally and that Pursh may have dismembered it for his own purposes. He named the plant *Clarckia pulchella*,

Clarkia pulchella

probably believing that Lewis had been adequately honored by the many other plants that bore his name in both generic and specific epithets, and thinking that Clark, too, deserved recognition. One must wholeheartedly agree and be thankful that Pursh chose such a lovely little plant for the purpose.[38]

167

LAMIACEAE (MINT FAMILY)

Collected on the "Kooskooskee" (Clearwater) River, Camp Chopunnish, Kamiah, Idaho County, Idaho, June 5, 1805

NARROW-LEAF SKULLCAP, *SCUTELLARIA ANGUSTIFOLIA* PURSH

The narrow-leaf skullcap is not a particularly conspicuous plant, but Meriwether Lewis, stuck in Camp Chopunnish while waiting for the snow to melt, apparently collected every flowering plant that he saw. This little plant and other members of the genus *Scutellaria* take their common name "skullcap" from a fancied resemblance of the calyx (the cup that contains the corolla and the generative parts of the flower) to a helmet with the visor raised. The odd shape of the calyx is also responsible for the generic name *Scutellaria*, a word that was derived from the Latin word *scutella*, meaning "little tray" or "saucer," terms that refer to the spur-like appendage on the upper part of the calyx (most noticeable in the fruiting plant). While the skullcap that Lewis collected is indigenous to the Pacific

Scutellaria angustifolia

A. SCOTT EARLE

Northwest, other species are found throughout the Northern Hemisphere (there are an estimated 350 *Scutellaria* species worldwide, of which more than 100 are found in the New World).

Frederick Pursh recognized Lewis's specimen as a new species and gave it the same species name *angustifolia* ("narrow-leaved"), which it has today. Pursh noted only that it was found "on the river Kooskoosky" and that he had examined the dried specimen "*in Herb. Lewis.*"[39] Our plant, var. *angustifolia*, is restricted to portions of southern British Columbia, eastern Washington, northern Oregon, and central Idaho. A closely related, somewhat smaller-flowered, but otherwise similar species, *Scutellaria antirrhinoides*, is found a bit farther to the south, and the two may intergrade.[40]

CRASSULACEAE (STONECROP FAMILY)

Collected on the "Kooskooskee" (Clearwater) River, Camp Chopunnish, Idaho County, Idaho, June 5, 1806, and in the valley of "Clarks River" (Bitterroot River) near Travelers' Rest, Missoula County, Montana, July 1, 1806

LANCE-LEAF STONECROP, *SEDUM LANCEOLATUM* TORR.

WORM-LEAF STONECROP, *SEDUM STENOPETALUM* PURSH

The sedums take the name "stonecrop" from related Old World plants, most notably the European houseleek, *Sempervivum tectorum*, an edible plant—"wall-pepper" is

another name—that grows on walls and roofs (*tectorum* is Latin for "of the roof"). The word *sedum* was probably derived from the Latin *sedes*, meaning "seat," from the ten-

Sedum lanceolatum

JAMES L. REVEAL

Sedum stenopetalum

JAMES L. REVEAL

dency of related plants such as the "hen and chickens" plant (*Sempervivum globiferum*)—to grow low and stay put. "Sedum" is used rather promiscuously for various Crassulaceae, but it should properly be restricted to the genus *Sedum* to which our two plants belong.[41]

As with many of the plants that Meriwether Lewis collected during the spring of 1806, the worm-leaf stonecrop was a plant new to science. Pursh appreciated this when he examined Lewis's dried collections, and he included them in his *Flora* when he established *Sedum stenopetalum* ("narrow-petaled"), the species name that it bears today. Pursh failed to recognize that there were two different species, although Lewis probably knew that when he collected the plants.[42] The two sedums are much alike. Both grow from low elevations almost to tree line. These attractive little plants are succulents, characterized by fleshy, pointed, closely arrayed leaves. They spread by means of an underground root system and from seed. Both of our sedums flower from late spring to early summer, depending on elevation, producing clusters of attractive bright yellow, five-petaled flowers. Although there are several morphological differences between the two species, the most obvious one is that the lance-leaved sedum sheds its leaves so that its stem is naked when the plant flowers. The worm-leaf species retains its leaves, at least from midstem upward. Later in the year one can see that the pointed fruit of *Sedum lanceolatum* stands upright, whereas that of *Sedum stenopetalum* protrudes outward at right angles to the stem. The fleshy young leaves of our plants, especially those of *Sedum stenopetalum*, are said to be edible and tasty when eaten in moderation.[43] Both *Sedum stenopetalum* and *Sedum lanceolatum* are western plants that are found along the Pacific coast east to the Rocky Mountains. Both occur along the Lewis and Clark Trail near Kamiah, Idaho, and Lolo, Montana.[44]

CAPRIFOLIACEAE (HONEYSUCKLE FAMILY)

Collected on the "Kooskooskee" (Clearwater) River, Camp Chopunnish, Kamiah, Idaho County, Idaho, June 5 and 16, 1806

TRUMPET HONEYSUCKLE, *LONICERA CILIOSA* (PURSH) DC.

Lonicera ciliosa

JAMES L. REVEAL

The trumpet honeysuckle's clustered flowers, with their long flaring petals, give them the trumpet shape reflected in their common name. The flowers are a bit irregular; two petals join to form an upper lip, and the other three form a lower lip with three distinct lobes. The vine's upper two opposing leaves are joined immediately below the flower cluster and the flower stems pass through the center of the leaves, a feature that—in company with the characteristic bright orange flowers—helps in identifying the plant. Lewis collected so many plants during the several weeks the expedition waited at Camp Chopunnish that his descriptions are often brief or lacking, yet Frederick Pursh managed quite well. The margins of the leaves of this plant, for example, are lined with very fine hairs or "cilia" (best seen by holding a leaf up to the light), a feature that Pursh noted and that inspired him to give the trumpet honeysuckle its scientific name, *Caprifolium ciliosa*.[45] Lewis apparently wanted to be sure that this attractive vine was represented in the expedition's collection, for he gathered it twice, first on June 5 and again on June 16, 1806, while the Corps of Discovery marked time in Camp Chopunnish.

FABACEAE (PEA FAMILY)

Lupinus argenteus collected on "Cokahlaishkit" (Blackfoot River) in the vicinity of Lewis and Clark Pass, July 7, 1806;
Lupinus sericeus collected on the "Kooskooskee" (Clearwater) River, Camp Chopunnish, Kamiah, Idaho County, Idaho, June 5,
1806, and on the Blackfoot River in the vicinity of Lewis and Clark Pass, July 7, 1806

SILVERY LUPINE, *LUPINUS ARGENTEUS* PURSH
SILKY LUPINE, *LUPINUS SERICEUS* PURSH

Apparently three of Lewis's collections of lupines reached Philadelphia (for the Great Plains species, *Lupinus pusillus*, see p. 62). The two shown here, the silky lupine and the silvery (or silver-stem) lupine, are common throughout much of the Pacific Northwest. Both species were new to science, and Frederick Pursh gave them scientific names that were derived from Latin words that mean exactly the same thing as their common names. Fortunately, Lewis and then Pursh could compare the two species directly and see that they differed significantly (when seen individually, however, the two

Lupinus argenteus

JAMES L. REVEAL

Lupinus sericeum

JAMES L. REVEAL

have been proposed; most are now considered synonyms. The problem for both botanist and amateur is twofold. First, lupines are adaptable plants, and their morphology and flower colors vary greatly depending on their surroundings. Second, lupines hybridize, and examples turn up that give evidence of complete intergradation between various species and varieties.[47]

That said, the two species that Lewis collected, and that Pursh described, can often be distinguished by the presence of hairs on the back of the two fused upper petals (the "banner") on *Lupinus sericeus* and the lack of hairs on *Lupinus argenteus*.[48]

It is strange that Lewis collected so few species of lupines along the Columbia and Snake rivers, especially since there are so many diverse species. Possibly he gathered some in 1805; if so, the specimens were lost.

Most lupines are lovely flowering plants, and many striking cultivars now hold a prominent place in ornamental gardens. It should be noted that lupines, and other legumes as well, form pealike seedpods, and that the seeds of many species are poisonous.

blue-flowered plants are enough alike that one might think that they were the same species). Identification of lupines is not always easy. The artist and designer Margaret Armstrong, who wrote and illustrated one of the first books on western wildflowers, noted that "There are so many western kinds of *Lupinus* that it is hopeless for the amateur to distinguish them."[46] Nothing has changed. Hundreds of species names

---

BORAGINACEAE (BORAGE FAMILY)

Collected on the "Kooskooskee" (Clearwater) River, Camp Chopunnish, Kamiah, Idaho County, Idaho, June 7, 1806

VARIABLE-LEAF PHACELIA, *PHACELIA HETEROPHYLLA* PURSH

There are three specimens of phacelia (or scorpion weeds) in the Lewis and Clark Herbarium, and two are of the variable-leaf phacelea that Meriwether Lewis collected at Camp

Chopunnish on June 7, 1806, while the other, the thread-leaf phacelia, was gathered a month and a half earlier at The Dalles in today's Oregon (see p. 124). Not surprisingly, when

Frederick Pursh examined these plants, he placed them in different (although related) genera, for they are so dissimilar in appearance that one may be surprised to learn that they belong to the same genus. He saw that these were new to science and assigned the thread-leaved plant to *Hydrophyllum* (reclassified in 1895 into its present genus) and the variable-leaved plant to *Phacelia*.[49]

The variable-leaf phacelia is a plant that favors dry ground. It grows all along the route that the expedition followed between the eastern end of the Columbia Gorge to Camp Chopunnish. It occurs in western Montana as well. The plant is upright, bristly, relatively colorless, and not particularly attractive. Its leaves vary, as its common and

Phacelia heterophylla

JAMES L. REVEAL

species names suggest, from simple lanceolate leaves to leaves that have one or two paired lobes at their base. The foliage is covered with fine hair, giving it a lusterless, gray appearance. Small bristly flowers are born in helicoid cymes (a fiddlehead configuration) located above the leaves at the top of the plant's stem.

The variable-leaf phacelia is so much like a closely related plant, the silver-leaf phacelia (*Phacelia hastata*), that the two are considered to be varieties of a single species by some botanists. It may be difficult to distinguish between the two plants. As the silver-leaf phacelia, *Phacelia hastata*, is commonly seen all along the Lewis and Clark Trail in the Pacific Northwest, Lewis may have considered them to be the same as well.

ROSACEAE (ROSE FAMILY)

Collected on the Weippe Prairie, Clearwater County, Idaho, June 12, 1806

PRAIRIE SMOKE, *GEUM TRIFLORUM* PURSH VAR. *CILIATUM* (PURSH) FASSETT

While many families of plants are well represented in the Pacific Northwest, few can match the rose family in number and diversity of members. These range from tiny ground-hugging plants to tall shrubs and even good-sized trees. *Geum triflorum*, also called "old man's whiskers," is one of the more unusual members of the family. It is easily identified by the nodding, vase-like shape of its flowers, its red color, and prominent recurved bracteoles (the sharp outward-turning little leaves that arise at the base of each of the flower's five petals).[50] Prairie smoke is a common spring flower. It grows from Canada south to California, Arizona, and New Mexico in the West and across the northern tier of the United States in the East. Given its unusual appearance, it is a plant that Meriwether Lewis would not have passed by. It often grows in large patches along stream banks and in damp, shady meadows. It can also be found occasionally on open, dry sagebrush slopes. Imagine what a field of fruiting plants, like the one shown here, would look like. It is not hard to see how the common names "prairie smoke" and "old man's whiskers" were derived.

Geum triflorum var. ciliatum

A. SCOTT EARLE

Geum triflorum var. ciliatum

A. SCOTT EARLE

Pursh described the species twice in his *Flora*. He gave the name *Geum ciliatum* (for the cilia, or fine hairs seen on leaf-margins) to the plant Lewis gathered on "the banks of the Kooskoosky." He described it a second time in the supplement to his *Flora*, calling it *Geum triflorum*, for the plant's characteristic three flowers to a stem. The second species had been found by botanist John Leigh Bradbury (1768-1823) "in upper Louisiana" (remembering that this then extended north nearly to the Canadian border), but he had not had an opportunity to describe the plant himself.[51]

Asteraceae (Aster Family)

Collected on the Weippe Prairie, Clearwater County, Idaho, June 12, 1806

Pineapple weed, *Matricaria discoidea* DC.

The pineapple weed is, as Frederick Pursh noted in his *Flora*, per Lewis's notes, "A small plant of an agreeable sweet scent; flowers yellow," that grew "On the banks of the Kooskoosky."[52] He gave it the name *Santolina suaveolens* (the species name means "agreeable," apparently in deference to Lewis's description). There is nothing in the expedition's journals about the plant, but it would seem that there was little reason for Lewis to collect the two specimens that he brought back other than for its "agreeable sweet scent." It is otherwise an unremarkable, rayless member of the aster family. The plant's smell, when crushed, is not the same as that of a pineapple, but it is close enough to explain its common name. The plant belongs to a small genus of perhaps thirty-five species that grow in the Northern Hemisphere. The generic name, *Matricaria*, was derived from the Latin

Matricaria discoidea

A. SCOTT EARLE

word *matrix*, used by herbalists to denote plants of presumed medical importance.[53] Ours is related to a similar European plant, *Matricaria recutita* (to which the name *Matricaria chamomilla* has long been misapplied), one of several related fragrant herbs that have been used for millennia to brew chamomile tea—a fragrant infusion with supposed calmative properties. The pineapple weed deserves its appellation, for it is a common weed—although a relatively innocuous one—that grows in disturbed places, along roadsides, and as an unwanted garden guest.

POLYGONACEAE (BUCKWHEAT FAMILY)

Collected at "Quamash Flats," in the vicinity of Weippe Prairie, Clearwater County, Idaho, June 12, 1806

AMERICAN BISTORT, *POLYGONUM BISTORTOIDES* PURSH

Polygonum bistortoides

JAMES L. REVEAL

Polygonum bistortoides growing in old Indian travois grooves at summit of Lewis and Clark Pass

A. SCOTT EARLE

The expedition was stalled. They had moved up to Weippe Prairie from Camp Chopunnish and were still waiting for the snow to melt in the nearby Clearwater Mountains. In three days they would make their abortive attempt to cross the more eastern and even higher Bitterroot Mountains, but for now Lewis had time to look for plants. On June 12, he added the American bistort to his collection. Frederick Pursh knew the Eurasian bistort, *Polygonum bistorta*, and saw that Lewis's plant resembled it, so he gave it a species name *bistortoides*, a term that means "like the bistort."[54] His distinction between the Old World bistort and the one that Lewis collected was sound and his name, *bistortoides*, is in current use although some botanists have suggested the bistorts ought to be assigned to their own genus, *Bistorta*.

The American bistort grows in wet meadows and along streams at montane to subalpine elevations in western North America—essentially, it is a mountain plant. Like its Eurasian relative, the American bistort has a large root all out of proportion to its slender stem and sparse foliage. The name "bistort" was derived from the Old World plant's large and twisted root (Latin *bis*, for "twice," and *torta*, for "twisted"). The twisted root is also presumably the source of the plant's other common name, "snakeweed."

It is an interesting plant. At the elevations where the American bistort is found, growth periods are short, and to

174

get a jump-start in the spring it relies on the energy stored in its large root system. Bistort blooms in the spring, although its "spring" depends on conditions and not on calendar dates. It often blooms in prodigious numbers well into August at tree line and even higher in the company of paintbrushes and other subalpine flowers. Native Americans ate both the roots and the young plants, deer browse on the foliage, and bears dig up the meadows searching for roots.

ONAGRACEAE (EVENING PRIMROSE FAMILY)
Collected on "Squamash Flats" (Weippe Prairie), Clearwater County, Idaho, June 14, 1806
LONG-LEAF SUNCUP, *CAMISSONIA SUBACAULIS* (PURSH) RAVEN

This sunny little four-petaled spring flower has gone by several names since Meriwether Lewis collected the type specimen on the Weippe Prairie in June 1806. Frederick Pursh examined Lewis's specimen and realized that it was a hitherto unknown plant. He named it *Jussieua subacaulis* in his *Flora*, noting incorrectly that it was found "On the banks of the Missouri." In 1964, the combination *Camissonia subacaulis* was published and the plant has been known by this name since then.[55]

Pursh's use of *subacaulis* requires some explanation. The Latin term means "not much of a stem." In this instance the term refers to the flowers and not the leaves. This is confusing, for in examining the plant one sees that its flowers appear to have stems. However, in common with many other plants in the evening primrose family, the "stems" are actually long flower tubes; the flower's ovaries actually lie stemless at the level of the basal leaves. The suncup's flowers fade in late morning, another characteristic common to the family as a whole. Confusingly, some

Camissonia subacaulis

JAMES L. REVEAL

classify the long-leaf (or northern) suncup as an evening primrose, placing it in the genus *Oenothera*, and it is so listed in many guidebooks. All parts of the plant are said to be edible.

RANUNCULACEAE (BUTTERCUP FAMILY)

Collected on an affluent of the "Kooskooskee" (Clearwater) River, Lolo Trail, Clearwater or Idaho County, Idaho, June 15, 1806

PIPER'S ANEMONE, *ANEMONE PIPERI* BRITTON EX RYDB.

On the fifteenth of June 1806, the expedition set out across the mountains but turned back two days later, defeated by the deep snowpack. Surprisingly, Lewis managed to col-

Anemone piperi

A. SCOTT EARLE

lect seven more plants during this brief mountain foray. About ten anemones (other common names include thimbleweed and windflower) are native to the Pacific Northwest. (One is *Anemone canadensis*, a plant collected along the Missouri River; see p. 29). There are differences among the species—leaf shape, configuration of the flowers and root systems, growth patterns, and so on—but they also have common attributes that help in classifying them correctly. First, in all anemones, the "petals" are actually petal-like sepals, for the flowers lack true petals (they are *apetalous*). Next, the sepals vary in number. Usually there are five or six, but some flowers will have up to nine, unlike most wildflowers, where numbers are relatively constant. The sepals are fairly large and showy, usually white but sometimes pink, blue, or purple. All of our anemones have a whorl of three leaves on an otherwise naked stem that bears a single flower.[56] The leaves may be simple (one blade) or compound (made up of several leaflets).

Piper's anemone has three compound leaves. Each consists of three entire leaflets (that is, smooth-edged, without teeth or lobes) or occasionally toothed ones. Its flowers are white to pinkish. The plants spread from seeds and from ascending rhizomes (specialized underground stems).[57]

Piper's anemone ranges from the low mountainous region where Oregon, Washington, and Idaho meet, across Idaho, and to extreme western Montana. Disjunct (isolated) populations occur in southeastern British Columbia and northern Utah. The label on Lewis's specimen of Piper's anemone, which Pursh copied from Lewis's original note, says only "on the waters of the Kooskooskee Jun: 15th 1806." Pursh wrote nothing in his *Flora* about this plant, believing that it was the common eastern North American species *Anemone quinquefolia*.[58]

Liliaceae (Lily Family)

Collected on an affluent of the "Kooskooskee" (Clearwater) River, Lolo Trail, Clearwater or Idaho County, Idaho, June 15, 1806

Purple trillium, *Trillium petiolatum* Pursh

On June 15, the expedition members set out on their first, abortive attempt to cross the Bitterroot Range by way of the Lolo Trail—and on the seventeenth they turned back. The snow was too deep to continue, and they needed to find a guide before trying again. One would think that Lewis would have been too occupied with the journey to collect plants, but there were so many spring flowers in bloom that he kept right on adding to his collection. On June 15 and 16, he added seven new plants.

The purple trillium was the second species of trillium, or wake-robin, that Lewis collected. As with the western wake-robin that he found on an island in the Columbia River (see p. 128), he would have recognized this plant as a trillium immediately, given its similarity to those that he knew from the East, where they are common. The roots of at least two of the eastern species, *Trillium grandiflorum* and *Trillium erectum*, were used in herbal medicine, as he had probably learned from his herbalist mother, Lucy Lewis Marks.[59] Neither of the dried specimens of the purple trillium in the Lewis and Clark Herbarium has retained its flower, although they were present when Pursh saw the collections; meanwhile, the leaves are so characteristic that there is no question of their identification.

Lewis, noting that the western species differed from those that he knew, probably suspected that they were new to science. Frederick Pursh doubtless would have seen this immediately. Pursh's description of the two plants served to establish both species. While the plant from the Columbia has a bright white flower, fading to pink or purple, the one that Lewis found on the Lolo Trail has a flower that is brown to purple. Both have three large leaves—everything about trilliums come in threes, hence their name. The leaves of *Trillium petiolatum* have a long stem or petiole (from which

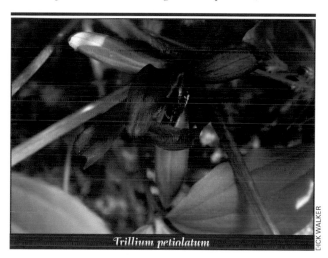

Trillium petiolatum

DICK WALKER

the species name is derived) and are round; further, its flower is nearly stemless. *Trillium ovatum* has a stemmed flower that is raised above broad, pointed leaves. Finally, *Trillium ovatum* is a common plant that occurs along the Lewis and Clark Trail from the Oregon coast to the mountains of western Montana, whereas *Trillium petiolatum* is less common, and one has to search to find it. Pursh's description of this plant notes that it was found "On the waters of the Kooskoosky" and that it was a "singular species," whose flowers resembled those of a dark flowered eastern plant, *Trillium sessile*.[60]

MELANTHIACEAE (BUNCHFLOWER FAMILY)

Collected in the Rocky Mountains, Lolo Trail, Clearwater or Idaho County, Idaho, June 15, 1806

BEAR GRASS, *XEROPHYLLUM TENAX* PURSH

On June 15, the explorers left the Weippe Prairie on their first attempt to cross the Bitterroot Range. They encountered bear grass (also known as Indian basket-grass) as they moved

Xerophyllum tenax

A. SCOTT EARLE

Xerophyllum tenax

JAMES L. REVEAL

into the Clearwater Mountains, although neither of the captains mentioned anything about it on June 15, the day Lewis collected his two specimens. Only when they started east for the second time did he mention the plant, writing, "there is a great abundance of a speceis of bear-grass which grows on every part of these mountains."[61]

The men of the expedition had known of the plant for some time. On October 22, 1805, at the Columbia's Celilo Falls, Clark wrote that the Indians stored their pounded salmon in a "speces of basket neetly made of grass and rushes." Then, on October 31, the captains saw two canoes on their way down

river loaded with "fish & Bear grass for the trade below." Subsequently they had plenty of opportunities to admire the watertight baskets, cups, ornaments, and hats that the Indians crafted from bear grass, although they still had not seen the plant in flower.[62] Certainly they would have been curious about its appearance, and that would have insured their collecting it when they finally did see it. The unusual appearance of its flowers would have particularly intrigued Lewis and Clark— tall, leafy stems surmounted by a large, white-to-cream-colored halo of tiny, six-tepaled, onionlike flowers. The leaves, growing in large tufts at the base of the plants, are long, even-sized over their full length, tough, and wiry—perfect for the uses to which Native Americans put them. Bear grass, like salmon, western red-cedar, and camas roots, was important in the lives of Native Americans in the Pacific Northwest.

The two Lewis and Clark specimens have relatively small flower heads, understandable given the distance they were destined to travel, but they allowed Frederick Pursh to describe the new species. They were also adequate enough for him to have an illustration made for his *Flora*. He gave the species name *tenax*, a Latin word that means "tenacious," for the plant's strong leaves. Pursh's description noted that it grew "On high lands near the Rocky-mountains" and that the "plant is very useful to the natives: out of its very tenacious leaves they weave their water-tight baskets, which they use for cooking their victuals in."[63] He did not mention how the natives cooked food in their baskets. To place them directly over a flame would have been asking too much of the vegetable fiber; instead, they dropped heated rocks into the liquid-filled baskets, and these transferred enough heat to cook the food.

Subsequently, in 1818, Thomas Nuttall established the genus *Xerophyllum*, a word that means "dry-leaf." *Xerophyllum tenax* occurs only in the mountains of western North American (British Columbia and Alberta south to northern California and east to Wyoming). *Xerophyllum asphodeloides*, the only other member of the genus, is a plant of the southern Appalachian Mountains.

MELANTHIACEAE (BUNCHFLOWER FAMILY)
Collected on Hungery Creek, Lolo Trail, Idaho County, Idaho, June 25, 1806
CALIFORNIA FALSE HELLEBORE, *VERATRUM CALIFORNICUM* DURAND

If ever a herbaceous (nonwoody) plant can be called "stately," this one qualifies. It may be as much as five feet high. It has gracious, smooth-edged, plicate (ribbed) leaves that wrap around one another as they ascend the plant's stem. It is a plant that immediately catches the eye. California false hellebore (or corn lily) was not blooming when Lewis saw it on the Lolo Trail (although he must have seen it earlier—possibly he even saw plants in bloom). If he collected a specimen, it did not survive. The plants that he saw in June 1806 were not blooming, but he plucked a leaf anyway and brought that back as a specimen. Surprisingly, the plant remained unclassified for half a century—no knowledgeable plant hunter had managed to catch it in flower.

A note on the herbarium sheet in Frederick Pursh's hand, taken from Lewis's field note, reads: "A plant growing in wet places with a Single Stem, & leaves clasping around one another; no flowers observed.—On the

Veratrum californicum

JAMES L. REVEAL

Kooskooskee Jun: 25th 1806." Pursh may have recognized the leaf as that of a *Veratrum*, but lacking a flowering part, he would have assumed that it was the related American false hellebore, *Veratrum viride*, a plant that he included in his 1813 *Flora*.[64]

The California false hellebore is an interesting plant for several reasons. Its closely clustered, six-tepaled, green-centered flowers are striking, and this, with its overall appearance, has found it a place in ornamental gardens. Because it grows in moist places where it spreads by rhizomes, animals may graze on its leaves. Unfortunately, the leaves contain poisonous alkaloids that cause cattle and sheep (and presumably other animals as well) to abort or to bear deformed progeny. The alkaloids, in minute doses, do have some therapeutic value, and until recently the leaf of *Veratrum viride* was used in small amounts to treat hypertension; the same alkaloid is present in our plant. The leaf is also effective as an abortifacient, as an insecticide, and as a pediculicide

Veratrum californicum

A. SCOTT EARLE

(a substance that controls lice). There is some suggestion that Native Americans also used veratrum therapeutically.

The word *hellebore* is derived from the Greek *helleboros*, and, like the Latin *veratrum*, means "hellebore." Both terms were used in antiquity for now unknown poisonous plants. In the process of classifying the plant kingdom, Linnaeus assigned the name *Helleborus* to a genus of poisonous plants in the buttercup family, and *Veratrum* to what is now the bunchflower family. Thus "true" hellebores are in the Ranunculaceae, and "false" hellebores are in the Melanthiaceae. Both are poisonous. "Corn lily" is another common name for our plant, explained by the appearance of its leaves, which resemble corn husks, and its closely ranked budding flowers, which resemble immature grains of corncobs.

POLEMONIACEAE (PHLOX FAMILY)

Collected on Hungery Creek, Lolo Trail, Idaho County, Idaho, June 26, 1806

SCARLET GILIA, *IPOMOPSIS AGGREGATA* (PURSH) V. E. GRANT

This bright red, trumpet-shaped wildflower is not a plant that one passes by without a second look. Although

Ipomopsis aggregata

JAMES L. REVEAL

Meriwether Lewis collected it while homeward bound, he probably saw it the previous summer, for it grows throughout the Rocky Mountains, blooming from late spring well into the summer at higher elevations. If he collected it earlier, his specimen would have been lost while cached at Camp Fortunate. In any event, the scarlet gilia became part of his collection of plants during the expedition's transit of the Clearwater Mountains. Except for the various Indian paintbrushes (*Castilleja* spp.), scarlet gilia is the only truly red flower commonly encountered in the mountains. The arrangement of its flowers in a loose cluster along the stem explains its species name, *aggregata*.

When Frederick Pursh examined Lewis's dry specimen, he saw that it was a hitherto undescribed plant. He wrote in his *Flora*—incorrectly—that Lewis's plant grew on "the banks of the Mississippi," and he assigned it to the genus

Cantua, one that included a look-alike that grows in the Carolinas.[65] Subsequently, our plant was reclassified as a *Gilia* (a genus proposed by Linnaeus to honor the Spanish botanist Felipe Luis Gil), and again in 1956 as an *Ipomopsis* (a term that means "looks like a morning glory"). Regardless of the genus, this colorful plant has been known as "scarlet gilia" for so many years that the name will probably persist—despite attempts to standardize common names to reflect such taxonomic changes, as in the proposed common name "scarlet skyrocket." Another, rather inelegant common name for this attractive plant is "skunk flower," used because both flower and foliage give off an acrid odor when crushed.

The species is composed of numerous varieties found from British Columbia to northern Mexico. Var. *aggregata* grows mainly in Idaho and Montana, south to Nevada, Utah, and Colorado.

ANTIRRHINACEAE (FIGWORT FAMILY)
Collected on Hungery Creek, Lolo Trail, Idaho County, Idaho, on June 26, 1806
WESTERN MOUNTAIN KITTEN'S-TAIL, *SYNTHYRIS MISSURICA* (RAF.) PENNELL

This attractive little plant is hard to miss, for the bright blue color of its numerous flowers stands out in the deeply shaded, moist woods where it grows. Frederick Pursh concluded that Lewis's dried specimen represented a new plant and named it *Veronica reniformis* (the species name means "kidney-shaped") in his 1813 *Flora*. Pursh wrote that the plant had been "Collected by Messrs. Lewis and Clark in boggy soil, on the banks of the Missouri."[66] Unknown to Pursh, Rafinesque had already used the name *Veronica reniformis* in 1808 for another plant, so a decade later Rafinesque corrected Pursh's error by proposing *Veronica missurica* as a substitute name. Eventually our plant was reclassified as *Synthyris missurica*.

The genus *Synthyris* is a complex group of nine species found in the mountains of western North America. The seven members of the genus that occur in the Pacific Northwest all have tightly clustered four-petaled flowers whose petals are usually unequal, the upper one being larger than the others. In our species the flower cluster is borne on a single stem that has several small leafy bracts growing below the inflorescence. Several long-stemmed, dentate (toothed), kidney or heart-shaped leaves arise at the base of the plant. Our kitten's tail blooms from April on, depending on the elevation, and is found mainly in the Blue and Wallowa mountains of Washington and Oregon, and eastward into the mountains of central Idaho. Small, disjunct populations occur farther to the south. The generic name *Synthyris* is derived from two Greek words and means approximately "little joined doors," referring to the valves of the seed capsule. Rafinesque's use of the name *missurica* was his way of referring to the Missouri River.

Synthyris missurica

A. SCOTT EARLE

RHAMNACEAE (BUCKTHORN FAMILY)

Ceanothus sanguineus collected between Bald Mountain and Spring Hill, Lolo Trail, Idaho County, Idaho, June 27, 1806
(date and exact location are uncertain)
Ceanothus velutinus collected on an affluent of the "Kooskooskee" (Clearwater) River (date and exact location are uncertain)
REDSTEM CEANOTHUS, *CEANOTHUS SANGUINEUS* PURSH
SNOW-BRUSH CEANOTHUS, *CEANOTHUS VELUTINUS* DOUGLAS EX HOOK.

The buckthorn family is a relatively small one, made up of shrubs, small trees, and vines. Most grow in warm to tropical climates, although several species are found in the Pacific Northwest. We have already met one species, the cascara (*Frangula purshiana*), whose purgative properties are well known. This property is shared to some extent with many other related Eurasian plants as well as with the two buckthorns described here. Also, various dyes are abstracted from the bark and fruit of some of the Old World species, but we have found no evidence that ours have been used for this purpose.

The two buckthorn specimens now in the Lewis and Clark Herbarium were gathered while crossing the Clearwater and Bitterroot mountains in the spring of 1806. Both specimens are incomplete, but presumably they were flowering when Lewis gathered them and this likely was his incentive for adding them to his collection. Both shrubs are, in fact, good ornamentals, although other members of the family are more often used for this purpose.

Frederick Pursh recognized that the redstem ceanothus (sometimes known as the Oregon teatree) was a new plant, and he described it in his *Flora*. Lewis probably first saw the plant on June 10 but he did not collect a specimen until June 27, according to the information on the label. Wherever it was found—near Kamiah, Idaho, or along Collins Creek on the Lolo Trail—Pursh incorrectly interpreted the location to be near "the Rocky mountain on the banks of the Missouri."[67]

Lewis found the snow-brush ceanothus (also called mountain balm, or tobacco-brush), *Ceanothus velutinus*, somewhere along the Clearwater River—most likely in the fall of 1805—as the specimen lacks both flowers and fruit. Lacking these critical features, Pursh was unable to place the plant taxonomically.[68]

Ceanothus sanguineus

JAMES L. REVEAL

Ceanothus velutinus

A. SCOTT EARLE

Our two buckthorns are quite similar. They differ in that the redstem ceanothus is deciduous, while the snow-brush ceanothus has sticky, rather shiny, evergreen leaves. The leaves of both plants are oval; the leaves of *Ceanothus sanguineus* have fine serrations. Both form attractive spring-blooming sprays of tiny, white, five-petaled flowers. The flowers of the snow-brush ceanothus have a strong, distinguishing odor—not exactly unpleasant, but not pleasant, either. The redstem ceanothus is an important plant in reestablishing vegetation after forest fires. As one proceeds west along U.S. Highway 12 just west of Lolo Pass, one encounters a large burn area dotted with *Ceanothus sanguineus*. Its seeds are able to germinate after being buried for several decades, and the shrubs spring up in the bare areas left by wildfires.

LAMIACEAE (MINT FAMILY)

Mentioned, but not collected, Camp Chopunnish, Idaho County, Idaho, May 24, 1806

WESTERN HORSEMINT, *AGASTACHE URTICIFOLIA* (BENTH.) KUNTZE

It is hard to guess why Lewis chose to collect certain plants while seemingly passing others by. A good example of this is the "horse mint" that he used in Camp Chopunnish to treat William Bratton. Bratton's was the most mystifying of all of the ailments suffered by the men of the expedition. It had started in the winter of 1806, while he was working at the saltworks. He was in so much pain that the captains had him transported back to Fort Clatsop. On February 16, Lewis noted in his journal that Bratton was "very weak and complains of a pain in the lower part of the back when he moves which I suppose procedes from dability."[69] Thenceforth, the journals mention Bratton's illness many times, for it was more than debilitating—the man was completely disabled.

More than three months later (May 24, 1806) in Camp Chopunnish, Lewis noted "William Bratton still continues very unwell; he eats heartily digests his food well…yet is so weak in the loins that he is scarcely able to walk…nor can he set upwright but with the greatest pain." At the suggestion of one of the men who had seen the following treatment used successfully, Bratton was placed in a "sweat hole" and alternately "sweated" and "plunged in cold water" all the while drinking "copious draughts of a strong tea of horse mint."

Heroic physical therapy, unquestionably, yet it served to break a cycle of painful muscle spasm. The patient was greatly improved and soon was well.[70] What part the horsemint tea

Agastache urticifolia

A. SCOTT EARLE

may have played in this miraculous cure is open to conjecture. Various diagnoses have been postulated for Bratton's illness. We suggest that he may have suffered a compression fracture or collapse of one of the lower dorsal or lumbar vertebrae—an injury compatible with his symptoms. If so, then time, rather than horsemint tea, would have healed the physical injury,

183

while the sweat probably reduced the muscle spasm.

Several members of the mint family are known regionally as "horsemint," but there is only one plant, *Agastache urticifolia*, in the mountains of Idaho that fits that description. A more precise common name for it is "nettle-leaved giant-hyssop."[71] It is a strongly mint-scented plant, common from British Columbia to northern California, and eastward to Montana and Colorado. It grows from midelevations nearly to tree line, and it begins to flower in early summer. The plants prefer moist to moderately dry terrain and are often seen along today's hiking trails. One can only guess why

Lewis did not gather it as a specimen, as the species was unknown to science, and was not named until 1829. Possibly Lewis believed that it was the same as a giant hyssop that he knew from Virginia (*Agastache nepetoides*).

The name *Agastache* was derived from two Greek words, *agan* and *stachus*. Together, these refer to the "large wheat-like spike" of the plant's inflorescence. The species name *urticifolia* means "nettle-leaved," from the resemblance of its leaves to those of various nettles (*Urtica* spp.). As with many members of the mint family, an aromatic tea may be made from its leaves; its seeds are also said to be edible.

POLEMONIACEAE (PHLOX FAMILY)
Collected between Bald Mountain and Spring Hill, Lolo Trail, Idaho County, Idaho,
on an affluent of the "Kooskoosky" (Clearwater) River, June 27, 1806
WESTERN POLEMONIUM, *POLEMONIUM CAERULEUM* L.
SHOWY POLEMONIUM, *POLEMONIUM PULCHERRIMUM* HOOK.

On June 27, 1806, the expedition was on the Lolo Trail. According to the calendar, it was summer, but at that elevation, it was early spring. Lewis noted in his journal: "met the main party at the Quamash glade on the head of the Kooskooske river. from this place we had an extensive view of these stupendous mountains principally covered with snow like that on which we stood." Despite the difficulties of their passage, Lewis collected several specimens that day. All are subalpine, early-blooming plants. At some point Lewis found a species of Jacob's ladder and added it to his collection.[72]

Unfortunately, the plant in the Lewis and Clark Herbarium, labeled originally *Polemonium caeruleum*, has fallen on hard times. It consists today only of a cluster of flowers, a short stem, and leaf fragments—not enough material for a positive identification. Further, there is

Polemonium caeruleum

A. SCOTT EARLE

Polemonium pulcherrimum

A. SCOTT EARLE

nothing in the captains' journals that helps us to identify the plant. It may even have been in poor condition when Frederick Pursh saw the specimen, for he did not include it in his *Flora*, noting only on the specimen sheet (from Lewis's original notes) that it was found on the "Head waters of Kooskoosky."

In 1999, the Lewis and Clark specimen was identified as *Polemonium pulcherrimum*, a totally different species, described originally by Hooker in 1830.[73] The reasoning was as follows: On the day the plant was collected—and we assume that the date was correct—the expedition traveled at a fairly high elevation and did not pass through any swampy meadows that would favor the growth of *Polemonium caeruleum*. They consistently traveled where they should have found *Polemonium pulcherrimum*, a more compact sub-alpine-to-alpine plant that grows on drier ground. In 2002 we followed portions of the expedition's path and found that only *Polemonium pulcherrimum* grows where Lewis and Clark traveled that day, a finding that bolsters our opinion that the specimen in the Lewis and Clark Herbarium is that plant.

WHERE TO SEE LEWIS AND CLARK PLANTS TODAY
DeVoto Grove: US 12 West of Lolo Pass

Pink wintergreen, *Pyrola asarifolia*

JAMES L. REVEAL

Bead lily, *Clintonia uniflora*

JAMES – REVEAL

Arrowleaf ragwort, *Senecio triangularis*

JAMES L. REVEAL

Ninebark, *Physocarpus malvaceus*

JAMES L. REVEAL

Fairy-bell, *Prosartes trachycarpa*

A. SCOTT EARLE

Baneberry, *Actaea rubra*

A. SCOTT EARLE

BITTERROOT	*Lewisia rediviva*
THREE-LEAVED LEWISIA	*Lewisia triphylla*
THIN-LEAF OWL'S-CLOVER	*Orthocarpus tenuifolius*
BITTERBRUSH	*Purshia tridentata*
BESSEY'S LOCOWEED	*Oxytropis besseyi*
AMERICAN SILVERBERRY	*Elaeagnus commutata*
SHRUBBY CINQUEFOIL	*Dasiphora fruticosa* subsp. *floribunda*
COMMON GAILLARDIA	*Gaillardia aristata*
TWINBERRY HONEYSUCKLE	*Lonicera involucrata*
YELLOW MONKEY-FLOWER	*Mimulus guttatus*
ROCKY MOUNTAIN IRIS	*Iris missouriensis*
ELEGANT DEATH CAMAS	*Anticlea elegans*
WILD BLUE FLAX	*Linum lewisii*
PINK ELEPHANTS	*Pedicularis groenlandica*
FERN-LEAVED LOUSEWORT	*Pedicularis cystopteridifolia*
NEEDLE AND THREAD	*Hesperostipa comata*

Travelers' Rest to Great Falls
June 30 to July 11, 1806

On June 30, 1806, the Corps of Discovery arrived at Travelers' Rest, its former campsite on Lolo Creek two miles west of the Bitterroot River, in present-day Lolo, Montana. While the members of the expedition prepared for the next segment of their journey, the captains firmed up a plan that they had been considering for several months: They decided to split the party. Lewis and nine men would follow today's Blackfoot River to the Continental Divide and go from there to the Great Falls of the Missouri. He planned to leave a few men at the falls to retrieve the canoes and stores that they had cached the year before, while he explored Maria's River (we know it as the Marias River).

Clark, in turn, would retrace the previous summer's route to Shoshone Cove near Camp Fortunate on the Beaverhead River. He would recover their cached material and then follow the Beaverhead to the Jefferson River. From there, he would proceed to the Three Forks of the Missouri. Clark would then head due east until he came to the Yellowstone River while Sergeant Ordway and a small party floated cached canoes down the Missouri to the Great Falls. Clark's men, reaching the Yellowstone, would stop to make dugout canoes at the point where the river became navigable and work their way down to the Missouri. With luck, the parties would meet there.

On July 3 the two groups left Travelers' Rest to pursue their separate ways. Clark completed his trek as planned, crossing Montana by way of today's Bozeman Pass, and then traveled down the Yellowstone River. The most notable event that occurred on his journey downriver was when stealthy Indians stole many of the horses that the captains had planned to sell at the Mandan villages.

Lewis collected plant specimens as he went, even though he and his men were moving rapidly. First, he traveled a short distance downstream along Clark's River (today's Bitterroot) to the future site of Missoula, Montana. From there, he followed the Blackfoot River upstream. As the explorers followed the Blackfoot upstream, they passed through a scenic patchwork of forest and prairie, covering twenty-five to thirty-five miles a day. Lewis continued to make notes along the way, describing the terrain and the plants, animals, and birds that he saw. When the Blackfoot divided into two branches, he decided to go northeast along present-day Alice Creek to its origin. This brought the party to the Continental Divide. On July 7, they crossed the divide over present Lewis and Clark Pass to emerge onto a seemingly never-ending, grassy prairie, covered with vast herds of buffalo.[1] The party continued to travel northeast to a stream that proved to be the Dearborn River—they had named it the year before, and it has the same name today. The party followed the Dearborn downstream for a short distance and then resumed their northeast course across open prairie until they came to what they called the Medicine River (our Sun River), which empties into the Missouri River at the Great Falls. They arrived there on July 11, having made excellent time. Their greatest problem had been the dense swarms of mosquitoes that they encountered. Lewis had added at least seventeen new plant specimens to his collection, first at Travelers' Rest and from there to the Great Falls. Three of these plants bear his name today.

PORTULACACEAE (PURSLANE FAMILY)

*Lewisia rediviva collected near "Clark's River" (Bitterroot River), Travelers' Rest, Missoula County, Montana, on July 1, 1806;
Lewisia triphylla collected between Bald Mountain and Spring Hill, Lolo Trail, Idaho County, Idaho, on an affluent
of the Clearwater River, on June 17, 1806*

BITTERROOT, *LEWISIA REDIVIVA* PURSH
THREE-LEAF BITTERROOT, *LEWISIA TRIPHYLLA* (S. WATSON) B. L. ROB.

Meriwether Lewis collected bitterroot, *Lewisia rediviva*, in early July 1806, after the expedition returned to Travelers' Rest.[2] Oddly, Lewis mentioned the plant only once in his

Lewisia rediviva

JAMES L. REVEAL

journal—on August 22, 1805—and then without knowing what it was. He sampled a root highly esteemed by the Shoshones. He said that the root "appeared to be fibrous; the parts were brittle, hard of the size of a small quill, cilindric and as white as snow throughout....[T]his the Indians with me informed were always boiled for use. I made the expurement, found that they became perfectly soft by boiling, but had a very bitter taste, which was naucious to my pallate, and I transfered them to the Indians who had eat them heartily."[3]

The bitterroot is one of our loveliest wildflowers. There are a number of other spring-blooming members of the purslane family (Portulacaceae), including the small spring beauties that the men saw along the Columbia River (see p. 127)—but the bitterroot is a different plant. Although it is edible and has an irregular flower in which the number of sepals seems unrelated to the number of petals, that is where the resemblance ends. Each stem bears one to several buds. These bloom one at a time to become showy flowers, subtended by whorls of small bracts (tiny leaflets). The flowers have many petals (usually twelve to eighteen). They are radially symmetrical, showy, and up to an inch and a half or so across. Their color ranges from a pure white to a deep pink. The bitterroot also differs from the spring beauties, for although they all bloom in the spring while the soil is moist, the gravelly ground that bitterroot prefers soon dries out, the plants disappear, and only sagebrush remains. Then, in late summer, leaves appear. These, in turn, disappear with the frost. Finally, in the spring, the flowers bloom again.

Back in Philadelphia, Bernard M'Mahon, a nurseryman, planted a root that Lewis brought back. Frederick Pursh noted in his *Flora*: "The specimen with roots...vegetated for more than one year: but some accident happening to it, I had not the pleasure of seeing it flower."[4] The plant that Lewis collected was apparently still alive, and so was given the name *rediviva* ("back to life"). Unable to fit the bitterroot into any existing genus, Pursh created a new one that he named *Lewisia*. The genus now has about eighteen species ranging from Alaska to the Southwest. It is gratifying to note that the Idaho and Montana state flowers both bear Lewis's name, the syringa or mock-orange, *Philadelphus lewisii*, and the bitterroot, *Lewisia rediviva*—both are beautiful plants.

As it happened Lewis collected another member of the

genus, the three-leaf bitterroot, *Lewisia triphylla*, on June 17, the day the expedition set out to try for the first time to traverse the Lolo Trail from west to east. It was a preview of the bitterroot that the men would find at Travelers' Rest two weeks later. The three-leaf bitterroot is a fairly widely distributed but rather rare mountain plant that grows from the Cascade Range of British Columbia south to California and east to Colorado and Montana. It grows—as do most bitterroots—on ground still moist from the snowmelt, often in sandy soil, in open ponderosa pine forests and on sagebrush slopes as high as the subalpine zone. It is a small plant with a cluster of pink flowers.[5]

A ticket on the specimen sheet in Frederick Pursh's handwriting records Lewis's location on that date as "On the waters of Kooskooskee within the Rocky mountains Jun: 27th 1806." Pursh did not include the plant in his *Flora*, as he probably thought it was a previously described spring beauty.[6]

OROBANCHACEAE (BROOM-RAPE FAMILY)

Collected in the valley of "Clark's River" (Bitterroot River), Travelers' Rest, Missoula County, Montana, July 1, 1806

THIN-LEAF OWL'S-CLOVER, *ORTHOCARPUS TENUIFOLIUS* (PURSH) BENTH.

The stay at Travelers' Rest was a pleasant hiatus for the Corps of Discovery, marking the completion of the west-to-east crossing of the Bitterroot Range; it was a time during which the expedition could prepare for its journey back to the United States. The camp was sited in a pleasant cottonwood-bordered meadow on the banks of Montana's Lolo Creek, an ideal spot for a layover while the captains planned their return journey.[7] The layover also gave Meriwether Lewis an opportunity to collect several plant specimens, including the owl's-clover.

The thin-leaf owl's-clover was obviously a new plant, as Lewis, and later Frederick Pursh, recognized. Pursh noted, making use of Lewis's information, that it was found "On the banks of Clarck's river....About a foot high; flowers deep yellow; floral leaves

Orthocarpus tenuifolius

A. SCOTT EARLE

tinged with purple." Pursh assigned the plant to *Bartsia*, as good a place as any at the time, for Lewis's plant was both a new species and a new genus.[8] Thomas Nuttall described the genus in 1818, based on specimens he found near the site of Fort Mandan in 1811.[9] The origin of the common name "owl's-clover," a name used also for several other unrelated plants, is obscure, although we suspect that it was derived from the closely clustered, cloverlike heads seen in some of the other species of *Orthocarpus*.

Orthocarpus is derived from two Greek words, *orthos* and *karpos*, and means "straight fruit," describing the symmetrical shape of the plant's seed capsules. Pursh's species name means "thin-leaf." Some of the owl's-clovers are inconspicuous little plants, but others (like this one) have colorful bracts and flower structures. As the appearance suggests, owl's-clovers are closely related to Indian paintbrushes (*Castilleja* spp.), plants also found mostly in the American West. The relation is close enough that nomenclatural confusion once existed as to whether certain species of *Orthocarpus* should be classified as *Castilleja* or *Orthocarpus*.[10]

ROSACEAE (ROSE FAMILY)
Collected at "Prairie of the Knobs" (Nevada Valley), Blackfoot River, Powell County, Montana, July 6, 1806
BITTERBRUSH, *PURSHIA TRIDENTATA* (PURSH) DC. EX POIT.

Bitterbrush is a large, many-branched shrub found throughout much of the arid American West. Meriwether Lewis collected it along the Blackfoot River in an area he

Purshia tridentata

JAMES L. REVEAL

termed "the prarie of the knobs," because of the small hills found there. *Purshia tridentata* grows in many places along the Lewis and Clark route, usually on sagebrush slopes. When in bloom during spring and early summer of a good year, sagebrush country is enlivened by the bright yellow of many blooming bitterbrush shrubs that seem to rival sagebrush in their numbers. It may be seen today almost anywhere in the Far West, from the eastern end of the Columbia Gorge through Idaho and Montana, and south to Arizona and New Mexico.

Frederick Pursh originally named the species *Tigarea tridentata*. Three years later, in 1816, the French botanist Jean Louis Marie Poiret proposed that the plant be given the name *Purshia*, as suggested initially by Augustin-Pyramus de Candolle, who was at the time a foremost authority on world flora. He recognized that the western American plant was unrelated to *Tigarea*, a tropical genus no longer recognized by botanists. Curiously, when he described it in his *Flora*, Pursh wrote that the shrub was also found along "the Columbia river."[11] Bitterbrush certainly does occur along the Columbia, but we do not know whether he knew this from a specimen collected there, or whether it was something Lewis told him.

The plant typically flowers from late April until early July and grows in sagebrush communities on arid foothills and mountain slopes. It is one of the most important browse plants for deer and other animals, explaining another common name, "antelope-brush." In good years, the shrub is completely covered with bright yellow flowers. It is attractive enough to make a nice ornamental, although it is used less frequently for this than the related shrubby cinquefoil (*Dasiphora fruticosa* subsp. *floribunda*, see p. 201). Its short, three-lobed leaves give the plant its species name, *tridentata*. A slightly sticky style remains attached to the seeds, so the fruit sticks to the fur of grazing animals, which helps to disperse the plant.

Fabaceae (Pea Family)

Site of collection uncertain; possibly on the Blackfoot River, Missoula County, Montana, July 1806

BESSEY'S LOCOWEED, *OXYTROPIS BESSEYI* (RYDB.) BLANK.

Bessey's locoweed is a perennial western plant in the pea family that grows from Alberta and Saskatchewan south to Nevada, Utah, and Colorado. Its clustered pinkish red papilionaceous flowers borne on naked stalks surrounded by grayish green odd-pinnate leaves are typical of the pea family in general.[12] *Oxytropis* and several related genera in the pea family are poisonous. The common names locoweed and crazyweed reflect the early symptoms that horses and cattle display after eating the plants—symptoms that are often followed by the animals' death. Many *Oxytropis* have colorful flowers that, like those of Bessey's locoweed, stand out on the sagebrush slopes where the plants commonly grow. Our plant's red flowers probably caught Lewis's eye, prompting him to collect it. Unfortunately, the red color turns to a washed-out blue when the plant is dried, a result of a change in pH, so the plants are best left in the wild. Occasionally one finds Bessey's locoweed as a nursery plant or—with perseverance—it can be grown from seed.

We do not know exactly where Lewis found his specimen. Bessey's locoweed grows along the Blackfoot River to east of the Continental Divide. Lewis probably gathered it somewhere between today's Missoula, Montana, and the prairie to the east of Lewis and Clark Pass.[13] The label on the specimen in the Lewis and Clark Herbarium (copied by Frederick Pursh from Lewis's original notes) says only "Near

Oxytropis besseyi

the head of Clarcks River Jul. 1806." Pursh identified the plant as *Oxytropis argentata*, a species found in Siberia, and included it in his *Flora* under that name.[14]

Elaeagnaceae (Oleaster Family)

Collected at "Prairie of the Knobs" (Nevada Valley), Blackfoot River, Powell County, Montana, July 6, 1806

AMERICAN SILVERBERRY, *ELAEAGNUS COMMUTATA* BERNH. EX RYDB.

We like Lewis's common name for this plant, "Silver tree of the Missouri." He would be disappointed today if he saw how the exotic Russian olive (*Elaeagnus angustifolia*) has become the dominant tree along streams in Montana and northern North Dakota where the silverberry once reigned. Our native shrub has oblong or egg-shaped leaves that are two to three times longer than wide. The leaves of the Russian olive—widely planted as a windbreak and ornamen-

191

tal—are narrower and three to eight times longer. The silverberry's young branches are densely covered with golden brown scales, whereas those of its introduced relative are a silvery gray. Finally, the silverberry lacks spines, while the tips of branches in the Russian olive become sharp and spinelike.

The American silverberry is still found in parts of Montana. It ranges north to Alaska and the Yukon Territory, south to Utah and Colorado, and eastward in Canada to Quebec. The Russian olive, on the other hand, is now found throughout most of North America. Lewis collected his specimen of silverberry on the same day that he collected bitterbrush

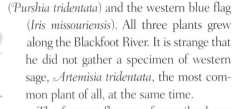

(*Purshia tridentata*) and the western blue flag (*Iris missouriensis*). All three plants grew along the Blackfoot River. It is strange that he did not gather a specimen of western sage, *Artemisia tridentata*, the most common plant of all, at the same time.

The fragrant flowers of our silverberry have four petal-like sepals. These are silvery gray and densely hairy on the outside and smooth and yellow on the inside. Although Hitchcock notes that the silverberry's fruits are "more mealy than juicy," they are usually considered to be inedible.[15]

MARY VAUX WALCOTT, (1860-1940),
SMITHSONIAN INSTITUTION'S *NORTH AMERICAN WILD FLOWERS*

ROSACEAE (ROSE FAMILY)

Collected at "Prairie of the Knobs" (Nevada Valley), Blackfoot River, Powell County, Montana, July 6, 1806

SHRUBBY CINQUEFOIL, *DASIPHORA FRUTICOSA* (L.) RYDB. SUBSP. *FLORIBUNDA* (PURSH) KARTESZ

Dasiphora fruticosa subsp. *floribunda*

JAMES L. REVEAL

The shrubby cinquefoil, or yellow-rose, grows all across the northern part of North America, ranging from Alaska and Labrador south to California and New Jersey.[16] It is a common montane to subalpine plant, usually found growing in open meadows and on sagebrush slopes as high as tree line. Our North American shrub is closely related to the Eurasian species (*Dasiphora fruticosa* subsp. *fruticosa*). Numerous cultivars (human-selected garden variants) of both plants are available in nurseries. The shrubby cinquefoil that Lewis collected is easily grown as a garden ornamental and is often used in industrial landscaping. The plant is deservedly popular, not only because it is attractive, but also because the plants bloom for a long time. The flowers are deep yellow, five-petaled, and have a simple roselike appearance. The fruit (an achene) is small and hairy. As the common name "cinquefoil" suggests, its compound leaves usually have five leaflets.

Lewis wrote in his journal that "the southern wood and two other speceis of shrub are common in the prarie of knobs. presrved specemines of them."[17] His "southern wood" was the common big sagebrush (*Artemisia tridentata*)—a plant that for some reason he did not collect. The two other shrubs probably were the American silverberry (*Elaeagnus commutata*) and bitterbrush (*Purshia tridentata*). Pursh identified Lewis's plant as *Potentilla fruticosa*, the name of an Old World species. The name has been used until recently for our plant and it is still found in some guidebooks. He noted that Lewis had collected it "on the waters of the Rocky-mountains"—a rather curious expression, although it shows that he knew that Lewis's specimen was not found along the Missouri River.[18] Pursh also described what he thought was another new species, *Potentilla floribunda*, at the same time. He believed that it was a plant that grew only in the mountains of eastern Canada, New York, and New Jersey. His two plants are actually the same.[19]

The shrubby cinquefoil blooms in the spring and summer throughout the high country of the American West and may be seen today along the Blackfoot River in Montana. It is likely that Lewis gathered the specimen on the sagebrush slopes near today's Montana State Highway 200, just west of Ovando.

ASTERACEAE (ASTER FAMILY)
Collected in the vicinity of Lewis and Clark Pass, Lewis and Clark County, Montana, July 7, 1806
COMMON GAILLARDIA, *GAILLARDIA ARISTATA* PURSH

Meriwether Lewis's label (as copied by Pursh) on the herbarium sheet of *Gaillardia aristata* in the Lewis and Clark Herbarium says "Rocky mountains Dry hills —Jul 7th 1806." It is usually assumed that Lewis collected the specimen. His journal for that day says nothing about collecting plants, but it notes that he crossed "the dividing ridge between the waters of the Columbia from those of the Missouri" (over today's Lewis and Clark Pass in Lewis and Clark County, Montana) onto the plains to the east. The common gaillardia (also known as blanket flower) still grows there today.[20]

JAMES L. REVEAL

Gaillardia aristata

There are about a dozen species of *Gaillardia*.[21] The plants favor grassy plains from southern Canada to northern Mexico, with one species native to Argentina. Five grow on our Great Plains.

Pursh had no trouble placing the Lewis and Clark plant in the genus *Gaillardia*. He gave it the species name *aristata*, a term that means "awned" or "bristly" (awn is a botanical term that refers to stiff hairs).[22] The inflorescence of composite plants, such as this one, are made up of "ray flowers" and "disk flowers." The inflorescence of *Gaillardia*

Gaillardia aristata

JAMES L. REVEAL

aristata is striking. Its orange-yellow ray flowers, and its prominent, deep red disk, make identification easy and explains the plant's common names—Indian blanket and blanket-flower. There are usually thirteen ray flowers, and each has a three-lobed tip. The plants are hairy perennials with rather narrow, upright, irregularly toothed leaves. Gaillardias are popular as ornamentals and may escape into the wild, so they are often found growing outside of their natural range.

CAPRIFOLIACEAE (HONEYSUCKLE FAMILY)
Collected in the vicinity of Lewis and Clark Pass, Lewis and Clark County, Montana, July 7, 1806
TWINBERRY HONEYSUCKLE, *LONICERA INVOLUCRATA* (RICHARDSON) BANKS EX SPRENG.

The better acquainted one is with Lewis and Clark's journey, and the plants that the explorers—primarily Meriwether

Lonicera involucrata

JAMES L. REVEAL

Lewis—collected, the more inclined one is to second-guess their actions. For example, why did they gather certain plants at certain times? Lewis did not collect the twinberry honeysuckle until 1806, yet it was a shrub that the explorers had to have seen repeatedly as they worked their way through the mountains of today's Idaho and Montana. It is a common plant along streams throughout the northern Rocky Mountains, growing to twelve feet or so in height. We suspect there were two reasons that Lewis collected this shrub (also known as bearberry and four-line honeysuckle) when he and his men crossed the Continental Divide in the summer of 1806.

First, the plant would have just been starting to form its fruit. Its small, paired yellow flowers are inconspicuous earlier in the season, but its mature berries are not. It would be easy to pass by the shrub when it was flowering, but nobody can miss the twinberry when it is fruiting. In a good, wet year, as 1806 was, the plant has many conspicuous, twinned, blue-black berries that are borne immediately above two pairs of shiny red, leaflike bracts.[23] A second reason for collecting this specimen, at this time and place, is that Lewis and his men were about to leave the mountains. It was their last chance to collect plants that they might never see again.

Lewis's characterization of the twinberry, as copied by Pursh on the specimen's label in the Lewis and Clark Herbarium, is "A Shrub within the Rocky mountains found in moist grounds near branches of riverlets." The specimen is a forlorn collection of three small twigs that give no idea whatsoever of the plant's appearance. Pursh—probably because he did not have sufficient material—did not include it in his *Flora* of 1813.[24]

Lonicera involucrata

JAMES L. REVEAL

PHRYMACEAE (LOPSEED FAMILY)
Collected on the Blackfoot River, above its confluence with the Clark Fork, in Missoula County, Montana, on July 4, 1806
YELLOW MONKEY-FLOWER, *MIMULUS GUTTATUS* FISCH. EX DC.

Meriwether Lewis's journey from Travelers' Rest to the Great Falls of the Missouri was botanically rewarding. He saw numerous plants that he had never seen before, and others that he had seen but realized would be unavailable to him when he reached the plains. He had to have seen the yellow monkey-flower before. Also called the seep monkey-flower, it is an attractive flower similar (except for its color) to the lovely pink-to-purple Lewis's monkey-flower, *Mimulus lewisii*, that he collected in 1805 (see p. 72). Both grow close to seep springs and along smaller, fast-moving mountain streams throughout the northern Rocky Mountains. The yellow monkey-flower may be found in many places along the trail that Lewis and Clark followed in the summer of 1805. (Look for it today on both sides of Lemhi Pass, along U.S. Highway 93 over Lost Trail Pass, and all along U.S. Highway 12 over Lolo Pass.)

The flower is large, bright yellow, five-petaled, and irregu-

Mimulus guttatus

JAMES L. REVEAL

lar. It has a prominent three-petaled lower "lip" with a raised hairy "palate" that obstructs the flower tube. The species name, *guttatus*, means "spotted," for the several carmine spots that dot the base of the lip. The plants usually are low, less than two feet tall, and often sprawling along moist ground. They have rich green, opposite, oval leaves.[25]

Frederick Pursh examined Lewis's specimen and listed the species as *Mimulus luteus*, an Old World plant. It grew, he wrote, "On the banks of Clarck's River…On the north-west coast…Flowers golden-yellow. The plant has lately been introduced as a garden ornamental, and will be a worthy addition to our hardy perennial plants."[26]

IRIDACEAE (IRIS FAMILY)
Collected at "Prairie of the Knobs" (Nevada Valley), Blackfoot River, Powell County, Montana, on July 5, 1806
ROCKY MOUNTAIN IRIS, *IRIS MISSOURIENSIS* NUTT.

Rocky Mountain iris, or western blue flag, is the most widespread wild iris native to western North America. It grows in mountain meadows and along slow-moving streams

Iris missouriensis

JAMES L. REVEAL

throughout most of the western United States, southwestern Canada, and as far east as Minnesota. The plant occurs frequently along the trail that Lewis and his men followed as he crossed western Montana in the early summer of 1806. Its lovely blue and white flowers are borne atop a stem that is just a bit taller than its parallel-veined, "equitant" leaves (the leaves are folded, overlapping adjacent leaves and stem). Blue flags add color to moist meadows in late spring and early summer just as the camas (*Camassia quamash*) fades away. The Rocky Mountain iris looks like an iris, and one will recognize it easily when first seen (think of a garden iris on a diet).

On July 5, Lewis's party followed the Bitterroot River (his "Clarck's River") downstream to Clark Fork, and then northeast along the Blackfoot River, paralleling present-day Montana Highway 200. That evening, the party camped a short distance east of today's Missoula. The next day, he wrote in his journal that he had seen "the common small blue flag."[27]

Lewis's specimen did not fare well. Obviously it still had a flower when Frederick Pursh examined it. He did not recognize it as a new species, and he classified it as a similar Eurasian plant (*Iris sibirica*). Today, only a few pieces of the leaves of Lewis's specimen remain. Thomas Nuttall, then on the faculty of Harvard University, studied specimens of the Rocky Mountain iris that the Boston merchant Nathaniel Wyeth collected—probably in southeastern Idaho—during the spring of 1833. Nuttall recognized that Wyeth's iris was new to science, and he described it the following year as *Iris missouriensis*, in the *Journal of the Academy of Natural Sciences* (1834), giving it its present scientific name.

Today, *Iris missouriensis* is cultivated although the plants are not always easy to obtain or to grow, for they require the intermittent moisture of montane, moist grassy meadows.

Although Lewis did not mention it, the Shoshone Indians used the western blue flag medicinally to treat a variety of illnesses, including toothache, earache, burns, and infections. It was also included as an unofficial remedy in pharmacopoeias until relatively recently, and used—probably with no benefit—to treat venereal diseases and other conditions.

Melanthiaceae (Bunchflower Family)

Collected on the "Cokahlaishkit" (Blackfoot) River in the vicinity of Lewis and Clark Pass,
Lewis and Clark County, Montana, July 7, 1806

Elegant death camas, Anticlea elegans (Pursh) Rydb.

The elegant death camas, also called the mountain death camas, was until recently known as *Zigadenus elegans*. It is a montane to subalpine plant that blooms from late spring into late summer depending on location and elevation. The flower stem arises from a basal whorl of long, parallel-veined leaves sometimes reaching a height of two feet or more. The (usually) single stem bears three—or often more—loosely clustered flowers. Its six oval tepals appear to be identical. All have heart-shaped green spots (glands) at their base. The plant favors moist mountain meadows, where it often grows in large numbers. Meriwether Lewis gathered this attractive plant as he traveled up the Blackfoot River and Alice Creek on his way to the Continental Divide.[28]

Frederick Pursh wrote in his *Flora* that he had seen Lewis's dried specimen; its flowers were white, and the plant had been found "On the waters of the Cokahlaishkit [Blackfoot River], near the Rocky-mountains."[29] In his Latin description, he noted that the tepals had two glands at the base; the plant was consistent with the genus *Zigadenus*, so he named the plant *Zigadenus elegans*. It has recently been reclassified as

Anticlea elegans

A. SCOTT EARLE

Anticlea elegans

JAMES L. REVEAL

Anticlea elegans.[30] There are two death camases, and both are now placed in the genus *Toxicoscordion*. Lewis had to have seen these common plants along the expedition's trail, but—for whatever reason—he apparently did not collect them.[31] The elegant death camas is said to be less poisonous than the *Toxicoscordion* species. It is usually not implicated in livestock poisoning, as the others often are—perhaps because it grows at higher altitudes where domestic animals seldom graze.

LINACEAE (FLAX FAMILY)

Collected on the Sun River, Lewis and Clark, Teton, or Cascade County, Montana, July 9, 1806

WILD BLUE FLAX, *LINUM LEWISII* PURSH

Lewis and his men were moving rapidly. They covered the sixty miles or so from the Continental Divide to the Great Falls in only two days. Along the way Lewis stopped to gather specimens of the lovely wild blue flax that now bears his name.[32] As with related flaxes, wild blue flax bears five-petaled flowers. Their color seems to vary somewhat according to the plants' environment, ranging from light blue-gray to a deep blue. The flowers bloom for several weeks or more from early to late summer. Each of the older blooms forms a single globular fruit that remains fixed on the flower stalk well into the winter. Pliable narrow stems bear alternating short linear leaves.

Frederick Pursh examined Lewis's specimens several years later. Today they consist of nearly complete plants that include both flowers and fruit mounted on two herbarium sheets. When Pursh described the plant in his *Flora*, he noted that he had seen the plant growing in cultivation. Since flax blooms and fruits more or less simultaneously, seeds would have been available to anyone who had access to the collection. It is possible that Lewis collected seeds separately, but it is more likely that the plants Pursh saw growing in England came from seeds that Thomas Nuttall had gathered in 1811. Today, a fruiting specimen that Nuttall gathered in "Upper Louisiana" is mounted on the same

BARTON'S *FLORA*

Linum lewisii

herbarium sheet as the Lewis and Clark specimen that Pursh took with him to London.

When Pursh described Lewis's wild flax in his *Flora*, he used the explorer's name for the species name.[33] In his *Flora*, Pursh also mentioned another species of flax, *Linum usitatissimum*, the cultivated European flax, a plant that grew then—and still does—in the wild as an escape from ornamental gardens.

The story of flax is a fascinating one. It has been used by man—both for its fibers, obtained from the plants' stems, and for the oil expressed from its seeds—for millennia. Finely crafted remnants of linen have been found in Swiss lake dwellings and in Egyptian tombs. The ancestral plant is believed to be the Eurasian wild flax, *Linum perenne*, from which the cultivated plant, *Linum usitatissimum*, probably evolved as a cultivar over the ages. It is surprising that Pursh did not mention the Eurasian wild flax when he described our wild blue flax, for the two are so similar that opinion varies as to whether or not they are the same species.[34]

The scientific generic name *Linum* is the Latin word for flax. From it (or more likely from an etymological precursor) we get our words "linen," "line," and "linseed" (the last two words are old terms for the flax plant itself). In addition to the fiber (linen) obtained from the stems, cultivated flaxseed may contain as much as 40 percent oil. Linseed oil is used in large amounts by the paint industry because it hardens with exposure to air. It is interesting that the plant was of such importance in the Old World, yet so far as we can learn, Native Americans did not use it either as a source of oil or for its fiber. The beautifully woven cloths from Mesoamerican sources were made from cotton or wool (the latter, especially, was—and still is—used by North American Indians in their weaving).

Two yellow-flowered species of flax (*Linum digynum* and *Linum rigidum*) also grow along the Lewis and Clark Trail. Apparently they were not seen, or, if specimens were gathered, they did not reach Philadelphia.

OROBANCHACEAE (BROOM-RAPE FAMILY)

Collected on the Blackfoot River, above its confluence with "Clark's River" (the Clark Fork), Powell County, Montana, July 6, 1806

PINK ELEPHANTS, *PEDICULARIS GROENLANDICA* RETZ.
FERN-LEAVED LOUSEWORT, *PEDICULARIS CYSTOPTERIDIFOLIA* RYDB.

Three days after leaving Travelers' Rest, Lewis's party was working its way up the Blackfoot River, above today's Missoula, Montana. Many early summer wildflowers were in bloom, and on that day alone Lewis gathered five specimens of plants that he had not seen before, including the two odd-looking louseworts described here. Although only about two dozen grow in the Pacific Northwest, louseworts are found throughout the Northern Hemisphere and are assigned to a genus of several hundred species. Their old, unattractive common name means "lousy." The name originated, probably in medieval times, in Europe, where farmers believed that sheep browsing on certain plants—including *Pedicularis sylvatica*, the common European lousewort—became infected with lice. While that peculiar folk belief has long since been disproved, the common name lingers on. In addition to the odd configuration of their flowers, louseworts are peculiar in other

Pedicularis groenlandica

JAMES L. REVEAL

Pedicularis groenlandica

JAMES L. REVEAL

ways. Many grow only at higher elevations. They are "hemiparasites," a term that implies that they are dependent on neighboring plants for nutrients, making them difficult to grow in the garden.

199

The scientific name, *Pedicularis cystopteridifolia*, means the same thing as the common name "fern-leaved lousewort." The name does not help much when it comes to identification, for many plants in the genus, including the other lousewort that Lewis gathered that day, have fernlike leaves. A peculiarity of the bracts—the small leaves that grow below the inflorescence and above the fern-shaped leaves—is more helpful in identifying this plant. They have three lobes in this plant, of which the middle one is greatly elongated. The purple flowers are irregular, in common with those of other Orobanchaceae. The lower petals are fused to form a three-lobed "lip," and the two upper petals are joined into a long overhanging projection known as the "galea." The stemless flowers are tightly clustered around the upper stem so that the inflorescence is known botanically as a "spike."[35]

Lewis's other plant, *Pedicularis groenlandica*, has several common names: "little red elephants," "pink elephants," and "bull elephant-head." The plant grows all across the northern part of North America from Alaska to Labrador, and to California, northern Arizona, and northern New Mexico (the species name is a misnomer; the plant does not grow in Greenland). Pink elephants takes its name from the peculiar configuration of its dull purple-red flowers. The galea is greatly elongated in this plant so that it resembles a curved elephant's trunk. If either Lewis or Frederick Pursh saw the resemblance, neither mentioned it.[36]

When Pursh examined the two louseworts that Lewis collected, he correctly placed them in the genus *Pedicularis*. He got the species right, too, at least for *Pedicularis groenlandica*—a plant the Swedish botanist Anders Johan Retzius (1742-1821) described in 1795—but Pursh noted incorrectly that it "occurred on the low plains of the Columbia."[37]

POACEAE (GRASS FAMILY)
Collected in Lewis and Clark or Teton County, Montana, on July 8, 1806
NEEDLE-AND-THREAD GRASS, *HESPEROSTIPA COMATA* (TRIN. & RUPR.) BARKWORTH

Meriwether Lewis was catholic in choosing plants to add to his traveling herbarium. He included specimens of trees, various wildflowers, berries, ferns, and grasses. He seems to have had several criteria for collecting specimens of grasses, including their use as forage plants, importance in Native American crafts (however, the "bear grass" that he collected is not a true grass; see p. 184), and unusual qualities, as in the decorative but weedy *Hordeum jubatum* (see p. 209). The needle-and-thread grass that he found growing on grassy hills just east of the Continental Divide in today's Montana is best included in this last category.

Frederick Pursh clearly examined Lewis's specimen, for he copied Lewis's original note: as "Valeys of the Missouri on the Rocky mountain." Pursh eventually identified the specimen as *Stipa juncea*, a similar Eurasian species.[38]

The needle-and-thread grass takes its name from its appearance. It is of average height—from one to two feet—with thin, curvy leaves. The flowering portion of the plant is a complex inflorescence called a "panicle," where the flowers, and ultimately the fruit, are borne in a spikelet that is surrounded by a thin, sheathlike structure that is pointed at the top to form the "needle." Each of its many fruiting bodies ("florets") ends in a threadlike, spiny process known as an "awn." The awns in this grass are extremely long, and because they are bent they form a loose tangle of "threads." These are common to all of the genera related to the Old

World genus *Stipa*, but the threads are especially pronounced in our American species, now assigned to *Hesperostipa*.

Hesperostipa comata is common throughout much of western North America, from the Yukon to Mexico. It is a two-faced plant; animals browse on the young grass with impunity before it fruits, and it is a useful forage grass. After it ripens, however, it becomes a troublesome and dangerous weed, especially to sheep, for its seeds are hard and their sharp points enable them to penetrate skin and mucous membranes. They may blind—or even kill—those animals that are unfortunate enough to

Hesperostipa comata

JAMES L. REVEAL

come in close contact with fruiting plants. The tendency of the fruit to become entangled in the wool of grazing sheep represents a lesser but still troublesome problem. Needle-and-thread grass is not a welcome plant on anyone's grazing land.

Interestingly, the long awns of this plant are hygroscopic; that is, they are sensitive to moisture in the air. Once lodged in a spot where the upper part of the awn cannot move, the lower part— and thus the floret to which it is attached—twists as the structure dries. In this way, the seed is drilled into the ground.

Where To See Lewis And Clark Plants Today
Lewis and Clark Pass area east of Lincoln, Montana, north of State 200.

Fuzzy penstemon, *Penstemon erianthus* var. *redactus*

A. SCOTT EARLE

Cliff anemone, *Anemone multifida* var. *saxicola*

A. SCOTT EARLE

Pasqueflower, *Anemone occidentalis*

A. SCOTT EARLE

Clustered broom-rape, *Orobanche fasciculata*

JAMES L. REVEAL

201

GREASEWOOD	*Sarcobatus vermiculatus*
GREAT PLAINS COTTONWOOD	*Populus deltoides* subsp. *monilifera*
NARROW-LEAVED COTTONWOOD	*Populus angustifolia*
BLACK COTTONWOOD	*Populus balsamifera* subsp. *trichocarpa*
SNOW-ON-THE-MOUNTAIN	*Euphorbia marginata*
FOXTAIL BARLEY	*Hordeum jubatum*
FALSE INDIGO BUSH	*Amorpha fruticosa*
LEADPLANT	*Amorpha canescens*
FRAGRANT INDIGO BUSH	*Amorpha nana*
SCARLET GLOBE-MALLOW	*Sphaeralcea coccinea*
RIGID GOLDENROD	*Oligoneuron rigidum*
WHITE MILKWORT	*Polygala alba*
GUMBO EVENING PRIMROSE	*Oenothera cespitosa*
RACCOON GRAPE	*Ampelopsis cordata*
PIN CHERRY	*Prunus pensylvanica*

Great Falls to St. Louis
July 11 to September 23, 1806

On July 11, Lewis and his men arrived at the Great Falls of the Missouri. Their stay was not a happy one. During the first night, seven of their seventeen horses mysteriously disappeared—Indians had neatly made off with them. The party crossed to the east side of the river the next day and opened up the cache that they had deposited the year before on White Bear Island (on July 26, 1805). Lewis found his "bearskins entirely destroyed by the water, the river having risen so high that the water had penitrated. all my specimens of plants also lost." The damage did not stop there; most of the medicine left in the cache was also ruined. Next, one of the men narrowly escaped being mauled by an aggressive grizzly, and the mosquitoes at the falls were so thick that Lewis noted that his dog "howls with the torture" and "we...get them in our thrats as we breath." He was understandably stressed when he wrote, "there seems to be a sertain fatality attached to the neighbourhood of these falls, for there is always a chapter of accedents prepared for us during our residence at them." The loss of his plants alone would have justified his lament—that was a calamity. Cutright has pointed out how much work and time must have been involved in preparing the specimens collected between Fort

Mandan and the Falls.[1] And it was a loss for us, too, for the collection would have reflected the flora of the Great Plains as it was two hundred years ago. There is no way of estimating how many plant specimens were lost.

On July 17, Lewis crossed to the north side of the river with three of his best men. He sketched the several falls in his journal and described the prairie as he saw it that day—both are now irrevocably changed. He wrote: "the grass is naturally but short and at present has been rendered much more so by the graizing of the buffaloe, the whole face of the country as far as the eye can reach looks like a well shaved bowlingreen, in which immence and numerous herds of buffaloe were seen feeding attended by their scarcely less numerous sheepherds the wolves." Then he set out to explore the river he had named the year before for his cousin, Maria Wood, whom he described with some feeling the year before, as "that lovely fair one."[2] Lewis had several reasons for wanting to explore the Marias River northward. First, it was a large tributary of the Missouri, and he hoped that it might lead to an easier passage to the west. Second, he hoped that it might connect with the "Suskashawan" [Saskatchewan] River, providing a trade route from the Louisiana Purchase into Canada.

Lewis's detour up the Marias would better have been omitted. The men spent four wet, miserable, mosquito-ridden days, twenty miles west of present-day Cut Bank, Montana, in "Camp Disappointment," so named because they had found no river road into Canada and no easy Northwest Passage. The worst was yet to come. The party headed south on July 26. An encounter with the Blackfeet ended with two Indians dead, and Lewis and his men in headlong flight toward the mouth of the river. There he turned up the Missouri to warn the rest of his men of the Indian presence. Although one can impugn his judgment in this affair, Lewis was a lucky leader throughout, and his luck held now. Shortly after the party reached the Missouri, the men who had left Clark at Three Forks and Lewis at Great Falls arrived. Lewis's small party, stiff and sore from their long ride, turned their horses loose, joined the men in the canoes, and headed down the Missouri. Surprisingly, the plants that Lewis collected at the falls and on the Marias survived the long ride. A few more were added during the journey home.

On August 7 Lewis reached the mouth of the Yellowstone River. Clark had left four days earlier to find a more suitable camp with fewer mosquitoes. The Corps of Discovery was reunited on August 12. The reunion was well timed, for Meriwether Lewis had been shot accidentally through the buttocks and thigh the day before. His luck held—his injury was serious and painful, but he sustained no bone or nerve injury and the wound did not become infected. Lewis stopped writing a journal on August 12, 1806: "as wrighting in my present situation is extreemly painfull to me I shall desist untill I recover and leave to my frind Capt. C. the continuation of our journal."[3] Still, before ending, he noted, "however I must notice a singular Cherry which is found on the Missouri in the bottom lands about the beaverbends and some little distance below the white earth river," and so it was that he completed his journal by describing *Prunus pensylvanica*. Two weeks later he was getting about.

As the party worked its way downriver, Clark's journal records noteworthy happenings. They visited Fort Mandan and returned to Sergeant Floyd's grave. They had an unpleasant but peaceful encounter with the Teton Sioux. They ran into old acquaintances on the river, and on September 21, they arrived at St. Charles, Missouri, met by "great numbers of the inhabitants." The party arrived in St. Louis, and Clark's final journal entry, on September 26, 1806, said simply, "a fine morning we commenced wrighting &c."[4] And so ended one of the most remarkable—and successful—undertakings ever recorded in the annals of American history and botanical exploration.

Populus deltoides subsp. *monilifera*
Missouri River near the Lewis & Clark Interpretive Center in Great Falls, MT

A. SCOTT EARLE

Sarcobataceae (Greasewood Family)

Collected on July 20, 1806, on the Marias River, Toole County, Montana

Greasewood, *Sarcobatus vermiculatus* (Hook.) Torr.

Sarcobatus vermiculatus

JAMES L. REVEAL

Although the Corps of Discovery encountered greasewood on its outbound journey, and Lewis described it in considerable detail, calling it "fleshey leafed thorn," he did not collect it until he encountered it again on the Marias River.[5] Frederick Pursh's transcription of Lewis's original note reads "A small branchy shrub from the plains of Missouri— Jul 20th 1806." On that date Lewis and his men made their camp on the Marias near today's Shelby, Montana. The plant was new to science and available for Frederick Pursh to examine, but the specimen lacked reproductive parts, so he could not classify it and he did not include it in his *Flora*.[6]

Greasewood is one of those plants that seem to characterize the American West, along with sagebrush (*Artemisia* spp.) and creosote bush (*Larrea tridentata*). Greasewood prefers saline or alkaline soil, where it often becomes either a dominant plant or a codominant plant with various species of saltbush (*Atriplex*).

It is considered a weed not so much because it drives out other plants, but because it may poison livestock. Greasewood has much in common with the saltbushes—the leaves contain a considerable amount of oxalic acid, so much that a few pounds of leaves may be sufficient to kill a cow. Otherwise it is a relatively benign member of the prairie community. On several occasions its woody, thorny stems and dense growth made passage difficult for members of the expedition. For this reason, too, it is sometimes used to fence in livestock. Both male and female flowers bloom at the same time, in middle to late summer. The male flowers resemble tiny pinecones; the female flowers are more conspicuous for their yellow sepals. The leaves, which give the plant its species name (*vermiculatus* means "wormlike"), are full of water; this might seem surprising, considering the dry surroundings in which it grows, although this is typical of other succulents as well.[7]

Salicaceae (Willow Family)

Described along the Missouri River between the Marias River and the Great Falls, Chouteau County, Montana, and collected at unknown sites in June and August 1806

Cottonwoods of the Expedition

A dozen species of *Populus* grow in North America, including the common quaking aspen, *Populus tremu-* *loides*, a tree that is so widely distributed that the explorers had no reason to collect a specimen. The cottonwoods, however, are less well known in the East. Three cottonwoods grow along the Lewis and Clark Trail. Lewis first mentioned seeing cottonwood trees on November 23, 1803, near Cape Girardeau on the Mississippi, even before the expedition began.[8] He noted that the trees changed morphologically during the expedition's westward course. The three species shown here represent a spectrum. Confusingly, all may interbreed with one another, making their identification difficult.

Cottonwood trees were of great importance to the expedition. They provided comfort and shade in the otherwise treeless expanses that extend for hundreds of miles along the Missouri River. The trees also provided firewood and transportation, the latter in the form of the pirogues (dugout canoes) that the expedition used on the rivers above the Great Falls of the Missouri. Interestingly, the bark of living cottonwood trees was used regularly by Native Americans as fodder for horses, and the animals apparently relished it. Clark wrote on September 22, 1804, while in present-day South Dakota, "I observed a number of Indian Camps in a Conicel form,—they fed their horses on Cotton limbs as appears."[9] Cutright, who is the undisputed expert on the natural history of the expedition, documented at some length the use of cottonwood bark as fodder.[10]

Collected at an unknown place, August 1806

GREAT PLAINS COTTONWOOD, *POPULUS DELTOIDES* BARTRAM EX MARSH. SUBSP. *MONILIFERA* (AIT.) ECKENW.

Populus deltoides subsp. *monilifera*

JAMES L. REVEAL

The Great Plains cottonwood's species name is derived from its large, more or less triangular leaves (described botanically as "deltoid," like the Greek letter Δ). It grows along the full length of the Missouri River and most of its tributaries well up onto the eastern slope of the Rocky Mountains. It is the largest (in terms of girth) of the three cottonwoods that the expedition encountered. It was well known to science, whereas the other two species were not. The specimen in the Lewis and Clark Herbarium consists today of only of one large, triangular leaf. Frederick Pursh's note on the specimen sheet (copied from Lewis's original) says only that it was a "Cotton tree of the Misisippi & Missouri.—Augst. 1806." Pursh makes no mention of the Lewis and Clark collection in his *Flora*.[11] Given the date, Lewis's specimen was not gathered along the Mississippi River, but it could have come from almost anywhere along the upper Missouri, Marias, or Yellowstone rivers from western Montana to the border of South Dakota and Nebraska. Clark mentioned the Great Plains cottonwood as covering the river bottom of the Missouri River on September 9, 1806, on today's Nebraska and Missouri border.[12]

The Great Plains cottonwood, *Populus deltoides* subsp. *monilifera* (known also, especially in the forestry literature, as *Populus deltoides* var. *occidentalis*), like most other cottonwoods, prefers stream banks and other permanently moist places. It is usually easily identified by its leaves—

large, with a more or less rounded triangular shape, with fine serrations along the sides, and with a broad base—although where species overlap geographically, intermediate forms occur.[13] There are other, mostly technical differences among the various cottonwoods, but leaf shape and location are usually all that is needed to distinguish the Great Plains cottonwood from the other two species that grow along the Lewis and Clark Trail.

Seen and described, but not collected

NARROW-LEAVED COTTONWOOD, *POPULUS ANGUSTIFOLIA* JAMES

If Meriwether Lewis collected a specimen of the narrow-leaved cottonwood tree, the dominant Rocky Mountain species, it was lost in one of the two caches destroyed by the winter floods of 1805-1806. Its leaves, like those of the others, are distinctive, making identification easy. The leaves of this tree are lance shaped, considerably longer than they are wide, and are noticeably different than the leaves of the other two species. The narrow-leaved cottonwood is by no means a small tree when it is fully mature. The trees grow as tall as the other cottonwoods, but they are more slender, and it would have been difficult, for example, to find ones large enough to use for the dugout canoes that the party required for river travel. The narrow-leaved cottonwood occurs throughout the mountainous west, appearing first at the edge of the Great Plains, then becoming more common in the foothills, until it is the only cottonwood that one sees in the mountains. Its range is extensive, for it grows in the Rocky Mountains from

Populus angustifolia

JAMES L. REVEAL

Alberta, Canada, to Chihuahua, Mexico. Its scientific species name, *angustifolia*, translates to its common name, "narrow leaved."

Collected at an unknown place, June 1806

BLACK COTTONWOOD, *POPULUS BALSAMIFERA* L. SUBSP. *TRICHOCARPA* (TORR. & A. GRAY. EX HOOK.) BRAYSHAW

The black cottonwood gradually replaces the narrow-leaved cottonwood in the western Rocky Mountains to become the dominant species along the Columbia River and its larger tributaries. While it shares the same stocky, rough-barked appearance, its leaves differ from the other two. They are smaller and spade-shaped, with a rounded base and wide body, tapering to a point, and with fine serrations along the edges. This species may grow to be exceedingly tall, and while such specimens are seldom seen today, they may grow to be 150 feet or more high with trunks in excess of five feet in diameter. Although—as with the other species—the black cottonwood is most often seen along streams and on the

Populus balsamifera subsp. *trichocarpa*

A. SCOTT EARLE

banks of lakes, it will sometimes grow in drier situations than the others. It is found in all of the western coastal states and provinces as far north as Alaska, south to Baja California, and east to the Rocky Mountains. As with the other cottonwoods, the best way to identify this one is by location first and then by leaf shape.[14]

Pursh's copy of Lewis's ticket appended to the specimen sheet reads, "Cotton tree of the Columbia River.—Jun: 1806." Given the date of collection, Lewis probably collected the plant near present-day Kamiah, Idaho, where the tree is common today. The specimen consists of a twig and thirteen leaves; Pursh did not include it in his *Flora* as a new species, probably because the specimen did not include catkins.

EUPHORBIACEAE (SPURGE FAMILY)
Collected in Rosebud County, Montana, July 28, 1806
SNOW-ON-THE-MOUNTAIN, *EUPHORBIA MARGINATA* PURSH

Euphorbia marginata (the Latin species name, *marginata*, means "enclosed by a border") was one of two species belonging to the spurge family, Euphorbiaceae, that the explorers collected. The other plant, fire-on-the-mountain, *Euphorbia cyathophora*, was added on October 15, 1804, while the expedition was between the Bad River and Fort Mandan, near today's Fort Yates in Sioux County, North Dakota (see p. 47). The common names of the two spurges relate to the bright white bracts ("snow") of the first and the reddish, poinsettia-like bracts ("fire") of the second. Snow-on-the-mountain is a fairly common plant, found today on the Great Plains and eastward—farther to the east today than formerly, for the plant is sometimes used as a garden ornamental and may escape. Lewis and Clark would have seen other spurges along their route, but apparently he did not gather them. All members of the family have milky latex, obvious when a stem or branch is broken. Individual species may be annual or perennial herbs, shrubs, trees, and even cactuslike plants (the last are found in Africa). Many of our spurges are roadside weeds.

There is scant direct evidence either in the Lewis and Clark journals or elsewhere that would suggest that William Clark collected any of the expedition's plant specimens. Some have even questioned those species that Clark almost certainly did collect. Snow-on-the-mountain (*Euphorbia marginata*), a plant that was new to science, is an example. Pursh described it in his *Flora* as being found "On the Yellow-stone river" and that it was "A very handsome species; the white margin of the involucre and white petal-like appendices have a fine contrast with the elegant soft green leaves." Both the label on the Lewis and Clark specimen sheet in Pursh's handwriting, and the plant's distribution as given in the *Flora*, show that Clark found this plant along the Yellowstone River on July 28, 1806.

Lewis was on the Marias River on that date, far to the north and beyond the plant's usual range. Nevertheless both Coues and Cutright suggest that Lewis gathered the specimen.[15]

Clark was fully aware of nature's curiosities. It is clear from his journal writings that he gathered some of the spec- imens that Lewis later preserved. There is also evidence to suggest that he encouraged the collection of plant specimens during his return trip across Montana and down the Yellowstone River. He may not have gathered, pressed, and dried the specimens himself, but he did oversee that task.

POACEAE (GRASS FAMILY)

Collected in the vicinity of Fort Clatsop, Clatsop County, Oregon, on March 13, 1806,
and on White Bear Islands, Cascade County, Montana, on July 12, 1806

FOXTAIL BARLEY, *HORDEUM JUBATUM* L.

The definition of a weed is usually "a plant that grows where someone does not want it to grow." Foxtail bar- ley (*Hordeum jubatum*)—growing almost anywhere—qualifies. This native grass has probably been a weed since pre-Columbian times. It is found throughout North America and now also has become a troublesome weed in the Old World. Foxtail barley is a beautiful grass, but it should not be cultivated or dispersed.

There are two specimens of *Hordeum jubatum* in the Lewis and Clark Herbarium. Pursh copied Lewis's notes for two specimens. The label on the Fort Clatsop specimen, gathered on March 13, 1806, reads: "Grass common to the open grounds." The label with the specimen collected on White Bear Islands on July 11, 1806, says the grass is "Called golden or silken Rye." Pursh's comment in his *Flora* mentions only that the plant was found "On the islands of the Missouri river. *M. Lewis*." At first he considered the species to be new, but "on examination

Hordeum jubatum

A. SCOTT EARLE

of the specimens in the Herbarium of A. B. Lambert, Esq., I found it to be the same as the *Hordeum jubatum* of the Hortus Kewensis."[16]

Foxtail barley is an aggressive peren- nial weed. It invades disturbed sites and prevents other perennials from growing. The long, hairlike awns asso- ciated with the plant's seeds promote its spread, for they easily become attached to animal fur. In addition, the awn and its attached seed complex can work its way into the soft tissues of the mouth of a grazing animal—if the ani- mal is hungry enough to browse on the plant—and cause infection and death. In this grim way the seeds are moved to new areas. Wind and water also play their part in dispersing the seeds.

Several other species of *Hordeum* have been introduced into North America, and these imported plants are also a problem for ranchers, farmers, and their livestock.

Lewis did not mention *Hordeum* in his journal at either location. His party camped on the banks of the Missouri opposite White Bear Islands on July 11, 1806. While there he wrote in his journal "I sincerely belief, that there were not less than 10 thousand buffaloe within a circle of 2 miles around that place."[17] The following day, he noted that the grasses and weeds were luxuriant, and two days later he sent men to hunt on the island, so if the location—as noted on the specimen label—is correct, one of the men may have gathered the grass for him there.

The scientific name was derived from the Latin; *Hordeum* means "barley," and *jubatum* is derived from the word *iuba*, which means "mane" or "crest," referring to the plant's long awns.

FABACEAE (PEA FAMILY)

Amorpha fruticosa collected at the Big Bend of the Missouri River, Lyman County, South Dakota, August 27, 1806; Amorpha nana collected at an unknown place and date; Amorpha canescens presumed seen, but not collected

FALSE INDIGO-BUSH, *AMORPHA FRUTICOSA* L.
FRAGRANT INDIGO-BUSH, *AMORPHA NANA* NUTT.
LEADPLANT, *AMORPHA CANESCENS* PURSH

Lewis's last journal entry was on August 12, 1806, the day that his party joined Clark and his men. Lewis had suffered a painful gunshot wound the day before when Pierre Cruzatte—a good man with poor eyesight—had mistaken the unfortunate captain for an elk.[18] Although Lewis's wound was deep and painful, it was not otherwise serious. He was probably happy to let Clark take over the journal-keeping responsibility.

On the evening of the twenty-seventh, the party camped on an island at the lower end of the big bend of the Missouri River. Lewis went for a stroll; Clark later wrote, "My friend Capt Lewis hurt himself very much by takeing a longer walk

Amorpha fruticosa
JAMES L. REVEAL

Amorpha canescens
JAMES L. REVEAL

on the Sand bar in my absence at the buffalow than he had Strength to undergo, which Caused him to remain very unwell all night."[19] Lewis probably collected the two extant specimens of the false indigo-bush, *Amorpha fruticosa*, and its seeds while on this stroll, for one of the specimens has a label in Frederick Pursh's handwriting that says "Great bend of the Misouri. August. 27. 1806."

False indigo-bush (*Amorpha fruticosa*) is an extremely variable plant. It was originally restricted to the Great Plains but now grows as a weed in much of the United States. Linnaeus knew the plant, for it was grown in Europe; he named the species in 1753. Aware of its variability, he gave it the generic name *Amorpha*, which in Latin means "without form" (the species name, *fruticosa*, means "bushy"). Pursh also saw the plant growing in Europe, and he believed that Lewis's specimens represented a variant form, so he proposed the name *Amorpha fruticosa* var. *angustifolia* (the varietal name means "narrow leaves"). We know the plant today by the name Linnaeus gave it, and no varieties are recognized.[20]

Lewis and Clark also encountered the fragrant indigo-bush (*Amorpha nana*) in the same general area. As Pursh noted, this species, with its fragrant purple flowers, is a "very elegant little shrub." We know that Lewis collected it because Pursh wrote in his *Flora* that he had seen Lewis's plant, although the specimen has since disappeared.[21] The false indigo-bush described above may grow to be ten feet high; its leaves are often covered with downy hair. The dwarf wild indigo (*Amorpha nana*), on the other hand, has smooth leaves and is usually less than three feet tall.

A third species, the leadplant (*Amorpha canescens*) is one that Lewis and Clark would have seen, although they did not collect it (unless they gathered it in 1804 and it was subsequently lost). This plant is widely distributed on the Great Plains. Its hairy, gray leaves (*canescens* means "gray") explain its common name. Indians used the leadplant's leaves for a tea. It is also a favorite browse for cattle and other animals, so one seldom sees the plant growing in heavily grazed areas.

The leaves of all three *Amorpha* are typical of those found in the pea family, but their flowers and inflorescences are not. The latter consist of long, tapering spikes densely covered with small, atypical, seemingly single-petaled purple flowers that are unlike the usual papilionaceous flowers of the pea family.[22]

For centuries, a deep blue dye was extracted from indigo plants (*Indigofera* spp.) native to India. The dye was of great economic importance. Then, about a century ago, cheap synthetic dyes were synthesized and these replaced natural substances. A blue dye can also be extracted from our plants, explaining the common names of "false-indigo" or "bastard indigo." (Confusingly, species of the related genus *Baptisia* are also known as false-indigo and are also used as garden ornamentals; *Baptisia* is more appropriately called "wild indigo.")

MALVACEAE (MALLOW FAMILY)
Collected on the Marias River, Toole County, Montana, July 20, 1806
SCARLET GLOBE-MALLOW, *SPHAERALCEA COCCINEA* (NUTT.) RYDB.

After leaving the Great Falls, Lewis explored the Marias River. He collected several plants and somehow managed to get his specimens back in spite of his precipitous retreat following the party's unfortunate encounter with the Blackfeet.

One of the plants that he collected, the scarlet, or red, globe-mallow, *Sphaeralcea coccinea*, apparently impressed him, for this plant's specimen sheet has more material on it than is usual for the plants that he collected.[23] One can understand

211

Sphaeralcea coccinea

JAMES L. REVEAL

including various ornamentals (such as species of *Hibiscus* and *Malva*) and economically important plants (such as the various cottons, *Gossypium* spp., and okras, *Abelmoschus* spp.). Even so, the explorers might have seen three other mallows during the previous summer (1805), including the orange or currant globe-mallow (*Sphaeralcea grossularifolia*) in Idaho, and Munro's or white-stem globe-mallow (*Sphaeralcea munroana*) in Oregon, as both are fairly common plants. The less common stream-bank or mountain wild hollyhock, *Iliamna rivularis*, with its lovely pink flowers, grows in Idaho along watercourses at higher altitudes. Lewis may well have seen this plant in 1805 while the party was struggling upstream on the Jefferson River and later on the way to Lemhi Pass.

Frederick Pursh was aware that Lewis's specimens were the same plant that the Frasers (nurserymen located in Sloane Square in Chelsea, England) listed in their plant catalog, issued first before September 1813 (see p. 241, n. 21). Thomas Nuttall had named the plant *Malva coccinea*, and the seeds had arrived in England as a result of his travels up the Missouri River in 1811 with the overland Astorians.[25] Pursh, who saw the plant growing in London, said that it is found "On the dry prairies and extensive plains of the Missouri," noting also that "its bright scarlet flowers, makes this plant particularly interesting."[26]

his interest in the plant; it is attractive, with small clusters of bright reddish orange, five-petaled flowers with yellow centers. Its divided leaves range in size but are usually less than two inches long and somewhat hairy. The plants often grow in large numbers on the prairies, and Thomas Nuttall, who gathered it in 1811, noted that the mallow grew "over the plains in such quantities as to communicate a brilliant redness to thousands of acres."[24]

The mallow family is not well represented along the expedition's route. Most mallows grow in warmer climates,

ASTERACEAE (ASTER FAMILY)

Collected in Brule County, South Dakota, possibly on September 12, 1804; or more likely in Doniphan or Atchison County, Kansas, or Buchanan County, Missouri, September 12, 1806

RIGID GOLDENROD, *OLIGONEURON RIGIDUM* (L.) SMALL VAR. *HUMILE* (PORTER) G. L. NESOM

The genus *Solidago* includes the goldenrods—plants we all know. The common goldenrod, *Solidago canadensis*, is the one most of us think of, if we consider goldenrods at all. It has a long stalk with many pointed leaves, and drooping

inflorescences made up of a myriad of tiny golden blossoms. The rigid goldenrod (also known as hard-leaf and flat-top goldenrod) that the explorers gathered is different. Its basal leaves have long petioles (leaf stems). Then, ascending the main stem, the petioles become shorter until finally there is no stem at all and the leaves clasp the main stem directly. The plant's individual blooms are larger than one expects to see in a goldenrod. The flower head is made up of a tightly arranged cluster of small flowers, each looking like a tiny sunflower with disks up to a quarter of an inch across and with eight to fourteen small, well-formed rays. These features, coupled with other details of their anatomy and their chromosome numbers, exclude this and a few other species from *Solidago*. As a result, the former *Solidago rigida* var. *humilis* is now assigned to the genus *Oligoneuron* (meaning "few nerves" in Greek, referring to the limited number of rays in each flower).[27]

Lewis collected the rigid goldenrod on September 12 or 13 (the date is difficult to read on the specimen's label), but we do not know the year. Did he collect it going or coming? We do not know. Frederick Pursh's label on the expedition's specimen—copied from Lewis's original notes—reads only "High dry prairies Septb: 12 [13?] 1804," when the expedition was in South Dakota. However, the specimen was not included with those that Lewis sent back to President Jefferson in the spring of 1805, so it is more likely that it was collected in

Oligoneuron rigidum

JAMES L. REVEAL

Kansas or Missouri on the return trip in 1806. Not that it makes a great deal of difference, but it points up the problems one encounters in trying to be precise in dealing with specimens in the Lewis and Clark Herbarium. Strangely, Pursh failed to include Lewis's plant in his *Flora* with the fifty-odd species of *Solidago* that he listed, even though he recognized it as a plant that Linnaeus had named in 1753.[20]

POLYGALACEAE (MILKWORT FAMILY)

Collected in Williams or McKenzie County, North Dakota, August 10, 1806

WHITE MILKWORT, *POLYGALA ALBA* NUTT.

Six species of milkwort are found on the Great Plains. Superficially their irregular flowers resemble those of various legumes, although, because they lack pinnate leaves it is not hard to distinguish them from plants in the pea family. As both its scientific and common names suggest, *Polygala alba* has white flowers. These are borne on short stems, blooming from below upward (in "racemes"). The flower clusters are so tight that they look almost cylindrical on the plant's numerous straight, upright stems. Its basal leaves are smooth surfaced and lance shaped, but higher up they become linear and grasslike. This milkwort is only four to ten inches high. Its white flowers and closely ranked, straight stems make identification easy once one has seen the plant.

The note for the white milkwort (in Pursh's hand, copied from Lewis's field notes) confirms what we already know; Lewis learned about herbal plants from his mother, who was a well-known herbal healer in Arbemarle County, Virginia. The notation reads: "Polygala A kind of Seneca Snake root. On the Missouri R." The words "Yellowstone River" are lined out—which brings up an interesting question: Is this a plant that William Clark collected during his descent of the Yellowstone River? We do not know—although we suspect Lewis collected it, as he did most of the expedition's plants.

On August 10, both captains and their men were on the Missouri. Clark had camped at the mouth of the Yellowstone River to wait for Lewis and then moved downstream to get away from hordes of mosquitoes. Lewis was a day behind, near present-day Williston, North Dakota. The next day, August 12, he sustained a gunshot wound that ended his collecting activities for some weeks, but until then he would have noticed any interesting plants that he saw. The white milkwort is plainly similar to *Polygala senega*, the Seneca snakeweed, whose root herbalists used to treat snakebite. Given the similarity, the white milkwort was a plant that Lewis would have wanted to collect. *Polygala*, from the Latin, means "lots of milk." The English had once believed—erroneously—that if animals browsed on the common milkwort (*Polygala vulgaris*), their milk production increased.[29]

Pursh examined Lewis's specimen, and later in England he saw another example that John Bradbury had collected. Pursh listed Bradbury's plant as a variety of *Polygala senega* in a supplement added to his *Flora*.[30] In 1811, Thomas Nuttall later re-collected it and recognized that it was new to science, so he described the plant and gave it the name that it has today.

ONAGRACEAE (EVENING PRIMROSE FAMILY)
Collected near the Great Falls of the Missouri River, Cascade County, Montana, July 17, 1806
GUMBO EVENING PRIMROSE, *Oenothera cespitosa* NUTT.

Oenothera cespitosa

JAMES L. REVEAL

The gumbo evening primrose is a low, small, tufted, perennial plant that grows in most of our western states (although it is rare in Washington). It usually grows on dry ground—sand dunes, talus slopes, clay banks, roadcuts, and other disturbed places. As with many plants that have a wide distribution, several varieties are recognized. Its common name is taken from the heavy, slick "gumbo-mud" common to the hills along the Teton and Marias rivers in northwestern Montana, and elsewhere in the West. Other common names include "sand-lily," "moon-rose," "tufted evening primrose," and "desert evening primrose," reflecting the plant's varied habitats. No matter which name one uses, the gumbo evening primrose remains one of our more attractive western wildflowers.

The gumbo evening primrose is the second plant in the evening primrose family that Lewis collected (he found the other, the long-leaf suncup, *Camissonia subacaulis*, on the Weippe Prairie on June 14; see p. 175). There are two herbarium sheets for the gumbo evening primrose in the Lewis and Clark Herbarium at The Academy of Natural Sciences in Philadelphia.[31] Thomas Nuttall had named the species *Oenothera cespitosa* in a catalog of plants published by the Frasers (London nurserymen) probably in September 1813. When Pursh learned of this, he amended his original classification (in the appendix that he added to the *Flora*) to agree with Nuttall's.[32]

Pursh characterized this plant's flowers as "large purple, with dark veins," adding that other species of *Oenothera* are yellow.[33] The flowers of our plant are actually white, although they darken to pink or purple as they age, as with Lewis's specimen (this is true of several other *Oenothera* as well). Evening primroses are so named because their flowers open early in the evening, remain open throughout the night, and close usually in late morning. The flowers then quickly wilt, and their color changes from white to rose and eventually purple by midafternoon. Most evening primroses are pollinated by night-flying hawk moths (also called "hummingbird moths"). The pollen grains are held together in long, sticky chains (easily removed from the anther by the tip of a finger); by early morning, the moths are clothed in long strands of *Oenothera* pollen.

VITACEAE (GRAPE FAMILY)

Collected either at Council Bluff, Washington County, Nebraska, on September 8, 1806, or in Leavenworth County, Kansas, on September 14, 1806

RACCOON-GRAPE, *AMPELOPSIS CORDATA* MICHX.

As the expedition worked its way down the Missouri River, someone in the party—most likely Lewis—paused to collect one more plant, possibly the last one he gathered.[34] The specimen in the Lewis and Clark Herbarium consists only of fragments, including a length of vine with a half dozen heart-shaped leaves. It is a specimen of raccoon-grape ("possum-grape" is another common name, although because the plant is not a grape, a better name is "heart-leaf peppervine").

At first glance raccoon-grape resembles a true grape (*Vitis* spp.). Its simple leaves are somewhat like those on a grape plant (but not compound as in the grape), as is its fruit, although the berries of the raccoon-grape grow in tight clusters that are wider from side to side than they are long, whereas the fruit of true grapes grow in elongated bunches. Both produce immature green fruit that turns color in the fall. The fruit of *Ampelopsis cordata* becomes a striking turquoise blue, unlike any species of *Vitis*. Clumps of small white flowers appear in the spring on the raccoon-grape, noticeable only because many are bunched together into panicles (clusters in which the stems may branch repeatedly). The petals of *Ampelopsis* are free, whereas those of *Vitis* are fused. The serrated leaves of *Ampelopsis cordata* are more or less heart shaped (explaining the species name, cordata). Another difference is the smooth, nonshedding bark, unlike the shedding bark of true grape vines. Finally, raccoon-grapes are inedible, at least for humans. Some birds and possibly raccoons do eat them—if so, it would explain the plant's common name, although more likely the common name was bestowed because both the plant and raccoons are capable climbers. Look for *Ampelopsis cordata* in moist, disturbed sites along the lower Missouri River where the vines, supported by many tendrils, grow high on nearby trees. *Ampelopsis cordata* is native to the southeastern United States. It grows as far north as Nebraska and

215

west to Texas and Mexico. André Michaux established the genus *Ampelopsis* in 1803, deriving the name from two Greek words, *ampelos* for "vine" (with "grape-vine" inferred) and *opsis* meaning "view" or "looks like."

ROSACEAE (ROSE FAMILY)
Collected in Williams or McKenzie County, North Dakota, August 10, 1806
PIN CHERRY, *PRUNUS PENSYLVANICA* L.

Because of confusion in recording the dates on which Lewis and others collected their various plants, it is uncertain which plant was the last one that the men of the expe-

Prunus pensylvanica

JAMES L. REVEAL

dition collected—it may have been either the pin cherry (*Prunus pensylvanica*) or the raccoon-grape (*Ampelopsis cordata*). What is certain is that the pin (or fire) cherry, Prunus pensylvanica, was the last plant to rate a full botanical description. The specimen does not amount to much today—a twig, with one complete and several partial leaves. There are no flowers or fruit. This dearth of material probably explains why it was previously identified as an eastern chokecherry, *Prunus virginiana*. Its lanceolate, serrated leaves, while a bit narrow, are consistent with that diagno-

sis—but Lewis's description of the plant in his journal is not.

On August 12, 1806, Lewis described "a globular berry about the size of a buck-shot of a fine scarlet red…the pulp of this fruit is of an agreeable ascid flavour and is now ripe." He had collected a specimen of the plant two days earlier, on the same day that his vision-impaired hunting companion had shot him through the buttock—an unfortunate accident that was nevertheless understandable, given that the men's standard "uniform" at the time was fashioned from deer or elk skin. Despite his discomfort, Lewis managed to get in this one last botanical description. He closed by noting that "I have never seen it in blume."[35] This description of the plant that we know today as the pin cherry was included in his last journal entry. Lewis was unaware that his cherry was new only to the men of the expedition.

The Garrison Reservoir in present McKenzie County, North Dakota, now covers the place where Lewis's cherry tree grew. Carl Linnaeus the younger (1741-1783), son of the creator of our modern binomial system, had described the pin cherry in 1782, and Frederick Pursh knew the plant. Pursh noted in the *Flora* that it ranged from New England to Virginia.[36] At the most—if he had recognized Lewis's specimen for what it was—he might have extended the plant's range westward to the Missouri. Today, the pin cherry occurs from the western edge of the Rocky Mountains onto the Great Plains (where it is uncommon) and in the northeastern United States and adjacent Canada (where it is often found).

Epilogue

On the twenty-first of September 1806, the homeward bound Lewis and Clark expedition reached St. Charles, near the mouth of the Missouri, where Meriwether Lewis had joined the party in May 1803. William Clark noted that "the inhabitants of this village appear much delighted at our return and seem to vie with each other in their politeness to us all." Two days later, he wrote: "Set out decended to the Mississippi and down that river that to St. Louis…we were met by all the village and received a harty welcom from its inhabitants &c."[1] They had ended their journey

The return of the Lewis and Clark expedition was good news for the nation. Although Jefferson had kept faith, many feared the men had perished. A few centuries earlier, people had feared that mariners might fall off the edge of the earth. Although no one believed that in 1806, explorers indeed faced hostile natives, unkind elements, and dangerous terrain—and who knew what savage animals were prowling the wilds. Some scientists even believed that the expedition might encounter woolly mammoths in the unexplored lands to the west. And finally, there were the Spaniards waiting to put the Americans to work in the mines of California, for Spain claimed all of the land to the west of the Louisiana Purchase. Several Spanish military parties were in fact dispatched to head off Lewis and Clark, but fortunately they did not go north far enough to engage the Americans.

Back in the United States, there was no lack of recognition for what the expedition and its men had achieved. They were feted and exclaimed over by a nation that wanted to know what they had seen and what they had brought back. Botanists, especially, were anxious to examine the plant specimens, and horticulturists wanted to try out the seeds of new species; they were as eager to see the plants as twentieth-century scientists were to see moon rocks. This simile is not as far-fetched as it seems. The expanse of terrain that the expedition traversed was not as well known as was the surface of the moon, for that at least could be perused with a telescope.

Both Jefferson and Lewis received requests for seeds. Jefferson kept some and grew many in his gardens—those of the currant family (*Ribes* spp.) did especially well, as he recorded in his garden and farm books. The rest of the first batch of seeds, those sent from Fort Mandan, went to the American Philosophical Society. The society's minutes for November 15, 1805, read "Resolved that the seeds transmitted by the President be referred to Mr. Wm. Hamilton [per Lewis's wish in his letter to Jefferson from Fort Mandan] with a request that he plant them in due season and report as soon as may be to the Society the nature of the plants produced by them with such descriptions & specimens as may serve for the information of the Society or the Public."[2] William Hamilton (1745-1813) was a wealthy naturalist with a special interest in trees. His estate, Woodlands, located on the west side of the Schuylkill River, was a showpiece. Primarily an arborist, Hamilton introduced several important trees and shrubs into the United States, including camellia, ginkgo, Lombardy poplar, and Norway maple.

Jefferson also kept some of the seeds that Lewis brought back at the end of the expedition, and he sent many others on to Bernard M'Mahon in Philadelphia, a grower whom he trusted and with whom he frequently corresponded. All in all, Lewis and Clark seeds were broadcast fairly widely to botanists, to relatives, to Charles Willson Peale, and others. Some of the nineteenth-century images shown in this book are of plants whose pedigrees extend back to Lewis and Clark seeds.

Cutright, who wrote extensively on the naturalistic aspects of the Lewis and Clark expedition, referred to the material the expedition brought back as "the Lewis and Clark booty." Booty implies value, but this has to be qualified. The Lewis and Clark booty had little monetary, but great intellectual value. The story of what happened to the expedition's botanical specimens is a fascinating one, and only recently has an end, of sorts, been written. But what of the other items that the expedition brought back? The account, sadly, is not a long one, for not much has survived.[3]

The captains had sent some ethnological material to President Jefferson from Fort Mandan, including buffalo robes (one had a painted battle scene on it), a bow, quiver, and arrows, and more. Jefferson kept some items and sent others to Charles Willson Peale for his museum in Philadelphia, noting that he (Jefferson) was retaining "horns, dressed skins, utensils, &c." Those that he sent to Peale comprised, in addition to Indian artifacts, "2 skins of the white hare [white-tailed jackrabbit, *Lepus townsendii*], 2 skeletons of do. [ditto], A skeleton of the small or burrowing wolf of the prairies [coyote, *Canis latrans latrans*], A male & female Blaireau [badger, *Taxidea taxus*] 13 red fox skins [swift fox, *Vulpes velox hebes*]. Skins of the male & female antilope with their skeletons [pronghorn, *Antilocapra americana americana*], 2 skins of the burrowing squirrel of the prairies [black-tailed prairie dog, *Cynomys ludovicianus ludovicianus*], A living magpie [American magpie, *Pica hudsonia*] A dead one preserved." At the time, all were new to science. These were just the first installment; many more were added when the expedition returned.[4]

Charles Willson Peale (1741-1827) was a man of many talents and interests. He and his brother James (1749-1831) were portrait painters—Charles studied under both John Singleton Copley (1738-1815) in Boston and Benjamin West (1738-1820) in London—as were many of Charles's twelve children and two of his grandchildren. He had served with distinction as an officer during the American Revolution; he was also a noted naturalist and the founder of the nation's best-known museum, one that enjoyed quasi-governmental support, for it was housed in Independence Hall. After Peale died, the museum went into slow decline. Although it struggled along until 1850, various items were sold at auction over the years. In 1850, the showman Phineas Taylor Barnum (1810-1891)—P. T. Barnum—bought half of the remaining collection for his own museum,

including some of the Lewis and Clark material. Barnum's museum burned to the ground in 1858

The other half was purchased by Moses Kimball (1809-1895) for his museum, located at the corner of Tremont and Bromfield streets in Boston. The articles remained there until Kimball died. In 1899, Kimball's family offered Harvard University's famed Peabody Museum the pick of the Boston Museum's ethnographic collection. The Peabody acquired several fine Lewis and Clark Indian artifacts, including clothing, a bow made from elk horn, and the painted Mandan buffalo robe among other items. Still, much is missing. Some articles were lost in the Barnum fire, and the locations of the Jefferson items and ones that Clark retained for his own museum in St. Louis are not known. Many Lewis and Clark artifacts are surely extant in museum collections today, but because they are mixed with other collections, they lack provenance.

The expedition's botanical material made out better—but only by great good fortune. The plant specimens that the expedition collected may be divided into four lots. The first was sent to Jefferson from Fort Mandan in the spring of 1805. On receiving this in August, President Jefferson inventoried it, found sixty-some plants, and passed these on to the American Philosophical Society. The society's secretary confirmed Jefferson's inventory and turned them over to Benjamin Barton, who would supposedly prepare a scientific report describing the plants. At some point after Barton received them, thirty of the plants disappeared. Their fate is unknown.

The second lot of plants was cached on White Bear Island at the Great Falls of the Missouri in late June 1805, to be retrieved on the party's return. These were destroyed by floodwater in the spring of 1806.

The third lot was made up of the plants that Lewis collected between Great Falls and Lemhi Pass. These were cached at "Camp Fortunate," and all but one, a *Ribes* (wild currant), was destroyed by floodwater as well.[5]

The last lot is the group that Lewis brought back with him in September 1806. After his return, while he was still in

Washington, Lewis received a letter from Bernard M'Mahon. Reading between the lines, it appears that M'Mahon—while he does not come right out and say so—believed Lewis's specimens might be better evaluated by "a young man [presently] boarding in my house," rather than by the aging Barton. M'Mahon did not identify the young man further, but described him as being "better acquainted with plants, in general, than any man I ever conversed with on the subject; he was regularly bred to the business in Saxony."[6] M'Mahon was writing about the thirty-one-year-old Frederick Traugott Pursh, who was then employed by Barton as a plant hunter. Lewis, accepting M'Mahon's suggestion, came to Philadelphia and met Pursh. He was favorably impressed and turned all of his plants over to the young German. Lewis apparently planned to describe the material himself, with Pursh's help, as part of a scientific report to be published in conjunction with the expedition's journals. Two things support this supposition. First, in May 1807, he paid Pursh seventy dollars "for assisting me in preparing drawings and arranging specemines of plants for my work."[7] Next, Lewis visited Barton—who had done nothing with the specimens from Fort Mandan—and retrieved what he could (apparently the first thirty were already lost, although possibly Barton did give them to Lewis). Everything then went to Pursh. Now, for the first time, all of the surviving specimens were together and in Pursh's possession.

In the summer of 1807, Pursh completed his collecting obligations to Barton following a trip to New York and adjacent Vermont. Presumably he also worked on the drawings and the plant collection Lewis had entrusted to him. In 1809, while waiting for further instructions from Lewis, Pursh accepted a position in New York City with Dr. David Hosack (1769-1835) to work at the Elgin Botanic Garden.

Hosack had studied medicine as the apprentice of a prominent New York surgeon, Dr. Richard Bayley (1760-1835), who perhaps is best known as the father of Mother Elizabeth Seton (1774-1821), the first American to be canonized by the Catholic Church. He then attended and received his M.D. degree from the Philadelphia Medical College in 1791. After that, Hosack traveled abroad, as did every American physician who could afford to do so, attending lectures in Edinburgh and in London, where he met William Curtis (1746-1799), a successful apothecary whose love of plants led him into horticulture. Hosack was greatly impressed by Curtis, who was then lecturing at the famous Chelsea Physic Garden in London. A few years later, after returning to New York, Hosack became professor of botany at Columbia (1795). Six years after that, in 1801, he founded the Elgin Botanic Garden (named for his father's birthplace, Elgin, Scotland). Hosack had great plans for the garden, including a magazine patterned after Curtis's *Botanical Magazine*. Pursh was slated to be the magazine's editor. In the end, however, Hosack did not have enough money to carry out his projects. By now Pursh had completed some or all of Lewis's plant drawings. Then he learned that Meriwether Lewis had died on October 11, 1809, of a self-inflicted gunshot wound.[8]

When he left Philadelphia, Pursh gave all of the plant specimens that Lewis had given him to Bernard M'Mahon—or so M'Mahon believed. He did not know that the botanist had removed many specimens from the collection, including entire plants and portions of plants that he had snipped from intact specimens. At this point William Clark came to Philadelphia, to tie up loose ends left by Lewis's death and to arrange to publish the expedition's journals. He took back the plant specimens that Pursh had given to M'Mahon and gave them to the aging Dr. Barton to describe. Ill health, lack of organization, apathy, simple disinclination, or likely a combination of all of these kept Barton from completing the project—had he done so, it would have greatly enhanced his reputation in his final years. But he died in December 1815. The Lewis and Clark specimens in his possession went, with the rest of his botanic collections, to the American Philosophical Society. We do not know what happened to the drawings Lewis had commissioned. Some of Pursh's artwork is included with the Barton material in the society's archives, and may include the Lewis drawings—the likely ones were published for the first time by Moulton.[9]

Pursh apparently was a good conversationalist, but his social skills were otherwise minimal, as opposed to his reported drinking skill. The combination meant that Pursh rarely retained positions of employment for more than a few years. He was also blunt, self-centered, and talented. In each of his positions, initially in Baltimore, then Philadelphia, and finally in New York, Pursh left for a variety of reasons, including his inability to be social and remain sober. All of his moves brought him an improved standing in botany but at a harsh price.

Pursh left New York in 1811, taking with him a good working knowledge of the American flora and a large collection of plants. In London, he obtained the patronage of Aylmer Bourke Lambert, a wealthy, dedicated, and productive botanist, and the vice president of the Linnean Society of London. Lambert knew botanical publishing. He had written several books himself, including *A Description of the Genus Cinchona* (1797) and *A Description of the Genus Pinus* (1803). The latter went through three editions. Several of the conifers that Lewis and Clark had seen were formally described in the last edition in 1832. Lambert's book on the pines was typical of those published at the time by the very wealthy, for its plates, executed by the finest German artists, are superb—considered by many to be the finest botanical illustrations of trees ever made. Lambert deserves great credit, for he prodded Pursh to write—and to finish—his *Flora Americae Septentrionalis*.

Pursh is a controversial figure today. Nevertheless, he took great care in his evaluations of the specimens that Lewis and Clark had gathered. He omitted plants that he was unable to classify properly. Altogether, he proposed ninety-four new names in his *Flora* that were based, at least in part, on Lewis and Clark specimens. Forty of his new names are still in use, exactly as he proposed. Thirty-six are names that were subsequently reassigned to other genera. Only eighteen are considered synonyms for plant names that were already in use when *Flora Americae Septentrionalis* was published in late 1813.

By 1813, Pursh was a confirmed alcoholic and Lambert reportedly had to confine him while he worked on the *Flora*. When completed and published, the *Flora* was given to various individuals and institutions in December 1813, and it was released to the general public in early January 1814.[10]

It is hard, today, to evaluate Pursh's achievement accurately; was he a hero or a villain? He was a hero, because if he had not published the *Flora*, the Lewis and Clark plants would probably never have been used to describe new species, and the explorers would have received no credit for finding them. Yet he was a villain, too, because he divested both Thomas Nuttall and especially John Bradbury of the opportunity to describe and name their own newly made collections. That in itself was bad enough, but that he appropriated the Lewis and Clark specimens and made no arrangements to return them was worse. In the final evaluation, Pursh acted as if he believed "if not me, who else?" And in so doing—and we have to agree—he was right. We should add that he credited Lewis for all of the expedition's plants that he included in the *Flora*. But he did not extend that courtesy to Nuttall and only grudgingly gave credit to Bradbury.

There are so many "ifs" to this story: *If* Lewis had lived…*If* Barton had acted…*If* Jefferson had made it possible for Lewis to work on the journals…*If* Pursh had been adequately paid to work on the expedition's plants. But none of these things happened, and Jefferson, Barton, and other American botanists experienced the chagrin of having "their" plants described by a German in a book published in England. But at least the *Flora* was finished and published. One hundred and thirty-two Lewis and Clark plants are in it.

Anticlimactically, when the *Flora* was done, Pursh was pretty much done, too. His alcoholism took over. To get rid of him, Sir Joseph Banks, England's dean of natural history studies, supposedly gave Pursh money for passage to Canada, where he died in poverty in 1820, having recently lost his newly made collections, books, and manuscripts to a fire.

The saga of the Lewis and Clark plant specimens does not

end here—there is more. Bernard M'Mahon gave the specimens that he had to the American Philosophical Society, and they disappeared into the society's archives. Those that Pursh had "borrowed" were incorporated into Aylmer Lambert's herbarium in London, and that was broken up after Lambert's death in 1842. Lambert died poor, for his wealth had gone into botany. Sotheby's auctioned off the Lambert estate, and the Lewis and Clark plants were in at least two of the lots. As luck would have it, a young American botanist, Edward Tuckerman (1817-1886), purely by chance wandered into the auction and purchased one of the lots. We do not know whether he knew what he bid on, but sooner or later he recognized what he had, and in 1856 he donated the collection to The Academy of Natural Sciences. (Tuckerman's name is known today for his important work on lichens, *Genera Lichenum* [1872], but more widely for the eponymous Tuckerman's Ravine on Mount Washington in New Hampshire, a mecca for skiers and mountaineers.) The other lot ended up in the Royal Botanic Gardens at Kew, where nine specimens remain today.

Now, fast-forward to the 1890s. Most of the Lewis and Clark specimens were back in Philadelphia. Those donated by Tuckerman were at The Academy of Natural Sciences, while others—the ones that Pursh had left with M'Mahon—were stashed away in the American Philosophical Society's archives. We have already met the nurseryman and author Thomas Meehan (author of the *Handbook of Ornamental Trees* [1853] and *The Native Flowers and Ferns of the United States* [1878-1880]; see p. 104). In his later years, Meehan was associated with The Academy of Natural Sciences as a botanist. A colleague tipped him off to the possibility that the American Philosophical Society might be holding some of Lewis and Clark's botanical material. Meehan searched for and found the missing specimens. They are now on permanent loan to the Academy. For the first time in almost a century, the Lewis and Clark plants—or all of those that are in the United States—came together. Meehan cataloged and described the collection in 1898.

Over the last century, the 232 plant specimens that Lewis and Clark gathered have been studied usually in conjunction with new editions of their journals or studies on their discovery.[11] Two works require special mention. By providing a full and accurate rendition of the journals, Gary Moulton has made it possible for the plant specimens to be more accurately identified. A few that originally were thought to have been gathered by Lewis and Clark were actually specimens obtained by Thomas Nuttall in 1811. Others were cultivated specimens grown in Philadelphia from seeds or cuttings sent by the explorers. Then, in 1999, James Reveal, Gary Moulton, and Alfred Schuyler summarized the technical information on the collection. Later in the year, Moulton's twelfth volume of his work, *The Journals of the Lewis and Clark Expedition*, appeared, which was devoted entirely to the plant collection and included images and information on each of the actual and purported Lewis and Clark specimens. These two published works, and a new CD-ROM of the Lewis and Clark Herbarium by Earle Spamer and Richard McCourt, plus the web pages of The Academy of Natural Sciences in Philadelphia, now make the collection available for anyone who may be interested in this small portion of our national history.

More remains to be done. There are missing Lewis and Clark specimens—such as *Krascheninnikovia lanata*, *Mentzelia decapetala*, *Mimulus lewisii*, and *Phyllodoce empetriformis*, and others, and, more notably, the first thirty specimens that Lewis sent to Philadelphia in 1805. Every effort must be made to find them or at least learn their fate. Additionally, some fragmentary specimens require more careful study to determine their exact identity. Already tiny fragments of select Lewis and Clark specimens have been examined to determine air quality in the American West of 1806, and certainly even tinier amounts will be used in the future for DNA studies. The value of the collection is not monetary, for its worth is incalculable. Rather, its value is in what it reveals of our past. The Corps of Discovery is still promoting new explorations into the unknown.

Notes

PROLOGUE, PP. 5-17

1. D. Jackson, ed., *Letters of the Lewis and Clark Expedition, with Related Documents, 1783-1854*. Hereafter, irregularities in spelling, grammar, and punctuation will not be noted in the quotations.

2. Ibid., 10-13.

3. Ibid., 61.

4. Ibid., 61-66.

5. Ibid., 16-17.

6. Hyoscyamus, or scopolamine, extracted from the plant is a potent alkaloid related to atropine; scopolamine is still in use today as an adjunct to anesthesia and as a seasickness remedy.

7. G. W. Corner, *Two Centuries of Medicine: A History of the School of Medicine at the University of Pennsylvania*, 45.

8. Jackson, p. 70. Mueller changed his name to Miller after he settled in London.

9. Jackson, *Letters*, 50, 54-55.

10. Ibid., 51-60.

11. R. Dillon, *Meriwether Lewis: A Biography*, 44.

12. See Jackson, *Letters*, for a record of the items taken by the expedition, and for numerous letters of critical importance written during this period.

13. Although Clark is traditionally referred to as "captain," and we follow that tradition in this book, his actual rank was second lieutenant—a fact unknown to the men of the expedition, because in the reduced post-Revolutionary army an open captaincy did not exist. In 2001 President Clinton conferred the rank of captain on William Clark and made York and Sacagawea sergeants.

14. See J. L. Reveal, G. E. Moulton, and A. E. Schuyler, "The Lewis and Clark Collections of Vascular Plants: Names, Types, and Comments."

15. In preparing this book, we had access to both the original 1813 printing of Frederick Pursh's *Flora Americae Septentrionalis*, and the 1816 reprint, which was unaltered from the first edition printing. For anyone interested in the botanical history of the time, we recommend the introduction by the late Joseph Ewan (1909-1999) in the 1979 facsimile of the second printing, published by J. Cramer.

16. W. Greuter et al., *International Code of Botanical Nomenclature*.

CHAPTER 1, PP. 18-53

1. Dillon, *Meriwether Lewis*, 79-80.

2. We have given the wording here as written by Clark. Moulton suggested that Clark was referring to two plants, an unknown violet and something he termed "dove's foot" (G. E. Moulton, ed., *The Journals of the Lewis and Clark Expedition*, 2:210 n). However, we suspect that Clark referred to only a single species, bird's-foot violet (*Viola pedata*), a plant that is common even today in that area. The usual common name for *Geranium carolinianum* is Carolina crane's-bill. The term "bloe" is Clark's spelling of "blow," an old expression meaning "blossom" or "bloom."

3. Ibid., 2:266.

4. Tongue-grass is an old term used for garden cresses—York probably gathered yellow cress, *Rorippa palustris*, or watercress, *Rorippa nasturtium-aquaticum* (ibid., 2:278).

5. P. R. Cutright, *Lewis and Clark: Pioneering Naturalists*, 57. The goldenseal, a member of the buttercup family, was so important medicinally that it is now uncommon, the result of overharvesting. Many of the related Ranunculaceae contain potent alkaloids, and it may be that the goldenseal is therapeutically active when used topically, as Lewis suggested (it is, however, a known poison and should not be taken internally). Wild gingers have been used for many conditions, although the various species of *Asarum* have no proven therapeutic value.

6. Springtime along the lower Missouri River is still challenging because of the mosquitoes, gnats, and ticks. Poison ivy (*Toxicodendron radicans*) can also make life miserable. By late spring and summer, the plant is well established and easy to avoid. The beautifully colored leaves in the fall also make poison ivy easy to recognize. In the early spring, however, as the plants are just emerging, they can be easily overlooked—until later, when one feels their effect. The new growth is rich in the oils that cause the characteristic itchy skin eruptions.

7. Moulton, *Journals*, 2:346, 2:433.

8. Ibid., 2:436, 9:78.

9. Ibid., 3:66, 46, 48.

10. Ibid., 3:66.

11. Ibid., 3:90.

12. Ibid., 3:418.

13. Ibid., 10:53, 3:461; Pursh, *Flora*, 46.

14. Moulton, *Journals*, 2:292.

15. C. van Ravenswaay, *Drawn from Nature: The Botanical Art of Joseph Prestele and His Sons*.

16. Linnaeus proposed the name *Dalea* to honor Samuel Dale (1659-1739), an English pharmacologist. The French botanist André Michaux established *Petalostemon* (the name refers to the union of the stamens onto the petals).

17. Moulton, *Journals*, 3:456. "Tausel" was Lewis's variant spelling of *tassel*, for the compact inflorescence. The date and the place of collection for

these plants are uncertain because of discrepancies between Lewis's list and the label data on the herbarium sheets in the Lewis and Clark Herbarium (Reveal, Moulton, and Schuyler, "Lewis and Clark Collections," 17-18).

18. Moulton, *Journals*, 12:25.

19. C. L. Hitchcock, in C. L. Hitchcock et al., *Vascular Plants of the Pacific Northwest*, 3:346.

20. Pursh, *Flora*, 441.

21. H. D. Harrington, *Edible Native Plants of the Rocky Mountains*, 72.

22. Other species of gumweed also grow along the Lewis and Clark Trail in the Pacific Northwest, notably the Idaho gumweed (*Grindelia nana*). It has fewer rays (12-25) on each composite flower head, whereas there are 25-40 rays on the flower heads of *Grindelia squarrosa*. Several varieties of *Grindelia squarrosa* have also been described. Besides the biennial var. *squarrosa*, the explorers may have seen the perennial var. *quasiperennis* in western Montana in 1805.

23. Moulton, *Journals*, 3:464.

24. Pursh, *Flora*, 559.

25. Ibid., 386.

26. Moulton, *Journals*, 2:493.

27. Pursh, *Flora*, 327-28. Whatever the truth, from that point Nuttall's name is missing from the pages of *Flora Americae Septentrionalis*.

28. Harrington, *Edible Native Plants*, 120.

29. Moulton, *Journals*, 2:308, 3:459.

30. Pursh, *Flora*, 97. Pursh wasn't through with the four-o'clocks, for while he was in England preparing his *Flora*, he had access to a collection of plants gathered by John Bradbury for the Liverpool Botanical Society, plants that Bradbury had not yet had a chance to describe himself. Pursh took it upon himself to include two of Bradbury's four-o'clocks, found "In upper Louisiana." He named these *Allionia linearis* (known today as *Mirabilis linearis*) and *Allionia hirsuta* (now *Mirabilis hirsuta*), placing them, along with many other plants that Bradbury collected, in a supplement at the end of his book. He noted only that they were Bradbury's dried specimens (Pursh, *Flora*, 728). These plants are now—because of Pursh's unethical behavior—associated with his name rather than with Bradbury's. Finally, our wild four-o'clock was reclassified in 1892 by Conway MacMillan (1867-1929), who was the Minnesota state botanist, so the full scientific name is now *Mirabilis nyctaginea* (Michx.) MacMill.

31. Catlin, *North American Indians*, 67.

32. Pursh, *Flora*, 115.

33. T. Nuttall, *The Genera of North American Plants*, 2:240.

34. Hitchcock, in Hitchcock et al., *Vascular Plants*, 3.461.

35. Moulton, *Journals*, 4:388, 5:39.

36. Pursh, *Flora*, 540. The genus *Gutierrezia* was proposed in 1816 by a Spanish botanist, Mariano Lagasca y Segura (1776-1839), to honor members of the Gutierrez family in Spain. Pursh's species name was not used for decades, because Thomas Nuttall independently found the plant in 1811 and in 1818 proposed a different name (Nuttall, *Genera of North American Plants*, 30). Eventually Pursh's priority was recognized and the plant

assumed the scientific name by which it is known today.

37. During the winter of 1804-1805, while at Fort Mandan, Lewis prepared a catalog to accompany the plants that he was sending back to Jefferson. Unfortunately, the specimens represented by entries 33 to 99 are now missing—lost sometime between the time the plants were dispatched from Fort Mandan and the present. Jefferson received the plants and then gave them to John Vaughan of the American Philosophical Society. Vaughan's description on his accession receipt—clearly information that Lewis provided—reads only "The leaf of Oak which is common to the Prairies. 5 Sep. 1804." This same information, in Pursh's hand, is also on the two specimen sheets (Moulton, *Journals*, 3:464). A mystery surrounds the second of the two specimens. Most of the sheet is taken up by mature leaves, typical of those of the bur oak, and labeled in Pursh's handwriting, "*Quercus macrocarpus circinata* Common to the prairie." In the upper left corner, however, there is a separate specimen of an oak's catkins that had to have been collected at a different time. This is labeled, also by Pursh, "*Quercus macrocarpa* . . . Mississippi." If the place of collection—on the Mississippi River—is correct, this specimen was most likely collected when the expedition was camped at Wood River.

38. Pursh, *Flora*, 632.

39. Ibid., 564.

40. According to the rules of botanical nomenclature, Pursh's species name, *spinulosus*, cannot be used with *Machaeranthera* because of a pre-existing species already named *Machaeranthera spinulosus*.

41. Moulton, *Journals*, 3:457.

42. Ibid., 3:464.

43. Ibid., 3:98; Pursh, *Flora*, 370.

44. Thomas Nuttall also collected the plant at the same place in 1811. Pursh apparently saw Nuttall's specimen, for it was among those that Edward Tuckerman (1817-1876) acquired when he purchased Lambert's Lewis and Clark specimens at auction in 1842 (see p. 221).

45. Another species, the dotted gayfeather (*Liatris punctata*) is the one most commonly found on the Great Plains today (the species name, from the Latin, refers to its spotted leaves). It differs from the two that Lewis found, for its roots resemble the taproots of a carrot. This plant prefers drier, sandy places. It grows today along the Missouri River from Kansas to the site of the expedition's winter camp at Fort Mandan, North Dakota. Native Americans boiled the roots of gayfeathers to make decoctions or poultices, which they used medicinally.

46. Confusingly, another plant, *Rosa blanda*, is also known as a "prairie rose," although today it is also referred to as "smooth rose."

47. Given the fragmentary nature of the remaining material, we can understand why its identification was revised (also true of many other plants in the Lewis and Clark Herbarium). Initially, Thomas Meehan, the horticulturist who "rescued" the expedition's material from the archives of the American Philosophical Society, identified the leaves as those of Woods' rose (*Rosa woodsii*). It is not surprising that Meehan classified Lewis's specimen as a Woods' rose, for it and several other species are quite similar in

223

appearance. To make matters even more confusing, various species of wild rose may interbreed (R. L. McGregor, in Great Plains Flora Association, *Flora of the Great Plains*, 398). More recently, botanists have examined the specimen and concluded that the plant that Lewis collected was most likely *Rosa arkansana*, the prairie wild rose, as described above. Both this plant and Woods' rose grow on the Great Plains, neither is a vine, but *Rosa arkansana* (also known as the dwarf prairie-rose, or the Arkansas rose) best fits Lewis's description (Reveal, Moulton, and Schuyler, "Lewis and Clark Collections," 45).

48. Pursh, *Flora*, 472.

49. Moulton, *Journals*, 3:454. Moulton incorrectly reported this as var. *berlandieri*, a variant known only from Texas (3:467). Var. *paysonii* is found along Alice Creek in the Lewis and Clark Pass area of Montana, although Lewis made no mention of the plant when he was there in July 1806.

50. McGregor, in Great Plains Flora Association, *Flora*, 435.

51. There is no way of knowing today whether the plants that Lewis and Bradbury collected were the same, because Pursh discarded Lewis's specimens. Until 1964 the species was known as *Astragalus multiflorus* (*multiflorus* means "many flowers"), but modern rules of nomenclature require the use of Pursh's original name, *Astragalus tenellus* (the species name is also Latin; it means "delicate," referring to the plant's small flowers).

52. Whitson et al., *Weeds of the West*, 370-71.

53. Pursh, *Flora*, 19-20.

54. In his 1832 *Genera et Species Asterearum*, the German physician and botanist Christian Gottfried Daniel Nees von Esenbeck (1776-1858) established the genus to which the plant now belongs. As with many generic names, it is uncertain what *Symphyotrichum* means. Apparently Nees von Esenbeck derived it from the Greek words *symphysis*, meaning "a growing together," and *trichos*, for "hair." He apparently meant the name to refer to a perceived tendency of the pappus hairs that are attached to the achenes (the seeds) to be joined together before they fall away. Today, the majority of asters found in North America belong to this genus.

55. Joel Roberts Poinsett (1779-1851), American minister to Mexico in the 1820s, saw *Euphorbia pulcherrima* growing in Mexico and introduced it into the United States as an ornamental. Millions of the red-bracted plants are now purchased each year for Christmas holidays.

56. APG II, "An Update of the Angiosperm Phylogeny Group."

57. *Scurf* is a word that most of us have never used. It is an Old English term, derived from a verb that meant "to gnaw." The word *scurf* was used as a noun in the distant past for various scaly skin diseases (such as scabies). Today its most common use is as a botanical term to describe plants that are covered by scaly glands (*scruffy*, a word in common use, has the same derivation). It is an example of a common name that mirrors a plant's scientific name, for most scurf peas were, until recently, assigned to *Psoralea*, a genus established by Linnaeus. The name *Psoralea* was derived from the Greek word for "mange" (*psora*), a word that also carries the connotation of a scaling skin eruption (as in *psoriasis*)—a reminder of how closely related medicine and botany were in times gone by.

58. This plant is also known as Indian breadroot or silver-leaf Indian breadroot.

59. Pursh, *Flora*, 475. There are good reasons to doubt that Lewis collected the specimen of *Psoralidium lanceolatum* that is in the Lewis and Clark Herbarium. First, the abundance of material on the sheet in the herbarium is not characteristic of specimens that Lewis collected. Next, the specimens are of plants that are in full flower, but when Lewis supposedly found the plant near present-day Yankton, South Dakota, it was late August—neither the time nor the place were right for him to find the plants, especially flowering plants. Finally, Pursh did not attribute the specimen to Lewis, something he did faithfully. All things considered, it seem likely that the specimens in the Lewis and Clark Herbarium were actually gathered by Thomas Nuttall in 1811 (Reveal, Moulton, and Schuyler, "Lewis and Clark Collections," 42). By the time Pursh had reached page 475 in his book, he was no longer giving credit to Nuttall, but was unethically describing new species that Nuttall had collected. Nuttall—understandably—was not pleased when he found out what Pursh was doing. Two of the scurf peas that Lewis collected have recently been reclassified as *Psoralidium*, a genus proposed by botanist Per Axel Rydberg (1860-1931) in 1919, formed by adding -*idium* (a Greek suffix that denotes smallness) to *Psoralea*. The common name "scurf pea" is more appropriately applied to species of the southern African genus *Psoralea*. The same name is also frequently used for the much more widely distributed Old World genus *Cullen*. We have retained "scurf pea" here because it is widely used in older guidebooks and floras, the remnants of a time when all of the New World species were included in *Psoralea*.

60. Moulton, *Journals*, 3:465.

61. Pursh, *Flora*, 204-5.

62. An apocryphal anecdote relates that when Rudyard Kipling was told that there are only two words in the English language—*sugar* and *sumac*—in which the initial s was pronounced "sh," he answered, "Are you sure?"

63. Moulton, *Journals*, 3:160. Confusingly, another plant, *Lobelia inflata*, also goes by the name "Indian tobacco." It is unrelated, but both species contain poisonous, alkaloidal substances.

64. Pursh, *Flora*, 141.

65. Moulton, *Journals*, 3:460-61, 3:466, 472 n.

66. Botanist Per Axel Rydberg claimed to have seen *Nicotiana quadrivalvis* growing in North Dakota in 1932, but this is an uncertain claim, as he did not provide a specimen (Great Plains Flora Association, *Flora*, 637).

67. It is hard to say whether Native Americans used tobacco for the pleasure they received from an immediate nicotine rush, or whether they became truly addicted. The answer probably is both. Often tobacco was in short supply (which is why the Indians mixed it with adulterating barks; see p. 56); at such times addiction would have been unlikely. At other times, when tobacco was freely available, Native Americans smoked it frequently—ceremonially perhaps, but it is not hard to find an excuse for a ceremony; and in such times of plenty it is likely that users were addicted. The captains described in their journals how the Clatsop Indians used tobacco (the former var. *multivalis*). Lewis wrote on January 8, 1806: "The nativs in this neigh-

bourhood are excessively fond of Smokeing tobacco . . . they appear to Swallow it as they draw it from the pipe, and for maney draughts together you will not perceive the Smoke they take from the pipe, in the Same manner they inhale it in their longs untill they become Surcharged with the vapour when they puff it out to a great distance through their norstils and mouth; I have no doubt that tobacco Smoked in this manner becomes much more intoxicating, and that they do possess themselves of all its virtues to the fullest extent." He went on to describe what happened next: "[T]hey frequently give us Sounding proofs of its createing a dismorallity of order in the abdomen, nor are those light matters thought indelicate in either Sex, but all take the liberty of obeying the dicktates of nature without reserve" (Moulton, *Journals*, 6:179, 196). Hardly a description of casual users of the weed!

CHAPTER 2, PP. 54-65

1. Moulton, *Journals*, 3:27, 127, 140, 187.

2. C. L. Hitchcock, in C. L. Hitchcock, and A. Cronquist, *Flora of the Pacific Northwest: An Illustrated Manual*, 342.

3. Pursh, *Flora*, 283.

4. Moulton, *Journals*, 3:464. The explorers also found kinnikinnik growing at Fort Clatsop. On January 29, 1806, Lewis described it at length in his journal. This time he mentioned that the berries were "hung in [the Indian's] lodges in bags where they dry." If one has sampled the berries, it is not hard to interpret Lewis's additional comment that "in their most succulent state they appear to be almost as dry as flour" (6:246). Lewis made no mention at Fort Clatsop of Indians smoking kinnikinnik leaves, and at Fort Mandan he made no reference to their eating the berries.

5. Until recently, its species name was *stolonifera*, and the plant is so listed in many reference books.

6. This plant is known to many as *Coryphantha missouriensis* (Sweet) Britton & Rose, although it has recently been reclassified as *Escobaria missouriensis*. Its common names "nipple cactus" and "coryphantha" seem to be well established, but, as noted, another name, "Missouri foxtail cactus," has been suggested for the plant. Its present scientific name honors two Mexican brothers named Escobar.

7. Hitchcock and Cronquist, *Flora*, 301. Robert Sweet (1783-1835), a horticulturist and nursery owner in Stockwell, England, described the nipple cactus in his *Hortus Britannicus* (1826)—an ambitious work in which he attempted to account for all plants then in cultivation in Britain. Because he described the plant, his name is still associated with its scientific name. Nuttall also collected the spinystar cactus, *Escobaria vivipara* (Nutt.) Buxbaum (known also as *Coryphantha vivipara* (Nutt.) Britton & Rose). Lewis and Clark may also have seen this plant at Fort Mandan and along the Missouri in western North Dakota or eastern Montana. Thomas Nuttall also found this cactus in 1811 near the site of Fort Mandan. *Escobaria vivipara* (from the Latin *viviparus*, meaning "bearing live young") differs, however, for it forms clumps of two hundred or more individuals, each of which may produce one or two pink, red, lavender, or yellow flowers. The spines of both species are in starlike clusters on the individual segments of the fleshy stem. Species of *Escobaria* are less common than those of *Opuntia* on the Great Plains and may be difficult to find.

8. Pursh, *Flora*, 476. Although Pursh's illustration, one of fourteen included in his *Flora*, shows the flowering plant, the one shown here is better, for the bulbous root is included. It was painted by Isaac Sprague (see p. 24) and included in *American Wild Flowers*, published in 1879 by George Lincoln Goodale (1839-1923), Asa Gray's successor as professor of botany at Harvard University. Pursh's illustration was made from plants cultivated by Lambert in London; he had obtained his seeds from Lewis's 1804 collection (Reveal, Moulton, and Schuyler, "Lewis and Clark Collections," 37).

9. The generic name, *Pediomelum*, was derived from *pedion*, the Greek word for flat, open country or "plains," and *melon*, for "apple," referring to the plants' apple-shaped anatomy—in this case the root—thus another common name, "earth apple."

10. Harrington, *Edible Native Plants*, 204.

11. Moulton, *Journals*, 4:35.

12. *Artemisia* is said to honor queen Artemisia II (who died ca. 350 B.C.) of Caria, in Asia Minor. Artemisia is best known for the tomb she built for her husband King Mausolus (the mausoleum—whence our modern term—one of the seven wonders of the ancient world). She also had an interest in botany and in medicine.

13. Pursh, *Flora*, 521.

14. Several other sagebrush species occur along the route taken by Lewis and Clark, although their ranges are limited. Clark might have seen black sagebrush (*Artemisia nova* A. Nelson) and little sagebrush (*Artemisia arbuscula* Nutt.) in southwestern Montana in 1806. These, until recently, were considered small varieties of big sagebrush, and it requires careful observation to distinguish among them. Almost certainly Lewis saw three-tipped sagebrush (*Artemisia tripartita* Rydb.) along the Blackfoot River in Montana. In addition to the big sage that grows along the Columbia, the scabland sagebrush (*Artemisia rigida* (Nutt.) A. Gray) is found on the volcanic flats above the river. One of the easiest ways to recognize this species is by looking for the red lichens that frequently grow on old stems. Unlike the wormwoods, sagebrush species are not used medicinally—although it is said that transplanted westerners need an occasional whiff to retain their mental health.

15. Pursh, *Flora*, 468.

16. Ibid., 647.

17. Ibid., 646.

Chapter 3, pp. 66-75

1. Lemhi Pass (at 7373 feet) is located on today's Idaho-Montana state border about thirty miles southeast of present-day Salmon, Idaho. A memorial honoring Sacagawea is located adjacent to a spring, a short distance below the summit of the pass on the Montana (eastern) side. This may be the spring that Lewis observed. It is not, however, the origin of the Missouri River; that is located at the head of the Red Rock River, another stream emptying into the Beaverhead.

2. Moulton, *Journals*, 5:74.

3. It is quite possible that Lewis passed by some plants on his return journey in 1806, believing that these species were safely cached at Camp Fortunate.

4. Moulton, *Journals*, 5:30-31, 4:89.

5. It is possible that Lewis gathered a specimen of the currant that Sacagawea found on April 30, 1805, near present-day Brockton, Montana. If so, the specimen was lost when the White Bear Island cache flooded the following spring. That plant would have been the Great Plains golden currant, *Ribes aureum* var. *villosum* (also known as Missouri or buffalo currant, and as *Ribes odoratum*). The western golden currant, *Ribes aureum* var. *aureum*, is a slightly different plant. It has shorter flowers and is generally smooth and nonhairy (glabrous), with three-lobed leaves, whereas the more eastern variety, *Ribes aureum* var. *villosum*, has hairy leaves with many lobes (*villosum* means "covered with long hairs"). Lewis distinguished between the two, consistently referring to the latter as the Missouri currant. Thomas Nuttall also collected the Great Plains golden currant in 1811, and Pursh indicated in his description that he had seen the plant growing in a garden (Pursh, *Flora*, 164). It is unlikely that a shrub from Nuttall's seeds would be flowering by 1813, so it is possible Lewis and Clark had gathered seeds. On August 9, 1806, Clark obtained a "deep purple berry of the large Cherry of the Current Species" in western North Dakota that might have been *Ribes aureum* var. *villosum* (Moulton, *Journals*, 8:286).

6. For a century the onions (*Allium* spp.) have been classified as members of the lily family. Recent research, however, has shown the necessity of dividing the Liliaceae into numerous families, of which the Alliaceae is one (see APG II, "Update of the Angiosperm Phylogeny Group").

7. Moulton, *Journals*, 4:416. We are impressed in reading the journals with how much later plants bloomed two hundred years ago than we would expect today. Lewis's Onion Island was north and east of present-day Helena, Montana; it is now under Canyon Ferry Lake. Of the two onions mentioned above, *Allium brandegeei* is the more abundant.

8. Ibid., 7:309.

9. Etymology per *Oxford English Dictionary*, 2d ed. The lore and accounts of angelicas' reputed folk medicinal value are voluminous. As with most herbal remedies, angelicas probably have no real therapeutic value, but their roots and seeds have an aromatic fragrance that may make them effective as placebos. They have other uses as well; "angelica oil" is expressed from the seeds, and candy is made from the root and flowers of the Norwegian angelica (*Angelica archangelica*). The leaves of some species are eaten. Their seeds, including those of our native species, may be used as flavoring in place of related herbs such as cicely (or cecily, *Myrrhis odorata*) and chervil (*Anthriscus cerefolium*). Angelica has also been used as flavoring for wines and cordials, including chartreuse and Benedictine. In days past, a perfume known as "angel water" was made from angelica root.

10. The two Rocky Mountain plants discussed here, *Angelica arguta* (formerly *Angelica lyallii*, and still known as Lyall's angelica) and *Angelica dawsonii* (Dawson's angelica), both have names honoring individuals. David Lyall (1817-1895) was assistant surgeon and botanist on one of Captain James Ross's voyages of exploration to the northern Pacific and Arctic regions (1839-1844), and John Wyndham Dawson (1820-1899) was a paleobotanist and professor of geology at McGill College (now University) in Montreal. He discovered some of the most primitive of the land plant fossils known.

11. The genus *Mimulus* is no longer considered to be a member of the figwort family (Scrophulariaceae). It is now classified as a member of the Phrymaceae, a family related to the mint family, Lamiaceae (R. G. Olmsted et al., "Disintegration of the Scrophulariaceae").

12. Pursh, *Flora*, 426-27; Ewan's comment is on p. 85. Botanists have speculated about where Lewis found his example. Pursh gave the location as "On the head springs of the Missouri, at the foot of Portage Hill," which suggests that Lewis found the plant near today's Lemhi Pass, close to the Idaho-Montana state line, but on the Montana side of the border. There is further evidence that confirms this location. Clark's map in volume 1 of Moulton holds the key. There, the ridge of the Continental Divide in the Lemhi Pass area is labeled "Portage" and the trail over the pass is marked "road over the Portage." Also, as previously noted, plant specimens gathered before August 20 were cached at "Camp Fortunate," and only one specimen—the golden currant—survived. If Lewis had found the plant when he first crossed Lehmi Pass on August 12, the specimen would have been left behind at Camp Fortunate, and lost; obviously, since Pursh saw it, the plant was collected later. Given this information, it seems likely that Lewis found *Mimulus lewisii* along the trail over Lehmi Pass in late August. If one accepts the exact wording in Pursh's *Flora*, however, then most likely the specimen was gathered along Trail Creek at the eastern base of Lemhi Pass in Beaverhead County, Montana, on or about August 25, 1805.

13. A close relative, the Sitka mountain-ash (*Sorbus sitchensis*), is also used in landscaping, and the two shrubs resemble each other closely, although the leaflets of *Sorbus sitchensis* are blunt rather than sharply pointed. A second ticket on the sheet (presumably copied from Lewis's original note) says that the shrub grew "On the top of the highest peaks & mountains. Jun. 27th. 1806. In the Rocky mountains." This might have been *Sorbus sitchensis*, although it is rare today in the area in which he found the plant.

14. Moulton, *Journals*, 5:217. The bird was the varied thrush, *Ixoreus naevius*, and "shoemake" is an alternate spelling of "sumac," a plant with similar leaves.

15. The species names *sitchensis* and *scopulina* (and variations of them) occur in other places in this book. The first translates from the Latin approximately as "from Sitka," and the second is derived from the Latin *scopulus*, variously translated as "rock" or "boulder" (J. Morwood, ed., *The Pocket Oxford Latin Dictionary*, 1230), and "cliff" or "crag" (W. T. Stearn, *Botanical Latin*). When used with American plants, however, the term has come to connote "Rocky Mountain."

16. Moulton, *Journals*, 5:77.

17. Botanist Zacheus Collins sent a specimen from one of the Philadelphia-grown plants to Stephen Elliott (1771-1830) of Charleston, South Carolina. That specimen is now in the herbarium of the Charleston Museum, where it was mistakenly thought to be an authentic Lewis and Clark plant, and it is so listed in a recent catalog of all of the plants that Lewis and Clark collected (see Moulton, *Journals*, 12:165). The error was caught, but not in time to prevent its publication (Reveal, Moulton, and Schuyler, "Lewis and Clark Collections," 48).

18. Pursh, *Flora*, 162. Another species, *Symphoricarpos orbiculatus*, or coral-bell, also grows along the Missouri River, although it is not as common as the other. Pursh's brief description provides no clue as to which one Lewis gathered.

19. Curiously, there is an additional label in Pursh's hand that suggests the specimens were gathered on June 16, 1806. Given the mature nature of the specimen, it is more likely that the plant material on the sheet (a twig and five leaf fragments) was gathered in 1805. Although the specimen was misidentified in the past, it is now recognized as the Rocky Mountain honeysuckle, *Lonicera utahensis*, described here. The specimen had previously been annotated *Lonicera ciliosa* by Jesse More Greenman (1867-1951), who examined the Lewis and Clark material in 1897. Thomas Meehan published the identification the following year in his report on the reassembled Lewis and Clark Herbarium. Sometime later, Charles Vancouver Piper (1867-1926) noted on the herbarium sheet that this was not *Lonicera ciliosa* but rather *Lonicera ebractulata*, a plant now known as *Lonicera utahensis* (Reveal, Moulton, and Schuyler, "Lewis and Clark Collections," 29).

CHAPTER 4, PP. 76-85

1. Moulton, *Journals*, 5:206.

2. Ibid., 5:209.

3. Ibid., 5:223.

4. Ibid., 5:201.

5. Douglas, *Journal Kept by David Douglas during His Travels in North America, 1823-1827*, 346.

6. Moulton, *Journals*, 5:204.

7. Ibid., 5:205. The line quoted here is the citation used by the *Oxford English Dictionary*, 2d ed. for the first printed use of the word *tamerack*.

8. Moulton, *Journals*, 5:205. Clark was usually careful to distinguish the various conifers, recognizing the difference between pine, spruce, fir, and tamerack. Lewis, however, called most conifers "pines," until he got to Fort Clatsop, where everything was a "fir."

9. Squirrels also may cache the whitebark's seeds; in fact, the best seed survival seems to occur when the squirrels bury the entire cone without removing the seeds.

10. Moulton, *Journals*, 5:145. Although Lewis thought the bird was a woodpecker, it is in fact a member of the crow family.

11. Ibid., 5:218, 226.

12. The common name "cedar" is widely misapplied to several genera of the cypress family in North America and elsewhere. In a strict sense the term should be used only for members of the Old World genus *Cedrus*. The common name most frequently applied to members of *Thuja* is "arborvitae," and thus *Thuja plicata* is termed "western arborvitae" in the more technical literature. Nonetheless, this common name is rarely used locally in the Pacific Northwest—nor is it likely to be—so we have retained its colloquial common name.

13. Moulton, *Journals*, 5:218.

14. Ibid., 11:328. *Crataegus* is a difficult genus taxonomically. Many can reproduce asexually, resulting in plants that are so different morphologically that—unless one has genetic knowledge—they may be regarded as different species. Various species also interbreed, adding to the taxonomic confusion. Fortunately, the hawthorns of the Pacific Northwest are less complex than those found elsewhere, although their identification still is not easy.

15. Pursh, *Flora*, 337.

CHAPTER 5, PP. 86-97

1. Moulton, *Journals*, 6:581.

2. The species name was proposed by Douglas, from the Latin *ponderosus*, meaning "heavy," because of its large size in old-growth forests. The varietal name, proposed by physician-naturalist George Engelmann, is the possessive form of the Latin *scopulus*, meaning a rock, crag, or cliff. It has come to mean "of the (Rocky) mountains" in the United States and Canada.

3. Moulton, *Journals*, 5:201.

4. Other naturalists had collected plants in other places along the Pacific Coast even earlier. In 1741, Georg Wilhelm Steller (1709-1746), a German physician with the Bering expedition (1733-1743), collected 141 specimens

on Kodiak Island off the coast of Alaska. Shipwreck and disaster prevented his Alaskan specimens from reaching Europe. (Steller's name is memorialized today in the form of the raucous Steller's jay, *Cyanocitta stelleri*, and the equally raucous Steller's sea lion, *Eumetopias jubatus*.) Next, the French gardener Jean-Nicolas Collignon (d. 1788), a member of the ill-fated Lapérouse expedition (which departed from France in 1785 and was lost off the Solomon Islands in 1788), had visited Monterey, California, in 1786. In 1791, the Czech botanist Thaddaeus Haenke (d. 1817), attached to Spain's Malaspina expedition (1784-1794), visited the same port before going on to Canada.

5. Moulton, *Journals*, 5:369, 6:103.

6. Hitchcock, in Hitchcock and Cronquist, *Flora*, 342.

7. Moulton, *Journals*, 6:287, 289.

8. Laurel (*Kalmia* spp.) and huckleberries (*Vaccinium* spp.) are, like salal, members of the heath family.

9. Pursh, *Flora*, 284.

10. Recent studies have conclusively shown that the maples do not constitute a distinct family (Aceraceae), and they have been returned to their traditional home, the mainly tropical Sapindaceae.

11. Pursh, *Flora*, 267.

12. Moulton, *Journals*, 6:294.

13. Ibid., 5:85, 8:28.

14. Pursh, *Flora*, 217-20. The illustration of *Berberis aquifolium* was drawn from material gathered by both Menzies and Lewis, whereas the one of *Berberis nervosa* was taken entirely from Lewis's collection (L. Rossi and A. E. Schuyler, "The Iconography of Plants Collected on the Lewis and Clark Expedition").

15. Various parts of these plants, as well as other *Berberis* species, apparently have been used in folk medicine, although there is no scientific evidence that they possess therapeutic value.

16. In 1818, Thomas Nuttall, impressed—as Pursh had been—with the unique combination of features that distinguished these American species from their Old World counterparts, proposed the genus *Mahonia*. Since 1818 some three hundred species of *Berberis* have been named. The apparent generic distinction recognized by Pursh and proposed by Nuttall cannot be sustained; as a result, the former *Mahonia aquifolium*, *Mahonia nervosa*, and *Mahonia repens* are all now considered members of the genus *Berberis*.

17. Pursh, *Flora*, 119.

18. Rafinesque's spelling of *Paxistima* is curious. The name is derived from two Greek words, "paxos" (παχοσ) meaning "thick," and "stigma" (στιγμα). In Greek, the letter χ (chi) is spoken with a hard "ch," as in "loch," not as an English x. (The Greeks have another letter that corresponds to our x; it is ξ, pronounced "ksee").

19. Both *Coreopsis tinctoria* var. *atkinsonia* and *Symphyotrichum eatonii* either are on, or are candidates for placement on sensitive plant lists, which is also true for several other of the Lewis and Clark plants mentioned in this book—probably because of alteration or destruction of their natural habitats. We were unable to locate Eaton's aster, and the golden tickseed used as an illustration for this section was a cultivated plant.

20. Pursh, *Flora*, 547.

Chapter 6, pp. 98-111

1. Moulton, *Journals*, 6:168.

2. The early death of some of the expedition's men in later years may have been due to syphilis contracted while they were with the expedition.

3. Cutright, *Pioneering Naturalists*, 272.

4. Moulton, *Journals*, 6:278.

5. In 1817 Constantine Samuel Rafinesque-Schmaltz, a man who was fond of naming plants, proposed, but did not publish, scientific names for the Fort Clatsop conifers. In 1832, he finally got around to publishing a brief article, entitled "Six New Firs of Oregon," basing this on the botanical notes that accompanied the 1814 edited journals. In the end, only one of the names that he proposed for the trees stuck, because in that same year, several others also proposed names for these trees—trees that had, for a quarter of century, remained scientifically nameless. It turned out that one of Rafinesque's "new" species had been named only two months earlier by a Russian botanist. Also, the manuscript names of David Douglas, who collected for the Royal Horticultural Society, were finally published. They appeared in a series of unnumbered pages inserted in the third edition of Aylmer Lambert's *A Description of the Genus Pinus*, published by David Don (1799-1841), the librarian of the Linnean Society of London. However, it is not known exactly when in 1832 this was published. If Don's edition appeared after October 1832, then Rafinesque's names of several of Lewis's conifers would be valid according to the rules of botanical nomenclature.

6. Today the genus *Tsuga* includes the hemlocks, and *Abies* the firs.

7. Moulton, *Journals*, 6:281.

8. Ibid., 5:191.

9. Ibid., 6:282.

10. Ibid., 6:284.

11. *Blechnum* is in the Blechnaceae (chain fern family); *Dryopteris* and *Polystichum* are in the Dryopteridaceae (wood fern family); and *Pteridium* is now in the Pteridiaceae (bracken fern family). All of these genera were once in the broadly defined Polypodiaceae, but the idea that ferns were all in the same family was abandoned more than fifty years ago.

12. Our species of deer fern has been known as *Streuthiopteris spicant* and *Lomaria spicant*. Linnaeus knew the plant from Europe and originally called it *Osmunda spicant*.

13. A French physician, Dominique Villars (1745-1814), knew it from the Grenoble area of France and named it *Polypodium carthusianum* in 1786. In most of our American literature, the fern was called *Dryopteris*

spinulosa, which explains the retained common name of spinulose wood fern. To make matters even more difficult, *Dryopteris carthusiana* (with 164 chromosomes) is rare in northwestern Oregon, whereas the closely related and much more common northern wood fern (*Dryopteris expansa*, with 82 chromosomes) also occurs.

14. E. E. Spamer and R. M. McCourt, *The Lewis and Clark Herbarium, Academy of Natural Sciences of Philadelphia (PH-LC): Digital Imagery Study Set*.

15. Moulton, *Journals*, 6:228.

16. Ibid., 6:304.

17. Ibid., 6:139.

18. *Equisetum* is the only modern genus of the Equisetaceae (horsetail family). Both *Glycyrrhiza* and *Lupinus* belong to the Fabaceae (pea family); *Sagittaria* is a member of the Alismataceae (water-plantain family); *Cirsium* is a member of the Asteraceae (aster family); and *Argentina* belongs to the Rosaceae (rose family). *Typha* is the only genus in the Typhaceae (cattail family).

19. Moulton has pointed out that Clark apparently confused two of Lewis's descriptions and combined the features of the wild licorice and seaside lupine; see Cutright, *Pioneering Naturalists*, 265, and Moulton, *Journals*, 6:230.

20. Moulton, *Journals*, 6:378, 402; 7:26-28, 30, 28.

21. Ibid., 6:366, 368.

22. *Vaccinium* belongs to the Ericaceae (heath family), *Sambucus* belongs to the Caprifoliaceae (honeysuckle family), and *Rubus* belongs to the Rosaceae (rose family).

23. Some believe that the common name "huckleberry" should be restricted to species in the genus *Gaylussacia* of eastern North America.

24. Moulton, *Journals*, 6:235.

25. The name *Vaccinium myrtillus*, long applied to Lewis's specimen, refers to a plant known only from montane and subalpine zones east of the Cascade Range and in the Rocky Mountains. The specimen was originally identified as *Vaccinium myrtillus* by Greenman, and while the identification was questioned by Meehan (1898), it was accepted without comment by Reveal, Moulton, and Schuyler ("Lewis and Clark Collections") and by Moulton (*Journals*, 12:54).

26. Pursh, *Flora*, 290.

27. Moulton, *Journals*, 6:237-39. See also Lewis's correction of his error in the entry for February 11 (6:297).

28. Ibid., 6:285.

29. Ibid., 6:103, 285. Moulton's note on p. 104 incorrectly suggests that Lewis is referring to the red elderberry (*Sambucus racemosa* var. *arborescens*). Rafinesque took Lewis's brief characterization of the color of the fruit and proposed *Sambucus cerulea* in 1838 without ever seeing a specimen. Some authors prefer to reduce both *Sambucus cerulea* and *Sambucus canadensis* to subspecies of the Old World black elderberry, *Sambucus nigra*.

30. *Rubus ursinus* is also known as the Pacific dewberry. It is the Northwest's only native blackberry. Ironically, there are more blackberries grown in the Northwest today than there were two centuries ago because of a troublesome but fruitful import, the Himalayan blackberry, *Rubus discolor*.

CHAPTER 7, PP. 112-147

1. Moulton, *Journals*, 7:106, 104.

2. Today, a large lumber mill occupies the site of Camp Chopunnish. A Kamiah resident told one of us, regretfully, "They just didn't know . . ." The mill is located immediately upstream from a city park, where US Highway 12 crosses the Clearwater River.

3. Cronquist, in Hitchcock and Cronquist, *Flora*, 333.

4. Reveal, Moulton, and Schuyler, "Lewis and Clark Collections," 29.

5. *Smyrnium* is a genus made up of similar European plants, one of which, *Smyrnium olusatrum* L., has edible flower heads, stems similar to celery, and a root like a parsnip.

6. Pursh, *Flora*, 196.

7. The authors searched for cous in the spring of 2002—including at the mouth of the Walla Walla River, where Lewis obtained his specimen—but were unable to find the plant.

8. Reveal, Moulton, and Schuyler, "Lewis and Clark Collections," 28.

9. Moulton, *Journals*, 7:264. Lewis may have been on to something, for aromatic umbellifers are known in folk medicine as "carminatives"—medications that assist in expelling gas.

10. Cutright, *Pioneering Naturalists*, 413.

11. Harrington, *Edible Native Plants*, 364.

12. We have sampled the root of a mature plant. It has a crisp consistency, but was—as Harrington noted—too strong to be edible except possibly as an emergency food. The roots of an immature plant would likely be more suitable.

13. Pursh, *Flora*, 197.

14. Ibid., 195.

15. Moulton, *Journals*, 5:172.

16. It was shown in 1969 that the name *Perideridia gairdneri* (Hook. & Arn.) Mathias applied to a plant from California, not the northern yampah of the Pacific Northwest. The plant most likely seen by Lewis and Clark is now known as *Perideridia montana* or as *Perideridia gairdneri* subsp. *borealis* T. I. Chuang & Constance. Taxonomic opinion is divided as to which name is correct. In our opinion, as long as tuni (*Perideridia lemmonii*)—a plant whose roots were also used for food by Native Americans—is considered a species distinct from *Perideridia gairdneri*, then our plant should be called *Perideridia montana*. Interestingly, the authors have crossed Lemhi Pass on various occasions throughout the growing season and have yet to find yampah growing in the vicinity.

17. Harrington, *Edible Native Plants*, 132-33.

18. *Dodecatheon* (from the Greek *dodeka*, twelve, and *theos*, god) is the name given to the primrose by Pliny the Elder. The common eastern North America species, *Dodecatheon media*, or pride-of-Ohio, was discovered in Virginia in the 1680s and was introduced quickly to European gardens. Initially the genus was named *Media* (for the fabled enchantress Medea), but in 1753 Linnaeus changed it to *Dodecatheon* when he adopted *Primula* as the genus name for primrose. Lewis and others on the expedition were well acquainted with pride-of-Ohio. The captains wrote that they saw the plants near St. Louis in the spring of 1804; see Moulton, *Journals*, 2:209.

19. Ibid., 3:481, 4:481.

20. The explorers would have encountered Cusick's serviceberry (*Amelanchier alnifolia* var. *cusickii*) along the Lolo Trail. Lewis would again see scattered specimens of var. *alnifolia* while crossing Lewis and Clark Pass (ibid., 4:392). Var. *alnifolia* has petals less than half an inch long and leaves that are serrated well over half of their length. With a hand lens, one can see the strongly hairy top of the ovary. Var. *alnifolia* occurs all along the Lewis and Clark Trail from mostly east of the Cascade Range to the Dakotas. Var. *cusickii* is the common expression in the Rocky Mountains and on the eastern slope of the Cascade Range. It has petals that are one-half to an inch in length. The top of its ovary is thinly hairy to glabrous. The plant was named for William Conklin Cusick (1842-1912), an Oregon botanist who collected mainly in that state and Idaho. Var. *semiintegrifolia* is often a small tree with petals more than a half-inch long and leaves that are serrate only on the upper quarter of the blade (thus "semi-entire," as implied by the name). The top of the ovary is hairy with longish hairs. This is the common phase in and west of the Cascade Range, but it can be found in scattered locations as far east as Montana. It grows today along the Clearwater River near Peck, Idaho, and ripe fruit would have been available when the Corps of Discovery worked its way down the river in 1805. A related species, the Utah serviceberry (*Amelanchier utahensis*) grows farther to the south. The explorers might have seen it while in the Rocky Mountains, especially when crossing Lehmi Pass and Lost Trail Pass in 1805. Its leaves and flowers are shorter, and the leaves are always densely hairy—unlike those of *Amelanchier alnifolia*, which are essentially glabrous (smooth and non-hairy) on the fully expanded, mature leaves. Its berries tend to be mealy, and yellowish or orange-tinged, whereas the fruit of the western serviceberries are fleshier and distinctly purplish. Both species occur on sagebrush slopes, on valley floors along edges of streams, and in meadows and aspen glades—localities where snowberry and chokecherry also grow.

21. Dioscoride's *Materia Medica* (ca. A.D. 77) was used in Europe as a standard medical text until the sixteenth century.

22. Moulton, *Journals*, 7:55, 61 n. Other species of *Delphinium* are in the area (including the two-spike larkspur, *Delphinium distichum*, and the upland larkspur, *Delphinium nuttallii*), but these flower later in the spring and in early summer, so Lewis and Clark may not have seen them. Several species of larkspur are also found in the mountains of Idaho and Montana. In addition to the two-spike larkspur, Lewis and Clark may have seen any, or all of them, including the slim larkspur (*Delphinium depauperatum*), two-lobe larkspur (*Delphinium nuttallianum*), tower larkspur (*Delphinium glaucum*), or Flathead larkspur (*Delphinium bicolor*). All form rather showy patches in the mountains or western edge of the prairie and can be locally common. The tower larkspur can be up to ten feet tall.

23. Flowers in the lily family do not have sepals and petals that can be differentiated. Their six segments are known as tepals.

24. Moulton, *Journals*, 7:101.

25. Pursh, *Flora*, 245.

26. Ibid., 230. The two plants are quite similar, as is the chocolate checker-lily, *Fritillaria atropurpurea*, that grows farther east in Idaho and Montana and onto the Great Plains.

27. Ibid., 134.

28. Unlike zoological nomenclature, the rules governing the naming of plants require that the species name agree grammatically with the generic name. Thus, when *lineare* is transferred from *Hydrophyllum* (neuter) to *Phacelia* (feminine), the specific epithet becomes *linearis*.

29. There is a mystery here. Pursh noted that he examined Lewis's Oregon specimen, yet he wrote in the *Flora* that the plant grows on the banks of the Missouri. In fact, he was correct for the plant ranges as far east as South Dakota, but how did he know that? Either he knew the plant from one of Thomas Nuttall's specimens or he simply made a mistake, substituting "Missouri" for "Columbia."

30. Moulton, *Journals*, 7:15-16. "Fanny" is believed to have been Clark's youngest sister, Frances. Moulton points out the "Fanny's bottom" became "Fanny's Valley," possibly "because Clark had second thoughts."

31. David Douglas collected the oak later (probably in 1825). His description was published in the last part of William Jackson Hooker's *Flora Boreali-Americana* in 1840. Hooker was aware that Archibald Menzies had found the tree while with the Vancouver expedition in 1792, but he was not aware of the Lewis and Clark collection of 1806. Douglas named the tree for Nicholas Garry, the deputy governor of the Hudson's Bay Company, who had helped make arrangements for his collecting efforts in 1825.

32. T. Nuttall, *North American Sylva*, 14-16.

33. Moulton, *Journals*, 7:19.

34. Nuttall did not know in 1842 that he had been antedated by botanist August Heinrich von Bongard (1786-1839), who based his description of the red alder on specimens collected on Sitka Island by a Russian expedition some years earlier. Bongard published his description in a Russian journal in 1832, giving it the scientific name by which it is known today, *Alnus rubra*.

35. Nuttall, *North American Sylva*, 29.

36. Clayton provided specimens of many American plants to Sweden's Carolus Linnaeus through a Dutch colleague, Jan Frederick Gronovius (1686-1762). In 1738, Linnaeus, at the suggestion of Gronovius, proposed *Claytonia* in *Hortus Cliffortianus*, a book used by Linnaeus's patron, the Dutch banker George Clifford (1685-1760), as a gift to guests visiting his estate at Hartekamp. The new genus was illustrated by the young Georg Ehret (1708-1770), who was destined to be the period's most significant

botanical illustrator.

37. Linnaeus also established and named the genus *Montia* for Giuseppe Monti (1682-1760). It is so closely allied to *Claytonia* that their various species seem almost interchangeable. Although the most recent classifications are as given here, some species may be found under different names in other guidebooks.

38. Pursh, *Flora*, 175.

39. We acknowledge with thanks the efforts of Kanchi N. Gandhi (Harvard University Herbaria), John McNeill (Edinburgh Botanic Garden), and John H. Wiersema (USDA, NPGS, Plant Taxonomy Laboratory) for discussions on the authorships of Peter Simon von Pallas's (1741-1818) names that Pursh mentioned, and for evaluating the image of *Claytonia lanceolata* that Pursh published in 1813.

40. Pursh, *Flora*, 176.

41. Ibid., 175-76. Pursh saw the similarity of Lewis's plant to the Siberian spring beauty, a plant named by Linnaeus in 1753 based on specimens that probably had been gathered by Georg Steller during the Vitus Bering expedition in the 1740s. Pursh believed, however, that Lewis's plant was sufficiently different to classify it instead as the recently described *Claytonia alsinoides* Sims. Subsequent research by Asa Gray published in 1877 demonstrated the two species were actually one, and this view has been accepted since then. Like *Claytonia perfoliata*, the Siberian spring beauty was classified throughout most of the last century as a *Montia*.

42. See our discussion of the berries seen at Fort Clatsop, p. 108.

43. Pursh, *Flora*, 248-49.

44. The alternate family name for Brassicaceae is Cruciferae, derived from the Latin *crux* for "cross," from the four-petaled, cross-shaped (cruciform) flowers that are a family characteristic.

45. Originally, when Lewis's plant was assigned to *Dentaria*, its correct name was *Dentaria tenella*, but when it was reclassified as a *Cardamine*, Pursh's species name could not be used, for there was already a plant with the name *Cardamine tenella*. Thus, when American botanist Edward Lee Greene (1843-1915) assigned Lewis's plant to *Cardamine*, he had to propose a new name. He chose *Cardamine nuttallii* in the mistaken belief that Nuttall had found the plant originally. The error was unfortunate but cannot now be changed.

46. The plant would have been in late fruit when Lewis crossed Lemhi Pass in the middle of August 1805. He would probably have seen it without taking particular note of it botanically.

47. Moulton, *Journals*, 7:121.

48. Specimens collected on both dates are mounted on the same herbarium sheet in the Lewis and Clark Herbarium, and all of Pursh's information would have come from Lewis's original notes, since discarded. He named it *Buphthalmum sagittatum* (the genus *Buphthalmum* is a small one made up of only a few Eurasian plants in the aster family; the word, from the Greek, means "ox-eye"); see Pursh, *Flora*, 564. Thomas Nuttall later assigned the species to a new genus, *Balsamorhiza*, that he proposed in 1840 for this and related species.

49. Plant parts, and particularly rays in members of the aster family, tend to conform to the numerical sequence known as Fibonacci numbers: 1, 1, 2, 3, 5, 8, 13, 21, etc., in which each number is equal to the sum of the two preceding numbers, named for their discoverer, Leonardo of Pisa (or Leonardo Fibonacci, ca. 1170–ca. 1241), an Italian mathematician.

50. In the most recent summary of the families of the flowering plants, most of the genera traditionally assigned to Scrophulariaceae were reassigned to the Plantaginaceae (APG II, "Update of the Angiosperm Phylogeny Group"). This same group of plants is also called the "Veronicaceae Clade (Olmstead et al., "Disintegration"). Here we prefer to exclude the genus *Plantago*, or common plantain, from the mix and to use the first available family name for the group published after 1789; thus, our use of Antirrhinaceae in this book.

51. Interestingly, an unnamed intermediate-sized variant of *Collinsia parviflora* with flowers over a quarter of an inch in length grows in northern Idaho—we have seen it growing east of Weippe, Idaho. Cronquist postulated that a Pleistocene remnant of the large flowered form was absorbed into a population of the small-flowered plant in that location; see Hitchcock et al., *Vascular Plants*, 4:328.

52. Pursh, *Flora*, 421. It is also possible that Archibald Menzies took back seeds to England in the 1790s. Unfortunately, when Nuttall proposed *Collinsia* in 1817 to honor his close friend, the botanist Zacheus Collins (1764-1831) of Philadelphia, he was not aware of the identity of Pursh's *Antirrhinum tenellum* and did not make the connection. David Douglas subsequently found the plant, and John Lindley, the librarian at the Royal Horticultural Society, published the name *Collinsia grandiflora*. By the time Charles Piper finally discovered the true nature of Pursh's *Antirrhinum tenellum* in 1915, there was already a *Collinsia tenella* and Pursh's early name could not be used.

53. This configuration is seen in other members of the borage family, and in related families as well. It is known botanically as a "helicoid cyme" (a cyme is a flower cluster in which the terminal, or highest flower blooms first; in a helicoid cyme, this flower stalk is shaped like a spiral).

54. In 1831, Johann Georg Christian Lehmann (1792-1860) of Hamburg, Germany, proposed the genus *Amsinckia*, naming it for a burgomaster of Hamburg, William Amsinck, a patron of the city's botanical garden. Several varieties of *Amsinckia menziesii* are recognized today, but Lewis's specimen appears to be var. *retrorsa* (retrorse is a botanical term implying that a plant's hairs grow backward). The history, both of the naming and of the determination of the identity of Lewis's fiddleneck, is complicated. Briefly, Pursh, in London, had access to Archibald Menzies's specimens from the Pacific Northwest, which were then in the possession of Sir James Edward Smith. Pursh apparently did not realize that the fiddleneck in that collection was also a new plant, and similar to the one that Lewis had collected. In 1831, in the very same publication in which Lehmann proposed the name *Amsinckia*, Lehmann also named Menzies's specimen *Echium menziesii*. He was, of course, unaware that Lewis had also found a specimen, for by then the Lewis and Clark specimens lay forgotten in the

231

rooms of the American Philosophical Society in Philadelphia. Eighty-five years later the combination *Amsinckia menziesii* was established. The identity of the Lewis specimen is still in doubt. Thomas Meehan (1898) believed it to be a species of *Krynitskia* (now a synonym of *Plagiobothrys*). Charles Piper suggested that it was perhaps *Amsinckia intermedia* (now treated as *Amsinckia menziesii* var. *intermedia*). All three varieties (var. *intermedia*, var. *menziesii* and var. *retrorsa*) occur in the vicinity of The Dalles where Lewis gathered his plant, each differing slightly in the degree and types of hairs along the stem and the size of the flowers. Further research may resolve the identity of Lewis's plant and related fiddlenecks. For more on the classification of these plants, see Reveal, Moulton, and Schuyler, "Lewis and Clark Collections," 8.

55. Nuttall, *Genera of North American Plants*, 1:126.

56. A description of the plant was formally published in 1851 when William Jackson Hooker printed a long letter from Geyer in *Hooker's Journal of Botany and Kew Garden Miscellany*, in which he described several plants that he had found. Subsequently Asa Gray, professor of botany at Harvard, a man who made a career of reclassifying plants, placed it in *Plagiobothrys*, a genus established by Russian botanists in 1836. The name *Plagiobothrys* was derived from two Greek words that referred to a pit (*bothros*) on the side (*plagi*) of the nutlet, a reference to a scar on the plant's mature fruit.

57. Pursh, *Flora*, 149.

58. Ibid., 478-79.

59. Ibid., 478.

60. The green rabbitbrush's species name was proposed, by William Jackson Hooker in his two-volume *Flora Boreali-Americana*, to reflect the sticky nature of the whole plant (including even the flowers). David Douglas finally collected good flowering material along the Columbia River in 1826, and that allowed Hooker to propose a name (*Crinitaria viscidiflora*; from the Latin *viscidus*, meaning "sticky," and *floris*, for "flower"). Nuttall transferred the plant to *Chrysothamnus* a few years later. Lewis's specimen is of var. *viscidiflorus*.

61. The lily family is now defined to include only a small number of genera (APG II, "Update of the Angiosperm Phylogeny Group"). In North America, these are *Scoliopus, Calochortus, Streptopus, Uvularia, Medeola, Clintonia, Erythronium, Fritillaria, Lilium, Lloydia*, and the introduced genera *Gagea* and *Tulipa* (J. L. Reveal and J. C. Pires, "The Classification of the Monocots: An Update"). With some justification the first three may be removed and assigned to the Calochortaceae.

62. Pursh, *Flora*, 231. Lewis collected the species twice. He gathered the May collection along the Clearwater River, between Big Canyon Creek in Nez Perce County and Little Canyon Creek in Clearwater County. The flowers of this specimen were considerably smaller than those on the plant Lewis obtained in June on the Lolo Trail, probably along Eldorado Creek near the mouth of Lunch Creek in Idaho County. The flowers of this specimen were far larger than flowers of other known species in the genus. Large-flowered plants may occasionally be seen in the Clearwater

Mountains, but most are like those found along the Clearwater River.

63. Harrington, *Edible Native Plants*, 178-79.

64. With the reduction of the Liliaceae in the early 1980s to just a few genera, several old families, such as the asparagus family (Asparagaceae, 1789) and the onion family (Alliaceae, 1797), were recognized. Continued work resulted in the separation of additional families, and the cluster-lily family (Themidaceae, 1866) is one of those recently removed from Alliaceae. Unlike the members of the onion family, with their distinctive odor and inflorescence, the genera assigned to Themidaceae lack these features (APG II, "Update of the Angiosperm Phylogeny Group"; Reveal and Pires, "Classification of the Monocots").

65. Before the Columbia was dammed, the river threaded its way through a narrow, rocky defile. This was named "The Dalles" by French voyageurs because of the resemblance of the nearby rock to flagstones (*les dalles*).

66. Moulton, *Journals*, 7:132.

67. Pursh, *Flora*, 223. In 1811 Sir James Edward Smith established the genus *Brodiaea* to honor Scots botanist James Brodie, basing it on a three-anthered (triandrous) plant that Archibald Menzies had collected in California. When Pursh saw Lewis's plant, he believed that it too was a *Brodiaea*. Lewis's plant had six anthers, however, so Pursh concluded that Smith had been wrong when he described Menzies's *Brodiaea* as being triandrous. What Pursh failed to realize was that Lewis's plant, although similar to the one that Menzies had collected in California, was actually different enough to be placed in a genus of its own. When David Douglas saw our *Triteleia* along the Columbia River in 1825, he wrote in his journal: "Pursh is correct as to it being hexandrous" (Douglas, *Journal*, 122). Douglas then sent seeds to the Royal Horticultural Society in England, and in 1830, after the plants had grown out, John Lindley, the society's librarian, realized that not only were there two different species but they deserved to be in different genera, and he proposed the name *Triteleia grandiflora* for Lewis's plant. Morphological evidence gathered since the 1950s has suggested that the genus *Triteleia* (the triplet lilies) does in fact differ significantly from the genus *Brodiaea* (the cluster-lilies) and that the two should be recognized as independent genera. Recent molecular studies have confirmed this view; see J. C. Pires and K. J. Sytsma, "A Phylogenetic Evaluation of a Biosystematic Framework: *Brodiaea* and Related Petaloid Monocots (Themidaceae)".

68. The word *strict* (cognate with *strait* and *straight* and Latin *strictum*) has an obsolete meaning of "straight and stiff"; it is used in this sense today only in botany and zoology.

69. Pursh, *Flora*, 321.

70. We have retained the common name that is used in Idaho, because it is the Idaho state flower. The name is inappropriate, however, because it is technically the genus name of the Old World common lilac, *Syringa vulgaris*, which is entirely unrelated, being a member of the oleaster family (Oleaceae). Elsewhere, the genus *Philadelphus* is known as mock-orange.

Only one other member of the hydrangea family, the yerba de selva or whipplevine (*Whipplea modesta*), is native to the Pacific Northwest. It is found west of the Cascades, from the Olympic Peninsula south to Monterey, California. Apparently it was not seen by the expedition's members.

71. Two other spring-blooming shrubs or small trees have what appear to be four-petaled white blossoms. Those of Nuttall's dogwood (*Cornus nuttallii*, p. 155) are large, whereas those of the red-osier dogwood (*Cornus sericea*, pp. 57, 234 n. 18) are small (a dogwood's "petals" are actually sepals—the true petals are tiny). Neither species is fragrant, so there should be no difficulty in separating them from syringa.

72. Pursh, *Flora*, 329.

73. Van Bruggen, in Great Plains Flora Association, *Flora*, 352; Hitchcock, in Hitchcock and Cronquist, *Flora*, 199. Numbers of species, when listed according to location, are necessarily approximate and vary according to how they are classified (as species or varieties). There is also some overlap of species between the two regions mentioned.

74. Pursh, *Flora*, 164.

75. The quote, from the *Transactions of the Horticultural Society of London* (7 [1830]: 515), is taken from one of eight scientific papers that Douglas himself authored. Four dealt with botanical matters (new species of *Pinus*, *Calochortus*, and *Ribes*), three were zoological, and his last, published in 1834, dealt with the volcanoes of the Sandwich (Hawaiian) Islands. Other botanists published descriptions of most of Douglas's new plant species after his death in Hawaii in 1834.

76. Hitchcock, in Hitchcock et al., *Vascular Plants*, 3:62.

77. Several other species of wild currants that grow along Lewis and Clark's route are worth mentioning. The wax currant, or squawberry (*Ribes cereum*), resembles the golden currant (*Ribes aureum*, p. 68) although its similarly ribbed and translucent berries are usually bright red and rather tasteless. Nevertheless, the members of the expedition probably ate them whenever they found them. Next, the widely distributed white-flowered

Hudson's Bay currant (*Ribes hudsonianum*, also known as the northern black currant or stinking currant) is common along streams and in moist meadows. The plant is easy to identify, for both its leaves and its large clusters of fruit have an acrid smell—some say that the plant smells something like the urine of a tomcat. The fruit, while it partakes of the odor, is really not that bad, particularly if one is hungry. Finally, bristly black gooseberry (*Ribes lacustre*) grows all across northern North America. It is very much an armed plant, covered with bristles. Its tiny bristly flowers are inconspicuous, but its shiny black and equally bristly berries are not. If you are tempted to try them, you will find them edible but hardly delicious.

78. The plant is common along the slopes above the Clearwater River. While the plant flowers in the early spring, Lewis's specimen is well past fruit, and Pursh's evidence suggests that Lewis might have gathered the plant in the fall of 1805 (see Pursh, *Flora*, 535). Pursh noted also that he had seen the plant growing in cultivation, meaning that Lewis's plant had mature seeds when he collected it. The herbarium specimen now in the Lewis and Clark Herbarium in Philadelphia was in Pursh's possession while in London, and the five leaves on the sheet certainly appear to be garden material. Only the three central fragments are Lewis's original plants. Pursh's Latin description applies only to Lewis's material, as no floral features are mentioned. However, in his comments, Pursh says that the ray flowers vary from "white to a lively pale red." Furthermore, the dates he gives (July and August) can only apply to a plant flowering in cultivation, for Lewis was not along the Clearwater during either month. Recently, scholars have concluded that Lewis probably found the plant near Lewiston in October 1805 (Reveal, Moulton, and Schuyler, "Lewis and Clark Collections," 21).

79. Pursh, *Flora*, 535.

CHAPTER 8, PP. 148-185

1. Moulton, *Journals*, 7.212.

2. The term "Camp Chopunnish" was first used by Elliot Coues (1842-1899), an ornithologist and historian and the editor of the *History of the Expedition under the Command of Lewis and Clark* (1893). It has been in general use since then.

3. Moulton, *Journals*, 8:22.

4. We can only guess what "uplands" Lewis was referring to. On June 6, Clark and a small group of men visited a Nez Perce camp about three and a half miles west, up nearby Lawyer Creek. They may have collected the plant then. Four days later the expedition traveled eastward to the Weippe Prairie. The two plants occur in both "uplands" today.

5. Pursh, *Flora*, 560.

6. A new family name for *Camassia* and its New World relatives is about to be published. Current research assigns the group to Agavaceae, well removed from its traditional home in Liliaceae, or in the principally Old

World family Hyacinthaceae; nevertheless, there is ample justification for placing *Camassia* in an independent family (see APG II, "Update of the Angiosperm Phylogeny Group"; and Reveal and Pires, "Classification of the Monocots").

7. Moulton, *Journals*, 5:222; Pursh, *Flora*, 227; Moulton, *Journals*, 8:17. It may be unfair to blame the plant for the men's illness despite what the explorers and many authors have written over the years. We believe that the men's illness more likely was caused—all or in part—by a bacterial infection such as salmonellosis or shigellosis contracted from tainted salmon or meat that the Indians gave them. The men's symptoms were certainly consistent with bacterial enteritis. Although Lewis did not find the plants "palleatable," Harrington—who has written extensively on the edibility of native plants—found that the roots were palatable but not exceptionally so. They were, he wrote, "gummy and mucilaginous" even when cooked (*Edible Native Plants*, 163). Recently one of us sampled camas root and found it rather

more palatable than Harrington suggests. Its taste is not unpleasant either raw or cooked, although the roots do have a rather gummy consistency not unlike that of okra; it is more noticeable when the bulb is eaten raw. With some culinary imagination, we can see where it could become an agreeable addition to one's diet. Admittedly our sampling was small, but nothing about the root suggested that it would produce the symptoms experienced by the explorers.

8. Moulton, *Journals*, 8:21. Lewis and Clark might have encountered several different varieties of camas during their western travels. The plants that they saw first in western Montana and then in and around the Weippe Prairie are *Camassia quamash* var. *quamash*. Near The Dalles, var. *intermedia* is common, while west of the Cascade Range they might have eaten var. *maxima*. They might also have seen var. *breviflora* in southeastern Washington, but they would not have encountered the loveliest of all, var. *utahensis*, which is more southern and is most often grown in ornamental gardens. They would not have seen var. *azurea*, with its pale blue-violet flowers, which grows in the Puget Trough region of northwestern Washington.

9. They got only as far as Lolo Creek the first night. Clark named this "Collins Creek" for one of the men in the party; Lolo Creek at the Montana end of the Lolo Trail is another stream.

10. Moulton, *Journals*, 8:7.

11. The specimen label suggests that he also saw the plant along the Columbia River. If so, it was probably a related species, Sandberg's bluegrass (*Poa sandbergii*). The *Poa secunda* complex is taxonomically difficult and most authors define that South American species to include not only *Poa canbyi* and *Poa sandbergii* but also several other North American species (Reveal, Moulton, and Schuyler, "Lewis and Clark Collections," 39).

12. *Poa canbyi* was named for William Marriott Canby (1831-1904), a botanist and banker in Wilmington, Delaware. He spent much of his later years collecting in the West. John Herman Sandberg (1848-1917) was born in Sweden and came to the United States in 1868, where he studied medicine, but he then became an agronomist and forester. He collected extensively in northern Idaho in the 1890s.

13. Richard Salisbury (1761-1829) proposed the name *Calypso* in a beautifully illustrated book, *The Paradisus Londinensis*, in 1808.

14. Two other saprophytes also grow in the mountain forests of Idaho and Montana. The Pacific coral-root (*Corallorhiza mertensiana*) has thin lines on its flowers instead of dots. The pinedrop (*Pterospora andromedea*) is not an orchid but rather a member of the heather family (Ericaceae). It is a tall, straight plant with numerous downwardly turned reddish flowers and roundish fruits. The two orchids bear elongated, brownish fruit.

Nonphotosynthetic plants are white, yellow, brown, or red because chlorophyll is not present. As when leaves change color in the fall, the other pigments, always present but masked by the green chlorophyll, become visible.

15. Moulton, *Journals*, 8:66, 80.

16. Frederick Pursh described *Orchis dilatata* in 1813, basing the name on a specimen collected in Labrador by an early British collector

17. Hooded ladies'-tresses takes its species name from Nicolai von Romanzov (1734-1826), the grand chancellor of the Russian empire, who sponsored—and funded—an around-the-world expedition (1815-1818) led by explorer Otto von Kotzebue (1787-1846).

18. The western dogwood (*Cornus nuttallii* Aud.) grows along the lower Columbia River and, as it flowers early in the spring, the men of the expedition would have seen it on their homeward passage. Several botanists collected the western dogwood after Lewis and Clark, but none noted that it was a new species. Thomas Nuttall recognized it as a new tree, however. He generously allowed John James Audubon (1785-1851) to use his collection of birds for Audubon's book *Birds of America*. Audubon included the western dogwood as a background in one of the illustrations. In this way, Nuttall had a species named for him, and the name itself was attributed to Audubon. Understandably, Audubon was extremely grateful to Nuttall for his generous help.

19. Pursh, *Flora*, 436. It seems likely that Pursh, while in England working on the *Flora*, examined an 1811 Thomas Nuttall specimen either of the western wallflower, *Erysimum asperum*, or the sand-dune wallflower, *Erysimum capitatum*. Both grow on the northern Great Plains, as does another species, the shy wallflower, *Erysimum inconspicuum*, so named for its small flowers. Lewis and Clark may have seen any or all of these plants on the Great Plains in the spring of 1805, although we have no evidence of this in their journals. All of these species are available today from specialized seed catalogs and nurseries. Care should be taken when growing wallflowers, for they may escape and become locally weedy.

20. A related plant, the green gentian or giant frasera, *Frasera speciosa*, grows a bit farther to the south and east in central Idaho and in western Montana. Lewis would have seen it while crossing Lewis and Clark Pass in 1806. He probably also encountered—and possibly collected—it in mid-August of 1805 near Lemhi Pass (if so, the specimen did not make it back to Philadelphia; the clustered elkweed is the only plant in the gentian family, Gentianaceae, in the Lewis and Clark Herbarium).

21. Pursh, *Flora*, 101. The generic names *Swertia* and *Frasera* honor respectively Emanuel Sweert, a sixteenth-century Dutch horticulturist, and John Fraser, 1750-1811, an English nurseryman who collected plants in North America.

22. The modern rules of botanic nomenclature were formulated in the 1860s, long after Pursh published his *Flora Americae Septentrionalis*. The rules require that each new species have a "type specimen," a preserved example of that plant to which the new species name is to be applied. This idea was traditional, and having a representative specimen for all new species was a common practice even before the 1750s when Linnaeus first established modern scientific names. Thus, many of the plants gathered by Lewis and Clark during their 1804-1806 transcontinental expedition are "types," the examples on which Pursh based his new species.

The rules require only that there be a specimen, but there is nothing in the rules that says that the specimen has to be a good one. The type of the clustered elkweed is an example. Unfortunately, herbarium beetles (or tobacco beetles, *Lasioderma* spp.) are fond of dried plants, and most likely they destroyed the flowering portion of Lewis's specimen, so today only one bug-damaged leaf remains. Nevertheless, it is still the type for Pursh's new species. It may not be the best specimen in the Lewis and Clark Herbarium, but it was carried across the continent to be named and described, and thus it has an honored place in botanical nomenclature.

23. Pursh, *Flora*, 240.

24. Hitchcock, in Hitchcock et al., *Vascular Plants*, 1:767.

25. Botanists recognize many subspecies and varieties of yarrow. These differ in morphology, time of blooming, degree of "woolliness" (*lanulosa* means "woolly"), and—at the cellular level—in chromosome numbers. Our native plants belong to subspecies *lanulosa*. This group may be further sub-divided into as many as eleven varieties; most of them grow in the American West. Lewis's specimen from Idaho is var. *lanulosa*, a plant common throughout most of western North America. Frederick Pursh included it in his *Flora* as *Achillea tomentosa* (however, *A. tomentosa* is still another plant, and it is known today as *Achillea millefolium* var. *occidentale*, the common variant in eastern North America); see Pursh, *Flora*, 563. In 1834, Thomas Nuttall named the western plant *Achillea lanulosa*, citing his own specimens as well as the ones that Lewis gathered.

26. Penstemons have been known in the United States as "beard-tongues" for nearly two centuries. Today, "penstemon" seems to be used more often as a common name, both in speech and in literature, than does "beardtongue." The derivation of the names is interesting. The flowers have five stamens. The plant's original name, "penstemon" (1748), was derived from the Greek words *pente* and *stemon* ("five" and "stamen," respectively), but the modern genus name was published as *Penstemon* in 1763, making that the nomenclaturally correct form of the name. Nonetheless, *Pentstemon* (and even *Pentastamon*) were used in both botanical and horti-cultural literature well into the early twentieth century.

Four of the stamens end in small anthers that open to distribute pollen to visiting insects. The fifth stamen is elongated, tonguelike, and sterile. It originates higher on the petals, and in many species the end is covered with hair so that a "beard" is clearly visible if one looks into the open flower—hence "beardtongue." The form of the anther sacs on the four pollen-bearing stamens and the extent of bearding of the fifth stamen are important in classifying the various species.

27. *Penstemon wilcoxii* was not recognized as a distinct species until 1901, for it was long thought to be the same as the coastal species *Penstemon serrulatus*, a plant that Archibald Menzies had discovered in the 1790s. Wilcox's penstemon was named by Per Axel Rydberg of the New York Botanical Garden. Rydberg had a special interest in Rocky Mountain plants, and he named this one to honor Earley Vernon Wilcox (1869–?), a western agriculturalist.

28. Pursh, *Flora*, 423. In 1846, England's George Bentham realized that Lewis's specimen was a beardtongue but improperly proposed a new species name, *Penstemon lewisii*. Since Pursh's name had priority, Edward Lee Greene restored Pursh's original species name in 1892 and the plant became *Penstemon fruticosus*.

There is a reference to a species of *Penstemon* in Pursh's *Flora* that remains unresolved. In 1810, Pursh's English patron, Aylmer Lambert, described *Penstemon frutescens*, a species from eastern Asia that is now known as *Pennellianthus frutescens*. Pursh included it in his treatment of North American plants, indicating that he saw it in Lewis's collection. Pursh described the plant as a "small shrub, about a foot or more high; flowers purple" (Pursh, *Flora*, 428). No such specimen exists in the Lewis and Clark Herbarium, and given the large number of penstemons in the Northwest, there are several species that it could have been. The prime possibility is a narrowly restricted plant of the Columbia River Gorge now known as Barrett's penstemon (*Penstemon barrettiae*). It is about the only species that Lewis and Clark might have encountered along their return route in 1806 with the right combination of features.

29. Pursh, *Flora*, 385.

30. One has only to check the Internet, searching on "cascara," to appreciate how popular the bark is. Some sites guarantee its effectiveness, providing the user with "a moving experience." The active ingredients in cascara are anthroquinones; the most important is the polycyclic compound emodin.

31. Pursh, *Flora*, 166.

32. *Holodiscus discolor* is uncommon east of the Cascade Range, where a related plant, the glandular oceanspray (*Holodiscus dumosus*), is more frequently encountered; it grows from central Idaho south to Arizona and Texas. *Holodiscus dumosus* has a thinly hairy lower leaf surface that is also glandular (sticky), unlike the hillside oceanspray, which has a densely woolly lower leaf surface. In addition, the leaves of *Holodiscus dumosus* seldom exceed three-quarters of an inch in length, whereas those of *Holodiscus discolor* are typically an inch or more long.

33. The present scientific name seems odd, given the redundant use of *disc-* in the binomial. The genus name *Holodiscus* was derived from the Greek prefix *holo-* and the word *discos*, together meaning "entire disk," for a ringlike disk that encircles a saucer-shaped hypanthium (the structure, typical of the rose family in general, that lies between the flower's stamens and its ovary). Pursh's species name, *discolor*, does not refer to a disk, however; it means "two-colored," referring to the bright green leaves with woolly, grayish green undersides.

34. The information on one of the specimens' labels reads "A shrub growing much in the manner of Nine bark." Lewis's use of ninebark implies he was familiar with the eastern Atlantic ninebark (*Physocarpus opulifolius*). Apparently he collected the Pacific ninebark (*Physocarpus capitatus*) along the Columbia River, and perhaps this was the plant he called "seven bark" on March 25, 1806 (see Moulton, *Journals*, 7:12). We say "apparently," for the specimen that Pursh "observed in the Lewisian Herbarium" has disappeared (Pursh, *Flora*, 342). At Camp Chopunnish, Lewis again referred to a shrub as "seven bark." If he meant ninebark, the shrub was the mallow-leaf ninebark (*Physocarpus malvaceus*). Lewis also mentioned seeing seven-bark near the Walla Walla River in southeastern Washington (Moulton, *Journals*, 7:335). This would also have been the mallow-leaf ninebark. Upon leaving Camp Chopunnish, Lewis yet again reported seeing "sevenbark"

(8:10, 12-13). Moulton suggested that Lewis was seeing mock-orange, or syringa, *Philadelphus lewisii*. Because we have observed *Physocarpus malvaceus* growing all along the route that Lewis and Clark followed to Weippe Prairie, we see no basis for this assumption.

35. Hitchcock, in Hitchcock et al., *Vascular Plants*, 3:161-62. We should mention var. *demissa*, which is shrubby and grows from the Cascade Range west to the coast of Oregon and northern California and north into British Columbia. If Lewis saw it, he did not gather a specimen.

36. If the specimen now in the Lewis and Clark Herbarium at The Academy of Natural Sciences in Philadelphia is any indication, Pursh could not possibly have described the species; this specimen consists of little more than two twigs and fragments of two leaves.

37. Moulton, *Journals*, 7:325, 323. The common name "ragged robin" is universally applied to *Lychnis flos-cuculi*, a garden flower in the pink family (Caryophyllaceae). Some feel therefore that the term "pinkfairies" would be more suitable for our plant. It seems unlikely, however, that "pinkfairies" will replace "ragged robin" at any time soon.

38. Pursh, *Flora*, 260. This plant was the only one in the genus when Pursh named it, but it has been joined by several other species that, like the ragged robin, have found a place in today's ornamental gardens—the godetia or farewell-to-spring, *Clarkia amoena*, is an example. Another, the four-petaled, pink small-flowered godetia (*Clarkia quadrivulnera*), a plant that Lewis apparently missed, is a common early-blooming flower that grows in the Columbia Gorge.

William Clark's last name often was spelled "Clarck." When Pursh published the genus, he gave it as *Clarkia* (*Flora*, 256), but when he later proposed the species name, he gave that as *Clarckia pulchella* (260). Pursh also implied that the name would appear in print in the *Transactions of the Linnean Society* before his book would be published. Fortunately he spelled the genus name *Clarkia*, and that established the spelling for the genus, so that his subsequent *Clarckia* is considered a typographical error.

39. Ibid., 412.

40. Cronquist, in Hitchcock et al., *Vascular Plants*, 4:273.

41. Further etymological links with this plant family suggest a long relationship with man. *Crassula*, for example, was a word used by long-ago herbalists for certain houseleeks, a name that came from the Latin *crassus*, meaning "thick" or "fat," for the plants' fleshy leaves. The scientific family name Crassulaceae was derived from this old name.

42. Pursh, *Flora*, 324. When the Lewis and Clark collection was curated after its move from the American Philosophical Society to The Academy of Natural Sciences, two labels were pasted onto a single herbarium sheet. The four fragments mounted on the sheet are specimens of the lance-leaf stonecrop. Broken fragments of another plant, the worm-leaf stonecrop, are in an attached specimen envelope. The two labels were pasted onto the sheet without reference as to which plant the labels referred to. The botanist who discovered that there were two species on the specimen sheet decided that the fragments of *Sedum stenopetalum* in the specimen envelope should be associated with the label that states "Valley of Clarks R. Jul.

1 1806," meaning that Lewis collected the plant at Camp Chopunnish.

43. Harrington, *Edible Native Plants*, 146.

44. Our fieldwork has shown that *Sedum stenopetalum* is far more common around Kamiah than *Sedum lanceolatum*, whereas near Lolo the opposite is true (recently we were unable to find *Sedum stenopetalum* near Lolo). The area around Lolo, Montana, has been developed over the last decade, resulting in modifications to plant habitats. It is impossible to guess what the members of the expedition might have seen there in 1806.

45. Pursh, *Flora*, 160. The French botanist Augustin-Pyramus de Candolle subsequently reclassified the plant as a *Lonicera* (a generic name, previously established by Linnaeus, that honors the German herbalist Adam Lonitzer, 1528-1586).

46. Armstrong, *Field Book of Western Wildflowers*, 250.

47. There is an additional problem of historical interest. Several species of lupines apparently were moved from one place to another during the westward migration of the 1830s through the 1860s. Most wagons had a bracket into which a container for flowers could be placed. As lupines last several days before wilting, they could be carried for some distance before being discarded. Even flowering lupines often have fruit with mature seeds, so it is not surprising that several species were transported and spread along these early western American trails.

48. Other features help to differentiate the two plants. The flowers of *Lupinus argenteus* are a deeper blue than *Lupinus sericeus*. Individual flowers are somewhat larger in *Lupinus sericeus*, and its flower clusters tend to be looser. Both plants are (inconstantly) hairy overall, but more so in *Lupinus sericeus* than *Lupinus argenteus*. All lupines have palmately compound leaves, but the individual leaflets of *Lupinus argenteus* tend to be narrower and sharper. Flower clusters in *Lupinus sericeus* often extend below the stems of the highest leaves. In *Lupinus argenteus* the lower leaves often dry up and fall away by the time flower clusters appear. The banner in *Lupinus sericeus* is frequently white. Finally, the shape of the calyx—the structure below the petals—differs between the two plants (it is humped in *Lupinus argenteus*).

49. Pursh, *Flora*, 134, 140.

50. *Geum* is an old Latin word for avens, a common European member of the rose family. Botanists recognize three varieties of *Geum triflorum*, but only one occurs in Idaho where Lewis collected his specimen, var. *ciliatum* (defined here to include var. *canescens*.) Another kind, var. *triflorum*, grows on the northern Great Plains and in Canada. Among botanists, the var. *ciliatum* is commonly called "ciliated prairie smoke."

51. Pursh, *Flora*, 352, 736. John Bradbury was in America as a plant hunter, under contract to the Liverpool Botanic Garden. He sent a sizeable collection of plants back to England in 1810. Pursh, in England working on his *Flora*, helped himself to Bradbury's collection and included several of Bradbury's plants in his *Flora* without Bradbury's knowledge or permission. Pursh knew his plants but seems to have been lacking in moral principle. Perhaps the idea of "intellectual property rights" was not so highly developed in the early nineteenth century as it is now.

52. Pursh, *Flora*, 520.

53. For those intrigued by the fine points of botanical nomenclature, the following may be of interest. European botanists now divorce the genus *Chamomilla* from *Matricaria*. If one agrees, *Chamomilla suaveolens* (Pursh) Rydb. becomes the correct name for our plant. This is only the latest genus that the plant has been in. First, Pursh assigned Lewis's specimen to *Santolina*, then Hooker placed it in *Tanacetum*, Nuttall assigned it to *Lepidanthus*, and Lehmann moved it to *Akylopsis*, only to have Ascherson put it in *Chrysanthemum*. All of this happened before Buchenau proposed that it be named *Matricaria suaveolens*, a disallowable name, because Linnaeus had already established *Matricaria suaveolens* for another European species! In other words, this tiny, inconspicuous, weedy little plant has been transferred from one genus to another, all in an attempt to settle it in its proper place once and for all. There is even more to this complicated story, but at this point we are inclined just to avoid the nomenclatural morass.

54. In his description Pursh (*Flora*, 271) inexplicably placed *Polygonum bistortoides* "On the banks of the Missouri, called '*Quamash flats*'."

55. Ibid., 304. For 125 years the long-leaf suncup was known as *Oenothera heterantha*. In the spring of 1833, Nathaniel Wyeth rediscovered the plant, probably in east-central Idaho, and Thomas Nuttall named it as *Oenothera heterantha* in 1840. Even when the Lewis and Clark herbarium was reassembled in 1899, Lewis's specimen was not recognized as being associated with one of the names in Pursh's *Flora*. Pursh's association of Lewis's specimen with the mostly tropical genus *Jussieua* was simply not noticed. When the specimen was examined in the early 1950s, it was realized that his specimen was the same as the one found by Wyeth.

The name *Camissonia* honors Ludolf Adelbert von Chamisso (or Louis Charles Adélaïde de Chamisso de Boncourt, 1781-1838), a French-born German naturalist who visited the Pacific Coast of North America with the Kotzebue Russian expedition (1815-1818). He is perhaps better known today as a composer, poet, and the creator of Peter Schlemihl, the hero of a romantic novella, *Peter Schlemihls wundersame Geschichte* (1814), about a man who sold his shadow to the devil for a bottomless purse. "Camisso" is an alternate spelling of the author's name, explaining why our plant is a *Camissonia*.

56. One species, the wide-ranging cliff anemone, *Anemone multifida*, has several stems, but each stem has the typical whorl of leaves below its flower.

57. The name *anemone* goes back to ancient Greece and means "daughter of the wind," explaining why "windflower" is a common name for many species of anemones. Piper's anemone honors Charles Vancouver Piper (1867-1926), a botanist and agronomist who was born in Canada, was educated at the University of Washington and at Harvard University, and in 1903 joined the Bureau of Plant Industry in Washington, D.C. He had a special interest in the history of botany and encouraged the publication of journals written by early plant explorers of the Pacific Northwest. In 1906 he published the *Flora of the State of Washington*. It was probably during this period that Piper examined the reassembled Lewis and Clark collection at the Academy of Natural Sciences in Philadelphia.

58. Three related species grow in the Cascade Range: the Columbian windflower (*Anemone deltoidea*), little mountain windflower (*Anemone lyallii*), and Oregon anemone (*Anemone oregana*). Lewis and Clark passed through the area just as these plants were starting to flower, so they may not have seen them in the Columbia River gorge.

59. *Trillium erectum* is known as the "birthroot," or "Indian balm." Indians and European settlers used it medicinally to aid childbirth. Native Americans apparently used the roots of western species in the same way—although we know of no scientific evidence that would suggest that any of the trilliums have therapeutic value.

60. Pursh, *Flora*, 244.

61. Moulton, *Journals*, 8:53.

62. Ibid., 5:323, 363. Lewis and Clark had seen bear grass growing from Lemhi Pass to the Weippe Prairie in 1805, and they probably had wondered if it was the same plant as the bear grass of the Appalachian Mountains. Without seeing it in flower, they would not have known that they were seeing two species.

63. Pursh, *Flora*, 243. Pursh placed the plant in the genus *Helonias*, one made up mostly of tropical plants, to go along with the related eastern turkeybeard (*Helonias asphodeloides*, now *Xerophyllum asphodeloides*).

64. Ibid., 242.

65. Ibid., 147.

66. Ibid., 10.

67. Ibid., 167.

68. The plant remained undescribed until David Douglas re-collected it. William Jackson Hooker, using the species name that Douglas suggested, described the species in the first volume of his *Flora Boreali-Americana* in 1831. The origin of the redstem buckthorn's name, *sanguineus*, is obvious; *velutinus* means "velvety," for the fine coating of hair found on the undersurface of the leaves. Linnaeus gave the genus the name *Ceanothus* in 1753 and, as with many Linnaean names, this one was used in antiquity for a now unknown spiny plant—possibly a species of thistle.

69. Moulton, *Journals*, 6:318.

70. Ibid., 7:282.

71. The name "nettle leaved giant-hyssop" is a botanical term proposed recently in an attempt to standardize common names. Like many such names, it is long and unwieldy and it is unlikely that anyone other than botanists will use it. That being said, there is some justification for a standardized English name because the term *horsemint* is confusing. It is used for several other plants, including European members of the family (such as *Mentha longifolia*, *M. sylvestris*, and *M. aquatica*), as well as for American plants, including the spotted bee-balm, *Monarda punctata*. Nevertheless, the common name "western horsemint," or sometimes "agastache," are names that are in common use wherever our plant grows.

72. Botanists encounter a number of problems in identifying plant specimens in general, and those in the Lewis and Clark Herbarium in particular. In the 1753 edition of *Species Plantarum*, Linnaeus gave the name *Polemonium caeruleum* to an uncommon Old World subalpine plant culti-

vated in Europe as a garden ornamental. The generic name was one that had been used in antiquity for what may have been a related plant. The origin of the word is unknown, but possibly it honored Polemon, a second-century B.C. Greek philosopher. The plant's common name, "Jacob's ladder," refers to its parallel leaflets. The species name, *caeruleum*, means "blue," in Latin for the plant's lovely deep blue flowers. Botanists, over the years, saw polemoniums similar to Linnaeus's plant growing in many parts of the world. While all are different, all also resemble to some degree the European plant (these include *Polemonium occidentale* in western America, *Polemonium vanbruntiae* in the eastern coastal states, *Polemonium acutiflorum* of eastern Siberia and northwestern Canada, and others as well). None of these overlap geographically. To circumvent the problems of classifying these, some taxonomists now consider all to be subspecies of *Polemonium caeruleum*.

73. Reveal, Moulton, and Schuyler, "Lewis and Clark Collections," 39.

Chapter 9, pp. 186-201

1. Lewis and Clark Pass is misnamed, for Clark was many miles to the south, near present-day Twin Bridges, Montana, having crossed the Continental Divide several days before. The pass is not shown on highway maps, but it is located about twenty-five miles north of Rogers Pass on Montana State Highway 200, a scenic route that runs between Missoula and Great Falls, Montana. The highway crosses Alice Creek nine miles east of Lincoln. There, an improved gravel road goes northeast for seventeen miles to end at a parking area. The last segment, a long mile and a half, must be negotiated on foot. In early July, one can see many of the plants that Lewis collected, as well as the persistent grooves and furrows in the ground made by the countless travois used by Native Americans as they traveled east to hunt buffalo and then returned over the pass with their winter's supplies of meat.

2. The specimen is dated July 1, but Lewis's journal indicates that he gathered plants only on July 2. Extensive development in the vicinity of modern-day Lolo, Montana, has resulted in the loss of much of the potential habitat where the plant might have grown. To our knowledge, it no longer grows near the site of Travelers' Rest.

3. Moulton, *Journals*, 5:183.

4. Pursh, *Flora*, 368.

5. We were unable to locate a specimen of *Lewisia triphylla* in the vicinity of the Lolo Pass during the spring of 2002. In fact, local botanists were not even aware of the species. Possibly the three-leaf bitterroot has gone undetected because of its similarity to the common lance-leaf spring beauty.

6. It was an understandable conclusion, for there is not much difference between the two genera. In *Lewisia*, the seed capsule splits along a smooth-edged lid. In *Claytonia*, the seed capsule splits open along three lines. Unlike *Lewisia rediviva*, *Lewisia triphylla* has just two sepals, as do the various claytonias. Also, like *Claytonia lanceolata*, the three-leaf bitterroot has a thickened underground stem (corm) from which stems arise. All other species of *Lewisia* in the Pacific Northwest have thick, fleshy taproots. Without careful observation and abundant material, it would have been impossible for Pursh to classify Lewis's specimen properly. In fact, when David Douglas re-collected the plant, he named it *Claytonia linearis*. Finally, Sereno Watson, a dishwasher (but soon promoted to naturalist) with the King expedition (1867-1869), saw the plant on Donner Pass in California in 1867 and realized that it was an undescribed species. Even so, he named it *Claytonia triphylla*. In 1897 it was finally assigned to *Lewisia*, where it remains today.

7. The State of Montana has recently opened a park at the site of Travelers' Rest (on U.S. Highway 93, close to the Lolo Pass turnoff). It is well worth visiting. Recent archeological research has revealed the camp's regular topology and confirms what we know—that this was from the beginning a military expedition.

8. Pursh, *Flora*, 429.

9. Lewis and Clark probably also collected *Orthocarpus luteus* in 1805 while along the Missouri River in Montana. If so, the specimen was destroyed when the White Bear Island cache flooded the following winter. One may reasonably ask why Lewis did not gather specimens of the several species of related Indian paintbrushes that he had to have seen blooming along his trail. It is difficult to believe that he simply ignored these (and other) showy plants. Although we will never know for sure, he might have gathered several in 1805 but lost the specimens when the two caches (White Bear Island and Camp Fortunate) flooded in the spring of 1806.

10. With the demise of the figwort family (Scrophulariaceae)—as traditionally defined—the hemiparasites (*Castilleja*, *Orthocarpus*, *Pedicularis*, etc.) are now classified with the parasitic genera previously assigned to the broom-rape family, Orobanchaceae (Olmstead et al., "Disintegration.")

11. Pursh, *Flora*, 333. The bitterbrush is one of the fourteen illustrations that Pursh included in his *Flora* (opposite p. 333). He drew it from the specimen now in the Lewis and Clark Herbarium. Initially he drew the entire fragment and then reduced this to a single branch, adding more flowers for publication (Rossi and Schuyler, "Iconography"; see also appendix C in Moulton, *Journals*, vol. 12).

12. The term *papilionaceous*, commonly used for flowers in the pea family, was derived from the Latin word *papilio*, meaning "butterfly," a reflection of the flowers' appearance.

13. Elliott Coues, who published some critical comments on Thomas Meehan's catalog of Lewis and Clark plants, suggested that Lewis collected it in the Bitterroot Valley, near Travelers' Rest (Coues, "Notes on Mr. Thomas Meehan's Paper on the Plants of Lewis and Clark's Expedition across the Continent, 1804-1806," 298).

14. Pursh, *Flora*, 473. In 1900 Per Axel Rydberg of the New York Botanical Garden named the plant *Aragallus besseyi*, in honor of his Montana collecting partner Ernst A. Bessey (1877-1957), whose father, Dr. Charles Bessey (1845-1915), was professor of botany at the University of Nebraska. Five years later Joseph William Blankinship (1862-1938), professor of botany at what is now Montana State University in Bozeman, classified it as *Oxytropis besseyi*.

15. Hitchcock, in Hitchcock and Cronquist, *Vascular Plants*, 302.

16. Those who would standardize common names prefer the name "golden-hardhack" for this plant.

17. Moulton, *Journals*, 8:93.

18. Pursh, *Flora*, 355.

19. Not until the 1950s did botanists realize that the New World plant—our *Dasiphora fruticosa* subsp. *floribunda*—is distinct from the Old World species, *Dasiphora fruticosa* subsp. *fruticosa*. Even so, the two can be distinguished consistently only on the basis of their chromosome number (14 in subspecies *floribunda* and 28 in subspecies *fruticosa*).

20. The question comes up. Could Clark, or someone in his party, possibly have collected this plant? Clark and his men crossed the Continental Divide over today's Gibbons Pass the day before, on their way to Camp Fortunate on the Beaverhead River to retrieve their canoes. (Gibbons Pass is adjacent to Lost Trail Pass, about sixty miles north of Lemhi Pass, where they had crossed the divide the previous summer. By crossing Gibbons Pass, Clark passed directly into the Missouri River drainage and avoided the Salmon River Valley.) Sacagawea knew exactly where they were and was able to direct them to Camp Fortunate. The party camped that night in the Big Hole Valley, a bit southwest of today's Wisdom, Montana. The next morning, on July 7, the explorers discovered that nine of their best horses had disappeared, spirited away in the night by Indians. They spent the day searching for their horses in the country around today's Jackson, Montana, and visiting the hot springs that bubble up there. This is high, cold, mountainous country, and despite the calendar date, it was still spring and camas was in bloom. It is extremely unlikely that they would have found *Gaillardia aristata* here; for sure, they did not find their horses.

21. The French botanist Auguste Fougeroux de Bondaroy (1732-1789) named the genus in 1786, basing his description on a plant gathered in Louisiana. He named it for a French magistrate, Gaillard de Marentonneau, said to be "a patron of botany"—and who, presumably, had no other connection to the plant. The species found in Louisiana, the "firewheel" (*Gaillardia pulchella*), has showy ray flowers of yellow to orange or red, mixed with purple. It became an immediate hit as a garden ornamental.

22. Pursh, *Flora*, 573.

23. The bright red, leafy bracts that subtend the flowers form an involucre (from the Latin *involucrum*, meaning "wrapper," "case," or "envelope") and provide the basis for the species name.

24. The species was described a decade later as *Xylosteum involucratum* by the English naturalist-explorer John Richardson (1787-1865). Richardson was a member of Sir John Franklin's (1786-1847) overland expedition to the Polar Seas (1819-1822) in search of a Northwest Passage. Two years later, the German botanist Kurt Sprengel proposed its present name, attributing it to Sir Joseph Banks, who sent him specimens with the name *Lonicera involucrata* written on their label.

25. An almost identical plant, the subalpine monkey-flower, *Mimulus tilingii*, grows higher in the mountains. It is a slightly shorter, few-flowered plant with slightly longer flowers than those of *Mimulus guttatus*, and it grows on creeping stems on the surface of the ground.

26. Pursh, *Flora*, 426. Pursh was unaware, when his *Flora* was published at the end of 1813, that the North American plant had just been described as a new species. *Mimulus guttatus* had been collected on one of the Fox Islands near Unalaska by the German explorer Baron Georg Heinrich von Langsdorff, the surgeon-naturalist to the Russian around-the-world, von Krusenstern expedition (1803-1806). Seeds arrived in England around 1810 and the plant was identified, incorrectly as it turned out, as *Mimulus luteus* by Sims, who illustrated it in the *Botanical Magazine* in 1812. Friedrich Ernst Ludwig von Fischer (1782-1854), a Russian botanist of German birth, as director of the St. Petersburg Botanical Garden (1823-1850), probably sent the seeds to England, for the plant had bloomed in Moscow before 1810. He may well have sent seeds also to Augustin-Pyramus de Candolle, who published a catalog of the plants in the botanical garden at Montpellier in early 1813. Although Fischer proposed the name *Mimulus guttatus* in 1812, he failed to provide a description. It was not until Candolle added a description in 1813 and attributed the name to Fischer that *Mimulus guttatus* was validly published according to our modern rules of nomenclature.

27. Moulton, *Journals*, 8:93. Their camp was located near the mouth of a creek that Lewis named for his dog, Seaman. Today it is called Monture Creek. The actual campsite was located just west of Scotty Brown Bridge on Scotty Brown Road. The iris is far less common today than it was in 1806, for much of the valley has been converted to grazing land for cattle. The large expanses of grassy, iris-filled meadows that Lewis described are now gone.

28. Lewis may have found the plant along the Blackfoot River, as his collection data suggests, but today it is only found at higher elevations. Look for it on the grassy slopes just below Lewis and Clark Pass.

29. Pursh, *Flora*, 241.

30. *Zigadenus* was proposed in 1803 by the French botanist André Michaux for the eastern sand-bog lily (*Zigadenus glaberrimus*), now the only member of the genus. Because each of that plant's petals has two glands at the base, Michaux used the Greek *zygos* ("yoke") with *aden* ("gland") to arrive at the name. Unfortunately his imagination was better than his Greek, for the name properly should be spelled with a *y* (*Zygadenus*), as it was sometimes in the older literature. Our plant, which has only a single gland, is a species of *Anticlea*, an old generic name that was established in 1843 for a Siberian species that differs only slightly from our American one. Its derivation apparently was based on the Greek word *anti*, one of whose meanings is "instead of," apparently implying that the plant was close to but not actually a *Zigadenus*. Still further confusion surrounds their family clas-

239

Kansas, on September 14. Pursh recognized the plant as one that André Michaux had described and named a decade earlier, although Pursh listed it in his *Flora* as *Cissus ampelopsis*, placing it in another genus in the grape family, without mentioning the expedition's specimen (Pursh, *Flora*, 169).

35. Moulton, *Journals*, 158.

36. Pursh, *Flora*, 331.

EPILOGUE, PP. 217-221

1. Moulton, *Journals*, 8:369, 370-71.

2. Cutright, *Pioneering Naturalists*, 358.

3. Ibid., 349-92.

4. Jackson, *Letters*, 260-61. Lewis arrived in Washington in late December 1806 and may well have resided at the President's House for an extended period. There is no question that the two men dined together often, so in all likelihood the president (of both the United States and the American Philosophical Society) examined the 1805-1806 collections in some detail. In April 1807, Lewis took his collections to Philadelphia. In 1999, three of the plant specimens returned, this time to the White House, at the request of President Clinton, after a detailed review of the botanical collection was published earlier in the year.

5. S. E. Ambrose maintains that Lewis was subject to depression and perhaps was manic-depressive (see *Undaunted Courage: Meriwether Lewis, Thomas Jefferson, and the Opening of the American West*, 311-12, 440-41, 471-75). There is no question that after 1807 Lewis drank heavily and by 1809 was perhaps an alcoholic. To what extent the loss of his 1805 collections may have contributed to any mental illness is impossible to judge. If Lewis did not suffer from depression to some considerable degree, one would think he would have been eagerly recollecting plants to replace as many specimens as possible, while on the Marias River and while heading down the Missouri. Yet few specimens were gathered, and it seems that there was no concerted effort by anyone to replace the lost material. Granted, the expedition was rapidly descending the Missouri River, yet it is almost as if Lewis gave an order for everyone not to bother.

6. Jackson, *Letters*, 398.

7. Jackson, *Letters*, 463.

8. For the gruesome details of Lewis's suicide, see Ambrose, *Undaunted Courage*, 475-78. Both Ambrose and Moulton (*Journals*, 2:36) discuss—and discount—the theory that Lewis was murdered.

9. Moulton, *Journals*, vol. 12, appendix C.

10. Pursh's alcoholism is described in several letters now in the Archives of the Ewell Sale Stewart Library at The Academy of Natural Sciences in Philadelphia. See also Moulton, *Journals*, 12:14.

11. See Thwaites, 1904-1905; and Cutright, *Pioneering Naturalists*.

Bear grass (*Xerophyllum tenax*) on the south side of Lost Trail Pass, Idaho

JAMES L. REVEAL

Bibliography

Ambrose, S. E. *Undaunted Courage: Meriwether Lewis, Thomas Jefferson, and the Opening of the American West.* New York: Simon and Schuster, 1996.

APG II. [B. Bremer, K. Bremer, M. W. Chase, J. L. Reveal, D. E. Soltis, P. S. Soltis, and P. F. Stevens.] "An Update of the Angiosperm Phylogeny Group Classification for the Orders and Families of Flowering Plants: APG II." *Botany Journal of the Linnean Society* 141 (2003): in press.

Armstrong, M., with J. J. Thornber. *Field Book of Western Wildflowers.* New York: C. P. Putnam's Sons, 1915.

Catlin, George. *Letters and Notes on the Manners, Customs, and Condition of the North American Indians.* 2 vols. London: Tosswill and Myers, 1841. Reprint, *North American Indians,* ed. P. Matthiessen, New York: Viking, 1989. [Page citations are to the reprint edition.]

Clarke, C. G. *The Men of the Lewis and Clark Expedition.* Lincoln: University of Nebraska Press, 1970. Reprint, Lincoln: Bison Books, 2002. [Page citations are to the 1970 edition.]

Corner, G. W. *Two Centuries of Medicine. A History of the School of Medicine at the University of Pennsylvania.* Philadelphia: University of Pennsylvania Press, 1965.

Coues, E. *History of the Expedition under the Command of Lewis and Clark.* 4 vols. New York: F. P. Harper, 1893.

———. "Notes on Mr. Thomas Meehan's Paper on the Plants of Lewis and Clark's Expedition across the Continent, 1804-1806." *Proceedings of the Academy of Natural Sciences at Philadelphia* 50 (1898): 291-315.

Cutright, P. R. *Lewis and Clark: Pioneering Naturalists.* Urbana: University of Illinois Press, 1969.

———. "Meriwether Lewis: Botanist." *Oregon Historical Quarterly* 69 (1968): 148-70.

Dillon, R. *Meriwether Lewis: A Biography.* New York: Coward-McCann, 1966.

Douglas, D. *Journal Kept by David Douglas during His Travels in North America, 1823-1827.* Ed. H. R. Hutchinson. London: Royal Horticultural Society, 1914.

Fifer, B., and V. Soderberg; maps by Joseph Mussulman. *Along the Trail with Lewis and Clark.* 2d ed. Helena: Montana Magazine/Farcountry Press, 2001.

Graustein, J. E. *Thomas Nuttall, Naturalist: Explorations in America, 1808-1841.* Cambridge: Harvard University Press, 1967.

Great Plains Flora Association. *Flora of the Great Plains.* Lawrence: University Press of Kansas, 1986.

Greuter, W., et al. *International Code of Botanical Nomenclature* (Saint Louis Code). Adopted by the Sixteenth International Botanical Congress, St. Louis, Missouri, July-August 1999. *Regnum Vegetabile* 138 (2000): 1-474.

Harrington, H. D. *Edible Native Plants of the Rocky Mountains.* Albuquerque: University of New Mexico Press, 1967.

Hitchcock, C. L., and A. Cronquist. *Flora of the Pacific Northwest: An Illustrated Manual.* Seattle: University of Washington Press, 1973.

Hitchcock, C. L., A. Cronquist, M. Ownbey, and J. W. Thompson. *Vascular Plants of the Pacific Northwest.* 5 vols. University of Washington Publications in Biology 17. Seattle: University of Washington Press, 1955-1969.

Jackson, D., ed. *Letters of the Lewis and Clark Expedition, with Related Documents, 1783-1854.* Urbana: University of Illinois Press, 1962.

McKelvey, S. D. *Botanical Explorations of the Trans-Mississippi West, 1790-1850.* Jamaica Plain, Mass.: Arnold Arboretum, 1956.

Meehan, T. "The Plants of the Lewis and Clark Expedition across the Continent, 1804-1806." *Proceedings of the Academy of Natural Sciences of Philadelphia* 50 (1898): 12-49.

Michaux, A. *Flora Boreali-Americana.* 2 vols. Paris: C. Crapelet, 1803.

Morwood, J., ed. *The Pocket Oxford Latin Dictionary.* Oxford: Oxford University Press, 1994.

Moulton, G. E., ed. *The Journals of the Lewis and Clark Expedition.* 13 vols. Lincoln: University of Nebraska Press, 1986-2001.

Nuttall, T. *The Genera of North American Plants.* 2 vols. Philadelphia: D. Heart, 1818.

———. *The North American Sylva; or, A Description of the Forest Trees of the United States, Canada, and Nova Scotia...* Vol. 1. Philadelphia: J. Dobson, 1842.

Olmstead, R. G., C. W. DePamphilis, A. D. Wolfe, N. D. Young, and P. A. Reeves. "Disintegration of the Scrophulariaceae." *American Journal of Botany* 88 (2001): 348-61.

Pires, J. C., and K. J. Sytsma. "A Phylogenetic Evaluation of a Biosystematic Framework: *Brodiaea* and Related Petaloid Monocots (Themidaceae)." *American Journal of Botany* 89 (2002): 1342-59.

Pursh, F. *Flora Americae Septentrionalis.* 2 vols. London: White, Cochrane, 1814 [December 1813]. Reprint, ed. Joseph Ewan, Braunschweig, Germany: J. Cramer, 1979.

Reveal, J. L. *Gentle Conquest: The Botanical Discovery of North America with Illustrations from the Library of Congress.* Washington, D.C.: Starwood Publishing, 1992.

Reveal, J. L., G. E. Moulton, and A. E. Schuyler. "The Lewis and Clark Collections of Vascular Plants: Names, Types, and

Comments." *Proceedings of the Academy of Natural Sciences of Philadelphia* 149 (1999): 1-64.

Reveal, J. L., and J. C. Pires. "The Classification of the Monocots: An Update." *Flora of North America* 26 (2002): 3-36.

Rickett, H. W. "John Bradbury's Explorations in Missouri Territory." *Proceedings of the American Philosophical Society* 94 (1950): 59-89.

Rossi, L., and A. E. Schuyler. "The Iconography of Plants Collected on the Lewis and Clark Expedition." *Great Plains Research* 3 (1993): 39-60.

Sargent, C. S. *Manual of the Trees of North America.* Boston: Houghton Mifflin, 1922.

Spamer, E. E., and R. M. McCourt. *The Lewis and Clark Herbarium, Academy of Natural Sciences of Philadelphia (PH-LC):*

Digital Imagery Study Set. Academy of Natural Sciences of Philadelphia Special Publication 19, 2002.

Stearn, W. T. *Botanical Latin.* 4th ed. Devon, England: David and Charles, 1992.

Thwaites, R. G., ed. *Original Journals of the Lewis and Clark Expedition, 1804-1806.* 8 vols. New York: Dodd, Mead, 1904-1905.

Whitson, T. D., L. C. Burrill, S. A. Dewey, D. W. Cudney, B. E. Nelson, R. D. Lee, and R. Parker. *Weeds of the West.* 5th ed. Laramie: University of Wyoming, 1996.

van Ravenswaay, C. *Drawn from Nature: The Botanical Art of Joseph Prestele and His Sons.* Washington, D.C.: Smithsonian Institution Press, 1984.

JAMES L. REVEAL

Lupines, cinquefoils and crane's-bill in a meadow along Alice Creek, Montana

Index

253